# Radicals, Secularists and Republicans

EDWARD ROYLE

# Radicals, Secularists and Republicans

## Popular freethought in Britain, 1866–1915

Manchester University Press

Rowman and Littlefield

© Edward Royle 1980

Published by
Manchester University Press
Oxford Road, Manchester M13 9PL

UK ISBN  0  7190  07836

First published in the USA by
Rowman and Littlefield
Totowa, New Jersey 07512

US  ISBN  0  8476  6294  2

*British Library cataloguing in publication data*

Royle, Edward.
    Radicals, Secularists and republicans.
    1. Secularism – **Great** Britain – History.
    I. Title.
    211'.6'0941          BL2765.G7

    ISBN 0–7190–0783–6

Computerised Phototypesetting
by G.C. Typeset Ltd, Bolton, Greater Manchester

Printed in Great Britain
at the Alden Press, Oxford

# Contents

# Tables and diagrams

# Abbreviations

Issues of periodicals have been identified by date in the notes; where a special issue of the *National Reformer* is undated, it has been identified by its issue number and given, in parentheses, an approximate date of publication. Where references have been gathered together they are given in the same order as the items to which they refer.

# Preface

The Secularists were a relatively small group of men and women from the working and lower middle classes whose mission was a radical restructuring of society by peaceful means. Their fundamental belief was that the evils of contemporary society were attributable to the baneful effects of religion, and their aim was to discredit Christianity and those social institutions which depended upon it. They were republicans in a country increasingly devoted to its Queen; and atheists in a society which, outwardly at least, was profoundly religious. Their hero was Thomas Paine.

For a hundred years after the publication of Paine's *Rights of Man* (1791–92), British radicalism was shaped by the ideas developed in Paine's writings concerning the twin evils of 'kingcraft' and 'priestcraft', but in the 1880s newer socialist ideas inspired by Karl Marx began to make an impact. Reformers appeared who were no longer satisfied with the old radical critique, and economic explanations were sought for the injustices of life. Social criticism was becoming secularised, leaving little room for the Secularists themselves.

Great changes were also taking place in the Churches in the later nineteenth century. The Secularists had thrived when attacking rigid Calvinism or biblical literalism, but theology was becoming more subtle as well as less central to the concerns of everyday life. The weakening of the Churches which many contemporaries detected towards the close of the century was accompanied by a decline among the Secularists.

Undoubtedly the golden age of Secularism came in the days of Charles Bradlaugh's leadership, from the 1860s to the 1880s. During these years Bradlaugh was able to push Secularism to the front of the political stage and his National Secular Society (established 1866) had branches throughout urban Britain. Politically, Bradlaugh and his followers stood on the extreme left of the

Gladstonian Liberal party, an expression of the consensus which had developed in British politics since the 1850s by which extreme radicals were attached to the political establishment. As an organisation Secularism could look something like a cross between a working men's club and a sectarian chapel.

The purpose of this book is to explore the history of Secularism as an organised expression of 'popular' radicalism—that is, 'popular' in the sense of being 'of the people' though not necessarily widely accepted by the people. It is a subject usually only touched upon in footnotes, and one which itself touches upon most aspects of radical activity. Charles Bradlaugh is the best-known leader, with his struggle to enter Parliament in the early 1880s, but beyond Bradlaugh there were other leaders, and beyond them was a movement of loyal supporters in the country. These deserve historical recognition: not only Mrs Annie Besant, remembered more as a socialist than as a Secularist, but also Charles Watts, who devoted a lifetime to radical agitations and yet who is remembered, if at all, as the father of Charles Albert Watts, the publisher, not in his own right; and G. W. Foote, Bradlaugh's successor as president of the National Secular Society, who was never able to fill the great man's shoes and who had the misfortune to preside over the decline of Secularism. His death in 1915 conveniently brings the story to a close, as the rationalistic optimism of his generation was submerged in the Great War.

The first section of the book (chapters 1–6) sets out the institutional history of Secularism between 1866 and 1915, building on the narrative of the years 1791–1866 which was provided in my earlier *Victorian Infidels* (Manchester, 1974). The aim is to set the framework within which the later chapters can be fitted. The second section (chapters 7–10) then explores the structure of the Secularist movement, its leaders and followers, their activities and ideas. The third section (chapters 11–16) offers a study of the campaigns in which the Secularists became involved, the emphasis being on perspectives which can be added to some well known themes from the Secularist viewpoint.

Contemporary terminology has been employed in its original meaning. Thus 'Secularism' as a proper noun is that system of beliefs and organisation which emerged in the 1850s, initially under the leadership of G. J. Holyoake; one thesis of this book is that it had little in practice to do with modern notions of the secular. 'Freethought' applies not to a mental process but to that historical phenomenon popularly known as 'freethought' in the days of Bradlaugh and Foote; it is virtually synonymous with Secularism. I have not attempted in this book to describe in detail freethinking among the higher social classes, which by the later nineteenth century was becoming known by Huxley's word, 'Agnosticism'.

The research for this book has occupied the best part of a decade, and the outlines of the work were conceived before the revival of the blasphemy laws in the *Gay News* trial of 1977. The events of that trial and the subsequent appeals may serve to remind the historian that his subject, however remote, is never dead. The present age is as concerned as its predecessors about moral consensus, the limits of tolerance, the nature of liberty, the rights of minorities, and the creative role (or otherwise) of dissidents within the community. Perhaps what follows may unwittingly contribute to the current debate.

A great many librarians and other individuals have made the work for this book less of a burden and more of a pleasure than might have been. Principally, but not exclusively, I should like to thank Mrs R. Corina, who generously allowed me to consult items from the library of her late husband; Mr W. McIlroy, former secretary of the National Secular Society, for whom nothing was too much trouble, and the executive of the N.S.S. for putting their society's library at my disposal and giving me permission to quote from their records; Mr and Mrs D. Rothwell, for their hospitality in London; Professor J. Saville, for allowing me to consult his copy of the *International Herald*; Mr N. Sinnott, for copies of his pamphlets; Dr F. B. Smith, who read through the manuscript and made many helpful suggestions; Mr N. Walter of the Rationalist Press Association, for allowing me access to the Association's library; and the librarians and staffs of the British Library, the Home Office Library, the Leicester County Record Office, Manchester Central Library, and the Public Record Office. Extracts from the records of the Leicester Secular Society are by permission of that society, transcripts of Crown copyright records in the Home Office library are by permission of the Departmental Record Officer, Home Office, and those in the Public Record Office appear by permission of the Controller of H.M. Stationery Office. Lastly I should like to thank my wife for her continued support and encouragement.

Part I

# The national organisation of freethought, 1866–1915

I

# The false dawn, 1866–74

*Introduction*

When Charles Bradlaugh launched the National Secular Society in 1866 he was attempting to give nation-wide coherence to a movement which had been struggling to find expression for twenty years. Since the early 1850s George Jacob Holyoake had been attempting to create out of the atheistic freethought pioneered by Richard Carlile a creed which would turn its back on transcendental religion and seek instead to explain and improve man's position in terms of the here and now. He had gained much from the teachings of Robert Owen and many of his early followers were Owenites, but they were also readers of Richard Carlile's publications, and through them of Thomas Paine. The ethical reformism of Owenism, stripped of its radical socialism, was combined in Secularism with the more widely held programme of anti-clerical ultra-radicalism. During the 1850s Holyoake hoped to reawaken the different forces for radical change inherited from the burnt-out agitations of the 1830s and 1840s, and to some extent he was successful: small groups of former Owenites and Chartists continued to meet, discuss and read the radical literature put out by James Watson, Edward Truelove, Holyoake and other publishers of 'advanced' material. Large numbers of adherents stirred themselves as in former days to hear a leader of national stature lecture against the evils of orthodox religion and the exclusiveness of élite politics. Still larger numbers—several thousands on occasions—attended summer-time camp meetings held at traditional meeting places close to the thriving industrial towns of Lancashire and Yorkshire, where all manner of radicalism found its surest home and most loyal support. But Holyoake was not entirely successful. Though he kept the embers glowing, he scarcely rekindled the fire. His periodical, the *Reasoner*, was issued weekly between 1846 and 1861, but its maximum circulation was only five thousand. Radicals were not ready for revival. Disillusioned by the failure of Chartism, distracted by the Crimean War, they were unable to offer any serious challenge to the stable political world dominated by Lord Palmerston. The radicals sought consolation championing foreign causes—the exiles of Poland or Italy could always count on a warm hearing and a resolution voted in their favour—and Palmerston himself could join in this enthusiasm when British diplomatic interests required it. Although the transformation of the Victorian economy from the booms and slumps of the 1830s and early 1840s to the stability of the 1850s and 1860s has been exaggerated, undoubtedly the edge was taken off the desperation and hunger of those skilled workers who invariably formed the backbone of any radical movement. The years 1850–65 were not good ones in which to launch a new progressive movement to shake the political, religious or social foundations of Britain.[1]

The history of freethought at the popular level is closely related to that of the contemporaneous political and religious worlds. The Secularist movement had its own internal dynamics but this often produced results which coincided with similar events in political or religious affairs. After 1849 the Methodists suffered a grave setback in both membership and confidence, no less momentous than that experienced by the political radicals, and for both the revival began in 1859. With the religious awakening which spread from northern Ireland in that year the golden age of Victorian institutional religion began, especially for the Nonconformists. Despite Darwin, and despite a failure to increase significantly the total proportion of the population habitually seated in the pew on Sundays, this was the period in which chapels were built larger and more resplendent, and were fuller, than ever before; and in which Nonconformist leaders challenged the Church of England for the spiritual leadership of the nation. Although Secularism was in opposition to Christianity it at times seemed just another religious group, a little more extreme than the latest Bible-based revivalist sect, but nevertheless bearing strong resemblances to it. At other times Secularism is best seen engaged in an antiphonal relationship with the Churches, thriving on their attacks and feeding religious groups with a justification for their existence.

The same sort of relationship is evident in the political world. Also beginning in 1859 with the general election of that year, the radical party in Parliament and its popular tail in the country, aided by the new cheap press, was at last able to make an impact on the Whigs and, in conjunction with the Peelite rump led by Gladstone, formed itself into the Liberal party. For the rest of the century the ebbs and flows of Secularism were to follow closely those of the Liberal party, with periods of greatest success after 1868, 1880 and, on a lesser scale, 1892, and with periods of disorganisation after 1873, 1886 and 1895. Despite its radical and republican political programme, freethought, in common with other expressions of radicalism, was a part of the great popular Liberal movement in the country, and can be interpreted in political as well as religious terms.

The most important reason for the weakness of Secularism in the 1850s was lack of leadership. Holyoake was not an inspiring person: scholarly, pedantic, cautious, placatory, he was not the man to stir the faint-hearted or rouse the indifferent. He was the William Lovett of Secularism, the man who created the movement and gave it its foundation documents, but who never moved on from being the pilot to being the captain of the ship. Cautious to avoid the rocks, he seemed in no hurry to make the actual journey. He did not appear to realise that political and social privilege and deeply entrenched religious beliefs would not be conquered solely by the intrepid might of self-educated artisan intellect. But in the late 1850s Secularism gained a new leader who was not afraid to smash the religious idols and political images of polite society—Charles Bradlaugh—and with his coming the ship of Secularism dropped its pilot.

*The foundation of the National Secular Society*

The revival of Secularism in 1859 and 1860 was based largely on Bradlaugh's provincial lectures tours and the *National Reformer*, a new Sheffield-based weekly Secularist newspaper which became Bradlaugh's personal property in 1862 when he transferred it to London, the principal scene of radical activity in the early 1860s. Here the builders' strike of 1859 had led to the formation of the London Trades Council and George Potter's paper, the *Beehive*; but it was foreign affairs rather than purely domestic matters which then kept political activity alive, with sympathy for the Federal cause in the American Civil War, for the Poles in the rising of 1863, and for Italy when Garibaldi came to Britain in 1864. The abrupt termination by the government of Garibaldi's visit brought together a group of radicals led by Edmond Beales and George Howell, who in 1865 founded the Reform League, which took the lead in the political agitation which swept the country following the death of Lord Palmerston in 1865, and led to the urban male household suffrage Reform Act of 1867.[2]

The National Secular Society (N.S.S.) was established in the midst of this political agitation by and for men who were deeply involved in the work of the Reform League. Whilst the N.S.S. was the fruit of twenty years' work, it ripened in a favourable season not of its own making. Despite Bradlaugh's considerable efforts on behalf of freethought, the suffrage and foreign republicanism during 1863–65, he was not able to maintain the initial impetus of 1859–62. He had his living to earn, he had a growing family to maintain, and he was in poor health.[3] In February 1863 he gave the *National Reformer* over to John Watts, who made it less of a newspaper and more of a weekly periodical like the *Saturday Review*, and its circulation fell by over half to about 2,500 in February 1866.[4] How far the *National Reformer* ought to be a newspaper was debated in its columns and among the leaders of freethought, raising issues of wider importance for the nature of Secularism. Bradlaugh wanted to keep the paper as a radical newspaper with a strong political flavour, but Watts thought of Secularism more in theological and philosophical terms, though he maintained some interest in politics. When he relinquished control of the *Reformer* in 1866 (he died of consumption in October), Bradlaugh had his way. In part this was in response to the events of 1866. The suffrage campaign was gaining ground and, as the Ashton Secularists informed their leader, two or three pages of political news would certainly advance the paper's circulation. Some readers, of course, did not agree with this view, and the question of whether Secularism should be directly involved in politics was contended throughout the rest of the nineteenth century and into the twentieth. Bradlaugh's policy, set out in reply to a complaint that he was making the *Reformer* 'a mere political journal', was that he had 'always intended the *National Reformer* to be an *avant courier* on political, social and theological questions, but never that it should deal with one to the entire exclusion of the others.'[5] He strove to keep this balance in the N.S.S. from its foundation in 1866 until his retirement from the presidency in 1890, but it was a balance which his successor, G. W. Foote, was unable to maintain once advanced politics came to mean socialism rather than radicalism. In 1866, however, the voice of extreme politics was still predominantly (if not entirely) radical, and Bradlaugh was determined that that voice should be his own.

Earlier attempts at uniting local Secularist societies had taken the form of regional or national federations. The initiative had lain with the provinces, and a central leadership had existed only on paper. The National Secular Society was different. Bradlaugh began to take soundings in June 1866; by August he was suggesting a national organisation; and by September he and Charles Watts were putting forward a programme and statement of principles. The aim of this and all subsequent programmes and activities can be summed up in the proposed fourth principle: 'That human improvement and happiness cannot be effectually promoted without civil and religious liberty; and that, therefore, it is the duty of every individual . . . to actively attack all barriers to equal freedom of thought and utterance for all, upon Political and Theological subjects.'[6] Bradlaugh announced himself temporary president, with Watts as temporary secretary, and a national conference was promised as soon as a thousand members had been enrolled. Membership was to be on an individual basis, and the subscription was to be 1s a quarter. Over a hundred members joined in a few weeks, but as early as October 1866 the Huddersfield society was suggesting that local groups should be able to enrol *en masse* for a reduced sum.[7] This had been the system previously used with little success, but the following year Bradlaugh evolved the ideal compromise, maintaining the individual membership, but permitting local societies to enrol their members for a third of the usual fee.[8] Not only did this give local Secularists an incentive to turn their independent societies into branches of the N.S.S., but it also encouraged Reform League members, once the excitement of the Reform crisis and the general election were over, to transfer their radical loyalties and energies to Bradlaugh's organisation.

After the first flush of enthusiasm, progress was slow until Charles Watts made a provincial lecture tour in the autumn of 1867. Commencing in Northampton, where John Bates, the local leader, had been one of the first N.S.S. members, Watts progressed up the east coast, across Scotland, and back through Newcastle, Yorkshire, Lancashire and the West Midlands to London over a period of four months.[9] The results of this tour were soon apparent. Four hundred individual subscriptions were collected, and branches were formed at Newcastle and Dewsbury. By November, when the first conference met in Bradford, the N.S.S. had over 500 individual members, and others joined at the conference when the plan for reduced branch membership was approved. The Bradford conference confirmed its self-elected president and secretary in office, and engaged Watts also as salaried lecturer.[10]

The impression should not be given, however, that the N.S.S. was immediately accepted for what Bradlaugh intended it to be, or that the mere fact of organisation implied success. Even the *National Reformer* was prepared to concede that there were as many committed Secularists outside the N.S.S. structure as inside it, and that, put together, these would represent only five per cent of those

who might turn up at lectures in London and the provinces. The
N.S.S. was regarded, even by its members, merely as 'the
organisation that has chosen Mr Bradlaugh for their president.'[11]
Other lecturers, such as G. J. Holyoake, Mrs Harriet Law or John
Maughan of London, stood largely on the sidelines. The strength of
the N.S.S., and its weakness, lay in its close identification with the
personality of Bradlaugh. Those who could not work with him, or
were unused to his forceful style of leadership, sooner or later found
themselves outside the mainstream of the movement.

The tremendous energy which Bradlaugh put into his
propagandism can be seen in the record for 1868. He was still
earning his living as a financial agent during the week and so could
go on lecture tours only at weekends; and from July he was nursing a
parliamentary seat at Northampton. Yet on 1–2 August he travelled
a thousand miles to deliver four lectures in Edinburgh and Glasgow;
on 22–23 August he covered six hundred miles to deliver three
lectures at Newcastle upon Tyne; and on 6 September he delivered
three major speeches in the Free Trade Hall, Manchester, on 'The
Irish Question', 'The Progress of Heresy' and 'The Political Crisis
and the Future of England' to total audiences of nine thousand
people. Charles Watts was at the same time pursuing a more
systematic countrywide campaign, but the credit went to
Bradlaugh.[12]

The pace over the next few years quickened. The circulation of the
*National Reformer* was increasing from an average of 3,000 in 1867 to
twice that number in 1872; Bradlaugh was establishing himself as
one of the foremost radicals in the country; and the N.S.S. became
one of the leading popular societies into which the popular cause
was channelled. In an attempt to capitalise on this, the subscription
in 1870 was reduced from 1*s* to 3*d* a quarter, as a result of which
Watts was able to announce nearly a thousand new members
enrolled by the end of the year. During 1870 he delivered 200
lectures, and Bradlaugh's figure was 170 for the second half of the
year alone. 'It is always one story,' he wrote. 'Enormous audiences,
great applause, few opponents, and fresh recruits for our ranks.'[13]

At both the national and the local level Secularism was thriving.
London was being stirred by outdoor lectures from 1869, while
Bradlaugh's famous Hall of Science in Old Street was opened the
previous year. Between 1867 and 1871 regional Secular Unions were
commenced (not always with prolonged success) in the South West,
the Black Country, Lancashire, Yorkshire, the North East and
Scotland. Sixty-eight local Secularist societies were recorded in
1870, but this represented the high point of the early N.S.S. By 1874

the number of societies had fallen by nearly half.[14] One reason for this
was the diversion of Secularist energies into the republican
movement, in which Bradlaugh and Watts took a leading part. At
the 1871 conference Bradlaugh declined to be re-nominated as
president, and the office went to the aged and respectable patron of
freethought, Arthur Trevelyan. Charles Watts similarly declined to
continue as secretary, and his place was taken by D. K. Fraser, a
regular contributor to the *National Reformer* over the pseudonym
'Freelance'.[15]

Without Bradlaugh and Watts to guide its fortunes the N.S.S.
collapsed. Historians have noted 1871 as the year in which
Bradlaugh was not president, but they have been so concerned with
the continuity since 1866 to notice that the N.S.S. had no real
existence at all during 1872 and 1873. Trevelyan was too old and
remote to be more than a figurehead, and his nomination had not
been seconded for these reasons in 1868. Fraser was not even present
at the 1871 conference. Watts did not hand on to him the minute
book, and when only two other persons besides himself attended the
Executive Committee he ceased to keep minutes at all. No annual
conference was held in 1872 or 1873, and the Council and officers of
the N.S.S. ceased to have even a nominal existence after September
1872. Fraser was seriously ill during the winter of 1872–73, and
actually begged members not to try to renew their subscriptions.
The work of sustaining and spreading freethought was undertaken
by Bradlaugh and Watts in their lectures and in the columns of the
*National Reformer* outside the framework of their defunct
organisation. By the summer of 1873 local societies were again
lamenting the lack of regional and national organisations, very much
as they had in the 1850s and early 1860s.[16]

*Notes*

1    E. Royle, *Victorian Infidels: the origins of the British Secularist movement
     1791–1866* (Manchester, 1974); L. E. Grugel, *George Jacob Holyoake: a
     study in the evolution of a Victorian radical* (Philadelphia, 1976), pp. 43–104.
2    R Harrison, *Before the Socialists: studies in labour and politics, 1861–1881*
     (London, 1965); F. M. Leventhall, *Respectable Radical: George Howell and
     Victorian working class politics* (London, 1971), pp. 17–92; F. E. Gillespie,
     *Labor and Politics in England, 1850–1867* (Durham, N. C., 1927; reprinted
     London, 1966).
3    D. Tribe, *President Charles Bradlaugh, M.P.* (London, 1971), pp. 67–86;
     *N.R.*, 31 January 1863.

4   *N.R.*, 27 February, 5 March 1864, 25 February 1866.
5   *N.R.*, 29 April, 22 July, 12 August 1866.
6   *N.R.* 10 June, 15 July, 5, 12, 19, 26 August, 2, 9 September 1866.
7   *N.R.*, 23 September, 28 October 1866.
8   *N.R.*, 14 April 1867.
9   *N.R.*, 21 April, 22 September, 10 November 1867.
10  *N.R.*, 13 October, 1 December 1867.
11  *N.R.*, 24 November 1867, 26 April 1868.
12  *N.R.*, 9, 30 August, 6 September, 3 May 1868.
13  *N.R.*, 4 August 1867, 7 January 1872, 5 September 1869, 29 May, 6 November 1870, 8 January, 12 November 1871.
14  See Appendix A.
15  *N.R.*, 1 October 1871.
16  *N.R.*, 20 December 1868; *S.C.*, 13, 20 June 1875; *N.R.*, 19 January, 16 February 1873; *S.C.*, 1 September 1873.

II

# New beginnings, 1874–80

*The reorganisation of Secularism*

With the collapse of the republican movement and the failure of the Liberal party at the general election of 1874, Bradlaugh again turned his attention to the N.S.S. In the *National Reformer* he requested London members to attend his lecture at the Hall of Science on 31 May 1874, after which, with their support, he temporarily resumed the presidency of the N.S.S. He then issued a list of Principles, Objects and Rules without further comment, and arranged for proper certificates to be issued to N.S.S. members. As before, Charles Watts was named as secretary and lecturer. Bradlaugh's initiative was ratified in the provinces at meetings held in Newcastle, in the Free Trade Hall, Manchester, and on Castle Hill, Huddersfield. Branches then began to reconstitute themselves, and lecture tours by Bradlaugh, Watts and G. W. Foote again rallied supporters to the cause.[1]

The impression of instant success which the *National Reformer* reports convey is dispelled by a contribution to the *Secular Chronicle*, written by the aptly named 'Verax':

Secularism is no better organised now than it was twenty years ago; nay, it is not so well organised now as then. Some new halls have been erected, but as an equivalent others have passed out of our hands. Many new Societies have been started but many also have died out. Both as regards numbers and organisation Secularists are themselves liable to be deceived. They go to the great meetings that assemble in the country to hear Mr Bradlaugh speak, and fancy that the numerical progress of Secularism is commensurate with the increase in his auditory, forgetting that Mr Bradlaugh is a great orator, and that the majority of his hearers are enamoured, not so much of what he says as of the way in which he says it.[2]

The *Secular Chronicle* called for a national conference and a fresh start.[3]

The N.S.S. Executive called a conference to meet in Manchester on Whit Sunday, 1875, but, though all Secularist groups were invited to send delegates, voting was to be restricted to N.S.S.

branches. This exclusiveness clearly infuriated the Birmingham men on the *Secular Chronicle*, and opposition was also expressed by the Glasgow Eclectic Society, which had joined the N.S.S. with great reluctance. Nevertheless Bradlaugh had his way, and the Manchester conference marked the beginning of the new N.S.S. By the time the next conference was held, on Whit Sunday, 1876, in Leeds, there were 1,192 members.[4]

Between 1870 and 1876 several changes took place in the lesser leadership of the movement. Death removed Austin Holyoake, Bradlaugh's printer, in April 1874; and George Reddalls, editor of the *Secular Chronicle*, in October 1875. Dr George Sexton, a prominent lecturer and 'Melampus' of the *National Reformer*, joined the International and then became a spiritualist; and D. K. Fraser also returned to religion. On the credit side, G. W. Foote emerged as one of the most promising young men in the movement; and in Annie Besant both Secularism and Bradlaugh acquired a rare gem. With the conversion to freethought of Joseph Symes in 1876 the N.S.S. completed a formidable lecturing team with which to rally the country.[5]

The death of Austin Holyoake from consumption at the age of forty-seven necessitated new printing and publishing arrangements. Austin had served the movement since entering into partnership with his brother, George Jacob, in 1851, and had had his own premises at 17 Johnson's Court since 1864. On his death the freethought party bought the business for Charles Watts. In December 1874 another distinguished freethought publisher, James Watson, also died and, as the Holyoakes had handled most of his business since his retirement in 1854, his plates and stock were also acquired by Watts, who now had in his hands the legacy of freethought publishing over the past forty years. Though this work compelled Watts to give up the secretaryship of the N.S.S. in 1876, he was clearly the second man in the movement, and in the absence of Mrs Bradlaugh (who was dying of alcoholism) Watts's talented wife, Kate, was first lady in the movement.

The position of both was challenged in the mid-1870s by the meteoric rise of Mrs Annie Besant, who succeeded also in alienating the ambitious G. W. Foote. The latter had begun contributing to the *National Reformer* in 1870, and at first had devoted himself mainly to youth work at the Hall of Science, and republicanism. He was a good speaker, a keen worker, and apparently had a promising future as a Secularist. His ideal of a leader at this time was a cross between the thoughtful, academic Holyoake and the powerful, passionate

Bradlaugh.[6] At first he was inclined to support Bradlaugh, but by 1875 he was growing restive. He dared to criticise Bradlaugh in the *Secular Chronicle*, and was immediately rewarded with a stern rebuke. Foote began to realise what many other radical and freethought leaders had still to learn: that the price of Bradlaugh's purposeful and successful leadership was strict obedience. 'Why does a democrat like Mr Bradlaugh,' wondered Foote, 'compare the party of which he is a member to a regiment of drilled machines, without will or purpose except to obey the word of command? I am not a soldier, but a citizen . . .'[7] What really upset Foote, however, was not just that he was being treated as a subordinate, but that Bradlaugh was showing excessive favouritism to his newest young colleague, Annie Besant.[8] Foote protested that he was being excluded, and began to move towards G. J. Holyoake, who, as the still respected founder of Secularism, had come to serve as a 'cave of Adullam' for discontented Bradlaughites. At the beginning of 1876 the two men issued their own periodical, the *Secularist*, but after two months they split up, Foote continuing the paper while Holyoake began his own *Secular Review*.

At the 1876 N.S.S. conference at Leeds, Foote launched an attack on the office of president and on its incumbent, but of the major figures in freethought only Mrs Harriet Law was prepared to support his demand for a broadening of the N.S.S. power structure. Every time he appealed to Holyoake for support the latter let him down. Foote was overwhelmingly defeated and Bradlaugh's position made more secure than ever.[9] At the meeting of the N.S.S. Executive on 24 June, Watts moved and Holyoake seconded the expulsion of Foote. Angrily, Foote responded in the *Secularist*:

The excommunication is a roaring farce, but that is not his fault; the man meant it seriously. Such an exquisite appreciation of his own dignity and of the necessary limits of democratic freedom, is ample evidence of Mr Bradlaugh's fitness for the post of President of the Coming Republic, which his well-advised advocacy does so much to hasten. A people under his sway would be truly united, for no dissentient would be allowed to live.[10]

This was not only ironic; it was prophetic, as Charles Watts was to learn at great cost when he dared to oppose Bradlaugh's will over the affair of the Knowlton Pamphlet.

*The Knowlton Pamphlet*

Among James Watson's stock which Charles Watts acquired in 1875 were the plates of *The Fruits of Philosophy, or the Private Companion of Young Married People* by Dr Charles Knowlton, a New England doctor who wished to give elementary contraceptive information to his patients. The book was originally published in New York in 1832, and in its first three years was subjected to three prosecutions, Knowlton himself being committed to three months' hard labour. James Watson brought out the first English edition in 1834, and it sold about a thousand copies a year, unmolested by prosecution. All the freethought publishers and booksellers handled the work in a cheap sixpenny edition. By 1876 it was superseded medically, and no one was really taking much notice of it. Watts had not even bothered to read it.[11]

This obscurity was destroyed by events in Bristol, where Henry Cook, a boot-closer who ran a bookselling business on the side, sent a catalogue of his wares under plain cover to a customer at his place of work. The man's employer opened the envelope and handed the contents to the police, who paid Cook a visit. Among the works they took away for examination was the Knowlton Pamphlet, and an information was laid against it under the Obscene Publications Act of 1857 (20 and 21 Vict., c. 83). Cook was tried at the Bristol Quarter Session on 29 December 1876. When Watts first heard of the prosecution, Bradlaugh was out of London, but after consulting Mrs Besant he advised Cook that the book was defensible as a medical work. What he did not know was that, though Cook had received his copies wholesale from Watts at 4*d*, to be sold at 6*d*, Cook had torn out the publisher's imprint, added some 'indecent' advertisements, and sold it for 1*s* 8*d*. Cook, who was not unknown to the police, was found guilty and given the maximum sentence of two years' hard labour. Watts immediately stopped selling the work, but on the night of Monday 8 January 1877 he was charged with being the publisher of an obscene work.[12]

At first he determined to fight the case, and he and Kate consulted Bradlaugh and Besant. Mrs Besant was eager to appeal to the Secularist movement for help, despite the known division of opinion about birth control, and Bradlaugh promised to look after Watts's business should he be martyred for the cause. But after reading the Knowlton Pamphlet carefully the Wattses decided they could not defend it. Both Bradlaugh and Besant were furious. They broke off all business arrangements with Watts, and Bradlaugh dismissed him from the sub-editorship of the *National Reformer*. On 8 February, at the Old Bailey, Watts pleaded 'guilty in law' and agreed to the plates and stock being destroyed. He was released on his own recognisances of £500 and ordered to pay the costs.[13]

Bradlaugh and Besant now began their own Freethought Publishing Company, and Bradlaugh and Watts separated amid mutual recriminations. The details of the split, as publicised in the *National Reformer*, the *Secular Review* and various pamphlets, were conflicting, but both sides appear to have acted in good faith. Bradlaugh felt that Watts had let down the cause of freethought; Watts felt that the pamphlet was not good enough to go to gaol for; Mrs Watts felt that Bradlaugh was too anxious to make a martyr out of her husband; Mrs Besant, who had already begun collecting funds for the defence, felt betrayed by Watts's capitulation.[14]

The members of the N.S.S. were shocked and bewildered by the conflicting claims on their loyalties. Watts and Bradlaugh had been close colleagues for over ten years. Together they had built, sustained and revived the N.S.S. Watts was a well liked figure who had few enemies in the movement. Bradlaugh was in a different position. His appeal was to the rank and file whom his lectures stirred; among those who knew him better there was a considerable feeling of resentment at his domination of the movement, despite Foote's failure to capitalise on it at the 1876 conference. Similarly with Mrs Besant. She was an exciting new lecturer to the rank and file, but to many older members she was an over-zealous upstart.[15]

The quarrel between Bradlaugh and Watts produced a fierce controversy in the Secularist press and in the local societies. Several issues were involved: supporters of Bradlaugh emphasised the need to defend freedom of publication at all costs; supporters of Watts defended his right to disagree with Bradlaugh and deplored his dismissal by Bradlaugh. The Walsall Sunday Reading Room came to the conclusion that Watts was wrong, but the Nottingham society (in which Kate Watts was brought up) received Watts 'with immense enthusiasm'. He was also supported by the Glasgow Eclectic Society, and the Dundee society went so far as to cancel Bradlaugh's lectures. But support for Bradlaugh came from Stourbridge and Bristol.[16] William Willis of London argued a 'domino theory' that 'if *The Fruits of Philosophy* be thus quietly surrendered, the others must of necessity follow'. On the other side, an even more prominent London freethinker, J. P. Adams, thought that 'by declining to defend the book [Watts] will best consult the interest of the party, respect his own dignity, and finally, purge our literature of a work which ought never to have been mixed up with it'.[17] Holyoake's *Secular Review* was generally favourable to Watts; Foote's *Secularist* liked Watts less, but Bradlaugh less still; Harriet

Law, who now ran the *Secular Chronicle*, was no friend to Watts but thought he should be allowed to do whatever he thought best without forfeiting his friends on account of it.[18] To Owen Balmforth, the leader of the Huddersfield Secularists, Bradlaugh's action was comparable to that of a mill owner who dismissed his bookkeeper for voting Radical against his instructions. 'How long will the Freethought Party permit Mr Bradlaugh 'to hold its flag,' when he commits such actions as these?' he wondered in the *Secularist*. The answer came from Walter Lewin of Birkenhead, the following week:

If by the Freethought Party, Secularism is meant, it is safe to answer—As long as he likes—or at least until he has succeeded in killing the Party. There will be secessions no doubt. The more thoughtful men and women will gradually withdraw from any such leadership, but the mass of Secularists will continue to declaim in the name of Freethought against the tyranny of kings and the superstitions of Christianity; . . .[19]

He was right. Some of those who regarded themselves as the more thoughful and responsible did withdraw. Holyoake handed his *Secular Review* over to Watts in February 1877, and Foote joined his *Secularist* to it in June. Around the new *Secular Review* a rival party to Bradlaugh grew up which was never completely reconciled to him, but by the time of the 1877 conference, held in Nottingham, there was little doubt that the bulk of the N.S.S. had remained loyal to Bradlaugh.

This was not only because of his personal hold over the rank and file. By June the whole issue had been transformed by the arrest of Bradlaugh and Besant. Objections to the *Fruits of Philosophy* were now forgotten. The issue had become the right to publish, and this was a cry to rally freethinkers. For most people, Bradlaugh's treatment of Watts sank into the background.

From the outset Bradlaugh and Besant were determined to make a test case out of the republication of the *Fruits of Philosophy*. The text was modified a little, and brought up to date with medical footnotes by Dr George Drysdale, but it was substantially the prohibited work. On Saturday 24 March at 4.00 p.m. copies of the new edition were offered for sale at the premises of the Freethought Publishing Company at 24 Stonecutter Street. The Guildhall authorities were notified in advance. Within twenty minutes 500 copies had been sold, and by 6.00 p.m. nearly 800, including some to the police. But on the Monday no warrant arrived for the arrest of Bradlaugh and Besant. Not till 5 April were they finally summoned to appear at the Guildhall Court, and on 17 April they were committed for trial at the Old Bailey. A defence fund had already collected £390, and the issue of the *National Reformer* which reported the hearing at the Guildhall sold an extra 2,500 copies. Public opinion was now mobilised both for and against the couple, and Bradlaugh succeeded in getting the case transferred to the Court of Queen's Bench before a special jury.[20]

While Bradlaugh and Besant were awaiting trial the police raided the premises of Edward Truelove, the veteran Owenite, radical and freethought bookseller, and on 23 May he was charged at Bow Street with selling birth control pamphlets by R. D. Owen and J. H. Palmer. Bradlaugh stood bail for Truelove and got his case also transferred to the Queen's Bench. Truelove agreed not to sell the prosecuted works, but he did continue to sell the Knowlton Pamphlet. C. H. Collette, solicitor for the Society for the Suppression of Vice, therefore brought a second case against him, which was held over pending the Bradlaugh–Besant trial.[21]

The case of Regina *v.* Bradlaugh and Besant came on at the Queen's Bench before the Lord Chief Justice, Sir Alexander Cockburn, on 18 June, with the Solicitor General, Sir Hardinge Giffard, leading the prosecution.[22] Both Bradlaugh and Besant conducted their own defence—an unusual enough event in any case, but remarkable for a woman. The trial lasted four days, whereupon the jury (chaired by Alfred Walter, whose father's *Times* had been hostile throughout) retired to consider its verdict. The prospects seemed good for the defendants, the Lord Chief Justice having summed up in what appeared to be a favourable manner. The jury was divided, six of the members not wishing to return an unqualified verdict of guilty, and agreeing to a special verdict on the sole understanding that, if it were not acceptable, they should retire to reconsider.[23] They therefore allowed Walter to report, 'We are unanimously of opinion that the book in question is calculated to deprave public morals, but at the same time we entirely exonerate the defendants from any corrupt motives in publishing it.' But the law, as laid down by Cockburn himself in R. *v.* Hicklin (1868), defined obscenity as that which was calculated to deprave and corrupt, irrespective of motive. Cockburn therefore took the verdict to mean guilty, and would allow no reconsideration by the jury. Even had he accepted the special verdict, this would not have vindicated Bradlaugh's right to publish the work. On 28 June the defendants came up to be sentenced. They expected to be fined, and Bradlaugh had drawn £250 out of his bank account in readiness. In fact Cockburn would probably have discharged them on their own recognisances, but for incidents at the Hall of Science between the verdict and the sentence.

On Sunday 24 June Bradlaugh as usual lectured at the Hall of Science, with Mrs Besant in the chair. Unfortunately, at that meeting copies of *The Fruits of Philosophy* were offered for sale in the hall; furthermore, Mrs Besant unwisely informed the audience that one of the jury had not agreed with the verdict, and she gave the impression that the Lord Chief Justice had summed up in favour of an acquittal. Cockburn took a very serious view of this contempt, and sentenced each of the defendants to six months as first-class demeanants in Holloway gaol, plus a £200 fine, plus entering into their own recognisances of £500 and providing sureties for a further £200 for good behaviour for two years thereafter. Bradlaugh immediately lodged an appeal, and stay of sentence was granted.[24]

He now displayed his mastery of English legal procedure, and finally on 12 February 1878 secured a ruling that the judgement should be set aside, as the wording of the original indictment had been insufficiently specific. Bradlaugh triumphantly compared himself to John Wilkes, who had challenged general warrants over a century before; in view of the later parliamentary struggle the comparison was unusually apt. No legal opinion, though, was given as to the *Fruits of Philosophy*, which could, therefore, still be the subject of new proceedings.[25]

Next came the Truelove cases. On the first charge he was found guilty after a retrial and sentenced to four months in prison and a fine of £50. On the second charge, involving the *Fruits of Philosophy*, Bradlaugh's name was entered as publisher, the question being whether the seized stocks should be destroyed. Bradlaugh again fought through the courts until in November 1878 he obtained a ruling that the stocks should be returned, and he then prosecuted an inspector of police for illegally detaining them. As no new case was brought against the work, Bradlaugh considered he had vindicated the right to publish it.[26]

What had been achieved? Apart from the implications for the advocacy of birth control (which will be examined in chapter 13), the consequences of the Knowlton trial for the freethought party were several, and, contrary to the fears of Bradlaugh's opponents, they were mainly beneficial. The real victims, apart from Truelove, were Bradlaugh and Besant themselves. The notoriety which the trial brought was one of the principal reasons behind the bitterness of the exclusion of Bradlaugh from Parliament in 1880, and was the means by which Mrs Besant's estranged husband was able to win custody of their daughter, Mabel, in June 1878.[27]

*The aftermath of the trial*

As the conference of 1877 approached, the Secularists realised that the constitutional issue about the dictatorial powers of the president would have to be faced once more. Bradlaugh's treatment of Watts had aroused too many anxieties among the second-rank leaders of the movement. If Watts and Foote were to make any impact on the future of the N.S.S. they knew they would first have to curtail Bradlaugh's powers as president. The one concession granted by the 1876 conference had been a committee chaired by Holyoake to review the rules of the N.S.S. and to report back to a general conference of freethinkers to be held at the same time as the next N.S.S. annual conference.[28] In view of the events of the past year, the scheduled debate took on a new interest. A proposal from George Millar of the Glasgow Eclectic Society, that the presidency be abolished, was debated at length. Millar, as a founder member of the Amalgamated Society of Engineers, pointed out that they had an executive chairman responsible to a committee, but no president with powers derived annually direct from the conference. Charles Cattell, the leader of Birmingham freethought and republicanism since the 1850s, supported this motion, and the members seemed about equally divided. For the proposal there were 110 votes, and against 117—though Mrs Law said she counted only 98. The *National Reformer* claimed that local Nottingham members, very few of whom were in the N.S.S., had flooded the hall and made up the bulk of those opposed to the presidency.[29]

In the open session of the conference Bradlaugh had come near to defeat, but in the closed N.S.S. session he successfully fought off an attempt not to re-elect him as president. The only achievement of his opponents came when the open session appointed a committee of distinguished Secularists to look into the case for a new organisation for freethought, showing that Watts was not alone in feeling that little hope could be entertained of a thoroughly free and secular organisation in connection with the N.S.S. The committee comprised Charles and Kate Watts, Mrs Law, Foote, and Josiah Gimson, the much-respected veteran Leicester leader. Holyoake, who had agreed to accept renomination as an N.S.S. vice-president, nevertheless lent them his support. In August 1877 they formed an anti-Bradlaughite organisation called the British Secular Union (B.S.U.), which took the *Secular Review* as its official paper.[30]

The bitterness between the *Secular Review* party and the *National Reformer* party never totally disappeared, though individual members moved from one to the other. In fact the division did little harm to the movement as a whole; nor did the split hurt Bradlaugh. As Walter Lewin had foreseen, the bulk of the ordinary members stayed loyal to Bradlaugh. His courageous fight for freedom of publication was irresistibly attractive, and his even more compelling campaign to enter Parliament in the 1880s completely outmanoeuvred his rivals of the B.S.U. In Bradlaugh and Besant the N.S.S. had two of the best platform orators of the nineteenth century, and there was to be no holding them back.

## *The revival of Secularism, 1876–80*

Just as the earlier period of Secularist expansion had coincided with a growing tide of popular Liberalism, so the revival can be dated from 1876, the year in which Mr Gladstone's Bulgarian Horrors agitation gave new heart to the Liberal cause. Whilst there is no apparent connection between the two (indeed, some Secularists were opposed to Gladstone's apparently pro-Russian policy[31]), and whilst the growth of Secularism after 1877 can more easily be attributed to the Knowlton trial, the coincidence remains instructive. Secularism was dependent upon a favourable 'climate of opinion'; and the political nature of Secularism under Bradlaugh linked it closely to the fate of general radical politics.

Each year until the mid-1880s the annual conference could be told of record numbers of recruits, and an ever increasing number of new branches. Though we are not given the annual figures for those who did not renew their membership, and are rarely told actual membership figures, there is no mistaking the general tone of optimism and expansion in these years. According to James Thompson (the poet 'B.V.'), an incidental remark of Bradlaugh's at the 1876 conference put the membership figure at 1,192 (excluding thirty-eight Glasgow members whose enrolment was not received in time). In October 1877 Bradlaugh was reporting 'that the audiences at our lectures are larger than ever, and that the sale of Freethought literature is more extended than at any time during the last thirty years'. Surveying the year 1878, George Standring noted that the N.S.S. had 'greatly increased in numbers' and that 'a large proportion of the persons enrolled during the year were women'. This can most likely be attributed to the Knowlton trial and the influence of Annie Besant. In 1880 Mrs Besant told the International conference of Freethinkers that the N.S.S. had 6,000 members 'on our books', compared with only 300 in 1875. Operating on a much smaller scale, the B.S.U. had enrolled 185 members from twenty-nine places by the end of 1877, and was said to have about six hundred members in 1879.[32]

The basic organisation of the N.S.S. in the later 1870s remained much as it had been ten years earlier. At the 1876 conference George Standring took over from Charles Watts as secretary, and in 1877 he was succeeded by his assistant, Robert Forder, who was to hold office until 1891. The subscription was restored to the original 1s a quarter, or 1s 4d a year for members of N.S.S. branches; and membership was either 'active' or 'passive', the latter category being reserved for those who did not wish to be associated publicly with freethought. Some members wanted the subscription to be payable only through branches, thus depriving Bradlaugh of the proxy votes of all the individual subscribers at the annual conference, but with the formation of the B.S.U. such critics were drawn off, leaving Bradlaugh all the more secure in the N.S.S.[33]

The split between the N.S.S. and the B.S.U. gave an additional incentive for branches to be formed. Most opposition to Bradlaugh came from independent societies which continued to see Secularism as a loose federation as in the 1850s. Bradlaugh intended the N.S.S. to be a much more disciplined body. As a society it was shaped in his image, and he was determined that any benefit which freethought might derive from his personality and efforts should be enjoyed only by those most loyal to him. An official N.S.S. lecturer could only lecture to local branches, and no disaffected group could employ him even when he was in the district. Before 1875 the only official lecturer had been Charles Watts, but from 1877 a number of lecturers were appointed, beginning with one of the most popular men in the North of England, Thomas Slater, who was given Lancashire, Yorkshire, the Midlands and Tyneside as his circuit. The issue of the 'boycotting' of non-affiliated societies, though, was to become much more important in the 1880s.[34]

The series of legal cases involved in the *Fruits of Philosophy* prosecution kept Bradlaugh and Besant in London much more than they would have wished in '1877 and 1878, though the number of other lecturers ensured that that the revival of Secularism was not lost. Whereas Bradlaugh's efforts on behalf of republicanism in the early 1870s had detracted from Secularism, in 1877 and again in the early 1880s his activities were closely associated with Secularism and so strengthened it. Apart from Slater, regular lectures were delivered for the N.S.S. by Joseph Symes, James Holmes (who was based in the Midlands), and Touzeau Parris (who worked mainly in the

South West). Central administration was looked after by Robert Forder and Bradlaugh's two daughters, Alice and Hypatia, who were beginning to be active in the movement. A further accession of strength came in 1879 when Edward Aveling joined the ranks.[35]

Meanwhile, in the country, the economic depression was deepening, dissatisfaction with Lord Beaconsfield's government was growing, and Mr Gladstone was stirring the embers of radicalism into new flames with his Midlothian campaign. Bradlaugh, who had fought the Northampton constituency on every occasion since 1868, prepared for the general election of 1880. As a radical and as spokesman for the unenfranchised, he had in the N.S.S. the best organised support of any popular leader outside the trade unions. He was to need all this and more in the next six years.

*Notes*

1   *N.R.*, 3 May, 7, 14, 21, 28 June, 6 September 1874.
2   *S.C.*, 1 September 1874.
3   *S.C.*, 3 January 1875.
4   *N.R.*, 24 January, 18 April, 2, 23 May 1875; *S.C.*, 4, 11, 18 April, 2, 23 May 1875; *Secularist*, 17 June 1876.
5   For biographical details see chapter 7, pp. 92–108.
6   G. W. Foote, *Secularism Restated* (London, 1874), pp. 4–5.
7   *S.C.*, 15, 22 August, 1875.
8   *S.C.*, 8 August 1875.
9   *N.R.*, 11 June, 1876.
10  *Secularist*, 29 July 1876.
11  P. Fryer, *The Birth Controllers* (London, 1965), pp. 99–105.
12  *Bristol Mercury*, 30 December 1876; Charles Watts to Henry Cook, [11 December 1876], B.L. 478; *N.R.*, 14 January 1877.
13  A. H. Nethercot, *The First Five Lives of Annie Besant* (London, 1961), pp. 119–23; D. Tribe, *President Charles Bradlaugh*, pp. 173–80; *N.R.*, 18 February 1877. The costs amounted to £162 4*s* 10*d*—*S.R.*, 13 October 1877.
14  *Secularist*, 27 January 1877; *N.R.*, 11 February 1877; *S.R.*, 18 February 1877; [G. W. Foote], *Mr. Bradlaugh's Trial and the Freethought Party*; Kate E. Watts, *Mrs. Watts's Reply to Mr. Bradlaugh's Misrepresentations*; see also printed circulars in B.L. nos. 490, 492.
15  This was also Hypatia Bradlaugh's opinion—D. Tribe, *op. cit.*, p. 177.
16  *N.R.*, 28 January, 4, 11, 18 February 1877.
17  *S.C.*, 21, 28 January 1877.
18  *S.R.*, 21 January, 4 February 1877; *Secularist*, 27 January 1877; *S.C.*, 28 January 1877.
19  *Secularist*, 3, 10 February 1877.
20  *N.R.*, 25 March, 1, 8, 15, 22, 29 April, 6, 13 May 1877.
21  *N.R.*, 20, 27 May, 3 June 1877.

22   See R. Manvell, *The Trial of Annie Besant and Charles Bradlaugh* (London, 1976), pp. 61–156; *N.R.*, 24 June, no. 26 [23 June], 1 July, no. 28 [30 June], 8 July, no. 30 [7 July], 15 July 1877. The *N.R.* was actually published about three days before its nominal date of publication, hence the apparent paradox of special numbers coming out before the preceding ordinary issue for the week.
23   *N.R.*, 12 August 1877.
24   *The Queen* v. *Charles Bradlaugh and Annie Besant* (London [1877]), pp. 313–16; *N.R.*, 1, 8 July 1877.
25   *N.R.*, 2 September, 11, 25 November, 30 December 1877; vol. XXXI, nos. 5–8 [3–10 February 1878], 24 February, 3 March 1878.
26   *N.R.*, vol. XXXI, no. 8 [10 February 1878], 17, 24 February, 3 March, 21, 22 July 1878; vol. XXXI, no. 23 [18 May], no. 25 [25 May], 2, 16, 23, 30 June, 17, 24 November, 15 December 1878.
27   *N.R.*, 12, 26 May, no. 25 [25 May], 2, 9, 23, 30 June, 11 August, 6 October, 10 November 1878; 26 January, 2 February, 30 March, 6, 13, 20 April, vol. XXXIII, no. 17 [26 April] 1879.
28   *N.R.*, 11 June 1876; *S.R.*, 26 November 1876.
29   *N.R.*, 27 May 1877; *S.R.*, 27 May 1877; *Secularist*, 26 May 1877; *S.C.*, 27 May 1877.
30   *Secularist*, 2 June 1877; *S.R.*, 11 August 1877; *S.C.*, 26 August 1877.
31   See below, pp. 209–10.
32   *Secularist*, 17, 24 June 1876; *N.R.*, 28 October 1877; *S.C.*, 1 January 1879; *N.R.*, 5 September 1880; *S.R.*, 8 December 1877, 12 July 1879.
33   *N.R.*, 30 May, 13, 20 June 1875, 5 May 1877.
34   See below, pp. 102, 112.
35   *N.S.S. Almanack* (1878), pp. 15–16; *ibid.*, (1880), pp. 17–18.

III

# The climax, 1880–85

*Bradlaugh and the oath*

Although the popular image of the infidel shoemaker might seem to find support in Bradlaugh's decision to try to enter Parliament as member for Northampton, the true explanation lies elsewhere. At the start of 1868 the Northampton branch of the N.S.S. had only twenty-nine members, and a year later after Bradlaugh's first contest it was still only sixty-one. If Bradlaugh were to succeed, it would have to be as a political radical, not as a freethinker.[1]

There is no doubt as to the amount of popular support Bradlaugh could arouse. The public meeting which adopted him in June 1868 was attended by 4,000 people, most of whom were his supporters. But in 1868, like most Liberal Associations which were sufficiently confident of success, the Northampton Liberals could ignore popular radical pressures. Nationally, the Reform League did not support Bradlaugh's candidature, and locally the League branch split, some members wishing to bring in F. R. Lees, the ex-Chartist temperance advocate from Leeds. Despite support from the London Trade Boot and Shoe Makers, who urged their fellows in Northampton to vote for Bradlaugh, the election result made dismal reading. Charles Gilpin, the Liberal candidate, topped the poll with 2,632 votes, but most Liberals gave their other vote to the Whig, Lord Henley, who polled 2,105. Then came the two Tories. Bradlaugh, with 1,086 votes, came nearly 300 votes behind the second Tory, leaving Lees bottom with 485.[2]

Bradlaugh very sensibly decided to persist at Northampton, rather than fight radical seats indiscriminately, but without official Liberal backing at a time when Liberal support throughout the country was weakening his chances of success in 1874 were small. A Tory topped the poll with 2,690 votes, pushing Gilpin into second place. Bradlaugh, with 1,653 votes, was bottom of the poll, but only 143 behind Henley, who was now in fourth position. With Henley thus out of the way, the *National Reformer* looked forward to a deal between Liberals and radicals.[3]

This is certainly what Gilpin expected, and when, late in 1874, he realised he was dying, he offered Bradlaugh copies of his old parliamentary papers in readiness for the succession. Gilpin died shortly afterwards, and Bradlaugh made a clear bid for the Nonconformist vote in his election address, but the orthodox Liberals were not interested in him and brought forward a Whig banker named Fowler. Bradlaugh fought again as an independent radical, and the Tory got in.[4]

Liberal Northampton now had two Tory M.P.s, and there were signs of a *rapprochement* between some Liberals and radicals; but others, led by the *Northampton Mercury*, would have no dealings with Bradlaugh, while John Bates for his part would have no dealings with Liberals. Bradlaugh was finally adopted as official Liberal candidate in 1880 only when the local Liberals found themselves with the prospect of no candidates at all just a few weeks before the poll. Then Henry Labouchere was brought in and, with his support, Bradlaugh.[5]

At the 1880 general election Northampton swung from having two Tories who believed in God to having two Liberal-radicals who did not, though, as Labouchere pointed out during the campaign, personal views as to religion were really irrelevant.[6] This was perhaps over-optimistic of him. The Nonconformist Liberals of Northampton (or, at least, sufficient of them) may have swallowed Bradlaugh, but the godly members at Westminster were to give a great deal more trouble.[7]

In 1869 and 1870 Evidence Amendment Acts had permitted non-believers in the Judaeo-Christian religion to make a secular affirmation in the courts of England and Wales. Bradlaugh believed that these Acts qualified him under the Parliamentary Oaths Act of 1866 as a person legally entitled to make an affirmation instead of the oath when taking his seat in the House of Commons. Accordingly, he informed the Clerk of the fact before he approached the table on 3 May to be sworn in, but the Speaker, Sir Henry Brand, was uncertain whether Bradlaugh really was qualified to make an affirmation instead of the oath, and put the matter in the hands of the House. On the precedents of 1833 and 1850, when similar cases had arisen with regard to the rights of Quakers and Jews respectively, Lord Frederick Cavendish moved for a Select Committee, and this was appointed on 11 May.[8]

The committee was equally divided on party lines, leaving its Tory chairman, Spencer Walpole, to cast his vote against Bradlaugh, who now prepared to take the oath, but this course of action was opposed by Sir Henry Drummond Wolff of the so-called 'Fourth Party', and a new Select Committee was set up. This second committee was opposed to Bradlaugh's being allowed to take the oath, but a majority was prepared to permit him to make an affirmation, subject to penalty in the courts. The relevant statute was 13 Will. III, c. 6 (as modified by 29 Vict., c. 19), which made any Member who voted without taking the oath liable to a penalty of £500 for each offence.[9]

The House was rapidly becoming confused by what was called 'The Bradlaugh case', especially after a motion from Labouchere to allow Bradlaugh to affirm was defeated on 22 June. The following day Bradlaugh entered the House and, after some argument, was allowed to speak at the bar. He delivered this, the first of four such speeches, in a manner demonstrating his own oratorical abilities, sense of the law, respect for Parliament, and determination not to yield. 'He had spoken,' the diarist Henry Lucy noted, 'without reference to note, for twenty minutes, often rising to heights of impassioned eloquence, but always with perfect command over himself and his audience.' He was frequently interrupted by applause, and at the end withdrew to loud cheers, but when the applause had subsided the House resolved to follow its earlier decisions not to allow him to take the oath or to affirm. Bradlaugh was recalled to hear the vedict, on hearing which he ignored the Speaker's command to him to withdraw. After further scenes, Sir Stafford Northcote moved that Bradlaugh be taken into custody, and he was duly confined to the Clock Tower.[10]

The Bradlaugh case was now a *cause celèbre*, and Bradlaugh's name became a household word. Telegrams of support flooded into the House of Commons, and a mass protest meeting was held at Northampton. The 'martyr' was kept in a room in the Clock Tower only for the night of 23 June, and a week later Gladstone's motion that Bradlaugh be allowed to affirm at his legal peril was carried by 303 votes to 249. On Friday 2 July Bradlaugh made his solemn affirmation, and immediately a writ was served against him by Henry Lewis Clarke, who claimed the informer's penalty of £500. Three days later another writ was served, this time in the name of Cecil Barber. It was the aim of Bradlaugh's opponents to break him financially: as a bankrupt he would be unable to sit in the House of Commons. Everything now depended on the legal outcome of Clarke *v.* Bradlaugh. Meanwhile Bradlaugh continued to take a full part in the proceedings of the House, speaking about twenty times and voting on ninety-one occasions before the end of the session.[11]

Bradlaugh was now, to all intents and purposes, an M.P. He was allowed full use of the House of Commons library, and was even allowed the usual patronage over government appointments in his constituency.[12] George Strandring thought the struggle was over, but on 11 March 1881 Clarke won his case against Bradlaugh, and three weeks later Bradlaugh lost his appeal against the verdict. He now commenced a further appeal on the grounds that Clarke was a common informer, while the House declared his seat at Northampton vacant.[13] As in the celebrated case of John Wilkes and the Middlesex election (1769), Bradlaugh contested the bye-election in the belief that as a new member he would be clear of all previous motions and prohibitions. The contest at Northampton was closely fought, with 153 former Liberals voting for the Tory candidate, and 237 Liberals abstaining, but the result still gave Bradlaugh 3,437 votes to his opponent's 3,305. With this fresh mandate from his constituents, on 26 April Bradlaugh again presented himself to take the oath, but was again objected to by the leader of the Tories in the House of Commons, Sir Stafford Northcote. Again Bradlaugh spoke at the bar of the House, and this time Mr Gladstone himself expressed himself in favour of Bradlaugh being allowed to take the oath, but to no avail. Bradlaugh therefore advanced to the table in front of the Speaker in open defiance, and the Serjeant at Arms escorted him back to the bar. Twice this pantomime was repeated before the House adjourned.[14]

Labouchere now sought leave to bring in an Affirmations Bill, but withdrew when Gladstone announced the government's intention of acting. Privately Bradlaugh promised Gladstone that he would abstain from further provocative acts provided the government introduced its Bill with reasonable speed. In the meantime he took his case to the country, where a widespread campaign had been mounting for the abolition of the oath. But the government was unable to find time in its schedule of legislation to give substance to Gladstone's cautious promise, and so on 3 August Bradlaugh came to the House of Commons at the head of a vast crowd of supporters to claim his rightful place. There followed one of the most dramatic scenes in the whole episode, as Bradlaugh was physically ejected from the House by its messengers and police.[15]

Ever the constitutionalist, Bradlaugh then used his power over the crowd to urge them to disperse peacefully. Annie Besant recalled with fierce pride, 'Ah! he was never greater than in that moment of outrage and of triumphant wrong; with all the passion of a proud man surging within him ... he was never greater than when he conquered his own wrath.'[16]

During the long autumn recess the first signs of hope came in Bradlaugh's legal battle. On 20 September he commenced an action against Charles Newdigate Newdegate, the ultra-Conservative M.P. for North Warwickshire, for 'maintaining' Clarke, contrary to 1 Ric. II, c. 4, sec. 2, and also the common law; and on 2 December he won a new trial of Clarke *v.* Bradlaugh on the grounds that Clarke's writ might have been obtained a few minutes *before* Bradlaugh cast his illegal vote. To follow the intricacies of the various hearings, demurrers, replies, rulings and appeals would require a volume of legal history, which would show Charles Bradlaugh to have been a brilliant lawyer. Clarke's case was conducted by the Solicitor General himself, Bradlaugh's old adversary Sir Hardinge Giffard. Despite many reverses, as when Clarke's appeal against the new trial was upheld in March 1882, Bradlaugh fought on, taking his case to the House of Lords. The more he fought, the more his legal costs mounted; he certainly would have been a bankrupt if he had ever acknowledged defeat. But Bradlaugh had the ability to take full advantage of the anomalies and absurdities of English law, and tried to beat the highest and most experienced legal brains in Britain at their own casuistical game. Only once, in 1881 when he was ill after his ejection from the House, did he contemplate settling with Clarke out of court, but Newdegate would not hear of it. Finally, after Bradlaugh had lost his legal points all along the way, the House of Lords ruled on 9 April 1883 that there was nothing in the Act under which Clarke had sued that gave a common informer the right to sue. The action therefore fell to the ground. A fortnight later Bradlaugh won his case against Newdegate and was eventually awarded £100 indemnity and costs.[17]

Bradlaugh was understandably relieved, but exhausted, for events had not stood still in Parliament while these cases and others were being heard in the courts. The 1882 session opened with Bradlaugh's third speech at the bar, followed by a further refusal to admit him to the oath or to declare his seat vacant. On 21 February he therefore astounded the Members by walking up to the table and administering the oath to himself. The House then expelled him, but his constituents sent him back again at the ensuing bye-election—though his majority was reduced to 108. The Duke of Argyll introduced an Affirmations Bill in the House of Lords, but it was defeated on its second reading.[18] In 1883 the government at last prepared its own Bill—the 'Bradlaugh Relief Bill', as its opponents called it. A majority of 131 was recorded at the first reading, when

Sir Stafford Northcote led his supporters out of the chamber, but on 3 May, despite an influential speech from Mr Gladstone, the Bill fell on its second reading by 289 votes to 292. Next day Bradlaugh spoke for a fourth time at the bar of the House, but when he presented himself to take the oath in July he was again excluded.[19] The pattern of events varied a little in 1884, for Bradlaugh again swore himself in, and then voted on Northcote's motion to exclude him, thereby hoping to find a new angle to test in the courts. He then applied for the Chiltern Hundreds, thus vacating his seat and clearing all the motions against him.In the next bye-election, for the first time, his majority over his Conservative opponent was increased, to 368. The Bradlaughite radicals were riding high, with Thomas Adams, Bradlaugh's agent, becoming mayor at the end of the year. In Parliament, though, the old story was repeated. Northcote's motion to exclude him was easily carried.[20]

The issue was now put to the test by the government, and Bradlaugh was prosecuted by the Attorney General, Sir Henry James, for five offences as an unsworn member on 11 February. Bradlaugh fought this case, as he had fought the others, meeting each defeat with a new appeal until once again he reached the House of Lords. While this was going on he held his hand, leaving the Commons to struggle with the problem of Ireland and constitutional reform. Gladstone's Ministry fell on 24 June 1885, with the Bradlaugh case no nearer solution. At the general election in November, Labouchere and Bradlaugh had a complete triumph against only one Conservative candidate, whom Bradlaugh kept in third place by 425 votes.[21]

The new Parliament met on 13 January 1886. The Speaker, now the youngest son of Sir Robert Peel, cut the Gordian knot and allowed Bradlaugh to take the oath. The government refused to institute any new prosecution while Bradlaugh's appeal was before the Lords. At the general election of 1886 Northampton was fought by two Conservatives but while Labouchere's vote fell slightly Bradlaugh's actually increased, and his majority over the nearest Conservative was now 503. It was clear that Bradlaugh had come to stay—a fact confirmed in the autumn when the Conservative government agreed to a *stet processus* of the action against Bradlaugh for voting in February 1884.[22]

## The National Secular Society

The Bradlaugh case was important in the constitutional history of

England, but it was also important in the history of popular radicalism and the Secularist movement. For many people of the 'popular' classes, Bradlaugh's name became synonymous with radicalism between 1880 and 1885. Whereas he had previously been only one leader among many, now he was indisputably *the* leader. Beyond the limits of Northampton, and beyond the confines of the N.S.S., Bradlaugh was the popular hero—the champion of the masses against the classes, of right against might, of the people against their corrupt, oligarchic masters. This did not, of course, turn the N.S.S. into a second Reform League, but it did win to it members who were broadly sympathetic to Bradlaugh's politics, and it brought the N.S.S. branches fully into the life of their communities as an active organisation for the promotion of radicalism. The Secularists could be in no danger of developing into an exclusively anti-religious sect, or of slipping out of the mainstream of radical action, while Bradlaugh was excluded from Parliament.

Between the annual conference in June 1880 and the following October the N.S.S. attracted 408 new members; by November the figure was 603 (more than in the whole of the previous year); and by Whitsuntide 1881 the annual total had reached 823. During the next twelve months the figure for new members was 1,304, and a further 1,022 were added in the second half of 1882 alone.This was the beginning of Foote's blasphemy trials and new membership figures for the whole of the year 1882-83 reached 1,883. The next twelve months almost matched this with 1,747, but the year 1884-85 saw a fall to only 1,367 new members. The number of new branches also grew in these years, and beyond the formal organisation vast numbers of adherents were attracted.[23]

The time and energy taken by the parliamentary struggle and its attendant legal cases restricted Bradlaugh's provincial lecture tours to occasional sallies during the vacations, and he most often spoke on political matters or his own case. For example, between 21 and 29 May 1881 he addressed fifteen meetings in nine towns, but only one of his lectures was on a freethought topic. His efforts were supplemented, however, by official lectures from Annie Besant, Edward Aveling, Touzeau Parris, Joseph Symes, Robert Forder, Thomas Slater and G.W. Foote—the latter having rejoined the Bradlaugh camp—as well as by a dozen or so freethought lecturers not directly sponsored by the N.S.S. The healthy condition of the movement fostered by all this activity and publicity was reflected in its literature. In the early 1880s the freethinkers were able to support

more periodicals than ever before, and in 1881-82 the circulation of
N.S.S. leaflets doubled. The Freethought Publishing Company was
so successful that it was moved from 28 Stonecutter Street to more
spacious accomodation at 63 Fleet Street.[24]

This was only the spearhead of Bradlaugh's cause: N.S.S.
branches gave the lead to a much wider movement. Exhorted by
Bradlaugh in the *National Reformer*, gripped by weekly episodes of his
superhuman struggles with the ogres of British justice, the
Secularists came into their own. Bradlaugh had his disciplined
army at last.

On 13 June 1880 he appealed through the *National Reformer* for
Secularists to petition Parliament on his behalf. By the end of the
month 405 petitions had been presented with 37,540 signatures. In
May 1881 Annie Besant organised a League for the Defence of
Constitutional Rights, which rapidly gained in popularity. The
enthusiastic members even suggested a Solemn League and
Covenant to abstain from tobacco and drink until Bradlaugh was
elected to Parliament. Meetings were held at St. James's Hall on 9
June and in Trafalgar Square on 2 August. Other radical and
Liberal associations threw in their efforts behind the agitation.
Delegates from forty-five London clubs (including nine N.S.S.
branches), representing 50,000 members, pledged their support for
the rights of the electors of Northampton at a meeting in the Hall of
Science in February 1882. Delegates from over a hundred towns
(many from Lancashire and Yorkshire) attended a rally in Trafalgar
Square on 10 May 1882, and four days later a crowd of 80,000
assembled in Hyde Park. The leading Manchester Secularists,
Thomas Slater and George Payne, formed an Electoral Rights
Defence Association in Manchester, which had ninety branches in
fifty-eight towns, mainly in Lancashire.[25]

The opposition to Bradlaugh was, of course, also active, but the
tally of petitions between 8 February and 2 December 1882 gives
some idea of the balance of forces: there were 520 petitions with
72,953 signatures against permitting Bradlaugh to take the oath,
and 1,153 petitions with 263,259 in favour.[26]

The same level of pressure was sustained each year during the
Bradlaugh case. After the rejection of Gladstone's Affirmations Bill
in 1883, Bradlaugh sent Gladstone a list of public meetings which
had *not* been reported in the London press: 6,000 had gathered in the
open air at Rawtenstall and were unanimously in favour of
Affirmation; crowed halls in Leeds were also unanimously in favour;
of 2,000 who gathered at Stockton, only forty were opposed; 6,000

Cleveland miners were unanimous; and of an audience at Dewsbury only two dissented; a mass meeting at Skircoat Moor, Halifax, with 30,000–40,000 present, had produced three opponents. There may be some pardonable exaggeration here, but Gladstone cannot but have been impressed by the scale of the agitation which continued throughout the summer—Woodhouse Moor, Leeds, in July; Trafalgar Square in August; and so on. Freethinkers predominated in the organisation of this agitation, just as they were behind Bradlaugh at Northampton, without actually constituting a significant proportion of the crowds.[27]

Sometimes it is difficult to know where to draw the line between radicals and freethinkers. A radical tea-party held near Halifax in 1886 to celebrate Bradlaugh's victory sang the radical/freethinking parody of the National Anthem from the *Secularists' Manual of Songs and Ceremonies*. Bradlaugh was able to draw on a common stock of populist ideas, anti-clerical and anti-aristocratic in the tradition of Thomas Paine.[28]

The freethinkers would not have been true to themselves, though, had they accepted Bradlaugh's actions uncritically. Rebels in the B.S.U. were unhappy about the prospect of an atheist fighting for the right to swear by the name of God and kiss the Bible. The popular success of Bradlaugh, and the public identification of Secularism with his cause, was more than sufficient to rouse the jealousies of those other leaders cast into the shade, particularly those patrician purists who doubted whether Bradlaugh's crowd tactics were calculated to enhance the intellectual reputation of Secularism.

The opposition to Bradlaugh centred on the *Secular Review*, where 'Saladin' (W. Stewart Ross) appointed himself chief pin-pricker of Bradlaugh and Besant bubbles. The B.S.U. and the older leaders, Holyoake and Watts, never made open warfare in quite the manner of Ross. Their roots in freethought were too deep for them not to appreciate what Bradlaugh was doing.

The position taken by Holyoake and Watts was that Bradlaugh should have quietly made the Quaker affirmation without drawing undue attention to himself. This was unrealistic advice. Further, they thought that, having been forbidden to affirm, he should not have sought to swear the oath, but should have taken a highly moral and principled stand. Foote was in agreement with the latter point, but more realistic on the former. Holyoake annoyed Bradlaugh by repeating his armchair advice in the public press. But, as the struggle dragged on, many of these attitudes were submerged. Foote was never reconciled with Annie Besant, but as a result of Bradlaugh's struggle he left the B.S.U. in the spring of 1881 and was received back as an N.S.S. lecturer, and even the Council of the B.S.U. supported a motion from Watts and Ross urging their members to join in the general campaign.[29]

At first the B.S.U. shared in the general expansion which the Bradlaugh case promoted: there was an increase in enquiries into the principles of Secularism, and requests for Secularist literature at Watts's shop increased in the first weeks of the struggle in 1880. General progress was reported to the Council in July 1880, and the annual conference reports convey the same impression of growth as in the N.S.S. Again, no membership figures are given, but what evidence there is suggests that at its peak the B.S.U. had no more than a score of branches, with only a few hundred members By 1884, when Watts emigrated to Canada, the organisation had faded away. Its emphasis was on quality, not quantity, with the Marquis of Queensberry as its first president.[30]

The fact was that, despite the general appearance of expansion and success, there was not enough room for two national organisations side by side. Local societies, such as that at Dundee, which had maintained their independence, had to endure the competition of an N.S.S. branch and did not want a B.S.U. branch in their town as well.[31] The *Secular Review* was a more appropriate centre of opposition, especially when Ross joined Watts as editor in 1882 and became sole editor two years later.

*Foote and blasphemy*

To set against Ross the Bradlaugh side had the services of G. W. Foote, a man of similar talents and wit who began his own paper, the *Freethinker*, in May 1881. If Bradlaugh had wielded the hammer of 'Iconoclast', Foote waved the feather of a quill pen. Some readers of the *Freethinker* were moved to laughter; others were not amused.

Foote meant well, but his flippant mockery of the Christian religion gave Bradlaugh's enemies just what they needed. Sir Henry Tyler, M.P., had noted that a person convicted of blasphemy was incapable of defending himself at law against the action of a common informer, or of initiating a prosecution. So a convicted Bradlaugh would have to concede in Clarke *v.* Bradlaugh and drop his action against Newdegate. Furthermore, as with bankruptcy, blasphemy was a bar on entry to the House of Commons. Accordingly Tyler set out to catch his man.[32] Foote's *Freethinker* was first published at the Freethought Publishing Company's address at 28 Stonecutter Street. Tyler illegally inspected the company's bank account and decided he had a case. The *Freethinker* for 28 May 1882 was prosecuted for an article, 'What shall I do to be damned', by William Heaford, and a cartoon of the Deity entitled 'Divine Illumination'. The indictment was against Foote as editor, W. J. Ramsey as manager, E. W. Whittle as printer, and Bradlaugh, whom Tyler believed to be the proprietor. The case against Whittle was dropped, but the other three appeared at the Old Bailey on 31 July 1882. Bradlaugh characteristically got the case transferred to the Queen's Bench, where he hoped for a fairer trial. His defence was that he had no connection with the *Freethinker* beyond publishing it for the first few issues in 1881, but he needed his co-defendant Ramsey to testify to this fact. He therefore applied for a separate trial. While these legal manoeuvres were going on, a second prosecution was brought against Foote, Ramsey and their printer, Henry Kemp, on account of their special Christmas number of the *Freethinker* in 1882.[33]

This second case came on at the Old Bailey on 1 March 1883 before Mr Justice North, a Roman Catholic. The jury was divided, but bail was refused and a retrial was held four days later. This time the jury was convinced by North's hostile summing-up, and the three prisoners were sentenced as common criminals—Foote to a year, Ramsey to six months and Kemp to three months—in Holloway prison. The freethought movement rallied behind its latest martyrs, but to no avail. During Foote's imprisonment the *Freethinker* and his other periodical, the monthly *Progress*, were edited by Edward Aveling, assisted by Annie Besant and Eleanor Marx respectively.[34]

On 10 April Foote and Ramsey were brought out of Holloway to stand trial at the Queen's Bench before Lord Coleridge. Despite his having been the prosecuting counsel at the trial of Thomas Pooley for blasphemy in 1857, Coleridge was expected to give the freethinkers a fairer trial than had Mr Justice North. He allowed Bradlaugh a separate trial on the grounds that the other two defendants already stood convicted of a similar offence, and he roundly condemned the prosecution for prying into Bradlaugh's bank account. On 13 April the jury's verdict was that Bradlaugh was not involved in any way with the indicted *Freethinker*. The trial of Foote and Ramsey took place on 24 and 25 April, and from it they gained two important points: firstly, Coleridge made a distinction between indecency and blasphemy, which were often confused in the minds of jurors and judges alike; secondly, he made legal history in his summing-up by distinguishing between the manner and the substance of an alleged blasphemy offence. The jury was divided, and the prosecution subsequently entered a *nolle prosequi*, thus abandoning any further attempt to secure a conviction.[35]

Coming as it did in the middle of Bradlaugh's parliamentary struggle, Foote's trial and imprisonment reinforced that sense of mission which attracted and sustained Secularist groups and won them sympathy in liberal quarters beyond their ranks; and it also established the *Freethinker* as the third major weekly Secularist paper. This success enabled Foote to maintain a balance within the freethought movement. The *National Reformer* was increasingly devoted to political and parliamentary issues, which it discussed in the sober terms of a respectable review. Foote, on the other hand, maintained the older freethought traditions of impious theological discussion and anti-Christian attack. The distinctive identity of freethought was thus preserved by Foote, and it was this, together with the crown of martyrdom, which ensured that he would inherit Richard Carlile's gavel, symbol of the presidency of the N.S.S., when Bradlaugh retired in 1890.

## Notes

1  *N.R.*, 10 January 1869; see also my article in *Northamptonshire Past and Present* (autumn 1979)
2  *N.R.*, 22, 29 November 1868.
3  *N.R.*, 15, 22 February 1874.
4  Charles Gilpin to Charles Bradlaugh, 4 August 1874—copy in B.L. no. 389; *N.R.*, 20 September, 11 October 1874.
5  *Northampton Radical*, 11 November 1874; W. L. Arnstein, *The Bradlaugh Case* (Oxford, 1965), pp. 26–9.
6  A. L. Thorold, *The Life of Henry Labouchere* (London, 1913), pp. 130–1; *N.R.*, 28 March, 11 April 1880.
7  The story of the Bradlaugh case is told most fully in Arnstein, *op. cit.* What follows is based largely on this and the very full reports which appeared in the *N.R.*
8  *N.R.*, 9, 16 May 1880.
9  *N.R.*, 23, 30 May, vol. XXXV, no. 23 [31 May], 6 June, no. 25 [6 June], 13 June 1880; vol. XXXVI, no. 2 [27 June–4 July] 1880.
10  H. W. Lucy, *A Diary of Two Parliaments* (London, 1886), pp. 37–8; *N.R.* vol. XXXVI, no. 2 [27 June–4 July], no. 4 [4–11 July] 1880.
11  See items in B.L. nos. 674–720, 21–26 June 1880; *N.R.*, vol. XXXVI, no. 4 [4–11 July], 11 July, 26 September, 3 October 1880.
12  E.g. R. Grosvenor to [Bradlaugh], and Bradlaugh to T. Adams, 21

March 1881, Bradlaugh collection, Northampton Public Library.

13  *Republican,* January 1881; *N.R.*, 20 March, 10 April 1881.

14  *N.R.*, 17 April, vol. XXXVII, no. 22 [1–8 May] 1881.

15  *N.R., loc. cit.*; Bradlaugh to W. E. Gladstone, 22 June 1881, B.M. Add. Mss. 44, 111, ff. 93–7; *N.R.*, 10, 24 July, 14 August 1881; Lucy, *op. cit.*, pp. 194–5.

16  A. Besant, *An Autobiography* (London, 1893), p. 268.

17  *N.R.*, 11 December 1881, 5 March 1882; 15 April, vol. XLI, no. 17 [15 April], 29 April 1883; 27 January 1884.

18  *N.R.*, 26 February, vol. XXXIX, no. 11 [26 February–5 March], no. 13 [5–12 March], 16 July 1882.

19  *N.R.*, 25 February, 13 May, 15 July 1883.

20  *N.R.*, vol. XLIII, no. 8 [17 February], 19, 24 February, 2 March, 16 November 1884.

21  *N.R.*, 16 March, 6 April, vol. XLIII, nos. 27–30 [17–21 June] 1884; vol. XLIV, no. 1 [1 July], 6 July, nos. 26, 28 [14, 21 December], 28 December 1884; vol. XLV, nos. 6–9 [1–7 February], 21 June, 6 December 1885.

22  *N.R.*, 24 January, 11 July, 3 October 1886.

23  *N.R.*, 24 October, 21 November 1880, 9 January, 12 June 1881, 4 June 1882, 7, 14 January, 20 May 1883, 8 June 1884, 31 May 1885. See also Table 1 and Appendix A.

24  *N.R.*, 29 May, 5 June 1881; *N.S.S. Almanack* (1881), pp. 15–17; *S.R.*, 3 July 1880; *N.R.*, 4 June, 24 September 1882.

25  *N.R.*, 11 July 1880, 22 May, 5, 19 June, 7 August 1881, 26 February, 21, 28 May 1882.

26  *N.R.*, 24 December 1882.

27  C. Bradlaugh to W. E. Gladstone, 11 June [1883], B.M. Add. Mss. 44, 111, ff. 134–6; *N.R.*, 15 July, 12 August 1883.

28  *N.R.*, 14 November 1886, reprinted in E. Royle, *The Infidel Tradition from Paine to Bradlaugh* (London, 1976), pp. 117–19. Gladstone once innocently quoted this same parody in a speech praising the virtues of self-help—*N.R.*, 5 November 1871.

29  *S.R.*, 15, 22 May, 19, 26 June, 3, 10 July 1880, 13 March 1881.

30  *S.R.*, 3 July 1880; *N.R.*, 25 July 1880; *S.R.*, 7 August 1880, 6 August 1881, 4 March, 12, 19 August 1882, 11 August 1883. Queensberry had been an elected Scottish peer until 1880, when, against convention, he was not re-elected. This was attributed to his rejection of orthodox religion—see *S.R.*, 24 April 1880; *N.R.*, 2 May 1880; and p. 270 below.

31  *S.R.*, 15 October 1881.

32  *N.R.*, 16, 23 July; vol. XL, no. 5 [23–30 July] 1882.

33  *F.*, 16 July 1882; *N.R.*, 30 July, 6 August 1882; *Republican,* August 1882.

34  *F.*, 11 March–15 April 1883; *N.R.*, 11 March; vol. XLI, no. 11 [11 March] 1883.

35  *N.R.*, vol. XLI, no. 17 [15 April], 22, 29 April, 6 May 1883; *F.*, 15 April–6 May 1883; see also below, chapter 14, pp. 273–4.

# IV

# Decline and fall, 1885–1915

*Secularism under Foote*

The N.S.S. reached its peak in 1883 and 1884. Thereafter there were signs of decline, to be written off annually by the conference. In 1884–85 the number of fresh recruits fell from 1,747 to 1,367, and the number of new branches from sixteen to eight. In his annual report Bradlaugh attributed this to 'the severe depression prevailing in various industries throughout the country', which had diminished the number of renewals and hindered fresh accessions. A year later a further fall was still being attributed to 'the continued dullness of trade', and Bradlaugh was undoubtedly right that, in common with other voluntary societies, the N.S.S. was vulnerable to trade depression. The following year, 1887, saw an even more serious fall in the number of new members, from 988 to 505, and a parallel drop in the number of branches from 99 to 84. With the ending of the depression in 1888 only a temporary revival could be reported, for in 1889 the number of branches fell again, to only 59, half the peak total in 1883.[1]

The decline of Secularism was therefore becoming apparent from the mid-1880s, though later critics of G. W. Foote were to blame his presidency after 1890 for the contrast between latter-day freethought and that of the golden age under Bradlaugh. Reports that all was not well in the later 1880s were quickly passed over, and any suggestions that Bradlaugh was ceasing to be a true and active radical after his acceptance by Parliament were dismissed as absurd. Bradlaugh was indeed as hard at work as ever promoting both radicalism and freethought, but his parliamentary duties were taking up an increasing amount of his time, as he himself recognised in 1889.[2] By this time the day-to-day running of freethought had passed to G. W. Foote, who was largely responsible for staving off an even more rapid decline until after Bradlaugh's death.

In response to this serious falling-off in the size and membership of the N.S.S. in the later 1880s, Foote successfully proposed to the 1888 conference that a committee should be appointed to find out what was going wrong. In his speech he recognised that the earlier growth had been unusual—the consequence of Bradlaugh's parliamentary struggle and his own prosecution for blasphemy. Now, with the ending of persecution, the N.S.S. would have to adopt new ideas. In his annual report a year later Bradlaugh himself returned to this theme. He now attributed the decline of Secularism to three things: the rival attraction of Home Rule; the diversion of local energy from propagandist work into clubs and other recreational activities; and the changed times. As with the earlier explanation in terms of depression, there was an element of truth in all this, though Bradlaugh would have done well to have recognised that the most successful rival issue was not Home Rule but socialism.[3]

Foote's committee of 1888 reported in 1889, putting forward a plan for 'greater cohesion and intercommunication'. None of this was new, and it had indeed been the spirit behind the moves in the 1850s and 1860s which had led to the foundation of the N.S.S. in the first place. The industrial centres of Lancashire, Yorkshire, Tyneside and the Midlands were urged to form their own federations with their own lecturers, modelled on the London Secular Federation which Foote had started in 1888. 'The propaganda of the streets' was recommended to the provincial branches, which were also assured that it was not the committee's intention to interfere with their autonomy. Nevertheless this is what the committee's suggestions amounted to, with a proposal that 'the Secular organisation should be vigorously worked from a trusted centre' which would have the executive power to send a representative 'to form new branches or energise old ones'. Such a representative would be paid by and under the control of a new Organisation Committee, with funds coming from a reorganised Propagandist Fund.[4]

Bradlaugh had himself been in effect a one-man organisation committee for many years. He had often taken the initiative through his lectures, stirring up members to found branches or awaken old ones; and branches had not been slow to criticise his despotic control of N.S.S. lecturers. But between Bradlaugh and Foote there was a difference in style as leaders. Bradlaugh was a crusader: he attributed the earlier success of the N.S.S. to its great campaigns, and thought the good times would come again if the members would only throw themselves into a new campaign against the blasphemy laws. Foote was a bureaucrat, who put his faith in reorganisation and rationalisation. He later recognised, 'With the death of the late

Charles Bradlaugh it may be said that the "heroic period" of English Freethought came to an end . . . From the time when I became president . . . I have always seen and felt that the triumphs of Freethought in the immediate future were to be won in the field of organisation.'[5] In the event, neither Bradlaugh nor Foote had the answer. The N.S.S. members could not be roused to campaign without an active persecution to stir them; and Foote was to spend the rest of his life, largely in vain, trying to reorganise the N.S.S. and to centralise its operations.

The Organisation Committee, chaired by Foote, was theoretically subordinate to the N.S.S. Executive, but in fact it took over many of the functions of that Executive and so put Foote in charge of the running of the N.S.S. a year before Bradlaugh formally resigned as president.[6] The committee set to work with enthusiasm, but not always with tact. Its activities, involving as they did a great deal of interference with local societies, could only be justified by success. Foote was at first confident, and in the short term his confidence was justified.[7] The number of new recruits rose from 492 in 1889 to 709 in 1890, 794 in 1891, and 1,074 in 1892, the highest figure since 1885, while in these four years the number of new branches rose from five to eleven, fourteen and twelve respectively. This recovery might partly be attributed to the Organisation Committee, and partly to the lowering of the subscription in 1890 from 4s and 1s 4d to 1s and 6d; but the recovery also coincided with the revival of wider radicalism in the early 1890s, leading to the Liberal election victory of 1892. The recovery was as short-lived for the freethinkers as it was for the Liberals, and by 1893 all the indicators had turned downwards once more.[8]

Bradlaugh's power had rested on popularity and success. The attempt by Foote to challenge him in the 1870s had failed for these reasons, but when Foote himself was in power in the 1890s things were very different. As he candidly admitted in 1891:

All history shows us, too, that leadership is indispensable. Abolish responsible power, and you only get irresponsible power. In my younger days I thought otherwise. I believed in 'parliamentarism' pure and simple. But age has brought experience, and I hope wisdom, and I see that some kind of subordination—perfectly voluntary, and therefore perfectly honourable—is necessary to the success of every enterprise.[9]

This candidness and belief in commonsense authority, as opposed to anarchistic idealism, were to be the hallmarks of the mature Foote as president of the N.S.S. and as a leading spokesman of popular Liberal–radicalism during the next quarter of a century. They make him an interesting commentator on political events, but did nothing to commend him to his followers.

The two main problems which dogged Foote throughout his presidency (1890–1915) were money and Bradlaugh's reputation. From the start he was determined that the N.S.S. should be his, not Bradlaugh's, but the Society had for so long been associated with its 'Chief' that he had no hope of success. He wrote in the *Secular Almanack* for 1894 with reference to Bradlaugh's death and the failure of Secularism, 'A party's vitality does not depend on such personal events; indeed a great movement cannot continue without serious changes; the one indispensable thing is its power of adjustment.'[10] Despite assertions to the contrary, the N.S.S. did not have this power. The golden age of Bradlaugh had rested on personal achievement and the Society was bound to suffer by his death.

Money was central to the problems of the later N.S.S., almost becoming an obsession with Foote. The decline of the Society meant a falling off of income, yet without money the organisation could not be revived. Increasingly Foote's dealings with his members appeared to be one long appeal for money, with little to show for it.

The two problems came together in a dispute over the future of Bradlaugh's famous Hall of Science, on which the lease had expired. In 1891 Foote paid Robert Owen Smith £250 for the use of the premises for a further season, but Hypatia Bradlaugh Bonner then proposed that the movement should subscribe to purchase a freehold Bradlaugh Memorial Hall. She was supported by John Robertson, now the editor of the *National Reformer*, and those of the 'old guard' whom Foote dubbed the 'Liberal Unionists of our party'. Foote wanted the N.S.S. to reach a further and more permanent arrangement for the use of the Old Street Hall of Science, but he failed to raise the money even for this, and in 1895 the Hall was permanently lost. It was hardly his fault, but that proved no excuse when Bradlaugh's headquarters passed into the hands of the Salvation Army.[11] The one consolation Foote had was the support of Charles Watts, who returned home from Canada shortly after Bradlaugh's death in 1891. Throughout the 1890s Watts worked as in the old days, but in 1902 Foote suspected him of supporting his son's newly formed Rationalist Press Association against the interests of the N.S.S., and for the second time in his life Watts found himself cast out by a president of the organisation to which he had given so much.[12]

A further difficulty which Foote had to face in the 1890s, and which was a major cause of the weakness of the N.S.S., was the

relationship between Secularism and socialism. Bradlaugh had been
fortunate to die when he did, for the N.S.S. had been built on ultra-
radicalism, and the ultras of the 1890s were mainly socialists. Foote
would not commit the N.S.S. to their cause, and, although the
criticisms of Foote arose out of his autocracy, financial problems and
general lack of success, many of the critics themselves were also open
to socialist ideas and attributed Foote's failure to his reactionary
ideas on 'the social question'.

The opposition was focused in London by two little freethought
journals: the *Jerusalem Star*, an impious four-page monthly edited by
W. J. Ramsey from June 1895 to September 1896; and a more
serious production of the same size called *Secular Work*, founded
anonymously 'for the purpose of criticising the N.S.S. and its
President' in May 1896.[13] The *Jerusalem Star* put the case against
Foote as follows:

Charles Bradlaugh was known throughout Great Britain long before his
parliamentary struggle, and wherever he went to lecture he had splendid
gatherings, although a charge was made for admission. At one time he was
leader of the extreme Radical and Democratic party, and people who heard
him on political questions went on to hear his anti-theological lectures, and
soon became Secularists. It is a well-known fact that hundreds of members
of the Secular Society were gained in this way, although quite
unintentionally.

Why do not our leading orators adopt the same policy at the present day?
They seem afraid to speak on social and political questions, or if they do
they give us a bit of ancient history—something about Cromwell, or was
Melchizedek a Social Reformer? Surely our leaders have some views on the
questions that affect the welfare of humanity, or are they completely
indifferent to worldly affairs and given themselves up entirely to God and his
book?[14]

Some of these criticisms were very old. The Holyoake school of
Secularism had always maintained against Bradlaugh and Foote
that constructive secular work was the true task of Secularists. The
truth was that Foote did have views on the social question, but he
knew that the socialist half of·his audiences would not agree with
them. The editorial opinion of *Secular Work* does not seem to have
been wholly socialist, but the paper gave voice to both socialist and
non-socialist complaints about the N.S.S. under Foote. Eventually,
in August 1896, a new national organisation was launched, called
the Freethought Federation. Its leader was George Standring, who
had resigned from the N.S.S. in 1894 after sixteen years of
membership, as a protest against the state of paralysis into which
the Society had fallen since Bradlaugh's death. The Federation was

founded at the appropriately named Bradlaugh Club and Institute, which met at the Ball's Pond Road Secular Hall, the home of a former N.S.S. branch, and its committee included several former leading members of the N.S.S., including Standring, W. H. Reynolds, Mrs Bradlaugh Bonner, her husband Arthur, and James Anderson, the former manager of the Hall of Science Club, who had been expelled from the N.S.S. for accusing Foote of financial malpractice.[15]

Despite such influential backing, the Federation made little progress, and its paper, *Reason*, which Standring launched in March 1898, ran for only a few issues and was able to report only four affiliated societies—the former N.S.S. Finsbury branch (which had come out in sympathy with James Anderson), the Regent's Park Freethought Society, the Westminster Secular Society and the Nottingham Freethought Society.[16] It was the N.S.S., therefore, not the Freethought Federation, which survived into the next century, and in 1899 Foote could still comfort himself with the belief that the success of the Bradlaugh years had been an illusion, and that a hard core of freethinkers still remained. He was probably right, but in 1899 it was under a thousand strong, and was about to be further reduced by the crisis which hit all radical organisations during the Anglo-Boer War. By 1904 the total number of branches had fallen for the first time to below thirty, where it remained, except for a brief revival in 1906, until the First World War temporarily halted almost all activity.[17]

Between the death of Bradlaugh in 1891 and that of Foote in 1915 the N.S.S. underwent a complete change in character. From being a large national organisation with branches throughout the country and a strong presence in London centred on the personality and activities of Bradlaugh, it became a small pressure group with no secure indoor lecturing place in London, and only a handful of branches in the provinces. Of these, those which were still active tended to resent interference from London, which no longer seemed to have much to offer them. In fact many of the branches ceased to send the Executive its share of the membership subscription (1*s* a year after 1897), and by 1902 most of the annual subscription income was in fact coming from individual, not branch, members.[18] The logic of this situation led Foote to consider abolishing the branches, but the war intervened before anything could be formulated. The N.S.S. was not to be turned finally into a national pressure group with an entirely central membership until the 1960s.

*The Ethical movement*

As the N.S.S. struggled in the 1890s, some remaining support was being drawn off by the Ethical movement, which was undoubtedly proving attractive to some of the younger generation of freethinkers like F. J. Gould and Harry Snell.[19]

The roots of the Ethical movement were partly American and partly English. Felix Adler of the Free Religious Association in the United States had founded an Ethical Culture Society in New York, and his ideas were brought to England by Stanton Coit in 1888 when he succeeded his fellow American, Moncure D. Conway, as minister of the South Place Chapel. Under Conway, between 1865 and 1885, the chapel had been a centre of progressive theology and politics not far removed from Holyoake's brand of Secularism. As a condition of his coming in 1888, Coit required the chapel congregation to turn itself into the South Place Ethical Society. Although they did this, the South Place members were too slow for Coit, who left them in 1891 to found Ethical societies elsewhere in London and then in the provinces. Some of these, like the London Ethical Society, which had been started as early as 1886 by J. H. Muirhead at Toynbee Hall, and the Cambridge Ethical Society, founded by Henry Sidgwick, were socially beyond the reach of the Secularists. Others, notably that in East London, were very similar to a Secularist organisation and appealed to the same sorts of people. The East London Ethical Society began meeting in a private house in 1889, and then in a Mile End dancing saloon. When evicted by their landlord in 1891 the members raised £200 and built themselves an iron hall in Libra Road, Old Ford, which was opened in 1894. F. J. Gould was the leader here until he moved on to run the Leicester Secular Society. Meanwhile other societies were established by Coit in West London (1892), South London (1892) and North London (1895). His ambition was to unite all this Ethical work in one great movement. In 1895 the four London societies were linked in the Ethical Union, and gradually both Labour Churches and Positivist Societies were drawn into its orbit. By 1915 over seventy societies had been formed, though the maximum membership of the Ethical Union was twenty-six, in 1905–06.[20]

In a lecture to the St Pancras Ethical Society in 1902, Charles Watts said that 'the spirit of the Secular movement and of the Ethical movement is fundamentally one and the same'. This led Coit to urge former Secularists from the days of Bradlaugh to re-form their societies and join the Ethical Union, though the move was viewed by Foote and others as a bid to take over the Secularist movement. Despite Coit's protestation to the contrary, it probably was. Relations between the Ethical and Secularist movements were ambiguous—what G. Dawson Baker in the *Freethinker* in 1898 likened to the difference between church and chapel. Coit himself in 1901 distinguished between the two schools of Rationalism: the individualistic Bible-smashers, and the more cohesive Ethical groupings. Foote's N.S.S. obviously belonged to the former category, but even the Ethical movement, which had looked for a moment in the 1890s as though it might succeed as the religion of the coming age, was, like Secularism, in decline before 1914.[21]

### The Great War

The war ended an era. For Rationalists the conflict brought to a climax the 'Revolt against Reason'. *John Bull*, edited by Holyoake's nephew, Horatio Bottomley, went religious and the tide flowed with him. Publication costs rose; lecture audiences fell. Just before his death Foote was proposing to lecture at Leicester on 'Religion, the War and Humanity', saying to Sydney Gimson, the Leicester president, 'One mustn't get very far from the war, I fear, if one wants to get an audience.'[22] Yet for Secularists to think and speak freely about the war was to invite public wrath and official suppression. Foote was refused the use of the Queen's Hall for a lecture because he would not undertake not to refer to the war. Chapman Cohen, who succeeded Foote, was visited by *agents provocateurs* in 1916 because he refused to make the *Freethinker* anti-German. He was also sent an official letter after publishing some notes on Russia; and on another occasion was asked for a list of his subscribers. He refused; the *Freethinker* was being sent to the trenches. In vain the N.S.S. protested against censorship in Britain 'as if she were a conquered country'. Foote's death in 1915 indeed marked an end to the world as his generation knew it. Chapman Cohen was left to rekindle the embers after the war in the context of a new age.[23]

### Notes

1  *N.R.*, 31 May 1885, 20 June 1886, 5 June 1887, 27 May 1888, 16 June 1889.
2  *N.R.*, 13 March 1887, 6 January 1889.
3  *N.R.*, 27 May 1888, 16 June 1889; *F.*, 27 May 1888, 16 June 1889.
4  *N.R.*, 5 February 1888, 16 June 1889.
5  *F.*, 16 July 1899; see also 12 October 1890.

6  This makes nonsense of George Bernard Shaw's claim that he was invited to become N.S.S. president in 1890—*F.*, 28 April 1912.

7  N.S.S. Organisation Committee, Minute Book, 1889–95. For an example of Foote's optimism see *F.*, 13 October 1889. Optimism, however unwarranted, was essential to any popular leader, as H. M. Hyndman cynically noted—*The Record of an Adventurous Life* (London, 1911), p. 341.

8  *N.R.*, 16 June 1889; *F.*, 1 June 1890, 24 May 1891, 12 June 1892.

9  *F.*, 10 May 1891.

10  *Secular Almanack* (1894), p. 17.

11  *N.R.*, 13 September 1891, 13 March, 5 June 1892; *F.*, 5 July, 13, 20 September 1891, 7, 14, February, 13 March, 15, 29 May, 16 October 1892, 10 May 1896. See also B.L. no. 184 (notes on the Hall of Science, from 23 August 1868); also B.L. nos. 2303–7, 2313–14, 2320–2, 2371–3, 2377, 2385, 2391, 2394–5, 2401–2, 2404–14, 2416–25, 2427–30, 2505, 2515, 2522–3, 2554–5 (18 June 1891–January 1896).

12  See below, pp. 166, 183.

13  *Secular Work*, January 1897.

14  *Jerusalem Star*, December 1895.

15  N.S.S. Minute Book IV, 3, 31 October 1895; *Radical*, February 1897.

16  *Reason*, 3 April 1898.

17  *Secular Almanack* (1900), p. 9; *ibid.*, (1901), pp. 9–10; see also Appendix A.

18  *F.*, 13 June 1897, 25 May 1902.

19  See F. J. Gould, *The Life Story of a Humanist* (London, 1923); H. Snell, *Men, Movements and Myself* (London, 1936).

20  Sidney Warren, *American Freethought, 1860–1914* (New York, 1943), pp. 96–109; S. K. Ratcliffe, *The Story of South Place* (London, 1955), p. 55; *N.R.*, 1 January, 9 September 1888; *F.*, 1 January 1888; F. J. Gould, *op. cit.*, pp. 76–7; G. Spiller, *The Ethical Movement in Great Britain* (London, 1934), pp. 114–15.

21  *Ethics*, 3 May 1902; *F.*, 11 December 1898; *Ethics*, 30 November 1901; G. Spiller, *op. cit.*, p. 115.

22  *R.P.A. Annual* (1915), pp. 81–6; *F.*, 20 September 1914; C. Cohen, *Almost an Autobiography* (London, 1940), pp. 119–21; S. A. Gimson, 'Random Recollections of the Leicester Secular Society', Part 1 (March 1932), p. 71.

23  *F.*, 11 October 1914; C. Cohen, *op. cit.*, pp. 124–5; *F.*, 28 February, 7 March 1915; N.S.S. Minute Book VI, 26 November 1914.

V

# Local freethought

*London*

The point at which local and national organisation met was undoubtedly at the Hall of Science. At first this was at 58 City Road, near Wesley's Chapel and opposite Bunhill Fields cemetery. In its hey day this hall had provided a platform for Rowland Detroisier and the Owenites, and in 1843 it had been secured for freethought and radicalism on a lease held by William Bendall. In the 1850s the City Road Hall of Science was the home of the London Secular Society and the principal centre for freethought in the eastern part of the metropolis.

In 1865 a new Hall of Science Company was launched by Bradlaugh, J. P. Adams, Charles Watts and Mrs Law to raise £10,000 to build a new lecture hall somewhere near the old one. Bradlaugh delivered the last lecture in the old hall on 18 March 1866, and the freethinkers then transferred temporarily to Day's Auction Rooms (now grandly called the 'New Discussion Hall') at 207 City Road. But by the end of 1866 the Hall of Science Company had raised only £100, and so the following year it was wound up.[1]

An alternative scheme was broached in 1868 whereby a twenty-one-year lease was to be purchased on a hall being built at the back of 142 Old Street. The leaseholder was to be Robert Owen Smith, a freethinker and son of an old radical (his brother was called Thomas Paine Smith). Smith was to have complete control and be responsible for the finance, but the N.S.S. was to pay £350 towards the furnishings and this was to secure the Secularists the use of the hall on Sundays, Good Friday and Christmas Day. Beyond this the exact nature of the agreement was hazy, a fact which was to cause G. W. Foote a great deal of trouble when it expired. The freethought party gradually acquired a larger and larger share in the use of the hall, and expended several thousands of pounds in extensions and improvements, while the lease still remained Smith's personal property.[2]

Still only half ready, the hall was opened by Bradlaugh on 4

October 1868. The capacity was about 700, but by 1869 plans were already in hand to double the capacity. Gradually what had been domestic premises with a stable-like building at the rear, covered with a temporary tin roof, was transformed into a set of buildings which, according to the *Weekly Dispatch* in 1879, 'might well be an evangelical chapel or a provincial theatre without altering its facade in any one respect'. By 1870 there was a large lecture hall built to hold 1,200; a small hall for 220 people; dressing rooms, school and class rooms, and a coffee and refreshment room. The cost to the Secularists had been £1,400, of which half had already been paid off. In 1871, evening audiences at Bradlaugh's lectures were filling the large hall to capacity, and further galleries were added to accommodate 400 more people. In the summer of 1880 the premises were given a new front, a new roof, and a new platform at a cost of £1,000.[3]

Here it was that Bradlaugh celebrated his greatest triumphs and Secularism became most notorious. Situated in St Luke's, Finsbury, at the heart of artisan/small shopkeeper radicalism, it set the tone of the whole area for friend and foe alike.[4] It was to Bradlaugh and freethought what the South London Tabernacle was to Spurgeon and the Baptists, or the City Temple to Joseph Parker and the Congregationalists. The audience, observed the *Freethinker* in 1885, 'does not reside around the Hall, but travels there from all parts of London'.[5] Like the N.S.S. itself, which had its headquarters at the hall, its impact was in great measure as an extension of the activities of Charles Bradlaugh. This was the pulpit from which he made his pronouncements and fought his campaigns for republicanism, birth control and his right to enter Parliament.

Apart from the Hall of Science, London also had its local societies like any other centre of urban population. Some of these, such as that in Battersea, had a long and stable existence; some, like that in Ball's Pond Road, had their own premises; others, like W. J. Antill's Religious Discussion Society, were on a more humble scale. Antill was an undertaker, and the society met in his cellar workshop, the audience sitting on planks spread between coffins while the speaker stood on the trolley used to carry corpses. When W. S. Ross wished to refer to disreputable Secularists, one name he called them—rather unfairly—was 'plank-and-coffinites'.[6]

In the 1860s and 1870s there were in any one year about a dozen identifiable freethought societies in existence in the London area, spread out within an arc swinging north-eastwards from Chelsea, through Paddington and Euston, to Hoxton and Hackney Road, with outlyers in Stratford and West Ham. South of the river, groups met in Battersea, Southwark and Greenwich, with an outpost in Woolwich. There were also societies in Kingston and Brentford. During the 1880s and early 1890s the number of societies increased to between sixteen and twenty-nine, the peak year being 1886, and not until the very end of the nineteenth century did the numbers fall again to below those reached in the 1870s.[7] The period of growth saw the extension of Secularism deeper into the suburbs, themselves expanding rapidly at this time. Groups were now also to be found from Kensington and Kilburn, through Camden Town, Holloway and Hackney, to Old Ford and Mile End, while another arc stretched northwards from the West Ham and Stratford societies, through Leytonstone and Walthamstow, to Edmonton, Wood Green and Southgate. In the south the older centres of Southwark and Lambeth gradually gave way to Walworth, Camberwell and Peckham, while new groups appeared out in Wimbledon, Streatham and Forest Hill. As the inner London societies began to decay (though the Finsbury society lasted until 1905), Secularism lost its traditional footholds on the fringes of the City and became increasingly a disparate, suburban movement. This development partly reflected the change in Secularism itself, but was also a part of the wider change in London radicalism as the inner areas became socially depressed and skilled workmen moved out to the more salubrious suburbs.[8]

Before the association of Bradlaugh with the Hall of Science, the centre of freethought in London was the John Street Institution, first opened by the Owenites in 1840, and replaced by the Cleveland Hall in 1861. Although built with an Owenite legacy from W. D. Saul, the Cleveland Hall was controlled by its shareholders, who over the years changed in composition and sympathy. Several attempts were made in the 1860s, by G. J. Holyoake, Harriet Law and other lecturers who did not accept Bradlaugh's leadership, to make this hall a rival to the Hall of Science, but in 1869 it passed into other hands, was then regained for freethought for two years by Mrs Law in 1876, but finally passed out of the freethought movement and eventually into the hands of Hugh Price Hughes and the West London Mission.[9]

Elsewhere in West London there were only a few and relatively weak societies, the most notable being in Paddington.[10] North and East London, by contrast, were far more congenial areas for freethought, particularly Finsbury, with its tradition of radical small shopkeepers and artisans. One of the earliest groups in this area in the 1860s was the Freethought Propaganda Society, founded at the Finsbury Hall in 1862, which moved to the Goswell Street Hall in 1863 and to the Metropolitian Coffee House, City Road, in 1865. Here it was renamed the Independent Secular Society. A second group meeting in the City Road in 1865 was the London Eclectic Secular Society, which merged with the Independents in 1867 to form the East London Secular Freethought Society at the old City Road Hall of Science. The Independents nevertheless lived up to their name and also met separately until both groups appear to have been swallowed up by the Old Street Hall of Science in 1869.[11] The Finsbury Secular Society was able to resist the pull of the parent hall largely because it had its own permanent premises in the London Patriotic Society's club on Clerkenwell Green. The Patriotic Society had grown out of the Holborn branch of the Reform League in 1871 and had obtained its club premises at 37a Clerkenwell Green in July the following year. The Finsbury Secular Society was started here in 1880 under the auspices of the N.S.S., and had a continuous existence as an N.S.S. branch until 1905, except for a brief period in the mid-1890s when it joined the Freethought Federation instead.[12] The link between the Society and one of the foremost of the London radical clubs is an important example of the way in which Secularism became the practical creed of London working-class club life.[13]

Farther east, towards the river Lea, other Secularist groups were started in the 1870s, many of them as a result of the efforts of the United Secularists Propagandist Society, founded in 1869 by W. J. Ramsey to promote outdoor work in East London. A branch was formed in Stratford in 1870, meeting at the Two Brewers public house, while the parent body took the Perseverence Hall, Goldsmith's Row, Hackney Road for indoor lectures during the winter of 1871. It was here that the Reverend C. M. Davies came across them in 1874 when he described one of their meetings in his series, *Heterodox London*. He found them debating whether the Hackney Secular Association (the indoor group) should amalgamate with, or simply co-operate with, the Propagandist Society. Of such niceties was Secularism made: fiercely local, stubbornly independent, and much concerned with constitutional proprieties, a veritable training ground in political procedures as little societies were formed and dissolved, amalgamated and sundered, in a ceaseless ebb and flow. Davies would not have been at all surprised to read in the *National Reformer* in 1875 that the Hackney Secularist Association had 'fallen into a disorganised

state', only to reappear a year later 'doing very good work'.[14]
Meanwhile in 1875 a branch of the N.S.S. was started in Mile End
which, usually under the title of East London Secular Society,
survived until 1903; and the Stratford branch of the Propagandist
Society re-emerged in 1877 as a branch of the N.S.S. which, in this
case, lasted only until 1881.[15] The strongest group in this area was in
West Ham, where a society made a brief appearance in 1875, and
then emerged as a branch of the N.S.S. in the early 1880s,
continuing right through until 1915 with its headquarters at the
Cromwell Club, Plaistow—another example of the close links forged
between the radical clubs and freethought. West Ham was, as G. W.
Foote noted in 1888, a new working-class suburb, populated by
families from Finsbury who had been attracted by the low rents and
the ease of travel offered by workmen's trains. The same was true of
Forest Gate, where a Secular society was founded in 1892 by the
former secretary of the West Ham branch.[16]

The same movement out from the centre can be seen in North
London. In the 1870s Secularism was based in the Euston/St
Pancras area, and the Claremont Hall in Penton Street was acquired
in 1876 for Sunday evening lectures. Here the North London Secular
Society met, with an initial membership of nearly a hundred, and
continued to meet until 1886. The area was also able to support
activities by the North London Secular Society under the Midland
Railway arches in the 1870s and 1880s, and in 1882 a North West
London branch of the N.S.S. was founded at the Milton Hall,
Kentish Town. This branch lasted until 1901 and for a time
provided a central home for the N.S.S. after the closure of the Old
Street Hall of Science in 1895.[17] Another active group met in the
Finsbury Park, Islington and Ball's Pond Road areas of North
London. The Bradlaugh Club and Institute in Ball's Pond Road,
however, proved to be more secular than Secularist in outlook, and
the branch there was dissolved in 1892, though an independent
society continued until 1899 and supported the Freethought
Federation.[18] The extension of Secularism farther north into the new
suburbs of Tottenham and district was largely the work of George
Standing's brother, Sam, who started the North Middlesex Secular
Federation in 1890 to bring together the societies he had been
forming in Hornsey, Edmonton, Tottenham and Old Southgate.
The Edmonton branch was the most successful, lasting from 1889
until 1901.[19]

South of the river there were not as many societies as to the north,
though the story of their development was similar. When a

conference of South London branches of the N.S.S. was called in 1884, at what was probably the height of Secularist organisation, representatives attended from Bermondsey, Rotherhithe, South Lambeth, Camberwell, Battersea, Peckham, Crystal Palace, Croydon and Woolwich. The oldest centre of freethought lay to the south of Blackfriars Bridge, where radicals had been meeting since the days of Richard Carlile's Rotunda, and the usual home for such groups in the 1860s was the South London Secular Hall at 132 Blackfriars Road. In the mid-1870s the focus seems to have moved outwards a little to Walworth, home of Mrs Harriet Law and her husband, Edward, who was the organiser of the Walworth Association of Freethinkers. The Society drew members from both Walworth and the rapidly expanding new suburb of Camberwell, where a new South London Secular Hall was built in 1885. The society here became one of the strongest and most successful of all the N.S.S. branches in London, and, despite many vicissitudes, was still in possession of its hall in 1915.[20] A similar success story could be told of the Battersea branch, founded in the early 1880s and lasting until 1905. Like Camberwell, Battersea was a new suburb: 'Twenty years ago,' recalled G. W. Foote's *Radical Leader* in 1888, Battersea was 'a semi-rural district, just emerging from the market-garden and brickfield state of existence,' but in 1888 it had a population of over 100,000. 'Here it is,' wrote Charles Booth the following year, of the Shaftesbury estate in Battersea, 'that the intelligent portion of the Socialism of the district is chiefly to be found, and the colony represents perhaps the high-water mark of the life of the intelligent London artisan.' This was good breeding ground also for Secularism, and the Battersea branch acted as midwife to the socialism of the area.[21]

The task of the London Secularists was to hold together this mass of local, diverse and sporadic activity. Already by mid-century the size of London was making this a difficult task. By the end of the century it was impossible. G. W. Foote noted in the *Freethinker* in 1902, 'the very vastness of London makes it difficult to work. The Freethinkers in it are scattered over such a tremendous area that it is difficult to bring them together and induce them to co-operate.'[22]

In 1870 Bradlaugh called a conference at the Hall of Science to organise the many groups which had emerged in London during and after the Reform Bill agitation of 1866-67. He proposed open-air propaganda, the formation of a tract Society, and the creation of more N.S.S. branches; he also offered to lecture anywhere in London where a large hall could be obtained. The principle outcome of this meeting was W. J. Ramsey's Secular Propagandist Society.[23] Following the collapse of the N.S.S. in the early 1870s, Ramsey returned to the task in 1875, when Annie Besant chaired a meeting at the Hall of Science to form a propagandist organisation which would issue a monthly circuit plan and provide lectures, both indoors and out, at five shillings a time. The scheme did not really make headway until 1876, when, under the presidency of Bradlaugh, a deliberate attempt was made to help out the poorer East London branches and to provide them with lecturers.[24] Thereafter the rapid rise of the N.S.S. brought such activities directly under its control. During the summer of 1877 the N.S.S. had eleven London lecturers on its books and was responsible for Sunday lectures at the Hall of Science, the Walworth Freethought Institute, the South London Secular Hall, Claremont Hall and Deptford Temperance Hall, and on Mondays at the Phoenix Temperance Hall, Commercial Road; there were also outdoor lectures on Sunday mornings in Stratford, on the Mile End Road, under the St Pancras arches and at Gibraltar Walk, Bethnal Green; and also a Sunday evening lecture station at Blackheath.[25]

With the decline of the N.S.S. after the mid-1880s, the need was once more felt for some special effort of organisation on the part of the London branches. To this end, G. W. Foote formed the London Secular Federation in 1888 to strengthen the branches and to spread freethought generally in London. Sixteen branches were affiliated to the Federation, of which George Standring was secretary. The aim was not only to co-ordinate lectures, but to work with other radical groups over the provision of candidates for School Board elections. It was soon quite clear that London freethought was badly disorganised, but the branches resented Foote's attempts to rationalise them.[26] Gradually the level of indoor work fell, and, apart from central lectures delivered, after the closure of the Hall of Science, at the Milton Hall, St James's Hall, and the Athenaeum Hall, the bulk of the work was carried on out of doors in the London parks and other public places. These were free, though the London County Council did not always permit freedom of speech.[27] Only a few branches, notably those at Camberwell, Battersea and West Ham, were able to continue on their own with a traditional indoor lecture programme.

*Southern England*

In the whole of South Eastern and central Southern England

freethought was widely scattered, difficult to organise, and short-lived. A visit from Bradlaugh would produce a good audience, but without actively organised local support an extended mission was beyond the means of the Secularists. Sometimes a local incident helped, as at Kingston on Thames in 1869 when a local tradesman was refused the oath in court, because he was a freethinker; or as at Reading in 1890, when a local clergyman attacked Secularism and so drew attention to it.[28] In the south, Brighton had a branch from the early 1880s to the mid-1890s, with forty-five members in 1889,[29] but all the other centres with any activity worth reporting were sea ports—the Medway towns, Southampton and Portsmouth. This was also true of the South West, where Bristol had a record of almost continuous activity throughout the period 1866-1909, and Plymouth even had two branches, briefly, in the later 1880s. The *Secular Review* was scarcely exaggerating when it complained in 1877 that 'outside Bristol and Plymouth nothing is done'. G. W. Foote, who came from Plymouth, pointed out the problem in 1881 when he admitted, 'The Western and Southern counties are too much neglected' but 'the N.S.S. can do nothing unless local Freethinkers move for themselves'. Even in Bristol the branch had to be reorganised by the Organisation Committee in 1889 and totally refounded after lectures from Foote in 1892; the membership then was only between fifty and seventy.[30] The availability of premises was often of crucial importance. One of the few inland centres in the West was at Bath, with its long radical history, where the freethinkers were able to use the People's Club and Institute in the 1870s. At Plymouth the Secularists found themselves without a hall in 1894 when St George's Hall in Stonehouse was acquired by the Corporation, who would not let it to them.All the Secularists could do was 'to lie low and wait for the dawn of a better day'.[31] Sometimes that day never came, or when it did the followers had melted away or the leaders had moved on to other things.

## Wales

One abiding challenge to the freethinkers of Bristol lay across the Bristol Channel in the unredeemably religious valleys of South Wales. The first Welsh Secular society appeared at Abergavenny in 1864; it lasted until 1868 and the town made no further appearance in the records. In 1869 J. Moss of Bristol started a West of England and South Wales Secular Union, which resulted in a society at Cardiff, and the Union was revived at Cardiff in 1872, with the aim

of covering Monmouth, Glamorgan, Gloucester, Wiltshire and
Somerset, supplying lectures to villages whether or not they had
Secularist groups. Charles Watts lectured in the valleys, attracting
audiences of 300 at Merthyr, but his cause was republicanism, not
Secularism. A Merthyr Republican Club was started, but the
freethinkeres were unable to hire a hall. At Aberdare and Cardiff
Watts's audiences were not large.[32] This he attributed to clerical
pressure, and certainly the Secularists had an uphill struggle in an
area in which working-class opinion, the chapel, and the Welsh
language stood together against what could be seen as the alien
intrusion of English rationalism.[33] It was a rare event when the
*Secular Review* carried a report from T. E. Owen and T. Evans of a
small society at Rhybydd—in Welsh. At another revival of the
District Secular Association in 1882, the main centres were given as
Cardiff, Bristol, Aberdare, Newport, Merthyr and Pontypool, but
outside Cardiff the only Welsh branch to last for any time at all in
the later nineteenth century was at Swansea. In 1905, when Wales
had a record four societies in existence at the same time, these were
Cardiff, Mountain Ash, Pontypridd and Merthyr.[34] The whole of
Welsh Secularism was contained within an arc drawn through
Swansea, Merthyr, Abergavenny and Newport.

## The eastern counties

The failure of Secularism in Wales was part of a general failure in
the countryside. Where there was no industry there was no
freethought. Secularism was as weak in East Anglia and
Lincolnshire as it was in Wales. Only Grimsby had a society
throughout much of the period between 1866 and 1915; Norwich
had a branch of the N.S.S. in the 1870s and 1880s, and Ipswich had
a society in the 1860s and 1870s which emerged again as a branch of
the N.S.S. as late as 1892. As was so often the case, a major reason
for the longevity of the Grimsby society was that it owned its own
hall, erected by a Secular Hall Company in 1875.[35]

## The East Midlands

The association between Secularist organisation and towns is
brought out clearly by the experience of the East Midlands, where
prominent societies existed in Derby, Leicester, Nottingham and
Northampton, with occasional societies and N.S.S. branches in
smaller towns such as Chesterfield, Ilkeston, Mansfield, Kettering

and Luton. Even in the largest towns the Secularists could not easily
find premises. In Derby the society was refounded in 1874, but had
to meet in members' homes after their landlord had been compelled
by public opinion not to let them a room; and the following year
Harriet Law had to resort to Chester Green for her lectures. Often a
society resulted from such a visit, as at Kettering, where in 1868
Bradlaugh attracted an audience of 500 to his lecture in the Corn
Exchange. A society was then formed, but such efforts were usually
short-lived. By 1873 the Kettering Secular Society had become a
republican club, and a branch of the N.S.S. did not appear in the
town until 1885.[36]

The history of Secularism in Northampton was much conditioned
by the fact that this was Bradlaugh's chosen parliamentary seat,
which was to the disadvantage of the local Secularists. Northampton
inherited from the 1840s and 1850s a nucleus of dedicated radicals
and Secularists, led by Joseph Gurney, a draper turned accountant,
and secretary of the Northampton Freehold Land Society; John
Bates, basketmaker turned newsagent, who kept a shop in The
Drapery; James and Edward Pebody of the Admiral Nelson public
house on The Green; and Thomas Adams, a Congregationalist
master baker who became a Secularist in the 1860s.[37] Bates founded
the Northampton Secular Society in 1864, and in 1867 it became one
of the first branches of the N.S.S. The society was never very large,
and in the 1870s it was checked when most of the leaders devoted
their energies primarily to radicalism rather than Secularism in the
town. Gurney was elected to the town council in 1873 and Adams in
1874, each in turn becoming a distinguished citizen and mayor.
Bates broke away from them rather than sully himself with political
alliances with Liberals and Nonconformists. With R. S. Johnson,
another newsagent , he formed an 'Earnest and Thorough Radical'
association, but attracted little support — he once remarked he had
no more than the twelve apostles.[38] In 1879 a *Secular Review*
correspondent lamented that, although there was 'a great number of
freethinkers' in Northampton, 'no efforts [were] being made to
propagate Secular principles among the inhabitants'. The N.S.S.
branch almost disappeared after 1880, and Charles Watts reported
in 1882 that 'it would probably be difficult to select any provincial
place of importance where, during late years, so few efforts have
been made by the leading Secular advocates to expound their
principles', and when Bates died in 1883 he had little so show for his
efforts. The following year G. W. Foote opened a Secular Club and
Institute to remedy the deficiency, attracting 400 members, a

quarter of whom were in the local Secular society, but there is little evidence of them doing much. During his time as M.P. for Northampton, Bradlaugh gave his freethought followers there no assistance. Foote made another attempt in 1896, but the condition of this branch (and many others) was summed up by its secretary: 'Ours is all hard work, which falls on a few real earnest workers who are determined to keep the flag of Freethought flying in Northampton at any cost'. The flag ceased to flutter at the start of the new century.[39]

Northampton illustrates the problems of a society working without the support of Bradlaugh. Nottingham, where freethought was much more successful, with organisation in practically every year from 1866 to 1904, illustrates the problem of local conflicts and division. As in Northampton there was a hard core of local leaders, including William Nowlan, Charles Watts's father-in-law. In 1875 the town had both an N.S.S. branch and a separate Secular Propagandist Society which gave outdoor lectures, apparently in competition with the branch. The latter was, however, relatively strong, selling weekly about forty each of the *National Reformer* and *Secular Chronicle*. The division produced by Bradlaugh's treatment of Watts in 1877 naturally produced a strong reaction in Kate Watts's home society, and there was a move by the Propagandist Society to join the N.S.S., presumably to turn their votes against Bradlaugh. They were refused permission to form a branch and told to join their rivals instead. Once the bitterness had died down, in 1878, the two groups did amalgamate and thereafter the branch existed in a relatively equable fashion, bringing young Harry Snell into the movement in about 1881.[40]

The doyen of all the societies in the Midlands was at Leicester, where the Secularist cause exemplifies all that was necessary to local success. There was a keen sense of local independence, local leadership and influential patronage, the latter being provided by the Gimson family. There was also a tradition of organisation going back to the 1840s and 1850s, in which Josiah Gimson, engineer, and William H. Holyoak, tailor, had played leading parts; but it was not until 1867 that the Leicester Secular Society was permanently established. In 1869 the society acquired premises with a reading room at 43 Humberstone Gate, and in 1873 they moved to no. 77 in readiness for building their own new hall on the site.[41]

Malcolm Quin recalled the original premises at 77 Humberstone Gate as 'a low roofed, humble room above a stable' and he could clearly remember 'the odours of the stable which floated in through the half-opened windows'. A Secular Hall Company was launched in 1872, with John Sladen, of Sladen's Indigo Works, as president, Josiah Gimson, of Gimson's Engineering Works, as treasurer, and W. H. Holyoak as secretary. The whole affair was arranged in a businesslike manner, and, with the financial backing of prosperous manufacturers like Sladen, Gimson, and Michael Wright, an elastic manufacturer, one of the main problems of any such venture was overcome. In 1878 the Secularist architect from Leek, Larner Sugden, was asked to design the new premises, and in March 1881 these were opened with great ceremony.[42]

Meanwhile Leicester Secularism was passing through the same sort of division as was experienced in Nottingham and elsewhere. George Voss, a butcher, started a branch of the N.S.S., but the Gimson group maintained its independence and was always the stronger of the two. Lectures were delivered by Holyoake, Watts, Foote, Harriet Law and Joseph Symes, not Bradlaugh, Besant or Thomas Slater, who were monopolised by the N.S.S. In retaliation for the N.S.S. forbidding Thomas Slater to lecture to the society, the Gimson group refused to let their premises to the N.S.S. in 1878.[43] Gimson was a leading member of the B.S.U., and shared the *Secular Review's* criticisms of Bradlaugh's autocratic leadership. Bradlaugh's power rested on the support he could bring to struggling local societies. In Leicester there was no such need; the Secularists there could afford to take their own line, and, indeed, provide an alternative lead in the Midlands. In 1875 the societies at Leicester, Derby and Nottingham jointly resolved not to join the N.S.S. because they found Bradlaugh's militant atheism too negative.[44]

The Leicester N.S.S. members turned themselves in 1877 into the 'Leicester Organised Freethought Branch of the N.S.S. Association', but as elsewhere they made their peace once the bitterness of the late 1870s died down. George Voss bought one share in the Leicester Secular Hall, and became secretary to the local society in 1884, though the N.S.S. branch survived until 1886.[45] At the opening of the Secular Hall in 1881 the main speakers were Holyoake, Mrs Law, Bradlaugh, and Mrs Besant, though differences of interpretation remained between the 'positive' Secularism of Leicester and the 'negative' Secularism of Bradlaugh.

Like other societies, that in Leicester enjoyed mixed fortunes in the later 1880s and 1890s, though, thanks to its stable management and adequate finance, it prospered more than most. When G. W. Foote commented in 1890 that Leicester was concentrating on the social at the expense of the propagandist (an admitted danger in all societies), Sydney Gimson replied, with a sideways comment on Foote's frantic efforts to revive the N.S.S., 'Our Secularism is not intermittent, alternating grand revivals with seasons of sloth; we keep steadily at work month after month, and year after year, with the result that our influence is always felt in the town.'[46]

In the early 1890s, though, Leicester did experience something of a downturn, but later in the decade a concerted effort at revival was made at the very time when the N.S.S. was sinking into permanent decline. In 1898 a full-time organising secretary was appointed, one Father Antony, a former Franciscan priest, now known by his secular name of Joseph McCabe. The following year he was succeeded by F. J. Gould, who for nearly a decade guided the fortunes of Secularism in Leicester in the directions of positive freethought and athism, whilst at the same time himself becoming a prominent figure in local Labour politics. Membership of the society was 206 in 1900, there were a hundred scholars in the Sunday school, and Sunday lecture audiences fluctuated between 20 and 100. With a full range of social and educational activities, the Leicester society came close to the life and experience of a Nonconformist chapel.[47]

## The West Midlands

The West Midlands region can be divided into two parts, Birmingham and the Black Country in the south, and the Potteries in the north, with Hanley providing the strongest branch in the latter and Birmingham in the former. Most societies existed in these areas in the first decade under study, between 1866 and 1875, before the N.S.S. had made much impact. There were during several of these years vigorous societies in ten localities, including Birmingham (the only N.S.S. branch), Coventry, Wednesbury and Oldbury. Under the auspices of the Birmingham Secularists, led by Charles C. Cattell, a Midland Secular Union was set up in 1867 and revived at Oldbury in 1869 to provide lectures for the towns and villages of the Midlands (including, it was hoped, the East Midlands). The main drawback was the lack of lecture halls and suitable local lecturers. Without a sustained mission the impact of an occasional lecture was soon lost. A third regional effort was made in 1871 by Cattell, when he brought Dudley, Wednesbury, West Bromwich, Walsall, Wolverhampton and Bilston together in a South Staffordshire and East Worcestershire Secular Union, following lectures by Bradlaugh in Wednesbury. This initiative too appears to have faded, and local efforts were diverted into the republican cause.[48]

Birmingham was the only place in the region to preserve a continuous freethought presence from the 1860s until the First World War, though its fortunes fluctuated, its premises varied, and several new and false starts were made. As 'Julian' told the *National Reformer* in 1864, 'The society here occasionally languishes.'[49] A Sunday Lecture and Debating Society was begun in 1867, and the following year Birmingham had an early branch of the N.S.S., but it collapsed in 1869 and had to be revived by Cattell. Then, after thirteen years without a regular home, the Secularists acquired St George's Hall in Upper Dean Street, which was opened by Bradlaugh in September 1869 with his republican lecture on 'The Land, the People, and the Coming Struggle'. The hall would seat four or five hundred people, and there were club premises for about forty. But the building was in a poor area of town, and the hall was not big enough for the sort of audiences which Bradlaugh could attract.[50] In 1876 Daniel Baker, a prosperous steel-pen manufacturer, proposed a Secular Hall Fund to raise money for a new hall. Land was acquired in The Crescent, and in September 1877 Holyoake was able to open the society's new premises, named after Baskerville, the eighteenth-century Birmingham Rationalist printer. With a hall, club and hall-keeper's accommodation, Birmingham had achieved in 1877 what Leicester was to achieve in 1881. Also, as at Leicester, the group using the hall was decidedly less militant than the mainstream of national Secularism. A branch of the N.S.S. was formed in 1880, but it did not use the Baskerville Hall, where the Secular Club and Institute met and where a B.S.U. branch was founded in 1882. But, unlike Leicester, the Birmingham group were never strong enough fully to utilise their hall, which became something of an embarrassment to them. In 1891 Baker offered it to Charles Watts as a permanent mission centre, but his tenancy did not last long, and in 1897 the hall was being used as a store room by a bookseller while the local N.S.S. branch met at the Bristol Street Board School, until prevented from doing so by the Board in 1899. Overall, the record of Secularism in Birmingham in the later nineteenth century was disappointing, and the division of resources between the two separate groups was undoubtedly one cause of this.[51]

*Central northern England*

The largest number of freethought societies anywhere in Britain existed in the regions of Lancashire and Yorkshire, from Liverpool up the Mersey valley to the cotton manufacturing towns to the south, north and east of Manchester, over the Pennines into the woollen and worsted districts of the Aire and Calder valleys, and southwards to Sheffield and the Don valley, with an extension out eastwards to Hull. In most years at least half the recorded provincial societies were in these areas, Yorkshire having between eleven and nineteen in the peak years between 1877 and 1885, and the North West as many as twenty-eight in 1883.

The 1860s opened with a strong regional organisation in Lancashire, based on Ashton, Manchester, Oldham and Rochdale. The usual problem was experienced over acquiring suitable halls for lectures, but there was no Josiah Gimson or Daniel Baker to help provide a provincial central hall in Manchester. The most spectacular regional assemblies were often held out of doors in the summer months. In 1867 the men of Lancashire were showing little interest in the N.S.S., but were arranging instead with their friends in Yorkshire to offer a permanent lectureship to G. J. Holyoake. Their leaders regarded the N.S.S. as too negative, and were more interested in such positive features of Secularism as education.[52]

The Lancashire Secular Union succeeded more than most because, although lacking powerful patronage, it was able to draw on the collective leadership of a number of local men from the different adjacent towns and villages of the Manchester area, notably Thomas Oates of Middleton, Frank Field of Oldham, Nathaniel Ridgeway and Thomas Ellis of Manchester, and Thomas Slater of Bury. The two last named were engaged as lecturers for the Union. Despite the promise of the 1860s, however, the Lancashire organisation was not exempt from the general decline of the 1870s. Whereas there were thirteen local societies in 1871, there were only six in 1872 and 1873, and the scheme for employing Slater and Ellis as permanent lecturers was not adhered to. But in 1874, when there were eight societies, the Union was revived, this time calling itself the Manchester and District Secular Union, drawing on the support of societies in Failsworth, Stalybridge, Oldham, Bolton and Manchester. In the first year of revived operations, 162 lectures were given and four large open-air meetings held, each attracting about five thousand people. Mrs Harriet Law was engaged to give ten special lectures in 1876, and for the next few years the lecture plan and Union activities seem to have been successfully carried out.[53]

The check to the expansion of freethought in the mid-1880s brought about renewed concern for the effective operation of a

Lancashire regional organisation, the initiative coming this time from Liverpool, with the support of the Manchester society, and in January 1887 a delegate meeting created the Lancashire and District Freethought Federation for local N.S.S. branches. As with previous efforts, this succeeded for a time, but then dropped from the records, the next entry being an appeal from Liverpool in 1890 for the re-establishment of the Federation; and in 1892 Sam Standring was invited to become permanent organiser. He settled in Rochdale, where he made a characteristically energetic impact on the area until his premature death in 1895.[54]

The strongest of the Lancashire societies was in Manchester, but life was by no means easy for it, despite the strong freethought traditions of the region as a whole. Before 1867, when premises were acquired at 123 Grosvenor Street, Chorlton upon Medlock, the group had had no settled home and had had the usual problems, in the words of the secretary, of 'too few workers for the amount of work to be done'. When Charles Cattell tried to find the new premises in 1868 he met 'several gentlemen to whom the name of Owen is sacred', but they hardly knew of Secularism. Nevertheless he got an audience of about a hundred at his lecture; and after a visit from Charles Watts in 1868 the Manchester society decided to join the N.S.S. They then began a Sunday school and started a Secular Hall Building Society, with two veteran radical freethinkers, Alderman Abel Heywood and Councillor Samuel Ingham, among the trustees.[55]

After the revival of the N.S.S. in 1875, the Manchester society again affiliated, but there was always an uneasy relationship between the two. Though not so independent as Leicester, like the men of Nottingham and Birmingham the Manchester members were in two minds about Bradlaugh's organisation. They were unhappy about Bradlaugh's treatment of Charles Watts and at the general exclusiveness of the N.S.S. In August 1878 a majority of the society voted to become independent again, the minority moving out to the Temperance Hall, next door at 125 Grosvenor Street, and soon they had forty-five members. Bradlaugh and Besant now showed their power by lecturing only for the new branch, ignoring the old society, which rapidly fell into a disorganised and disillusioned state. By 1881 the branch had taken over the old society's premises for their club room. The same problem occurred again in 1886 when the Manchester branch refused to take sides in Bradlaugh's quarrel with Ross and the *Secular Review* group. The local leader, George Payne, was a Bradlaughite, but resented being told by Bradlaugh what he should or should not do. The quarrel was patched up the following year, when Bradlaugh gave the proceeds of three lectures to a New Secular Hall Building Company. This enabled the Manchester Secularists to purchase a former chapel in Rusholme Road, which would accommodate five or six hundred people.[56]

The history of the branch in its later years up to the First World War can be summed up in a comment sent to the *Freethinker* in 1901: 'The Manchester Branch seems to be doing fairly well, but not so well as could be wished, in spite of the active efforts of the officers and committee. It appears that really good audiences only assemble on the occasion of Mr Foote's visits.'[57]

This might well serve as fair comment on most of the branches for most of the time, though few survived like Manchester much beyond the Bradlaugh era. The Oldham branch disappeared in 1892, Stalybridge in 1902, Wigan in 1910, and Blackburn and Bolton in 1913 or 1914. Doubtless their fate was that of the Rochdale branch: Bradlaugh noted small audiences on his visit in 1888, and in 1893 the branch was too poor to keep its Secular Hall, which was sold off. Even Sam Standring could not put the clock back.[58] Only Liverpool really experienced a freethought revival after the Bradlaugh period, and this came at the beginning of the new century when Percy Ward, a former Wesleyan who had already enjoyed success in Yorkshire and was secretary of the British Secular League, came over as resident lecturer. After two years of work the society had a membership of just over a hundred and lecture audiences of over two hundred, but the work fell back, and when Ward emigrated to the United States in 1909, the Liverpool society had only fifty-two members. The other principal missionary work in Lancashire in these years also came from Yorkshire, under the direction of the British Secular League, which was centred on Bradford.[59]

The Yorkshire side of the Pennines experienced a similar history to that of Lancashire. Beginning in the 1860s with a tradition of regional organisation, the aim of co-operation between towns and villages to sustain lecturing work was more or less maintained, under a variety of different names, throughout most of the period. In the early 1860s there was a Yorkshire Secular Association, and in 1873 a Yorkshire West Riding Special Lecturing Circuit, based on Huddersfield, Bradford and Sheffield. By 1876 there were nine affiliated societies, with fourteen lecturers who delivered seventy-nine lectures during the lecturing season 1876–77. The Circuit then disappeared, but re-emerged as the North of England Secular

Propaganda Association in 1883 with 500 individual members. In 1890 came the Yorkshire Secular Federation, which was turned into the Yorkshire and Lancashire Secular Association in 1892 when Sam Standring came to Rochdale as lecturer.[60]

This sort of regional work helped many of the Yorkshire societies to struggle on into the new century, though the weakest of them, at Halifax, failed in 1893. In 1895 Chapman Cohen came on a lecture tour and revived five branches, and in 1901 Percy Ward became secretary of a new North of England Secular Federation, which, in eighteen months, was responsible for organising 120 lectures. This body then became the British-Secular League, the aim of which was to spread Secularism into areas where the N.S.S. was no longer active. It was very much a response to the provincial feeling that the N.S.S. had now become too much of a London organisation. The first conference, held in Liverpool in 1903, attracted delegates from all over the North, which remained the centre of operations, although a Southern Section was formed in 1905 to arrange lectures in the London parks. In July and August 1903 Percy Ward delivered thirty-six open-air lectures to audiences in Blackburn, Preston, Bolton, Wigan, Oldham, Liverpool, Birkenhead, Leeds and Crewe. The following year he decided to rejoin the N.S.S., but others, led by the treasurer, J. W. Gott of Bradford, took up the cause. In 1905 the B.S.L. had a lecture team of four in the North (George Weir of Leeds, F. Gazeley of Bradford, William Addison of Bolton, and A. E. Killip of Birkenhead), with Ernest Pack and William Heaford in London.[61]

Bradford, where the B.S.L. was based after Ward's departure, along with Bramley, Barnsley, Halifax, Heckmondwike, Huddersfield, Hull, Leeds and Sheffield, was one of the strongest Yorkshire societies, with a branch of the N.S.S. from 1877, and a tradition of freethought organisation going back to the 1850s. The Bradford Secularists had acquired their first hall as early as 1864; in 1878 they had a B.S.U. branch as well as the N.S.S. one; and, as so often happened, these reunited in 1880 at the time of the Bradlaugh case. The early 1880s, though, do not seem to have brought notable success, there being only sixty members (thirty of them new) in 1884. A generous policy of giving free lectures destroyed their finances, and little is heard of their activities until 1891, when a revival was led by J. W. Gott and John Grange. They gathered together about fifty members in the 1890s, and in 1898, after a lecture from George Standring of the Freethought Federation, a conference was held to form 'a local society to promote the mental and economic emancipation of the people'. This object shows the interests of both Gott and Standring, who were socialists, and this unusual combination of Secularism and socialism was thereafter to be a hallmark of the Bradford movement under Gott's leadership.[62]

From 1903 the Bradford freethinkers worked closely with their colleagues in Leeds, whose history was similar to their own. In Leeds also there was a tradition of organisation, with a branch of the N.S.S. from 1867. A hall was acquired in Northgate in 1875, where in 1878 the members brought upon themselves credit by running a soup kitchen for the poor, and discredit by letting their hall for a dance at which the police found illegal beer being sold, a man dancing almost nude, and others wearing female clothing. These 'Leeds orgies', coming just after the Knowlton Pamphlet 'obscenity' trials, were highly embarrassing for the Secularists, who appear to have been quite innocent themselves, but were never allowed to forget the happenings on their premises. In 1879 the society left the N.S.S., but rejoined when the ranks closed in 1880. A favourite place in Leeds for outdoor lectures was Woodhouse Moor, and here the local Secularists were described in 1887 as comprising a mixture of 'crafty gentlemen from headquarters', 'local gentlemen, some of whom wear their hair long and bushy', 'clever gentlemen, whose powers of verbosity and glibness of tongue intoxicate them', 'the discontented artizan', and 'one or two true believers in the doctrines of Secularism'. The bushy gentleman was clearly J. Greevz Fisher, an Irishman, who in 1888 led one of the many revivals which kept the society in action.[63]

With a further revival in 1903 to establish a branch of the B.S.L., Gott, Weir and Pack busied themselves on Woodhouse Moor and regularly appeared before the stipendiary magistrate, charged with breach of the bye-laws, profanity, obstruction, and even blasphemy. In 1911 Gott was entrusted with a six months' lecture mission for the N.S.S., but was then imprisoned for four months in Leeds for blasphemy. In 1912 he was involved in a new joint Leeds and Bradford Secular Society, and persuaded Foote's Secular Society Ltd to finance a three months' mission in Lancashire and Yorkshire. He and his friends were soon in trouble with the police in Blackburn, where, disowned by the N.S.S., they saturated the town with lecturers in the name of the B.S.L. In these years, under Gott's leadership, the independence of the North reached its limits, and nothing could illustrate more the relative ineffectiveness of the N.S.S. once the great days of Bradlaugh were over.[64]

*The North East*

Unlike Lancashire and Yorkshire, the North East had not been a noted centre of Secularist activity in the 1850s and 1860s, but from 1869 there was a remarkable quickening of the pace, with societies in Bedlington, Newcastle, Sunderland, South Shields, Jarrow, Windy Nook, Seghill and Spennymoor. In 1881 there were seventeen societies, and even in 1894 there were still ten, making it by this time the strongest region in the country.

The success of Secularism in the North East may at first sight seem surprising for an area in which Primitive Methodism was strong. In that other centre of Nonconformity, the valleys of South Wales, the reverse had been true, though there were strong economic as well as religious similarities between the two regions. What the North East does exemplify is that the relationship between Secularism and its supporters was not the obvious religious one, but a more complex political one, based on Bradlaugh's appeal as a Liberal and as a Republican.

'Mr. Bradlaugh's Atheism does not appear to injure his reputation with the Northumberland miners,' observed G. W. Foote in 1884 when Bradlaugh (with 109 votes) was second only to John Morley (113 votes) in the miners' ballot to decide whom to invite to their Annual Gala. In the same year the miners of Oakenshaw Colliery, who took the politically inclined *National Reformer* in their reading room, were deeply divided over the irreligious *Freethinker*. Ten years earlier, when Bradlaugh had attended the Gala at Seaton Delaval, he noted, 'There are scarcely any Freethinkers in the Seaton Delaval or New Delaval pits.' On the same occasion, in recognition of his political work, he was presented with an address from men and women of all denominations. When Bradlaugh came to Seghill to give his republican lecture on 'The Land, the People, and the Coming Struggle', in 1869, he was locked out of the colliery schoolroom, but Father O'Dwyer, the local priest, came to the rescue and let Bradlaugh use the Catholic chapel school at Annitsford. One may presume that, while Father O'Dwyer may well have been an Irish land reformer with no love for the House of Brunswick, he was no freethinker.[65]

Bradlaugh's close association with the miners of the North East was a political one. He was never a socialist, but neither were they: both were staunch Liberal/Radical/Labour in their politics, which made Bradlaugh the ideal political spokesman for the men of Northumberland and Durham. So far as religion was concerned, freethought could happily coexist with an anti-clerical populism not inconsistent with local Methodism. When G. W. Foote lectured at Easington Lane in 1875 on 'Our State Church', he noted that local parsons were 'not in the best odour just now, and the Disestablishment of the Church would be warmly welcomed'. On a Sunday in July 1880 a Methodist preacher held a meeting in a field near New Harrington Colliery to protest at the Tories' treatment of Bradlaugh—although the Methodists then removed the preacher from his post. In a demonstration to welcome General Grant to Newcastle in 1877, the Secular Society marched in procession with the Netherton Colliery brass band. The Secularists carried a banner with a portrait of Bradlaugh, and the famous flag of the Garibaldi Legion, lent to them by G. J. Holyoake, while their friends from the colliery bore a banner with a 'handsome picture of the Good Samaritan, and the inscription "He that reproveth the poor, reproacheth his Maker".' Admittedly some Secularist supporters were also outright freethinkers. One miner wrote to Hypatia Bradlaugh Bonner of her father in 1892, 'He helped to make an Atheist and a good citizen of me,' and Ralph Young, secretary of the Northumberland Miners' Association, was 'a staunch atheist' who received a secular funeral at his death in 1904. But the overwhelming majority of the supporters of Secularism in the North East were Bradlaughites rather than freethinkers. As G. W. Foote later argued, this was probably also true in other parts of the country, but nowhere is it more apparent than in the North East.[66]

Bradlaugh's first impact on the North East was made through the republican movement of the early 1870s, but he quickly went on to become involved with the miners' unions and was soon accepted as a spokesman for the miners' interest. He attended his first Northumberland Miners' Picnic in 1873, and his first Durham Miners' Gala the following year. On the latter occasion the South Tanfield Colliery banner depicted Bradlaugh trampling on a broken sceptre, with a crown lying at his feet. Republicanism was certainly strong in the area. In 1876 all but two of the miners at Hebburn Colliery signed the N.S.S. petition against a further grant to the Prince of Wales; South Brancepeth, with only 175 cottages, filled eleven signature sheets; Spennymoor sent in 140 names. Politics were also the point of contact with the Cleveland Miners, at whose Annual Demonstration in 1876 Bradlaugh proposed the motion for the assimilation of the county and borough franchises, a speech which he repeated for the Northumberland Miners at Blyth a month later. At the Durham Miners' Demonstration he proposed the successful motion in favour of arbitration rather than strike action after the miners' wages had been cut by 35 per cent in twenty-one months, and later in the same year he was asked to be an arbitrator at Silksworth Pit in a dispute between the hewers and the owners. With this background of co-operation in the cause of radicalism and labour, it is not surprising that in the early 1880s the miners rallied behind Bradlaugh in his constitutional fight. Not until 1887 did there enter a discordant note, when Bradlaugh would not support the Durham miners in their opposition to women surface workers. Then, in 1889, he moved into more serious conflict with them over the Employers' Liability Bill, which he consistently opposed.[67]

The place of Bradlaugh in the North East is best summed up by the Bedlington radicals, whose political creed was embodied in a 'Burns, Paine, Jones and Bradlaugh Social and Reform Club', the president of which was an aged Chartist, the vice-president a follower of Ernest Jones, and the treasurer a Bradlaughite. As the *Morpeth Weekly News* wrote after Bradlaugh's death, 'No public man so thoroughly represented the social and political opinion of the Northumberland miners as he did.'[68]

To turn from Bradlaugh as a popular leader to the organised freethought movement of the North East, is to move from the large scale to the small. Although there were thirty-two Secular societies in the region at some time between 1865 and 1915, the maximum number in any one year was almost half this. Most of this number were village societies, but the strongest were those of the towns—Newcastle, South Shields, West Auckland, the Hartlepools, Sunderland and Stockton. The only village societies to have a comparable life were those at Bedlington, Cramlington, Spennymoor, and Hetton le Hole (with Houghton le Spring and Easington Lane). Most of the village societies comprised a small knot of outright freethinkers who could form the nucleus of larger meetings convened on the occasion of a lecture from Bradlaugh or one of the other national leaders, especially when the topic offered was a congenial political one. This process was aided by the fact that many such freethinkers were already established radical figures in their communities—like Charles Mark of Wolsingham, who had been a leading Chartist and is described in his obituary as 'the father and founder of Freethought principles in this locality'. The initiative often rested with a single individual, such as M. Stitt, a grocer, of Crook, who issued a placard appealing to his friends in Wolsingham, Willington, Tow Law and districts to meet at his house to form a Crook Secular Society and elect a committee.

Sometimes the committee and the society were virtually co-terminous, as at Spennymoor in 1879, where B. Dawson raised the tricolor flag from his summer house and announced he was ready to receive N.S.S. members. In addition to himself, the president of his society, there were a secretary, treasurer, and three members. Yet, when Joseph Symes lectured at Spennymoor only a few weeks later, on the topics 'Toryism, the Curse of the Nations', 'What have the Great Landowners Done for the Poor', and 'Confederation of Labour and How to Obtain It', he had 'large and enthusiastic audiences'. A few weeks later still, when heavy rain and wind limited his audience to a mere thirty, Symes could report in a different mood: 'Apart, however, from wind and rain, I fear the Spennymoor people are much more deeply concerned about racing, coursing, the birth of a litter of puppy hounds, or the "shindies"[1] of Hallelujah Lasses than about any such trifles as the death-lock in agriculture, the dearth of trade, and the prospective sufferings of the coming winter.' Such moments of frank realism are rare in the periodicals of freethought, but the three faces of Spennymoor seem likely to represent three faces of Secularism anywhere in the country.[69]

Of the town societies the longest-lasting was, not unnaturally, the central one in Newcastle, where freethought had been organised since the 1850s, despite many fluctuations in its fortunes. After tea at one of the customary regional outings to Marsden Rock in 1864, the local Secularists discussed how to make their movement more effective in the area. 'Local societies had been formed in Newcastle and elsewhere,' it was reported, 'but they had all failed, chiefly through the apathy of Secularists and the smallness of their number.' A North of England Secular Union was formed to tackle this lamentable situation, the activities centring on Haslam's Dining Rooms in Clayton Street, Newcastle. This made the Secular Union in effect the Newcastle Secular Society. In 1867, following difficulty hiring a lecture hall, a Hall of Science Building Fund was started, and the Secular Union affiliated to the N.S.S. Later the same year a regional conference discussed setting up a Sunday school, which was opened in January 1869. Newcastle then appears to have run out of energy and into debt. In 1871, and again in 1873, Charles Watts commented unfavourably on some of the Newcastle leaders, and in 1874 Bradlaugh by-passed the Secular Union and started his own Northern Branch of the N.S.S. in Newcastle. A new Secular Hall Fund was started in 1875, and the branch amalgamated with the Secular Union, which arranged for local and national lectures, in March 1877.[70]

Those involved in Newcastle Secularism in the later 1870s can be divided into hardcore, and peripheral supporters. At the General Grant demonstration, for example, each trade society was represented, doubtless calling on the first loyalties of many freethinkers who thus did not appear in the Secularists' contingent: the *Newcastle Daily Chronicle* reported, 'The Secularists do not show in very strong numbers.' But the following year a *Newcastle Examiner* report of open-air preaching at Sandhill described the Secularists as having audiences of five to six thousand men. It was around this time that Malcolm Quin came from Leicester to Newcastle, and found only a 'small Secular Society'.[71]

The pattern of Secularist development in the North East in the 1880s followed the national trend, with expansion in the first half of the decade and contraction thereafter, but the revival in fortunes here at the end of the decade was more widespread and more lasting than in most other places. A new Sunderland branch was started in 1887 after a visit from Foote, the Newcastle branch secured a new hall in Newgate Street the following year, and in March 1889 a new attempt at regional organisation was made when Foote started the North East Secular Federation on the model of the London Secular Federation. The state of freethought in the North East on the eve of its revival was typical of many parts of the country: 'Some of the Branches of the N.S.S. merely existed in name from their isolated condition, small membership, and lack of funds. They were unable to do any active work, some of them not having been able to engage a lecturer for years past. The work of the strongest Branches was of an intermittent character, and some Branches had gone out of existence altogether, and yet this populous district teems with Freethinkers.' The new Federation comprised members in Newcastle, South Shields, Bedlington, Jarrow, Chester le Street, Stockton, Middlesbrough and West Hartlepool, and it was fortunate to secure the services of a number of lecturers from London, including Foote, Mrs Mary Sowden and Arthur Moss, who spent his annual summer holidays lecturing in the area. By 1890 the Newcastle society could report 'over a hundred financial members' and the annual Federation picnic to South Shields in 1891 had an attendance of around four hundred. When Charles Watts made an extensive tour of the area, two years later, freethought was still thriving, despite the trade depression; but, despite the hard work of S. M. Peacock of South Shields and Joseph Brown of Newcastle (Federation president and secretary, respectively), the usual decline set in after 1895, with the number of societies in the region falling from thirteen in 1891 to only five at the opening of the new century.[72]

*Scotland*

In Scotland, freethought was represented by a few, relatively strong societies. No more than seventeen localities had societies at any time between 1865 and 1915, and most of these were extremely short-lived. The only centres of any significance were Edinburgh, Perth, Dundee, Glasgow and Paisley, which, with Aberdeen and Greenock, all had societies in the early 1870s, the most successful times for the Scots. There were nine societies reported in 1871 and again in 1877; usually there were only six, even in the early 1880s, and two of these were in Glasgow.

Glasgow and Paisley had two of the longest-established freethought societies in Britain. The Wilson Hall, Paisley, was described in 1866 as 'the oldest Secular Hall in the Kingdom', while the Glasgow Eclectic Institution, which dated back to the zetetic societies of the 1820s, had been 'maintained in operation for a period of years of which there is no example in England'. The veteran Owenite, Alexander Campbell, was still active as a lecturer among the Glasgow freethinkers in the 1860s, and was honorary president of the Eclectic Society in 1867. Owenism was not dead here, with Campbell still performing the naming of infants according to the old Rational Society's practice of twenty years earlier. As was often true of Secularism where Owenite roots were strong, G. J. Holyoake retained his popularity among the Glasgow friends, and in 1865 was invited to move there (as he had in 1845–46) as permanent lecturer, but the illness of his wife forced him to cancel his appointment after only a few weeks. A branch of the N.S.S. was started among the Eclectic Society's members in 1867 at the instigation of Charles Watts, but after two halls had been lost in two years, Bradlaugh was disappointed when he visited them in 1870 to find that many old faces were gone and not enough younger men had been recruited to replace them. A split then seems to have developed between the N.S.S. branch and the Eclectic Society. The latter was meeting at the Wilson Street Hall, but the former moved out to the Democratic Hall, Neilson Street, where they held their own monthly and then weekly meetings. The Eclectics in 1872 issued a new set of principles which were remarkably Owenite in tone, stressing the positive Secularism of Holyoake against what was regarded as the negative frethought of Bradlaugh. As at Leicester, the branch came off the worse in this conflict, and even Arthur Trevelyan, when president of the N.S.S., appeared to favour the Eclectics, who went from strength to strength. Not surprisingly, in 1877 there was a strong party in favour of Charles Watts, and a B.S.U. branch was formed with thirty members. In the 1880s an N.S.S. branch was once more included within the Eclectic Society, but this did not prevent Charles Watts from being invited to open the Society's new hall in 1883.[73]

There was a similar division at Edinburgh at this time. In 1870 a Scottish Secular Union was formed to pioneer missionary work, especially in eastern Scotland. The Union was soon afterwards amalgamated with the Edinburgh Secular Society, and Thomas Slater was asked to lecture. The pace then slackened and the number of societies fell, until the Union was revived at Dundee in 1876. This time it seems that the Union was thought of as a Scottish equivalent to the N.S.S., with the same subscription of 1s 4d a year; it was not affiliated to the N.S.S., but members were free to join both organisations. The Union disappeared in the early 1880s, and with it the Aberdeen society, whilst those in Dundee and Edinburgh were divided among themselves. The Edinburgh society was not in the N.S.S., but there was a strong Bradlaughite contingent in the city led by John Lees, a rope and twine manufacturer who was a vice-president of the N.S.S. and personal friend of Bradlaugh. His branch merged with the independent society in 1884 to form what appears to have been a strong and healthy society with a club and Sunday school, but a further split occurred in 1888 when a new Scottish Secular Union broke away. This Union was not affiliated to the N.S.S., although it was organising lectures in the city rather like the regional federations of England.[74]

The leading figure in the later period of Scottish freethought was J. P. Gilmour of Glasgow, who joined the Eclectics in 1879 at the age of nineteen and continued active in both local affairs and the N.S.S. until the inter-war years. With characteristic Scottish independence, he was one of the main critics of G. W. Foote in the 1890s, associating himself with the Freethought Federation. At the beginning of the twentieth century the Glasgow freethinkers were more successful than the English branches, reporting large audiences even during the Anglo-Boer War. They survived a trade depression in 1909, although this meant that some people could not even afford to pay for seats at lectures, and they survived the destruction by fire in 1912 of their hall with its splendid Eclectic Society library, which included a complete 1768 edition of Voltaire's works. In 1915 Chapman Cohen could still get good audiences, both indoors and out of doors; and 'red Clydeside' was long to continue to have a freethought wing, personified by Guy A. Aldred, who settled in the city to propagate communism and the views of Richard Carlile.[75]

## Ireland

On the continent of Europe, not to be a Catholic was to be a freethinker, but in Ireland, not to be a Catholic was to be a Protestant, often of the fiercest, most aggressive and most unreasoning kind. There was no room for freethought in Ireland. As the *Freethinker* commented in 1882, 'Father Fennelly is proud that no "infidel societies" have been established in Ireland. Quite so. They go in for "assassination societies" over there. Murder isn't half as bad as infidelity. Better beat out your neighbour's brains than believe that Jonah was not swallowed by a whale.'[76]

At the 1861 census on Irish education and religion, only twenty-one freethinkers (including one woman), twenty Secularists (three women) and nineteen Deists (three women) stated their positions to be such.[77] Rarely does the historian get his perspectives set out in so clear a way. Organised freethought barely existed. Boyne managed a freethought society in 1875 and 1876; Cork had a branch of the N.S.S. in 1883. Otherwise, only Dublin and Belfast had anything to offer, which was very little. Secular societies appeared in both Dublin and Belfast in 1875, though neither lasted long. In March 1886 the *National Reformer* admitted that there was no organised freethought in Ireland, but in November of that year a branch was founded in Belfast, which lasted until the mid-1890s, and to which G. W. Foote paid a presidential visit in 1891. This society arose in reaction to the Belfast riots of the summer of 1886. It represented a small, untypical group of self-proclaimed 'sane' men in a sea of religious folly.[78]

## Notes

1 *N.R.*, 3 September 1865, 25 March, 23 December 1866, 29 September 1867. The lease expired on Lady Day 1866.
2 *N.R.*, 6, 27 September 1868, 10 January, 11 July 1869; notes on the Hall of Science, from 23 August 1868—B.L. no. 184. For R. O. Smith see *F.*, 4 June 1893.
3 *N.R.*, 4 October 1868, 1 August, 26 September 1869, 9, 30 January, 13 February, 6 March 1870, 5, 26 November 1871, 2 May 1880; *Weekly Dispatch*, 8 June 1879.

4   E.g. *Tablet*, 1 July 1871.
5   *F.*, 15 February 1885.
6   *S.R.*, 10 April 1886; C. M. Davies, *Heterodox London*, 2 vols. (London, 1874, reprinted New York, 1969), I, pp. 121–36. For Antill see *N.R.*, 27 April 1879.
7   See Appendix A.
8   P. Thompson, *Socialists, Liberals and Labour* (London, 1967), p. 242.
9   *Secular World*, January, February 1864; *N.R.*, 15, 22 October, 12 November 1864, 18 June, 15 October, 3 December 1865, 1 July 1866, 21 June 1868, 18 April, 23 May 1869, 30 January, 5 November 1876; *S.C.*, 27 August 1876; *Secularist*, 26 August, 2 September, 4 November 1876, 27 January 1877; *S.R.*, 3 September 1876, 7 July 1877; C. Booth, *Life and Labour of the People in London*, 3rd series: 'Religious Influences', 7 vols. (London, 1902–03), II, pp. 206–8.
10  *N.R.*, 2 September 1866, 30 October 1870, 15 January, 30 April, 6 August 1871, 15 December 1872, 19 January, 19 May, 2, 9 June 1873, 8, 22 November 1874, 7 November 1875, 29 October 1876.
11  *N.R.*, 13 December 1862, 4 July 1863, 15 January, 10 September, 1, 29 October 1865, 8 September, 20 October 1867.
12  *N.R.*, 2 May 1880; *Radical*, December 1887; *Secular Work*, February 1897. For the Patriotic Club see *N.R.*, 25 August 1872.
13  See *F.*, 9 February 1890, 11 January 1891.
14  *N.R.*, 1 May, 12 June 1870, 10 December 1871, 13 October 1872, 12, 26 October 1873, 10 January, 13 June 1875, 8 October 1876; C. M. Davies, *op. cit.*, I, pp. 351–63.
15  *N.R.*, 31 January, 14 March 1875; *N. S. S. Almanack* (1878), p. 33.
16  *Radical Leader*, 6 October 1888; *N.R.*, 19 October 1890, 8 May 1892.
17  *N.R.*, 10 September 1876, 7 January 1877; *F.*, 7 December 1884.
18  *N.R.*, 9 November 1890; N.S.S. Minute Book IV, 1 November 1892; *F.*, 31 May, 27 October, 3 November 1895; *Jerusalem Star*, November 1895.
19  *Radical*, April 1889; *F.*, 21 July 1889; *N.R.*, 26 October, 23, 30 November 1890.
20  *N.R.*, 6 January 1867, 30 April 1876; *S.C.*, 30 April, 14 May, 24 September 1876; *F.*, 12 October 1884; *N.R.*, 19 April 1885.
21  *Radical Leader*, 18 August 1888; C. Booth, *op. cit.*, 1st series: 'Poverty', 4 vols. (London, 1889–91, reprinted 1902), I, p. 294; *Secular Work*, July 1896. The Shaftesbury estate was a commercial housing development designed exclusively for skilled artisans; John Burns was brought up there.
22  *F.*, 5 October 1902.
23  *N.R.*, 27 March 1870.
24  *S.C.*, 28 November 1875; *N.R.*, 17 September 1876.
25  *N.R.*, 22 July 1877.
26  *F.*, 27 November 1887, 22 January, 17 June 1888; *N.R.*, 5 February, 17 June 1888; *F.*, 27 October 1889, 17 January 1891.
27  See below, p. 285.
28  *N.R.*, 24 January 1869; *F.*, 19 January 1890.
29  *Radical*, August 1889.

30 *S.R.*, 9 June 1877; *F.*, 30 October 1881, 27 October, 3 November 1889; *N.R.*, 1 May 1892; *F.*, 14 May 1893; N.S.S. Organisation Committee, Minute Book, 12 September, 10 October 1889, 13 February 1890, 16 April 1892.

31 *N.R.*, 31 May 1874; *F.*, 7 October 1894.

32 *N.R.*, 16 April 1864, 22 August 1869, 4 February 1872; *S.C.*, 1 October 1872.

33 See C. R. Williams, 'The Welsh Religious Revival, 1904–05', *British Journal of Sociology*, III (1952), pp. 249, 252.

34 *S.R.*, 31 May 1879; *F.*, 1 October 1882, 5 March, 6 August 1905.

35 *N.R.*, 24 March, 1 September 1867, 12, 19 January 1868, 10 January 1869, 3 November 1872, 12, 19 October 1873.

36 *N.R.*, 15 November 1874; *S.C.*, 18 July 1875; *N.R.*, 22, 29 March 1868, 2 March 1873.

37 For Gurney see *Dictionary of Labour Biography*, V (London, 1979); for Bates see *Northampton Daily Reporter*, 23 August 1883; also *Northampton Mercury*, 1 June, 20 July 1850; for Adams see *ibid.*, 15 February 1890.

38 *N.R.*, 13 February 1864, 21 October 1866, 17 February 1867, 10 January 1869; *Northampton Mercury*, 7 November 1874, 17 February 1922.

39 *S.R.*, 16 August 1879, 22 April 1882, 3 January 1885; *F.*, 4 January 1885, 3 May 1896; *Secular Work*, January 1897.

40 *N.R.*, 11, 25 July 1869; *S.C.*, 5 September 1875, 6 May 1877; *S.R.*, 9 June 1877, 9, 16, March 1878; *N.R.*, 24 March 1878, 27 November 1887; H. Snell, *Men, Movements and Myself*, p. 32.

41 *N.R.*, 9 May 1869, 15 December 1872. For the society, see F. J. Gould, *The History of the Leicester Secular Society* (Leicester, 1900), and S. A. Gimson, 'Random Recollections of the Leicester Secular Society' (unpublished Ms., Part 1, March 1932; Part 2, May 1935), Leicestershire C.R.O.

42 M. Quin, *Memoirs of a Positivist* (London, 1924), pp. 47–8; *N.R.*, 15 December 1872; Leicester S.S., Shareholders' Allotment Book, 1873–75, and Register of Members, Annual Lists, 1875–1904, Leicestershire C.R.O.; *S.C.*, 3 November 1878, 12 March 1881, *S.R.*, 31 May 1879; *N.R.*, 13 March 1881.

43 *N.R.*, 21 January, 21 October, 4, 11 November 1877; Leicester S.S., Minute Book II, 4, 17 March 1878, Leicestershire C.R.O.

44 *S.C.*, 18 July 1875. See also the replies to a questionnaire from Nottingham about the N.S.S.—Leicester S.S., Minute Book II, 28 May 1883.

45 *Ibid.*, 20, 27 April, 1881, 4 February 1884.

46 *F.*, 6, 27 April 1890.

47 *F.*, 24 April 1898; *Ethical World*, 19 May 1900; Leicester S.S., Scrapbook, 1872–1908: Annual Report (1900), pp. 7, 9–10.

48 *N.R.*, 10 March 1867, 14 February, 14 March, 11 April 1869, 6 March 1870, 9 April, 4, 18 June, 8 October 1871.

49 *N.R.*, 6 August 1864.

50 *N.R.*, 14 April 1867, 25 April, 13 June, 10 October 1869, 7 July 1872;

*S.C.*, 1 November 1872.

51  *N.R.*, 13 February 1876, 7 January 1877; *S.C.*, 3 June, 9 September 1877; *N.R.*, 9 September 1877; *S.R.*, 8, 29 September 1877; *N.R.*, 6 June 1880, 27 February 1881; *F.*, 9 August 1891; *Anti-Infidel*, June 1897; *Reformer*, 15 November 1897. See also C. Stephens, 'The Secularist Movement in Birmingham and District, 1850–1885' (B.A. dissertation, University of Birmingham, 1972).

52  *N.R.*, 30 April 1865, 14 January, 16 December 1866, 10 February, 6, 13, 20, 27 October 1867.

53  *N.R.*, 7 March, 11 April 1869, 20 February, 27 March 1870, 5 January 1873, 30 August 1874; *S.C.*, 13 June, 19 September 1875, 9 September 1876, 8, 15 September 1878; *N.R.*, 26 May 1878; *S.R.*, 7 September 1878.

54  *N.R.*, 5 December 1886, 23 January, 2 October 1887, 2 February, 13 July 1890; *F.*, 2 February, 13 July 1890, 29 May 1892; *Rochdale Observer*, 28 September 1895.

55  *N.R.*, 21 April 1867, 24 December 1865, 16 February, 8 March 1868, 6 June, 24 October 1869.

56  *N.R.*, 6 June 1875, 1, 8 September, 1 December 1878; *S.R.*, 11 January 1879; *N.R.*, 27 November 1881, 7 November 1886; *Watts's L.G.*, November 1886; *N.R.*, 10 April 1887, *F.*, 11 December 1887; George Payne to C. Bradlaugh, 1, 6, 18, 20 October 1886, G. Payne to [Annie Besant], 5 November 1886, A. Hemingway to C. Bradlaugh, 5 November 1886, B.L. nos. 1281, 1284, 1285, 1286, 1295, 1296.

57  *F.*, 26 March 1893, 24 February 1901.

58  *N.R.*, 2 September 1888; *F.*, 7 May 1893. In 1894 the Rochdale society applied as a society to affiliate to the N.S.S. but was refused; seven members then applied to form a branch—N.S.S. Minute Book IV, 30 August, 27 September 1894.

59  *F.*, 19 February, 24 December 1905, 7, 21 January 1906, 4 April, 5 December 1909; *Truth Seeker*, March 1906.

60  *Secular World*, 1 September 1863; *N.R.*, 15 September 1867, 6 February 1870, 5 October, 14 December 1873; *S.C.*, January 1874, 10 January 1875; *N.R.*, 6 September 1874, 31 October 1875; *S.C.*, 14 November, 12 December 1875, 19 March 1876; *N.R.*, 12 March, 10 September 1876; *S.C.*, 10 September 1876; *N.R.*, 9 September 1877; *S.R.*, 8 September 1877; *S.C.*, 20 October 1878; *N.R.*, 20 April, 16, 23 November 1884, 2, 9 March 1890; *F.*, 8, 15 June, 9 November 1890.

61  *F.*, 29 May 1892; *N.R.*, 12 June, 4, 11 December 1892; *F.*, 8 December 1895; *Truth Seeker*, August, December 1901, January 1902; *Secularist*, March 1902; *Truth Seeker*, March 1903; *F.*, 31 July 1904; *A.J.*, 6 August 1904; *Truth Seeker*, July–September, October–December 1905; *A.J.*, 27 May, 10 June, 15 July, 19 August, 16, 23 September, 7 October 1905, 10 November 1906.

62  *N.R.*, 19 December 1863, 13 February 1864, 8, 29 August 1880; *S.R.*, 31 July, 14 August 1880; *N.R.*, 13 April, 3 August 1884; *F.*, 2 August 1885; *N.R.*, 15 March 1891; *F.*, 10 January 1892, 5 February, 30 April 1893; *Reformer*, 15 December 1898; *Truth Seeker*, November, December 1898,

December 1900, August, September, October 1901, June 1903; *F.*, 24 November 1901, 3 August 1902. For John Grange see *Truth Seeker*, April 1897; for J. W. Gott see *Labour Annual* (1900).

63　*N.R.*, 11 April 1863, 4 August, 24 November 1867, 6 June 1869, 21 July, 4 August 1872, 17 August 1873, 29 August 1875, 13 February 1876; *S.R.*, 11 August 1877; *S.C.*, 19 August 1877; *N.R.*, 17 February 1878; *S.R.*, 9 March 1878; *S.C.*, 31 March 1878; *Leeds Daily News*, 6 September 1878; *Leeds Mercury*, 6 September 1878; *S.R.*, 12 April 1879, 27 March 1880; *Leeds Evening Express*, 18 August 1887; *F.*, 28 October 1888. For J. Greevz Fisher see *Truth Seeker*, July 1895.

64　*Truth Seeker*, June 1903; *F.*, 10 April 1904, 14 July, 4, 11 August 1912; *Truth Seeker*, new series, nos. 1–3 [1913]. For the blasphemy prosecutions see below, chapter 14, pp. 277–82.

65　*F.*, 22 June, 24 August, 16 November 1884, 25 January 1885; *N.R.*, 21 June 1874, 17 October 1869.

66　*S.C.*, 31 October 1875; *N.R.*, 25 July 1880; *S.C.*, 30 September 1877; *Newcastle Weekly Chronicle*, 29 September 1877; *Newcastle Daily Chronicle*, 24 September 1877; *N.R.*, 28 February 1892; *F.*, 25 December 1904.

67　*N.R.*, 6, 20 July 1873, 23 August 1874, 23 January, 14 May, 18 June, 9, 16 July, 29 October 1876, 25 July 1880, 20 February 1887, 30 June, 7 July 1889.

68　*F.*, 15 March 1891; *Reformer*, 15 July 1898.

69　*N.R.*, 23 February 1873, 28 August 1870, 18 May, 1, 15 June, 24 August 1879.

70　*N.R.*, 18 July 1863, 25 June 1865, 14, 21 April, 24 May, 9, 23 June, 6 October 1867, 3 January 1869, 29 October 1871, 14 September 1873, 28 June, 26 July 1874, 9 May, 26 December 1875; *S.C.*, 26 December 1875, 18 March 1877.

71　*Newcastle Daily Chronicle*, 24 September 1877; *N.R.*, 21 July 1878; M. Quin, *Memoirs of a Positivist*, pp., 62–3.

72　*F.*, 27 February 1887, 17 March, 7 April, 20 October 1889, 11 May 1890; *N.R.*, 7 April 1887, 18 August 1889, 19 July, 9, 23 August 1891, 22 January 1893; *F.*, 19 February 1893. For S. M. Peacock and J. Brown see *F.*, 7 May 1893.

73　*English Leader*, 14 July 1866; *N.R.*, 26 October, 2 November 1861, 12 July, 9, 16, 23 August 1862, 19 September 1863, 29 September 1867; *Reasoner*, 1 October 1865; *N.R.*, 28 January 1866, 22 September, 6 October 1867, 23 October 1870, 5 November 1871, 10, 17 November 1872, 13 April 1873, 24 May 1874, 9 May, 25 July, 29 August, 19 December 1875; *S.R.*, 6 April 1878; *N.R.*, 11 August 1878, 12 January 1879, 26 December 1880; *S.R.*, 6 May 1882.

74　*N.R.*, 21 August 1870, 20 August 1871, 7 April, 2 June 1872, 18 June, 10 September, 1 October 1876, 16 March 1879; *Secularist*, 30 September 1876; *N.R.*, 13 April 1884; *F.*, 28 October 1888. For J. Lees see *N.R.*, 5 October 1884, and *F.*, 27 December 1896.

75　*F.*, 29 September 1901, 28 February 1909, 15 December 1912, 17 October 1915; *Secular Work*, November 1896, January 1897. For J. P. Gilmour see F. J. Gould, *Pioneers of Johnson's Court* (London, 1929), pp.

134–5; for G. A. Aldred see his autobiography, *No Traitor's Gait* (Glasgow, 1955). Aldred was a London-born freethinker who at various times was a socialist, anarchist and communist.

76   *F.*, 8 October 1882.

77   *N.R.*, 10 December 1865. There were also four Socialists, two Materialists, two Rationalists, one Theist, one Philanthropist, one Positivist, one Atheist (all male), and one female Unbeliever.

78   *N.R.*, 6 June, 5 September 1875; *F.*, 14 May, 16 July 1882; *N.R.*, 14 March, 5 December 1886; *F.*, 24 February 1889, 20 April 1890, 19, 26 April 1891. For the Belfast riots see *F.*, 22 August 1886.

# VI

# International freethought

Britain led Europe in the organisation of popular freethought, for in most Continental countries the political régimes were not conducive to free discussion and publication. When criticisms were voiced, freethought was but part of a wider programme of political and social protest. As the American, Samuel Putnam, wrote in 1894, 'In Europe the terms Socialist, Republican, and Freethinker are, by the government papers and orators, employed to denote any person who expresses radical political and religious views, and hence it has come to pass that the public at large cannot conceive of a Republican or Socialist who is not at the same time a Freethinker, and vice versa.' Conservatism and the Catholic Church went hand in hand; so too did Liberalism and freethought.[1]

The first stirrings of freethought organisation came in the Low Countries in the 1850s, the first Belgian society being set up in 1854 and the first Dutch two years later; but there was no Belgian equivalent of the N.S.S. until 1885, and the Dutch *De Dageraad* had to be revived by its founder-president, R. C. d'Ablaing van Giessenburg, in 1880 when it had only a hundred members. The initiative for an international conference came from Belgium in 1879, where the freethought cause was represented by the Belgian Rationalist Federation (with eighteen societies) and La Libre Pensée of Brussels (a more middle-class but socialist society with 1,000 members). Invitations were sent to the N.S.S., the B.S.U., the Liberal League of America, and France and Holland, and the conference met in Brussels at the end of August 1880 to set up the International Freethought Federation. As the strongest society, the N.S.S. was host the following year, but the French socialists refused to co-operate and held their own meeting in Rome in 1882. Amsterdam was host in 1883, and thereafter international conferences became a regular event, providing the English leaders with an excuse for a Continental holiday in such places as Antwerp (1885), Paris (1889) or Rome (1904). By the end of the nineteenth century the Federation embraced members not only in most European countries and North America, but also in Spanish America and the West Indies.[2]

The spread of freethought closely followed the triumph of liberalism in Europe. In France, freethought flourished once the Third Republic was established under Gambetta. By 1885 La Ligue Anti-Clericale Union de France was claiming 300 branches and 10,000 members.[3] In Germany, Bismarck's *Kulturkampf* may have encouraged freethinkers, though the first organisations did not come until the more reactionary 1880s. In 1881 a German Freethought Society was started in Frankfurt, with the celebrated materialist philosopher and doctor, Ludwig Büchner, as president. By 1885 the *Freidenkerbund* had 1,000 members. Even more successful was the *Monisterbund*, founded by the followers of the Darwinian zoologist, Ernst Haeckel, in 1906, which, within a few years, had forty-two branch societies and 6,000 members.[4]

Freethought societies were also reported in Rome, Milan and Florence in the mid-1880s, while in Spain La Union Española de Librepensadores in Barcelona had thirty branches in 1885. The real spread of freethought here, however, came with the growth of free towns and the expansion of commerce following the war of 1898. The centre of Spanish liberalism and freethought was always Barcelona, and the British freethinkers showed great interest in the work there of Francisco Ferrer, whom the Spanish authorities executed on a trumped-up charge in 1909.[5]

## The United States

Charles Watts noted on his 1883 lecture tour of America how vastly different each part of the United States was from the rest and from Britain; he also commented on the general lack of organisation and fragmentation in the freethought movement.[6] Apart from the German-speaking societies, there was a multiplicity of English ones. The Free Religious Association was founded in 1867 by a group of conservatives, including R. D. Owen, under the presidency of Octavius Brooks Frothingham; its paper was the *Index*, edited first by F. E. Abbott and then by B. F. Underwood. In 1876 a group of radicals broke away to form the National Liberal League, led by D. M. Bennett's *Truth Seeker*, which had been started in September 1873. A third force was J. P. Mendum's *Boston Investigator*, which Abner Kneeland had started in 1831, and which Horace Seaver had edited since Kneeland's imprisonment for blasphemy in 1833. In

1884 an American Secular Union was established, which the National Liberal League joined two years later, but in 1891 a split occurred similar to that in the British movement, between those who favoured 'positive' Secularism and those who wanted militant freethought. The latter group, led by S. P. Putman and the *Truth Seeker*, founded an alternative Freethought Federation of America in 1892, which then absorbed the American Secular Union two years later. In 1901 the old A.S.U. name was readopted and the organisation was led by Eugene Macdonald, who now edited the *Truth Seeker*. Meanwhile the *Index* had been succeeded by the *Open Court*, which became more radical when edited by a German emigrant, Paul Carus, who was a follower of Büchner and Haeckel.[7]

Chief among the American freethinkers was Robert G. Ingersoll, who in many ways resembled Charles Bradlaugh. Like him he was an outspoken atheist, an outstanding orator, a lawyer (he had been Illinois State Attorney General), and a social conservative. He was probably a greater propagandist than Bradlaugh.[8]

The greatest problem which the American Secularists had to face was the fact that they were living in a nominally secular society. Indifference to theological teachings had been a cornerstone of the Republic. The only God worshipped by the American people, thought Charles Watts, was 'the almighty dollar'. Nevertheless, a little healthy religious prejudice occasionally broke the surface and gave the freethinkers a cause. The main controversies centred around the use of the Bible in public schools, the exemption of Church property from taxation, the provision of chaplains in state prisons, and the invocation of the Divine Blessing at sessions of Congress. The religious reaction worsened in the 1870s after Anthony Comstock, chief special agent for the New York Society for the Suppression of Vice, secured a law providing severe penalties for the sending of obscene (including contraceptive) materials through the post. D. M. Bennett challenged this law in 1878 and was imprisoned for thirteen months. This, and the scale of the Vice Society's operations, gave a great boost to the National Liberal League at the same time as the Knowlton prosecution was having a similar impact on the N.S.S. There were eighteen local Liberal Leagues in 1876, sixty-two in 1878, a hundred more in 1879, fifty more again in 1880, and 225 by 1881. The National Liberal League had 123 branches in 1879, and 240 by 1882. In addition a National Defense Association was started to counter the Vice Society, its most celebrated defence being that of Walt Whitman's *Leaves of Grass* in 1882.[9]

Charles Bradlaugh paid three visits to the United States in an attempt to restore his precarious financial position. His first tour, beginning in September 1873, was cut short by the need to be in Northampton for the general election of February 1874; he returned in October 1874 for a five-month tour of the eastern and mid-western states; and again in the autumn of 1875. G. J. Holyoake also visited North America, in 1879 and 1882; and Charles Watts went there in 1882, 1883, and 1884, staying in Canada on the latter occasion until 1891. He and Foote visited a National Convention of Freethinkers in Chicago in 1896, and he crossed the Atlantic for a final time in 1898–99. On the other side, Samuel Putnam visited Britain in 1895, and Ingersoll was planning to do so when he died in 1899.[10]

On his 1899 visit Watts was disappointed at the disorganisation of American freethought, for the golden age was over there as surely as it was in Britain. With Bennett, Mendum, Putnam, Ingersoll and Seaver all dead, and with the freethought movement as out of touch with socialism as it was in Britain, the organisations were in rapid decline. After 1910 the *Truth Seeker* carried no further record of their activities.[11]

### The British Empire

Apart from N.S.S. branches in India at Fyzabad (1883) and Madras (1884),[12] in the West Indies at Barbados and Port of Spain,[13] and among the Gibraltar garrison,[14] there was a small independent freethought movement in South Africa created by Edward B. Rose, an emigrant to Port Elizabeth in 1887. His audiences were small, however, and his lectures outside Port Elizabeth resulted in no lasting success.[15] By contrast, the Australian colonies, New Zealand and Canada all had thriving freethought societies.

### Canada

The Canadian movement, which had links with that in the United States, was much smaller than its neighbour to the south. The first society was that organised in Toronto in 1873, which took a lead in forming a Freethought Association in 1877 to campaign for the taxation of ecclesiastical property, secular education, the abolition of the judicial oath, and a free Sunday. Weekly meetings were held in the Albert Hall, Toronto, and a journal was started, called simply the *Freethought Journal*, edited by W. J. R. Hargreaves. In 1882

Charles Watts visited Canada and was invited to stay by the Toronto society. He did so in 1884, and started a new periodical called *Secular Thought*. The Toronto Freethought Society now took the name of Secular, and the Canadian Association was reorganised as the Canadian Secular Union under the presidency of William Algie. The period of Algie's presidency (1885–89) and Watts's lectureship (1884–92) saw the high point of Secularism in Canada. In 1884 small societies were reported at centres in Welland, St Thomas and Aylmer (to the north of Lake Eirie), Gananoque and Belleville (to the north of Lake Ontario), and at Ottawa. Apart from Toronto, the other main society was in Montreal, where a private and well patronised—and apparently English-speaking—Pioneer Freethought Club (1880) was formed under the presidency of Captain Robert C. Adams, who also succeeded Algie as president of the Canadian Secular Union in 1889. The latter's greatest successes were to challenge the ban by customs officials on such freethought works as Paine's *Age of Reason*, and to secure the Dominion Oaths Act of 1893, but after Watts's return to England the movement never again recovered the momentum of the 1880s.[16]

## New Zealand

A steady stream of freethinkers emigrated to Australia and New Zealand from the 1850s, carrying with them the way of life they had created at home. The Secularist movement in New Zealand was remarkable for producing two Prime Ministers, Robert Stout (1884–87) and John Ballance (1890–93), who laid the foundations of modern, Liberal politics in the country. Stout was to New Zealand what Ingersoll was to the United States and Bradlaugh to Britain.[17]

Freethought in New Zealand went back to the 1850s, but as elsewhere it was the 1870s and 1880s which saw the greatest successes. Christchurch became a branch of the N.S.S. in 1881, with ninety-three members; the numbers had increased to 174 by 1883, 120 of whom were reported 'active' the following year. Other societies existed in the mid–1880s, in Nelson (founded 1883 with sixty members); Auckland (where a Rational Association was started in 1884 with 200 members); Wellington; and Wanganui, Ballance's home town (where he published a sixteen-page monthly paper, the *Freethought Review*). These societies, and other groups in Waverley, Woodville, Patea, Inglewood, Lyttelton, Masterton, Nguire and Waitora were members of the Freethought Federal Union, founded in March 1884 under the presidency of Robert Stout. In the same year Stout became Prime Minister, breaking a long Conservative run, with Ballance as his Minister of Land, Native Affairs and Defence. Undoubtedly their prestige helped the cause, but as in Britain the political commitments of the leaders may have drawn off some of the energies of the movement.[18] New Zealand, like Ireland, continued to hold religious censuses, and in 1887 the record shows 3,925 Freethinkers, with a further 189 Secularists, 105 Atheists, 207 Agnostics, 83 Deists and Theists, 11 Materialists, and 668 of no religion. Four years later the figures were practically unchanged, with still under one per cent of the population declaring itself to be supporters of freethought.[19] During the 1890s the most vigorous campaigner was probably William Whitehouse Collins, grandson of the Chartist John Collins, who settled in Christchurch from Australia in 1890, became president of the local freethought association, and M.P. for Christchurch (1893–96, 1899–1902). The society in Christchurch long remained the strongest in New Zealand, with Collins publishing a monthly *Examiner* there from 1907 until his return to Australia in 1917.[20]

## Australia

The Australian freethought movement was larger than that in New Zealand, but none of its members reached such heights of political power.[21] As in Britain, societies were founded, faded, and were refounded on more than one occasion, the greatest successes coming in the 1880s with Joseph Symes, who emigrated to Melbourne in 1884, dominating the movement.[22]

The earliest freethought societies in Australia grew up in the Newcastle area of New South Wales in the early 1860s, but the most important centres were Sydney and Melbourne. A Secular society was started in Sydney in 1869, and soon ran into trouble when William Orlando Jones was prosecuted for lecturing against the Bible and gaoled for two years in 1871. Two thousand signatures were obtained on a petition for his release, which was granted after a few months. In the mid-1870s lectures were held in the Victoria Theatre, where John Tyerman, Charles Bright and Mrs Hardinge-Brittain were the principal lecturers, but these three were anti-Christian spiritualists rather than true Secularists, so the latter broke away in the late 1870s to form the Sydney Freethought Progressive Society, later renamed the Secular Society. Further stimulus came in 1881 when a Freethought Association was begun to defend the opening of the public library and museum on Sundays. In 1884 both wings of the movement in Sydney were thriving:

Charles Bright's Liberal Association of New South Wales was holding weekly Sunday lectures in the Theatre Royal while the Sydney Secular Society, now led by Thomas Walker from Melbourne, was holding Sunday morning 'social' services for 800 people and Sunday evening lectures for a thousand.[23]

In Melbourne, a Free Discussion Society was reported meeting at the Trades Hall in 1874, and regular reports appeared in the *National Reformer* during 1878 of the Eclectic Association of Victoria, which met at the Royal Society's Hall in Melbourne. In all, according to the secretary of the Free Discussion Society in 1878, there were three societies, each with membership rolls of between 30 and 100, the Free Discussion Society being the main one, able to attract an audience of 160 to its Sunday evening lectures at the Trades Hall.[24]

In July 1882 the Australian Secularists decided to emulate the N.S.S. and founded the Australasian Secular Association (A.S.A.). The Melbourne wing expanded rapidly, and in 1883, with 540 members, it invited Bradlaugh to send out a permanent lecturer. He chose Joseph Symes, a forty-two year old former Methodist preacher and vice-president of the N.S.S., who was a talented lecturer and vigorous journalist who had been an early and enthusiastic contributer to Foote's *Freethinker*. By the beginning of 1884, when Symes arrived, the A.S.A. had 730 members in Melbourne, 120 in Sydney, and a further seventy in Newcastle, where the society was revived by Daniel Wallwork, a Dudley Chartist and freethinker who had inspired every effort to organise freethought in Newcastle since his arrival in 1861. Thomas Walker, president of the A.S.A. and the regular Melbourne lecturer, had moved on to Sydney in September 1883, pursued by rumours that he had once fled from Canada to escape a manslaughter charge, and his place had temporarily been filled by a visit from Moncure D. Conway, until Symes's arrival on 10 February 1884.[25] Almost immediately, Symes started a periodical, modelled on the *National Reformer* and *Freethinker*, which he called the *Liberator*. It first appeared on 1 June 1884 and was to run for twenty years. Symes was a great success, as another emigrant, William Willis, reported home when he arrived in Melbourne later the same year. Sunday morning services were held for between two and three hundred people at a theatre in Swanston Street, while lectures were given at the Bourke Street Hall of Science on Sunday evenings. In September 1884 Symes was elected president of the A.S.A., and the following year he was joined by W. W. Collins from Birmingham, who lectured in Melbourne until

1886, and then moved on to Sydney, where Willis was now the local president.[26] Here Collins started a paper, the *Freethinker*, modelled on Foote's paper even to the extent of reproducing cartoons from *La Bible Amusante*. The following year when the government, led by Henry Parkes (an old friend of Holyoake from Birmingham), clamped down on the use of theatres in Sydney on Sundays, Collins moved on to Brisbane, while the Sydney men tried to persuade Aurelis B. Wakefield of Hipperholme to come out to lecture for them. Collins thought of leaving for New Zealand, but for a while returned to Sydney, where he was prosecuted for selling Mrs Besant's *Law of Population*, found guilty, but acquitted on appeal. In 1890 he laid the foundation stone of a new Sydney Freethought Hall, but then moved on to Christchurch. Meanwhile another English lecturer, Wallace Nelson, arrived in Brisbane for the good of his health.[27]

In Melbourne, Symes continued to thrive, though not without difficulties.In 1888 the A.S.A. split along lines not dissimilar from those which divided the Secularists in England. Like Bradlaugh and Foote, Symes was authoritarian, anti-socialist and vigorously pro-birth control.[28] All these attitudes made enemies, who, like Foote's, conspired against him. Between 1889, when the Symes faction built a new Hall of Science, and 1897, when their opponents collapsed, a long wrangle took place over possession of it , and by the time victory was secured Symes and his followers were exhausted.[29] The golden age was over in Australia as surely as it was elsewhere in the English-speaking world. In 1892 Wallace Nelson offered his explanation for the decline in Australia since his arrival in 1888: the prolonged trade depression, and 'the undoubted tendency of modern thought . . . to attach increasing importance to social and economic questions, and to relegate to a subordinate rank questions of a theological, or anti-theological, character'.[30] These two reasons, along with an increasing awareness of secular-fed apathy, seem to have been equally applicable in Britain, North America and Australia.

*Notes*

1   S. P. Putnam, *Four Hundred Years of Freethought* (New York, 1894), p. 612.
2   *N. R.*, 7 September, 14 December 1879; *S. R.*, 13 December 1879; *N. R.*, 29 August, 5 12 September 1880; *S. R.*, 4 September 1880; *N. R.*, 23 January, 2, 9 October 1881; *S.R.*, 1 October 1881; *N.R.*, 25 December

1882, 9 September 1883, 4, 11 October 1885; *F*, 7 June 1885, 18 September 1887; *N. R.*, 18, 25 September 1887, 22 29 September 1889; *F.*, 22 September 1889, 12 June, 7 August 1904; also S. P. Putnam, *op. cit.*, pp. 612-13, 615. For Belgian freethought see *S. R.*, 13 September 1879, 6, 20 November 1880; *N. S. S. Almanack* (1881), p. 56; (1885), p. 48. For Holland see *S. R.*, 18 September 1880; *N. S. S. Almanack* (1881), pp. 28-9; (1885), pp. 49-50; (1886), p. 52.

3   *F.*, 7 May 1882, 7 January 1883, 21 November 1886; *N. S. S. Almanack* (1885), p. 49; (1886), p. 51.

4   *Id; F.*, 4 August 1889; D. Gasman, *The Scientific Origins of National Socialism* (London and New York, 1971), pp. 19-26.

5   *N. S. S. Almanack* (1885), p. 50; (1886), p. 52; *F.*, 24 October 1909, 4 June 1911.

6   *S. R.*, 22 December 1883.

7   S. Warren, *American Freethought*, pp. 22-3, 34-6, 39-41, 73-4, 96-109, 156-175; *Republican*, September, October 1885; *N. S. S. Almanack* (1885), pp. 50-1; (1886), pp. 52-3. See also S. P. Putnam, *op. cit.*, pp. 672-80.

8   S. Warren, *op. cit.*, pp. 81-9, 95; J. M. Robertson, *A History of Freethought in the Nineteenth Century* (London, 1929), p. 446.

9   *S. R.*, 19 May 1883; P. Fryer, *The Birth Controllers*, pp. 117-18; S. Warren, *op. cit.*, pp. 176-205; S. P. Putnam, *op. cit.*, pp. 527-32, 536-47; *N. R.*, 14 September, 5 October 1879, 2 July 1882; *Adult*, March, April 1898.

10   Bradlaugh's visits are described in H. B. Bonner and J. M. Robertson, *Charles Bradlaugh*, 2 vols. (London, 1893, 2nd ed., 1895), I, pp. 380-91, II, pp. 1-11; see also his correspondence, September 1873–February 1874, October 1874–February 1875, September– December 1875, B. L. nos. 353-72, 399-417, 434-41. For Holyoake's visits see his *Among the Americans* (London, 1881) and *Travels in Search of a Settler's Guide Book of America and Canada* (London, 1884); see also his correspondence, August–November 1879 and July–November 1882, Holyoake papers, Co-operative Union, nos. 2533–63, 2740–95. For Watts see *S. R.*, 30 September 1882, 28 April, 25 August, 1 September 1883, 6 January, 30 August 1884; *F.*, 9 June 1895, 13 June 1897, 23 April 1899.

11   *F.*, 23 April 1899; S. Warren, *op. cit.*, pp. 117-55, 175. For obituaries of the leaders see *F.*, 24 December 1882 (Bennett), 8 February 1891 (Mendum), 3 January 1897 (Putnam), 30 July 1899 (Ingersoll), 15 September 1889 (Seaver).

12   *N. R.*, 1 November 1885; *N. S. S. Almanack* (1885), p. 53; (1886), p. 55.

13   *N. R.*, 6 April, 11 May 1890.

14   *F.*, 29 September 1889.

15   *F.*, 4 September 1887; *N. R.*, 1 January, 26 August 1888, 6 October 1889.

16   S. P. Putnam, *op. cit.*, p. 563-5, 582-6; *N. R.*, 20 May 1877, 7 July 1878, 27 July 1884; *N.S.S. Almanack* (1885), p. 50; (1886), p. 52. There are no reports of French-speaking freethought, even from Montreal.

17   *A. J.*, 15 July 1899; *N. R.*, 2 July 1893.

18  *N. R.*, 4 June 1882, 28 January 1883, 9 March, 20 April, 5 October, 29 November, 28 December 1884; *F.*, 23 March 1884; *N. S. S. Almanack* (1885), p. 52; (1886), pp. 54-5; *N. R.*, 1 March, 1 November 1885.
19  *N. R.*, 20 March 1887, 17, 24 April 1892.
20  *Watts's L. G.*, 15 February 1894; *F.*, 4 March 1900, 2 June 1907. For W. W. Collins, who died in 1923, see *Republican*, February 1885, *F.*, 3 October 1915, and the entry in G..H. Scholefield (ed.), *A Dictionary of New Zealand Biography* (Wellington, 1940).
21  Thomas Walker became an M. P. only after he had ceased to be a Secularist—see the article by F. B. Smith in G. Serle and R. Ward (eds.), *Australian Dictionary of Biography* VI (Melbourne, 1976).
22  For Symes in Australia see F. B. Smith, 'Joseph Symes and the Australasian Secular Association', *Labour History*, no. 5 (1963), pp. 26-47, and his entry on Symes in the *Australian Dictionary of Biography*, VI; also N. Sinnott, *Joseph Symes, the 'flower of atheism'* (duplicated pamphlet, Atheist Society of Australia, 1977).
23  *N. R.*, 17 October 1863, 7 May 1864, 6 August, 3 September 1865, 13 May 1866, 26 May 1867, 24 July 1870, 30 April, 7, 14 May, 4 June 1871, 7 July, 4 August 1878, 22 June 1879, 2 September 1883, 28 December 1884; *F.*, June 1881.
24  *N. R.*, 18 October 1874, 11 August 1878.
25  *N. R.*, 14 January, 23 September 1883, 20 January, 11 May 1884; N. Sinnott, *op. cit.*, p. 12.
26  *N. R.*, 27 July, 10 August, 28 December 1884, 27 September, 11, 18 October, 22 November, 6, 13 December 1885, 21 March, 7 November 1886.
27  *F.*, 30 May 1886, 21 August 1887; *N. R.*, 25 September, 2 October 1887, 14 July 1889, 27 July 1890, 25 September 1892; *F.*, 31 January 1892. For freethought societies in the 1880s see *N. R.*, 30 March 1884, 9 May, 7 November 1886; *N. S S. Almanack* (1885), pp. 51-2; (1886), pp. 53-5.
28  Symes was also, like Bradlaugh, having marital trouble, which alienated some support.
29  *F.*, 17 April 1898; *Ethical World*, 13 January 1900. Symes's own account is in *F.*, 23 September–18 November 1906.
30  *F.*, 31 January 1892.

# Part II
# Anatomy of freethought

# VII

# Leadership and strategy

## The national leaders

The men and women who led the freethought movement in Britain between 1866 and 1915 had at least one thing in common: they were indomitable. Whatever their enemies might say of them, and whatever criticisms the historian might make, their courage, determination, energy and enthusiasm were almost limitless. They all made considerable personal sacrifices - both financial and physical - in what they believed to be a righteous cause. In darker moments they had no faith to sustain them other than a trust in the inevitable triumph of reason. They often thought they glimpsed the light of the new dawn, and proclaimed it enthusiastically in the face of all indications to the contrary, but for them, as for liberals of all viewpoints, the skies grew darker, not lighter, as the twentieth century approached. Most of these leaders still lack a biographer, though Charles Bradlaugh, Annie Besant and G.J. Holyoake have received some attention from historians in recent years[1] Yet because their personalities meant so much to the freethought movement, and because the clashes between them were important in shaping freethought history, there is need to look individually at their lives and characters.

## Charles Bradlaugh ( 1833-91)

Bradlaugh was undoubtedly the greatest leader: there was much truth in the verdict of G. J. Holyoake, who was no admirer, that 'He was the greatest agitator, within the limits of the law, who appeared in my time among the working people'.[2] He attracted fierce loyalties and created strong aversions, but none could deny his power and effectiveness, whether or not they admired the purpose to which he applied his enormous talents.

He was born on 26 September 1833 in Hoxton, North London, the son of a solicitor's clerk who was scarcely able to give his family a standard of living above that of the labouring poor. Bradlaugh was always to think of himself as being of the poor and speaking on their behalf. His upbringing was orthodox, with Sunday school at St Peter's, Hackney Road, where he prepared for Confirmation in the Established Church. Only at this point did he question the belief in which he had been brought up, possibly under the influence of the open-air speakers in nearby Victoria Park. His theological questioning led to tension at home. He left and took lodgings with Richard Carlile's widow at the Warner Street Temperance Hall, where he had already been drawn into a group of freethinkers who were to constitute part of G. J. Holyoake's Secularist movement. He delivered his first major lecture, with Holyoake in the chair, in October 1850.[3]

After an unsuccessful attempt to earn his living as a coal merchant, he spent the next three years in the army, stationed in Ireland, where he witnessed scenes which shaped his attitude to English rule, before his family purchased his discharge in October 1853. He decided to follow his father's profession as a solicitor's clerk, and soon developed a flair for the law which was to serve him well in years to come. At the same time he adopted the pseudonym of 'Iconoclast' and devoted his spare time to freethought and radical lecturing. He rapidly became a favourite with London audiences and, after a provincial lecture tour in 1858, was just as popular in the country. In 1860, when the Sheffield Secularists started the *National Reformer*, he was invited to become one of the editors.

At the beginning of the 1860s he was in a position to challenge G. J. Holyoake for the leadership of the Secularist party and, with the *National Reformer* soon securely under his own control, many freethinkers were willing to accept his forceful leadership. In the 1860s he was at the high point of his personal life. He had married Susan Hooper, daughter of an old London freethinker, in 1855, and had three children - Charles (b. 1859), Alice (b. 1856) and Hypatia (b. 1858). They lived in the relative luxury of Northumberland Park, Tottenham, and in 1864 were even in the position to advertise for a second servant. There are happy pictures of Bradlaugh at this time as a suburban commuter, correcting proofs of the *National Reformer* on his daily journey into the City.[4]

His efforts were, however, beginning to take their toll on his health and happiness. The carefree young man had become rather sober and serious. His health was not good, and his attempts to set himself up as a company promoter were both hazardous and a constant worry. By 1869 he had come to realise that he must choose between private life and public career. He chose public career, and Susan, who was by now a chronic alcoholic, went to live with her parents at

Midhurst in Sussex, while Bradlaugh took cheap lodgings in Turner Street, Commerical Road, in East London. He devoted himself fully to freethought and radical propaganda, at the same time trying to sort out his now perilous financial position. In July his son died of scarlet fever. He must have felt like a freethought Job. In indifferent health himself, he soldiered on — he could not afford not to lecture. This was the man who in the early 1870s provided the energy behind the Secularist and republican movements. In what private life he could salvage he could still be relaxed and humorous, but little of this reached the outside world.

Physically Bradlaugh was an impressive person. Arthur Moss recalled him in his fortieth year, 'A fine commanding figure, slightly over six feet in height, with clean-shaven face, and long dark hair, in quite the professional style, like a great artist or musician; he wore a black frock coat, an open waistcoat, and a black bow.' Others commented on his almost clerical appearance in his black clothes, and all were agreed as to the rather harsh tone of his voice and the outstanding quality of his oratory.[5]

After the severe restraint and discomfort of the early 1870s, Bradlaugh's life began to open out once more as his daughters grew up and shared his life, and as Annie Besant came into it as a devotedly loyal partner - though suggestions that their relationship was other than perfectly 'proper' seem to be unfounded. He moved out of Turner Street in 1877 to a house in Circus Road, St John's Wood, where he was to live the rest of his life. His early teetotalism had given way after fourteen years, and he now had a liking for Continental wines. He indulged himself more in the 1880s and put on a great deal of weight. H. M. Hyndman was horrified in 1884 to see him drink 'a deep draught of cold claret' after their debate on socialism, and feared for Bradlaugh's health.[6] In fact this was already being undermined by hereditary Bright's disease. After his long parliamentary struggle he was beginning to pay the price for the pace at which he drove himself. In 1880, in just one week in July, he attended the House of Commons on three and a half days, he spent a day in his constituency, travelled 600 miles to be at the Northumberland Miners' Gala, and dealt with a correspondence of about a thousand letters.[7] By 1887 he would have liked the long rest of a journey to Australia, but he could not afford it. He was now admitting that he was feeling the strain. In 1889 his health collapsed completely with what the *National Reformer* described as 'fever and congestion of the lungs and kidneys'.[8] He was at last persuaded to take a long rest, and he sailed for India to attend a meeting of the

Indian National Congress. This merely postponed the end, and he died of uremia consequent upon Bright's disease on 30 January 1891.

In his later years, Bradlaugh's huge bulk was a formidable presence on the public platform. Hyndman remembered him, 'Tall, powerful, and well-shaped in body, his face was that of a huge bull-dog with the upper lip drawn down instead of being turned up. And he had all the qualities of the animal he resembled when fully roused.' This unusual facial characteristic reminded others — particularly those who recalled his pro-Darwinian views — of an ape. Hyndman's image is an apt one. There was no *finesse* about Bradlaugh. A sympathetic portrait in 1888 admitted that his oratory was 'of the rugged kind', lacking the 'peculiar polish and diffuseness of Mr Gladstone, and the sweet simple, but glowing, terseness of John Bright. But it is direct and effective.' Hyndman recognised that Bradlaugh posssessed neither the literary capacity of Charles Watts and G. W. Foote, nor the scientific knowledge of Edward Aveling or Joseph McCabe, nor the charm of Annie Besant. His learning, which was largely self-acquired, was strictly practical. He had a working knowledge of Hebrew and French but, according to Foote, he could not dance and had no taste for poetry: he loved Shelley for his atheism, and did not appear to have read a line of Shakespeare. He was a hammer; the pseudonym 'Iconoclast' was well chosen. As W. S. Ross recalled, 'His writing was third rate; but, on the platform his power was titanic.[9]

The words most often used to describe Bradlaugh are 'formidable' and 'indomitable'. William Morris recalled how, on one occasion when he and Bradlaugh went to Edgware Road police court to bail out a comrade, he was nervous but Bradlaugh 'behaved as if the whole place belonged to him, and was deferred to with awe by everybody'. Hyndman was shocked by 'the exaggerated deference paid to Bradlaugh personally by those immediately around him'. He was a proud man, strong-willed, not able to take criticism or accept challenges to his authority. Robert Ingersoll privately confided to Holyoake in 1891, 'He seemed insanely egoistic to me — entirely too pictorial and personal'. Only Annie Besant was able to remain on close personal terms: Holyoake, Foote, Watts and Ross all had their quarrels with him and, although there were faults on both sides, Bradlaugh's personality lay at the root of much of the difficulty. This was the price which the Secularists paid for success, and most reckoned it a price well worth paying.[10]

Bradlaugh's motivation was his almost obsessive hatred of

Christianity. In 1933 George Bernard Shaw recognised the 'passion and conviction' with which Bradlaugh viewed the question of religion; and Josiah Wedgwood remembered a friend telling how Bradlaugh 'described to us how the shadow of the Cross lay like a black curse across all history, and as he spoke of the horrors of Christianity great tears rolled down his face.' His personal experience had much to do with this, but not all. His passionate hatred of religion cannot simply be laid at the door of those who had mishandled his adolescent doubts. Hyndman was right when he saw individualism lying at the heart of Bradlaugh's creed: *unus contra mundum*, without God and without faith, except in reason and the capacity of his own will. Such a man was born to lead and to stamp his personality on those who followed him.[11]

*George Jacob Holyoake ( 1817-1906) and Austin Holyoake ( 1827-74)*
The oldest leader of freethought and founder of Secularism was G. J. Holyoake, but by 1866 he had been supplanted by Charles Bradlaugh; though Holyoake was to retain a certain amount of affection and a good deal of respect, he in fact now counted for very little.[12] In 1864 he was said to be lecturing to empty benches at the Cleveland Street Hall, while Bradlaugh's Hall of Science was overflowing. His style was too bland, his wit too dry, his arguments too subtle for most of his audiences and, lacking a commanding physical presence and loud voice, he had few of the attributes of a really successful orator. 'Though he could not steer the barque of Unfavourable Views through the troubled waters of popular opinion proudly, majestically, defiantly and rapidly; yet, he could guide it smoothly, gracefully, pleasantly, softly - but slowly,' reported the secretary of the Birmingham Secular Society in 1863. Only occasionally, as when lecturing at the Hall of Science on the death of President Lincoln, did he reach heights of passion and fervour as he whipped up his audience to tumultuous applause.[13]

After 1866 he remained a figurehead, sometimes inside the N.S.S., sometimes opposed to it. He supported Bradlaugh at the 1876 conference, and was appointed chairman of the committee to revise the laws of the Society, but a year later, after the Knowlton controversy, he helped rally the anti-Bradlaugh forces in the B.S.U. He was not an organisation man, though; and was too idiosyncratic to work with any group for long. He also had an irritating way of offering good advice when it was not wanted. During the Knowlton trial,he wrote to the *Daily News* and *The Times*, dissociating himself from the views expressed in the pamphlet. Bradlaugh thought that this probably counted against him with the jury, and he wished that Holyoake had stayed his pen until the trial was over. In 1881 Holyoake again intervened inopportunely to embarrass Bradlaugh by opposing his campaign to take the parliamentary oath, his argument being that a true Secularist would have stood his ground on secular affirmation. In 1883 he found a technical pretext not to petition on behalf of Foote and Ramsey. Such characteristic pedantry made many enemies, and at times Holyoake fully deserved Marx's gibe about 'the thin-voiced, instrusive, consequential Holyoake'.[14] Yet time was a great healer, and Holyoake's more attractive characteristics fortunately survived in the memories of his associates when the less pleasant features were happily forgotten. His stubbornness towards friends became resolution in the face of the enemy. His mistrust of organisation arose out of a genuinely libertarian streak which made him a more adaptable person than Bradlaugh. His witty journalism is readable, though infuriatingly inaccurate and superficial. His speeches made up in their felicitous choice of language and shafts of piercing sarcasm what they lacked in oratorical power. The impression he left on Harry Snell in the 1880s seems a fair summary of Holyoake's position in the freethought movement throughout most of the period under review:

By the time that I got to know him fairly well his work had for the most part been done, but he was always a welcome speaker as representing the heroism of earlier days. Young people loved him 'for the dangers he had passed,' while seasoned reformers regarded him with the affection due to a revered colleague and teacher. Holyoake was one of the best type of working class leaders in the nineteenth century, and he will occupy a distinguished place in the story of their fight for political and social freedom. He took a kindly interest in my work, but never failed to chide me for my limited faith in some of the causes that aroused his own enthusiasm. I remember the genial and gentle old man with great respect and some gratitude.'[15]

It was the fate of Austin Holyoake to live in the shadow of his more famous brother. Not until the emergence of Bradlaugh does he seem to have had the opportunity to break free of the family ties and loyalties of his youth. Even so he lectured only occasionally for the movement, prefering the quieter life of the back-room organiser. In 1864 he set himself up as a printer at 17 Johnson's Court, and in 1866 was nominated one of the vice-presidents of the N.S.S. The following year he took over the printing and publishing of the *National Reformer*, of which he became a sub-editor. Indeed, he and Charles Watts carried much of the burden of the early propagandism before Bradlaugh devoted himself full-time to the

N.S.S. in 1870. In the early 1870s Austin's health began to fail, and he died of consumption in April 1874.[16]

In character he had his brother's better points without his worse ones. There was the same courtesy, refinement and wit, but he was less touchy than George Jacob, a peacemaker who stood midway between his brother and Charles Bradlaugh. His calming presence was sadly missed when the Secularist leadership ran on to the rocks of the Knowlton affair. Austin was, said the *Secular Chronicle* in 1872, 'one of those quiet, unostentateous workers who are the real bone and sinew of the Secular body — like the stage manager, without whose work the play would be incomplete, but who seldom comes before the curtain to receive the plaudits of the audience.' He was, as G. W. Foote remembered him, 'a capital chairman'.[17]

### Annie Besant ( 1847-1933)

During the golden years of Secularism, Charles Bradlaugh was ably supported by Annie Besant, one of the most talented public lecturers of the century, and with good claims to be regarded as the most talented woman. Her background was middle-class, comfortable by the standards of most Secularists but not well-off, until the sudden death of her father, William Wood, reduced her mother to the necessity of keeping a boarding house for boys from Harrow school. Annie herself was educated at a private school run by Ellen Marryat (sister of the novelist), where she learned Latin, French and German in addition to the usual female accomplishments. In December 1867 she married the Reverend Frank Besant, by whom she had two children, Arthur Digby (b. 1869) and Mabel Emily (b. 1870). After the marriage she began to chafe at the restrictions imposed on her by Victorian conventions about women, sex, family life and religion which her husband appeared to embody. In her *Autobiography* she wrote, 'Nothing but an imperious intellectual and moral necessity can drive into doubt a religious mind, for it is as though an earthquake shook the foundations of the soul, and the very being quivers under the shock.' Hers was a religious mind, and her earthquake followed upon the serious illness of Mabel in 1871.[18]

Mrs Besant first entered the world of freethought when visiting her mother in London in 1872, where she heard the unorthodox preaching of Charles Voysey at St George's Hall, and became acquainted with Moncure D. Conway of the South Place Chapel; she also met Thomas Scott, the deistic publisher, for whom she wrote an anonymous tract on *The Deity of Jesus of Nazareth*. After passing through a storm of doubt, she left home in 1873, following a quarrel with her husband over her refusal to conform to the outward observances of the Church and to attend Communion. A formal separation secured her the custody of Mabel and a small allowance, which she supplemented by working as a governess.

She bought a copy of the *National Reformer* from Truelove's shop in High Holborn in July 1874, and sent her name in to Bradlaugh for enrolment in the N.S.S. On 2 August she attended the Hall of Science for the first time, and a week later her name was in the first batch of members since the revival of the N.S.S., along with those of Kate Watts and Susan Bradlaugh. Only two weeks later, on 25 August, at the Co-operative Institute in Castle Street, she delivered her first public lecture, 'On the Political Status of Women', in which she condemned religious influences for the subordinate position in which women were placed: the motivation clearly lay in her own bitter experience.[19]

As a public speaker Mrs Besant was immensely gifted, with a deep, rich, full voice and extraordinary fluency of speech. She was a remarkable acquisition for the Secularists — well bred, well educated, polished and charming; quite a contrast to that rough diamond, Mrs Harriet Law, who had hitherto been the foremost woman lecturer in the freethought movement.[20] Taking 'Ajax' as her pseudonym, Mrs Besant began a weekly 'Daybreak' column in the *National Reformer* from 30 August 1874. On 19 January the following year she lectured at South Place, and was then ready to begin her provincial appearances. The Secularists were delighted with her. On 21 February she appeared at the Glasgow Eclectic Institution, and the next week she made her first appearence at the Hall of Science with a lecture on 'The Gospel of Christianity versus the Gospel of Freethought'. Her meteoric career was well launched.[21] The Knowlton Pamphlet controversy made her name nationally, after which she became a central figure not only in freethought but also in the wider radical movement, ever at the shoulder of Charles Bradlaugh to strengthen him and to urge him on. She sub-edited the *National Reformer* from February 1877, and became co-editor in May 1881, a position she held until October 1887. By this time, although her personal commitment to Bradlaugh was no less strong, her political views had ceased to be compatible with his. From 1884 the socialist movement was attracting her sympathies, and in 1885 she joined the Fabian Society. Soon she was a leading activist in her new cause, but nevertheless retained her links with the N.S.S. until Foote became president in 1890. By this time she was well on her way to her Theosophic future.

George Bernard Shaw, who knew her well, described her manner and motivation as follows:

Annie Besant, a player of genuis, was a tragedian. Comedy was not her clue to life:she had a healthy sense of fun; but no truth came to her first as a joke. Injustice, waste, and the defeat of noble aspirations did not revolt her by way of irony or paradox: they stirred her to direct and powerful indignation and to active resistance.[22]

This is what made her such a powerful fighter for a succession of causes. But she was no leader. As Shaw wrote on another occasion, still pursuing the dramatic analogy, 'There was a different leading man every time: Bradlaugh, Robertson, Aveling, Shaw, and Herbert Burrows. That did not matter.'[23] But it was Bradlaugh who was her closest companion. He was, said W. E. Adams,

not so much her friend as her idol. Able as she was, and strong-minded as she appeared to be, she was yet the very creature of circumstances . . . While she was associated with Bradlaugh, she was so influenced by the vigorous intellect of her idol that she imitated his manners in private, his gestures and methods of argument on the platform.[24]

This claim to a special and intimate relationship with Bradlaugh infuriated the other leaders of Secularism, and accentuated the differences between the *National Reformer* group and the *Secular Review* group, who attacked Mrs Besant both in her own right and when they wished to attack her chief. She for her part stood loyally by him and he by her. Undeniably, though, her principal weaknesses were unconcealed ambition and intense pride. Thomas Scott, her earliest mentor, warned G. J. Holyoake in 1874, 'Mrs Besant is an ambitious woman and when the fit is on her will do and say any mad thing. She is very young, and in all wordly matters very foolish.' Those Secularists who were appalled by Bradlaugh's treatment of Watts in 1877 were in no doubt that Mrs Besant was behind it. It was her headstrong resolution which demanded that she and Bradlaugh should republish the *Fruits of Philosophy*, just as it was her courage which sustained radical, freethought and socialist campaigns in the 1880s. Although, as Adams said, 'she had lost none of her fine-lady airs by associating with the common people', yet those who knew her would have echoed — gladly or reluctantly — Arthur Moss's verdict in 1915 that 'she was unquestionably the most learned, the most eloquent, and the most powerful lady advocate of Freethought that this country ever produced.'[25]

### Charles Watts (1836-1906)

Charles Watts was the man whom Mrs Besant cast into the shadows in 1877 and who, historically speaking, has remained there ever since. Yet he gave forty years of his life to the freethought movement, while Mrs Besant gave fifteen. As Bradlaugh's lieutenant in the formative years of the N.S.S., and as Foote's colleague in the declining years, he deserves to be considered as one of the key figures in the British freethought movement of the later nineteenth century. When one considers most of the other leaders one can see why they made enemies, but Watts was always more sinned against than sinning. 'Whatever faults he may have had,' wrote Arthur Moss in 1915, '. . . I was never able to discover them.'[26]

He was born in Bristol in 1836, the son of a Wesleyan minister, and he made his *début* on the temperance platform at the age of fourteen, when he also joined a dramatic society. In 1853, at the age of sixteen, he came to London, where he heard Charles Southwell lecture and this completed a conversion to freethought which had begun the previous year in Bristol when he had heard G. J. Holyoake lecture. His elder brother, John (1834-66), became a freethinker shortly afterwards under Charles's influence, and came to join him in London. They appear to have settled in South London, and John became a printer with the Holyoake brothers at 147 Fleet Street, and started lecturing on Secularism. The first reference to Charles is to his playing Othello in 1858 in a dramatic evening at the South London Secular Institute, organised by brother John. He worked with John as a printer, and lectured part-time in South London until 1864, when he began to devote himself full-time to the work.[27] The previous year John had taken over the *National Reformer* from Bradlaugh, and Charles might have succeeded his brother, but instead gave way in favour of Bradlaugh on the understanding that he would remain sub-editor.[28] Thenceforward he was Bradlaugh's closest associate, and when they together launched the N.S.S., Watts was the obvious choice for secretary. It was he who toured the country in the early years, stirring up support and enrolling the first branches. He remained a key figure in the Society until the Knowlton Pamphlet bombshell landed in December 1876. After this he was fortunate to retain widespread support in the movement, and he had the resolute backing of his second wife, Kate. His first wife, Mary Ann, had died in 1870 aged thirty-one. Her death was closely followed by those of two of their sons: as with Bradlaugh, the early 1870s were personally difficult years and this may have been one reason why he declined to stand as

N.S.S. secretary in 1871. He still had one son, though — Charles
Albert (b. 1858) — who had served his apprenticeship as a printer
under Austin Holyoake, and who in 1877 was ready to begin sharing
his father's life and work.[29]

A hostile portrait of Watts, which appeared in the *Radical* in 1881,
described him as 'thick-set, black, podgy, round-headed, goggle-
eyed', an observation born out by sketches and early photographs.

He spoke *extempore*, and although his sentences were far deficient in force
and finish to those of Stewart Ross, yet they had less of the study and the
lamp about them. His elocution is vigorous and effective, but with just a
little leaning towards rant and tub-thumping.[30]

This same Stewart Ross in 1882 was a little more generous, but
similarly wrote:

His trunk is square and well-built, and in his walk there is something of
quiet and careless dignity. Although his frame is adipose rather than
muscular, it has a fine, free outline, and is far from flaccid. He meets you, he
recognises you. With a frank and jovial, but somewhat noisey and stagey
*bon-hommie*, he shakes you by the hand repeatedly, addressing you 'My
friend'. He uses this expression indiscriminately to everybody he knows, for
it does not seem to have occured to the genial and kindly man that anybody
who knows him can be less than his 'friend'.

In short, Watts had the common touch — of which Ross did not
wholly approve. His intellect, Ross went on,

is more powerful in its grasp than extensive in its range. It can lay little
pretence to exceptional qualities. It treads firmly the ground covered by the
thought and the work of the active world; but it walks not upon the slippery
strand of mental physics and abstract speculation . . .

Watts was, in fact, just short of greatness in everything: without the
ruthlessness of Bradlaugh, the culture of Besant, or the style of Ross
and Foote, he was *par excellence* the ordinary man's leader — effective
but limited; a little dull, a little plodding, and, as Ross recognised,
'deficient in originality of conception and boldness of generalisa-
tion'.[31]

In 1884 Watts handed his business over to Charles Albert and
emigrated to Toronto, where he remained until 1891. His old
colleague, G. W. Foote then received him back as an N.S.S. vice-
president, and for a further decade his familiar rotund, bewhiskered
face was to be seen on the dwindling number of Secularist platforms.
After his second fall from favour in 1902, he at least had the
satisfaction of seeing Charles Albert's work in the Rationalist Press
Association succeeding beyong his own wildest dreams. He died less

than a month after G. J. Holyoake in February 1906. As usual the obituaries paid generous tributes, and this time we may believe them.

*George William Foote (1850–1915)*

Foote was the man who, above all, enabled the rump of Secularism to survive until the present day. Born in Plymouth in June 1850, the son of a customs officer who died when he was four, Foote was brought up an Anglican but then adopted a Unitarian position under the liberalising influence of the Reverend J. K. Applebee. Like many other freethinkers the most significant event in his youth was his coming to London, where he found work at 25s a week in a West End library in 1868. Through an old schoolfriend he became acquainted with the Secularists, he heard Mrs Law and Bradlaugh lecture, and soon joined the movement.[32] At first he was involved mainly with youth work, as founder of the Young Men's Secular Association and superintendent of the Hall of Science Sunday School; but he then rose to national prominence as secretary of the London Republican Club in 1871, and of the National Republican League two years later. His first appearance on the Hall of Science platform was in 1873, after which he became an established member of the Secularist lecturing force.[33]

His *forte* was the pen and not the platform: 'He has a pleasant voice, a clear, fluent, forcible delivery, and a good, though perhaps not highly popular style,' noted Harriet Law's *Secular Chronicle* in 1878, contrasting this with the 'polished periods' and 'pitiless logic' of his written work. In the 1870s Foote thought of himself primarily as a man of letters, one of his first contributions to the *National Reformer* being on the poetry of William Blake. His ambition was always to be accepted as a writer and critic, and he certainly had the talent. Malcolm Quin thought him 'a wider-read man than any of the other Secularist leaders' who 'brought to his apostolate not only a poetic and historic sense, but the care and order of a deliberative mind'. A writer in the *Literary Guide* at the time of his death thought him 'the cleverest pamphleteer since Paine'. His literary and artistic tastes were catholic: he loved the works of Titian, Angelico and Turner; Beethoven, Wagner and Chopin; Shakespeare, Byron, Shelley and Browning. His favourite novelist was his friend, George Meredith, but he also included in his library Richardson, Fielding, Thackeray and George Eliot; among the poets he also thought highly of George Herbert, Cowper, Morris and Swinburne. His most surprising choices lay in theology. He possessed works by St Basil,

St Augustine, Thomas à Kempis, Erasmus and, his favourite, Hooker. He had a great admiration for seventeenth-century theology and some eighteenth-, but thought little of his contemporaries, J. H. Newman excepted.[34]

As a student, book-lover and writer he was closer in temperament to G. J. Holyoake than to Bradlaugh. The turning point in his life came with Bradlaugh's exclusion from Parliament in 1880. Foote now made a deliberate decision to sacrifice all that was dear to him: the bigotry shown to Bradlaugh convinced him that the fighting was to be done not in the study but on the streets. He became vulgar; he prostituted his wit to the service of scurrility; the *Freethinker* was born, and he went to prison for it. His treatment at the hands of Mr Justice North confirmed him in what might otherwise have been a passing phase. There were now two G. W. Footes: the blasphemous editor and popular lecturer; and the literary critic and armchair thinker. In the former capacity he became president of the N.S.S. in 1890 and never again had the time or opportunity to be his other self. His tragedy was that he failed in his appointed rôle. His enemies thought him an indolent dreamer. In fact throughout much of the last fifteen years of his life he was dogged by bad health and insomnia. In 1903 he moved from London to Southend on account of his bronchitis, but there was to be no respite. He died in October 1915, his projected *magnum opus* on his beloved Shakespeare still unwritten.[35]

Physically Foote was of a slightly above average height—five feet ten inches in his shoes—and of average build. His photographs give the impression of his hair being dark, but it was in fact yellow, turning to grey in his early fifties; and he always wore a beard. Though a careful writer, 'he would put off the task to the last moment, and write many an article with the "printer's devil" waiting at his elbow to take it slip by slip to the printer'. Yet those articles were often shrewd and stimulating. On the platform, F. J. Gould remembered his 'Victorian regularity in his frock-coat, black tie, and restraint of gesture'. A highly critical writer in the *Birmingham Weekly Post* in 1907 could not 'refrain from a feeling of wonder that so pleasant a voice from so peaceful appearing a man should speak as he does'. Henry Salt more kindly recalled, 'It was always an intellectual treat to hear him speak.'[36]

Foote married twice. His first wife, Henriette Mariane Heiman, a gifted musician and a linguist, died a few months after their marriage in 1877. His second wife appears to have taken little active part in the movement. Foote, being a modest man, did not return details of his life to *Who's Who*, or write an autobiography, and the historian must still say with Chapman Cohen in 1915: 'His biography will, I fancy, have to be dug out of the thirty-five years' issue of the *Freethinker* and other publications.'[37]

### William Stewart Ross (1844–1906)

Stewart Ross, alias 'Saladin', was the self-conscious 'joker' in the pack of Secularist leaders in that he deliberately stood apart from the mainstream of activity, sending darts of wit or cynicism into the midst from his editorial chair at the *Secular Review* or (from 1889) *Agnostic Journal* office.

Born on 20 March 1844 at Kirkbean, Galloway, he first attended the parish school at New Abbey, Kirkcudbright, at the age of nine. He then went on to Hutton Hall Academy, Caerlaverock, leaving at the age of seventeen to become master at Glenesslin School, Dunscore, but returning to Hutton Hall shortly afterwards as assistant master. His parents were orthodox Presbyterians, and at the age of twenty Stewart went to Glasgow University to study for the Church. At university his interests were more literary than theological, and he set out to make his name as a poet. He entered Thomas Laurie's publishing house in Edinburgh, and then went to London as manager of the branch there. In 1872 he started publishing on his own. Up to this point he still thought of himself as a poet and a writer, but at university he had come to doubt the orthodox creeds and his freethinking now grew, possibly influenced by his love for the poetry of Burns and by the philosophy of his childhood hero, Thomas Carlyle. His politics he took from Carlyle, not Burns, and it was this which detached him from the mainstream of the democratic freethought movement at the same time as that other aspiring man of letters, G. W. Foote, was being drawn towards it. The latter wrote of Ross at his death, 'Both his strength and his weakness marked him out as a solitary campaigner. He could never have worked with a party, and a party could never have worked with him. There was something in him of an Old Covenanter born out of due season.'[38]

His first involvement with the Secularists came in 1880 when, as president of the Lambeth Radical Association, he chaired a lecture from Bradlaugh which had been organised by the South West London N.S.S. branch.[39] He despised Bradlaugh's 'Knowltonism', and thoroughly disliked Mrs Besant. His place was clearly with the anti-Bradlaughites on the *Secular Review*, which became markedly more hostile to them after 1881, when Ross's contributions began.

In this quarrel he clearly had the support of young C. A. Watts, though less so that of the genial elder Watts, who must have had some trouble controlling his 'Saladin' when the latter became co-editor in 1882. When Watts emigrated in 1884, Ross became sole editor of the *Secular Review*, and Bradlaugh was to know no peace. Ross was a man of public hates. In this respect his freethought was totally negative. He hated the hypocrisy of his age: 'Ours is the Era of Dissimulation,' he told F. J. Gould in an interview in 1900. Like Carlyle he admired the genius of Cromwell, whom he called a 'practical mystic'. He had no such praise for Bradlaugh, whom he thought a hollow bombast. Ross lectured little until after 1886, when he offered to help those societies which Bradlaugh was boycotting, but when he did appear on the platform he seems to have been a startling performer.[40]

The end of his life was tragic. Private details of his life rarely creep into his journal, but from 1899 there are hints that Ross was suffering from an illness which impaired his walking. Not till 1904 did he admit that he was suffering from sclerosis. From the end of 1905 he was editing the *Agnostic Journal* from his bed, scarcely able to write except with two hands. He died in 1906, the third freethought leader to go in that year.[41]

Ross might seem to have little claim to be regarded as a true leader of the freethought movement; yet for twenty-five years he was a presence in his columns in the *Secular Review* and *Agnostic Journal*, and he was not a man to be ignored. A fierce critic of Bradlaugh, and a fiercer critic of all hypocrisy, he was a guide and inspiration to those rebels whom freethought inevitably attracted. In the 1880s he built up an alternative school of thought to the official one of Bradlaugh, Besant and Foote, attracting old hands like W. H. Johnson and young enthusiasts like C. R. Mackay, Ernest Pack and Guy Aldred. Even freethought, apparently, needed its guru.[42]

*The lesser leaders*

Senior among the lesser leaders of freethought was Mrs Harriet Law (1832–97), who had the distinction of being one of the few Secularists of whom Karl Marx approved. An ex-Baptist from Essex who had been converted to freethought by Charles Watts, she was an active lecturer in the movement from 1859 until 1879, when her health gave way. Throughout this time she stood resolutely outside the N.S.S., refusing offers of a vice-presidency in 1867 and 1876, and wisely remaining neutral in the 1877 dispute over the Knowlton Pamphlet.

Bradlaugh remembered her as 'earnest, brusquely honest'; to Ross 'She was a plain, blunt, honest woman, utterly free from all suspicion of humbug'. Apart from being a courageous freethinker, she was also an active radical, a member of the General Council of the International Working Men's Association, and an advocate of women's rights.[43]

Of the same generation, but quite different in character, was Thomas Collins Touzeau Parris (1839–1907), who was educated at Bristol Grammar School and Bristol Baptist College, became a Unitarian minister, patronised by Samuel Courtauld, and helped his father sell books in Bristol, before coming to London to join Bradlaugh during the 1877 crisis. He continued active in the movement until infirmity compelled his retirement shortly before his death. In his later years he joined the anti-Foote Freethought Federation, and was a friend of William Morris at Kelmscott House. By temperament he was more of a teacher than a lecturer and, although a regular performer on Secularist platforms, he never engaged in public debate.[44]

Two years younger than Parris was Joseph Symes (1841–1906), also trained as a Christian preacher, this time as a Methodist. During his probationary period in 1872 he began to change his views, and by 1876 he had been accepted as an N.S.S. lecturer instead. During the next five years he became one of the leading Secularist propagandists, until his emigration to Melbourne in 1883. Like Parris it was really the 1877 crisis which launched him in the movement.[45]

Not all the Secularist leaders had the advantage of such education and training for ministerial work. Two men born in 1844 came of a very different background: Robert Forder (d. 1901) and William James Ramsey (d. 1916). Forder was the son of a Norfolk agricultural labourer who was himself sent out to work in the fields when he was eight. At the age of sixteen he came to London and, after being rejected by the army because he was too puny, he worked as a labourer in the boiler-shop of a firm of marine engineers at Deptford. Whilst there he began attending open-air radical and freethought meetings, and became a freethinker and a republican. He next took a job in the Woolwich arsenal, where he became a Reform League organiser, his house being well known as a committee room for all advanced movements. In 1874, during the agricultural labourers' lock-out, he was secretary of the Aid Committee at Woolwich, and in 1876 he was tried but acquitted for his part in the struggle to save Plumstead Common from enclosure.

The following year he took over as general secretary of the N.S.S., a post he held until his death (although his appointment was purely nominal in his later years). He was also secretary of the Land Law Reform League in 1880; and, from 1883, when he took over Foote's business during the latter's imprisonment, he was a publisher and bookseller for the movement. Of all the leaders, Forder probably came closest to being typical of the rank-and-file membership of the movement.[46]

Ramsey was born in London, the son of a freethinking, Chartist shoemaker, but when his family moved to Norwich, he sang in the cathedral choir! A lecture from Bradlaugh in Norwich in 1859 brought him back to freethought, and in the 1860s he returned to London, joined the Reform League, and was present at the 'storming' of Hyde Park in 1866. He was a founder member at the Old Street Hall of Science, where he was a regular chairman at Sunday lectures, at which he also sold books and periodicals. At first he supported himself as a shoemaker, but in 1877 he became manager of the Freethought Publishing Company for Bradlaugh and Besant. In 1883 he was charged with blasphemy and sentenced with Foote to nine months in Holloway gaol. In the 1890s he became increasingly critical of Foote's leadership, and was a leader of the so-called 'awkward squad' which founded the Freethought Federation. He also edited the *Jerusalem Star* (1895–96) under the pseudonym 'Le Vitty Cuss'. In 1906 he worked to secure the return of his old Reform League colleague, W. R. Cremer, as M.P. for Hackney.[47]

The next group of leaders comprises seven men of G. W. Foote's generation, four of whom lived to carry freethought into the inter-war years. Slightly younger than Foote was the Reverend John T. Lloyd (1851–1928), a Welshman who had spent some time as a Presbyterian minister in Johannesburg. His 'conversion' came late, and not until 1903, when aged fifty-two, did he begin lecturing to the freethinkers. He rapidly became a stalwart of the freethought platform, and an active member of the Rationalist Press Association.[48]

Almost exactly contemporary with Foote was his closest and most loyal friend, Joseph Mazzini Wheeler (1850–98), the son of a radical journalist who, needless to say, was an admirer of the great Italian nationalist. As a prolific biographer of many of the early freethinkers, Wheeler appropriately enough wrote his own obituary in 1893, in which he attributed his atheism to his reading of Newman, Mill, Darwin and Spencer: like Foote, he was a distinctly bookish sort of person. He became a close friend of Foote in 1868, when, as Foote recalled, they 'talked and talked and talked, especially about poetry, capping quotations from Shelley and Swinburne, and always recurring to Shakespeare, who was ever the supreme god with us'. On the death of his father, Wheeler went to Edinburgh to work as a designer in a lithographic printing office, but he kept in touch with Foote and contributed to his early periodicals. In 1881 he threw up his job and came to work for Foote on the *Freethinker*, of which he became sub-editor at £1 a week. But Wheeler was not made of the same material as the other freethought leaders: suffering from nervous diathesis, he was prone to mental breakdowns with outbursts of uncontrollable mania, and Foote's relationship with him was almost a protective one. In 1883 he broke down while Foote was in prison (a fact which increased Foote's own bitterness) and had to be confined to an asylum. He broke down twice more in 1884, but with the help of his wife, Jennie, and Foote, he then recovered until a final breakdown in 1898. He was a gentle, honest scholar, interested in comparative religion, the history of Christianity, and the history of his own freethought movement. At his death, even the secretary of the Christian Evidence Society was moved to send a letter of condolence.[49]

Whilst everyone grieved for Wheeler, few tears were shed for the man who took over Foote's publications during his imprisonment and Wheeler's illness—Edward B. Aveling (1851–98). Aveling was a plausible rascal: G. B. Shaw had the measure of him when he wrote, 'If it came to giving one's life for a cause one could rely on Aveling even if he carried all our purses with him to the scaffold.' He was the son of a Congregationalist minister, a brilliant teacher, and lecturer on comparative anatomy at the London Hospital. In 1879 he was introduced to Annie Besant by J. H. Levy of the City of London College; she became a pupil of Aveling, and introduced him to Bradlaugh, who sent his daughter Hypatia for lessons too. Rapidly he rose in the N.S.S. In 1879 he began contributing articles to the *National Reformer* over the initials 'E.D.', laying claim to Bradlaugh's sympathy with a story that he had failed to get a Chair at King's College only on account of his freethought views. Doubtless softened by Mrs Besant, Bradlaugh was sympathetic, and in April 1880 he asked the impecunious young man for a full statement of his debts (£480 16s), which he proceeded to help him with. This price at first seemed well worth while: Aveling brought to the movement rich talents, on the platform, in the Hall of Science Schools, and in the columns of the *National Reformer*. By May 1880 he had already delivered over a hundred lectures and his reward was to be made an

N.S.S. vice-president—an honour which brought him credit in more than one sense of the word. By May 1883 Bradlaugh's patience had begun to run out, and in November he cleared Aveling's debts rather than have reproach cast on the movement: he was never to see his money again, although, like a bulldog, he was to snap at Aveling for small sums for the rest of his life. The 1884 conference was the last to appoint Aveling a vice-president. In July he announced to Bradlaugh that he was going to live with Eleanor Marx. Bradlaugh froze, and prepared to drum him out of the movement. He had gone on incurring debts, despite assurances to Bradlaugh that he would not, and the affairs of the Science School were in a muddle. Aveling had appropriated the microscope belonging to Mary Reed, one of the most promising pupils (and, if Shaw is to be believed, probably seduced her as well). Bradlaugh had received more than enough complaints; Aveling's career as a Secularist was over. He had been one of the brightest lights of the early 1880s, but only the intensity of his brief involvement can qualify him as a freethought leader of any significance.[50]

This was far from the case with the Standring brothers. Their father, Sam Standring (senior), was the son of a Lincolnshire farm labourer, and had been a leading pupil of F. D. Maurice at the Working Men's College, founded in the 1850s. He was a joiner and wheelwright by trade, who built up a prosperous business manufacturing school apparatus, wall maps and kindergarten toys. His elder son, also called Sam, was born in 1853 and the younger, George, two years later. Despite his connections with F. D. Maurice, Sam (senior) was what was later to be called an 'agnostic', but his wife was a Wesleyan, and this was how the two boys were brought up, though they later became Anglicans and sang in the church choir. After the death of their mother in 1870 George's faith began to weaken, and in 1873 he joined the Secularists, becoming assistant secretary of the N.S.S. in 1875 and secretary on Charles Watts's retirement in 1876. He then devoted himself to publishing and journalism, using a printing press at his father's works. Sam (junior) continued as a Christian, with ritualistic tendencies, for a further decade, and even considered entering the ministry, but he eventually declared himself a Secularist also. In the later 1880s both brothers were freethought activists in London, Sam spreading the word in Wood Green and Tottenham through the North Middlesex Secular Federation, which he started in 1889. Their father died in 1890 and the toy business was sold, though Sam still worked for the old firm as a traveller, as this gave him the opportunity to lecture in the country.

He then resigned and moved to Rochdale in 1892, but on returning to London a year later, he found it hard to re-establish his business in the face of German competition. George employed him in his printing and publishing business for a few months, but he then returned to Rochdale, where he supported himself manufacturing toys by day, and lecturing and teaching in the local Working Men's College at night, until his premature death in 1895. Both brothers had been attracted to socialism in the later 1880s, and had joined the Fabian Society. George increasingly devoted himself to socialism in the 1890s, was highly critical of G. W. Foote, and formed the Freethought Federation to oppose him in 1896. Bradlaugh, not Foote, was his hero, and his later years were devoted to the Fabian Society and the Malthusian League, rather than the N.S.S. He died in 1924.[51]

An exact contemporary of George Standring was Arthur B. Moss (b. 1855). His father was the manager of a large wharfe on the Thames, who secured a good education for all his children. Arthur attended the Queen Elizabeth Grammar School (later St Olave's) in Tooley Street, South London, until the age of twelve. His father then fell ill and lost his job, and Arthur had to go out to work, as an office boy, clerk, and then reporter on a South London paper. He was a devout Christian until the age of sixteen, when, after a dispute with an elder brother, he read Paine's *Age of Reason* and began attending lectures at the Hall of Science. This was in 1874, when Bradlaugh was beginning the great revival in Secularism. Moss commenced lecturing in South London, out of doors and then indoors, as he was to continue to do for the next thirty-six years. This public activity lost him his position as a journalist and, after some time as a freelance, he became a Schools Visitor in Southwark. He was also active in local politics in South London and was a pillar of the Camberwell Secular Society until his death in 1937.[52]

The final member of this generation born in the 1850s was John Mackinnon Robertson, the most successful of all the leaders at making his way in the world, though surprisingly he still has not found a biographer. He was born on Arran in November 1856, and first worked as a telegraph clerk on the railways at Stirling. He then spend nearly five years in a law office and two in an insurance office in Edinburgh, during which time he began to write for the press. By the age of twenty he was producing leaders for the *Edinburgh Evening News*. In the early 1880s he was active in the Edinburgh Secular Society, and in 1884 came down to London to work on the *National Reformer*, of which he became editor on Bradlaugh's death. He had one of the keenest intellects among the freethought leadership, and was almost alone in bringing fresh political thinking to the Secularists in the 1880s. It was he who first led Annie Besant to socialism, though he himself became a 'New Liberal'. In 1906 he was elected Liberal M.P. for Tynemouth, having previously failed to win Northampton, and in 1911 he was appointed Parliamentary Under-secretary to the Board of Trade, a position he held until the fall of Asquith's government in 1915, when he was compensated with membership of the Privy Council. After losing his seat as an Asquithian Liberal in 1918, he devoted himself to freethought literature until his death in 1933. The breadth of his writings on both freethought and political topics was outstanding and, although he was hardly a freethought leader in the narrow sense after the closure of the *National Reformer* in 1893, as an opinion-former he must be reckoned one of the most important of latter-day Liberals and Secularists.[53]

The final leader, Chapman Cohen, was of the first generation not to have known Bradlaugh. He emerged as Foote's successor in the Edwardian years, and was president of the N.S.S. from 1915 until 1949. He was born of a Jewish family in Leicester in 1868, and had the advantage of a public elementary education in a Board School, where he reached Standard V. He was a precocious reader, and by the age of eighteen he had read works by Spinoza, Locke, Hume, Berkeley and Plato. The history of freethought made him a freethinker. When he moved to London in 1889, he scarcely knew of the *National Reformer* or the N.S.S., and he never met Bradlaugh. He first lectured for the Secularists by accident: hearing a Christian Evidence Society lecturer in Victoria Park mimicking an old man with a speech impediment, Cohen intervened to rebuke the lecturer. The following week he himself opposed the Christian, and the local N.S.S. branch eagerly invited the young stranger to lecture to them. Thus the first freethought lecture he heard was his own. Only after he had been lecturing for some months did he meet Foote and join the N.S.S. The latter body then made good use of his talents. He became a prominent lecturer, both in London and the provinces, and his first experience of journalism was editing John Grange's Bradford *Truth Seeker* while its editor was ill in 1896. In 1897 he became more closely involved with the *Freethinker*, and, following Wheeler's death in 1898, he became Foote's assistant. He loyally supported Foote through all his troubles, and in 1915 he had his reward.[54]

Apart from Cohen, who was unusual by any standards, the

twenty leaders considered in this chapter had much in common, though it is doubtful whether any significant generalisations can be made about them. The sample is itself pre-selected: all were from London or based in London, for they were national leaders; all were originally Christians, for they were brought up in a country where most children were brought up Christians, and they were all Protestants for the same reason. It may be more interesting to note that all were *fervent* Christians who experienced 'conversions' to freethought—their freethinking was a positive reaction against a positive set of beliefs. Three (Lloyd, Symes and Parris) had been ministers of religion, and two (Ross and Sam Standring) had contemplated the ministry as a career. Three more (the Watts brothers and Aveling) were the sons of ministers. Most obviously, only two of the group were women. With the exceptions of Mrs Besant and the sons of the manse, who might be reckoned middle-class, all were drawn originally from lower-middle-class or working-class homes—though there was still a wide gulf between the Standrings' toy manufacturer father and Robert Forder's background as an agricultural labourer. None of the group appears to have been undergoing a psychological reaction against a father figure, or to have rooted his denial of God in the early loss of a father—though Ross, Besant, Foote and Moss were all left to be brought up by their mothers. The move to London, with its new intellectual horizons and open clash of ideas, appears to have been important for some. Bookish freethinkers, like Parris, Ross, Foote, Wheeler, Lloyd, Aveling, Moss, Robertson and Cohen, were largely converted by what they read; the others were influenced more by events, lectures they heard and people they met: none of this is surprising. Above all, this score of men and women were individualists: they were freethinkers because, for various reasons, they had been brought to think for themselves and consciously to adopt a position which was *different* from that of the common herd. This gave them a sense of freedom, from conventions and from authority, which also meant independence from one another.[55]

## Disputes and strategy

The history of the freethought movement was riven by disputes. Many of these now seem trivial, or at least of no importance to the historian, though they aroused great passions at the time. Others raised important issues of principle, and, although these too can be explained partly in personal terms, they are susceptible to deeper

analysis along lines suggested by such sociologists as Dr Colin
Campbell and Dr Susan Budd.[56] The main issues at stake were
twofold: the first concerned what might be termed questions of
strategy—which often resolved themselves into questions of mere
tactics: was Secularism synonymous with atheism, and was the
latter a necessary consequence of freethinking; ought Secularists to
adopt a militant or accommodating attitude in their propaganda;
was the movement helped or hindered by 'respectability'? The
second group of questions centred on authority: should the N.S.S. be
ruled by a president; how formal should the organisational
structures be; what restrictions were individuals prepared to accept
in order the achieve success? The issues were rarely put so starkly as
this, for the whole was overlain by those often trivial and intensely
personal quarrels which absorbed so many of the energies of the
freethinkers themselves.

The questions of strategy initially centred on the personalities of
the foremost leaders, G. J. Holyoake and Charles Bradlaugh, in a
conflict which lasted throughout their lives (and beyond, at the
hands of their daughters and disciples). That men of such differing
temperaments and personalities, each with something of the *prima
donna* about him, should quarrel is not surprising. Added to this,
there was plainly a resentment felt by Holyoake and his supporters
about the aggressive manner in which Bradlaugh had supplanted
the old leader at the head of the movement which he had, after all,
done more than anyone else to create.[57] Nevertheless, at the heart of
their quarrel the broader matter of strategy was at issue. Holyoake
wished to distinguish between Secularism, which embodied a
constructive attitude towards the affairs of this world; and atheism,
which was a philosophical proposition; and freethought, which was
a condition of mind open-ended in its conclusions. Moreover, the
true freethinker had to be tolerant, to argue his atheism (if such were
the conclusion of his freethinking) with philosophical calm, and to
participate in secular reforms without dragging in any of his
philosophical conclusions about the existence or otherwise of God.
Bradlaugh believed that in practice the three could not be separated,
but that, because Christianity was a barrier to secular reform, the
duty of freethinkers was to reach a philosophical conclusion which
would destroy Christianity when urged strongly enough, often
enough, and loudly enough. The *National Reformer* always
championed this policy of 'Thorough'.

These differences were fully aired in 1870 when Bradlaugh and
Holyoake debated their opposing views on two nights at the Hall of

Science, the propositions being 'The principles of Secularism do not include Atheism' and 'Secular criticism does not involve Scepticism'.[58] As in most such debates, neither side convinced the other. The discussion which followed in the *National Reformer* nevertheless suggests that dividing lines should not be drawn as clearly in practice as in theory. J. P. Adams, who was a long standing supporter of Bradlaugh and critic of Holyoake, recognised that Holyoake's approach had failed and that Bradlaugh's appeared to work, but hoped that the two men would learn to work together. Charles Watts resolutely failed to see any real difference of principle between the two men. It was left to Austin Holyoake to point out that his brother did appear to have unrealistically shifted his position, and that 'The garrison cannot "ignore" the presence of the army by disarming, and seeking, by the use of the hoe and the pruning hook, to reclaim the land that has been invaded; if they did they would be speedily overwhelmed and made prisoners.' G. J. Holyoake's position was, in fact, unrealistic. Most freethinkers knew in practice that religious opposition had to be fought even while at the same time secular alternatives were to be propounded. A contributor to the *Agnostic Journal* in 1906 reached a fair assessment of the *creative* conflict between the two men: 'Without the egotism of a Bradlaugh the work of a Holyoake would never have been made possible; robbed of the altruistic and nirvanic egoism of a Holyoake, the iconoclasm of a Bradlaugh would have been in vain. The character of the one was the completion of that of the other.'[59]

Less creative were some of the disputes which centred on questions of authority. This is what lay behind the attempts to abolish the N.S.S. presidency, which Foote led against the Bradlaughites in 1876, and which the old Bradlaughites led George Standring made against Foote himself twenty years later.

The Knowlton Pamphlet affair was an excellent example of Bradlaugh's abuse of presidential power, and it was this aspect which caused most concern among Secularists and had the most lasting repercussions, accounting for the popularity of the *Secular Review's* crude and bitter attacks on Bradlaugh and Besant in the 1880s. These attacks began in a column headed 'Flings and Stings', contributed by the 'The Wasp' from 31 December 1881. The identity of 'The Wasp' was never disclosed; the impression is given that it was not Ross, though the style and sentiments are very similar to his. After several weeks of taunting, Annie Besant eventually lost her patience and refused to place an advertisement for the *Review* in the *Reformer*. Delighted, 'The Wasp' dismissed her as a 'Drudging dabbler in school-girl examinations'.[60] The die was cast, and the *Review* took upon itself the task of collecting all the criticisms that could be levelled at the Bradlaugh group. Among the young men attracted to Ross's side were George Chetwynd Griffith-Jones ('Lara') and Charles R. Mackay; there was also William Maccall, a veteran of similar background to Ross, who had once dubbed Bradlaugh and Besant as 'Brassy Cheek' and 'Breezy Bouncer' respectively—unkind but not wholly unjust labels.[61] The culmination of hostilities came with the libellous *Life of Charles Bradlaugh, M. P.*, published in 1888, the main aim of which was to show that Bradlaugh was hypocritical, financially corrupt, had lived off the movement, and had brought it into disrepute through his advocacy of birth control.

Exactly who was really responsible for this work is unclear, as Mackay, Griffith-Jones and Ross soon fell out among themselves as to their various parts in the affair. The man who claimed to have supplied most of the material was W. H. Johnson, *alias* 'Antony Collins', who in the 1850s, had done much to destroy Holyoake's reputation and promote Bradlaugh's: he alleged that Mackay had then added the libellous passages without his knowledge, whereas Mackay alleged a conspiracy between Johnson and Ross. The matter will probably never be resolved.[62]

These excesses of criticism and muck-raking nevertheless conceal an important issue. The financial accusations are not dissimilar from those levelled at Holyoake in the 1850s and Foote in the 1890s; and the charges of profiteering from the birth-control issue are unjust but illustrate the deep disquiet which the events of 1877 caused. As a contributor to the *Secular Review* noted in 1882, 'The real cause of the split in the Secular ranks was the defence of the Knowlton pamphlet.' Ross's leadership enabled all the pent-up grievances against Bradlaugh to be released. Old wounds were reopened and new victims turned to Ross for support: when a former Unitarian minister from Glasgow was refused in his application to become an N.S.S. special lecturer because he had once contributed to the *Secular Review*, the latter took up his cause; and a move was started in 1886 among the discontented N.S.S. branches to start a rival organisation when Bradlaugh boycotted them for countenancing the *Secular Review*.[63]

Bradlaugh rode out the storm when the conspirators fell out among themselves over the libellous *Life*, but the issues themselves did not die. By 1894 Holyoake was attacking Foote for working on Bradlaugh's method, which was for 'anyone who expressed an opinion different from Mr Bradlaugh' to be 'put down by him with a fury of arrogance because he did not "understand the gravity" of differing from the President'.[64] Foote was quite unabashed, and in 1895 was telling his followers:

For the present, at least, I do not mean to be trammelled by committees. I want help, in money and in work; but I do not want people looking over my shoulders, and trying every minute to control my activities. Committees are never good at initiative.[65]

This may have been true, but was it politic? Only a few months later the 'awkward squad' had retaliated with their own Freethought Federation, and in 1902 the newly discarded Charles Watts felt obliged to remind Foote that he had lost the support of all his old colleagues except the late J. M. Wheeler: Holyoake, Robertson, Parris, Standring, Reynolds, Gilmour 'did not believe in "a one-man movement," hence they separated from you'. Such attacks went on in every generation. Guy Aldred recorded in his autobiography his feelings about Foote: 'I saw him as a would-be priest, even when they styled themselves Freethinkers and Atheists . . . Foote in particular, and Cohen as his lieutenant, had to be not only the priests but the popes of the Freethought movement.' The same thing had been said about Bradlaugh, and, before that, about Holyoake.[66]

Not all these disputes can be explained in general terms. Many of them were the result of personal clashes of little abiding interest. The followers in the country were much more inclined to take success as the sole criterion of good leadership, which meant accepting anyone who could attract a full lecture hall. This gave Bradlaugh a tremendous advantage. Most freethinkers would have agreed in theory with G. J. Holyoake, who in 1897 stated what had always been his policy, that 'organisation beyond a certain point is a fetter upon individuality. I am for federation—not chieftain organisation'. But it was the very failure of this policy in the 1850s which had prompted men to accept Bradlaugh's alternative of a presidentially controlled N.S.S., and the success of the period 1877-85 appeared to justify this policy. The failure of Foote to maintain this record was the principal reason why the issue was then successfully reopened by men who had previously supported Bradlaugh's personal rule.[67]

In the conflict over strategy, few positions, even at the top, remained static. Holyoake's own attitude was far from consistent, and he rarely gave that practical lead to opposition which his theoretical position appeared to require. Had he done so

consistently, the attempts which were made in every decade might
have produced a real alternative to the N.S.S., based on more liberal
principles. Charles Watts was almost as inconsistent, supporting
Bradlaugh in 1870, yet moving towards Holyoake's position in later
life, while Foote travelled in the opposite direction. Ross, who would
co-operate with Watts, but not with Bradlaugh or Foote,
nevertheless shared their attitude towards Church-fighting
throughout his life.[68]

Dr Susan Budd has attempted to consider the rival positions,
exemplified in the 1870s debate, in terms of 'militancy' and
'expediency'. The choice of terms is unfortunate, since expediency
implies lack of priciple, whereas both policies were seen to be both
highly principled and highly expedient—that is, they would achieve
the best results. Nevertheless she is right in pointing to these two
theoretical positions, which were indeed poles apart even though
most men for most of the time found themselves skirmishing around
a common equator.

The argument against Holyoake's position came most succinctly
from Belfast in 1876: 'Whilst endorsing the greater part of what is
laid down in your current articles on Secularism, your advice with
regard to theological controversy though theoretically good, is not,
in our town, practically applicable.'[69] This was irrefutable. The
purest form of the 'militant' approach was without doubt to be
found in the writings of Foote, Heaford, Symes and Aveling in the
early *Freethinker*,[70] which even the *National Reformer* found difficult to
take. In 1883 in *Our Corner*, Annie Besant expressed her distaste for
burlesquing 'other people's deities', and in 1888 J. H. Levy in the
*Reformer* reopened the whole question by seeking to meet the decline
in Secularism by returning to Holyoake's position: 'Freethought is
only useful as a weed-clearing. Secularism is more. It is a religion in
the best sense of that term.'[71] Bradlaugh and Robertson naturally
disagreed, and there is little doubt that theirs was always the
popular view. In 1876 S. L. Mosley was wanting to give his branch
positive lectures 'of service to the general community', but he found
that a lecture on 'Health' 'only draws a mere handful of listeners,
while a lecture on some anti-theological question (worn threadbare)
will draw a room-full, not because it contains the more common
sense, but because there is more thunder and lighting and more
appeal to passion.' G. W. Foote, then still in his moderate phase,
wisely advised his correspondent, 'Lecturers must, to some extent,
accommodate themselves to the average intelligence and taste of
their audiences.'[72]

An extension of the argument about militant or destructive work, and more positive or constructive work, centred on the use of the word 'atheist' and the adoption of the new word 'agnostic' which was emerging in the 1870s. Agnosticism, according to T. H. Huxley in 1884, 'is of the essence of science, whether ancient or modern. It simply means that a man shall not say he knows or believes that which he has no scientific grounds for professing or knowing to believe.' An atheist, wrote Holyoake in the same year, 'is one without knowledge of a Deity, and therefore without belief in one'. One might well sympathise with G. W. Foote's outburst that 'We may be very obtuse, but we fail to see in any straightforward statement of the Agnostic's position anything that distinguishes it from the Atheist's'.[73]

There were differences, though, as Huxley's definition went on to make clear: 'The theological "gnosis" would have us believe that the world is a conjuror's house; the anti-theological "gnosis" talks as if it were a "dirt pie" made by the two blind children, Law and Force. Agnosticism simply says that we know nothing of what may be beyond phenomena.' Bradlaugh would have agreed with the latter part of this, but as a definition equally true of atheism. In his *Plea for Atheism* he wrote, 'The Atheist does not say, "There is no God," but he says, "I know not what you mean by God; I am without idea of God; the word 'God' is to me a sound conveying no clear or distinct affirmation. I do not deny God, because I cannot deny that of which I have no conception." '[74]

This was too subtle for most freethinkers. Guy Aldred wrote of the above extract, 'To my mind this statement is mere playing with words. It is cautious, almost respectable rubbish. I prefer Richard Carlile's clear declaration that there is no such being as a God and no such place as heaven in which God could dwell. Bradlaugh's Atheism was a miserable pretence.'[75] Many Secularists, unable to cope with the finer points of philosophy, must have agreed with him. As ever, Charles Watts had the common man's touch for confusing everything when, after writing an article which appeared to support the claims of agnosticism against atheism, he replied to G. W. Foote's criticisms with the resounding words:

I am a pronounced Atheist - that is, I have no belief in the existence of any 'God'; I am an Agnostic - that is, I know nothing of the alleged supernatural, or of a future life. Further, I am a Secularist - that is, I believe in making the best, physically morally and intellectually of what is known, leaving conjectures as to the unknown to those imaginative individuals who prefer to indulge in speculations, rather than in the realities of life.[76]

Hammered out on the platform table, this message would have sent a freethought audience home happy, wondering what all the fuss was about.

Indeed, G. W. Foote had earlier suggested that the 'real difference' between the two positions was not intellectual or philosophical at all, but 'It is not far from correct to say that the Agnostic is a timid Atheist and the Atheist is a courageous Agnostic.' This may not have been fair to the poetic Ross, who was a courageous agnostic, prepared to speculate upon a future life, but it was generally true. Holyoake was willing to accept the label 'Agnostic' rather than 'Atheist' because it was more respectable and more in keeping with his non-militant approach to freethought. Foote thought the use of the word Agnostic was typical of England, 'the home of timidity and compromise in logic of thought'; Belfort Bax agreed that respectability was the significant difference between the atheist and the agnostic, a point underlined by the opposition shown by some agnostics to the advocacy of 'obscene' birth-control literature.[77]

Was this division between respectables/agnostics/non-militants and non-respectables/atheists/militants a matter of class? The utterances of Stewart Ross would indicate that it was—though, unfortunately for any neat theory, he remained, ideologically speaking, a militant. Attacking Holyoake for speaking in the Free Christian Church in Bolton in 1880, Ross expressed sympathy with 'the hard-working and much-suffering soldiers of Scepticism, who are too uncompromising to be permitted to speak in a Christian church, who are skilled only in plain English to express the truth, and who have a contempt for the finesse by which reprobated "Infidelity" can be transmuted into a mild aspect of fashionable heresy'.[78] But often Ross and his friends seem to have had even less time than Holyoake for the ordinary working man's rather crude and uneducated attempts at freethought. On one occasion Charles Watts had to repudiate the views of R. B. Hithersay, expressed in the *Secular Review*, that 'it is only the intelligent we ought to care about converting. The non-intelligent are to us of neither use nor ornament. Let orthodoxy take care of them.' This was all very well if 'unintelligent' meant no more than that, but in fact too often it really meant 'ill-educated', which was a matter of class rather than of intelligence. As Ross wrote in 1883, 'the uneducated mass are not Freethinkers. They are not thinkers at all, either bond or free . . . Secularism furnishes no theory of existence that can with advantage be shouted at street corners and under railway arches.' The same sense was expressed by a frustrated F. J. Gould in his first lecture on Secularism, in which he condemned habitually unthinking Secularists: 'It is enough for them to laugh when they hear fun poked at Noah's Ark and Balaam's Ass, or to hiss with indignation when they hear of Archbishops with £15,000 a year. But talk to them of plans for improving the world and increasing the moral happiness of mankind, and they show little or no interest in the subject.'[79]

The class basis of this attitude was brought out into the open in 1884 when Ross admitted that, 'although "the utterly debased" may be found amongst dukes and dustmen indiscriminately, the "utterly ignorant and utterly thoughtless" are more to be found among the dustmen than the dukes'.[80] The B.S.U., after all, had a marquis for its first president in 1880! This sort of argument produced an instructive retort from Bristol:

I am a constant reader of your journal, which I must say I admire very much, and there is no pen gives me so much pleasure as your own. Allow me, dear Sir, to inform you that I am only a poor working man; but, having thought and read myself out of supernaturalism, you may conclude that your remarks anent my class have given me some pain - although, in spite of myself, *I believe you are very near the truth*, taking into consideration the lower or lowest order of working men. But I would respectfully remind you of our merits. We work hard and live hard, and are, mostly, law-abiding; and, tell it not in Gath, thousands of us call ourselves Freethinkers, Atheists, and Agnostics, which you perhaps think a pity.[81]

Ross was unrepentantly convinced that there was no use in casting pearls before swine. After a semi-literate postcard attacking Ross had been received from J. W. Crowther of Halifax, a Halifax reader wrote:

J. W. C. is a 'big pot' on the Executive of the Halifax Branch of the N.S.S., and the postcard you have received from him is a fair sample of the magnanimity of the lot; and, unfortunately for Secularism—and Secularism stands very low in the social scale as at present represented—no man of influence or position will identify himself with the party here.[82]

The N.S.S. under Bradlaugh was clearly *felt* to represent a lower order of being than the intellectual agnostics of the *Secular Review*.

Though Bradlaugh and Foote could themselves be snobs, they never took quite this attitude towards their humble followers. The moderates were seeming to show an excessive desire for respectability; decent meeting places were wanted to mark the Secularists out as respectable, yet halls cost money, which meant that patrons would have to be attracted, which could only be done when the Secularists were respectable. Where this circle could be broken and premises were acquired on a semi-permanent basis, respectability often did set in—even at Bradlaugh's Hall of Science—but often with respectability came a decline in militancy, as Foote pointed out to the eminently respectable Leicester society in 1890.[83]

Whether one can actually establish a general correlation between class and attitude is a different matter. All the above can illustrate is that certain freethought leaders thought so; and the likelihood is that the more respectable, moderate, accommodating groups did attract people from the more respectable classes, and vice versa; though it cannot be demonstrated that this did happen to any significant extent. Any person who was really respectable would not be a Secularist at all—which was the point of Holyoake's continuing lament.

Can differences in strategy be related to age or generation? Did young, eager men join the militant freethinkers in the first flush of youth, only to grow wiser with age? This was undoubtedly the case in some instances, Holyoake and Bradlaugh (but not Foote) being good examples. When the Leeds Secular Society split in 1877, 'those who had been longest identified with the movement, withdrew in disgust, and left the management entirely in the hands of a few, young in years and young also in the Secular movement'.[84] Holyoake in the earlier period, and Bradlaugh in the later, not surprisingly seem to have retained the loyalties of some at least of their own generations. Personal loyalty was often of more importance than mere age, as in Nottingham in 1877, where Charles Watts was supported because of his wife's connections with the branch. There also seems to have been some relationship between support for Holyoake and surviving remnants of Owenism, as at Leicester, Huddersfield, Failsworth and Glasgow. G. W. Foote recalled how the Manchester and Glasgow societies had been founded by old Owenite socialists: 'almost to the last they were pro-Holyoake and anti-Bradlaugh'.[85] It is small wonder that the Glasgow Electics long favoured Holyoake: the opinion of many old Owenites was summed up by Alexander Campbell in 1868: 'I am heart-sick of theology, and consider it a great waste of time to discuss the old Book . . . When I compare the past Freethought platform with the present, it seems to me that there was more real progress made in the past when Robert Owen was propounding the old social ideas.'[86] Holyoake's Secularism was, in its origins and message, much closer to Owenism than Bradlaugh's freethought.

On the other hand, young men like Foote, F. J. Gould, Malcolm Quin, Harry Snell and Sam Standring all began as moderates and all—except Foote—continued as such. Indeed, Standring, Quin, Snell and Gould might be taken as representing a new generation for whom moderation was the true hallmark of youth. Writing in 1883, Standring declared that 'The Secularists have brought out no rule of life equal to that laid down by Christianity. As at present formed, Secularism is a dreary waste of vague expressions made up of negations and ridicule.' He went on, more significantly, 'The new Secular party which is gradually forming, and to which I claim to belong, finds in the secular life of Christ the true basis of a Secular life—rejecting any conceptions of a divinity, but accepting the grand doctrines of love towards all men.'[87] His brother George would not have endorsed this, but Quin, Snell and Gould would and did. By the 1890s the Ethical movement was beginning to respond to just such an appeal, and Quin and Snell joined it.

Two American sociologists, N. J. Demerath and V. Thiesson, have attempted to relate freethought strategies to the nature of different communities. In Wisconsin they conclude that militancy can be related to a differentiated community, where a freethought group might otherwise be unnoticed; whereas in a small, undifferentiated community, freethinkers might be likely to compromise with their neighbours in a search for legitimacy.[88] There seems no clear pattern of this nature in Britain: the N.S.S. had militant groups in small villages, like Bedlington in Northumberland, as well as in large towns like Manchester or Leeds. The B.S.U. had branches in the same sorts of places as the N.S.S. Holyoake could appeal to Glasgow and Failsworth alike. What does seem true, though, is that in towns and villages where the freethinkers could, for any reason, be accepted as a legitimate (if eccentric) part of the community, they were there likely to be less militant. Aggressive freethought was the response when survival appeared to be at stake.

E. Bittner has argued that radicalism — and here freethought might be substituted—could function either by abandoning 'the purity of doctrine through the slow assimilation of casuistic interpretations, the development of dogma and bureaucratisation'; or by imposing purity at the expense of increased resistance and hostility, by making participation in the movement psychologically satisfying by imposing an authority structure, by drawing rigid boundaries to monopolise members' interests, by the charisma of leadership, and other such features, so that radicalism should be seen 'not as a person's way of relating to his environment, but as a group's organised response to its peculiar disadvantage.'[89]

Some characteristics of the 'Holyoake' and 'Bradlaugh' aspects of the British freethought movement are recognisable in this model of radicalism: the first type adopts what C. B. Campbell has called a 'substitutionist' attitude towards religion, and seeks an accommodation with the world; the second adopts an 'eliminationist' attitude, and draws in on itself in response to Christian hostility. In religious language, the former approximates to a denomination, and the latter to a sect.[90]

This is helpful as a sociological model to distinguish the two trends within freethought; but as will be seen in the next chapter, two of the best examples of freethought denominationalism are to be found at the pro-Holyoake Leicester society and at Bradlaugh's Hall of Science. The actual struggle went on *within* each, rather than *between* each. Indeed, the struggle often went on within individual freethought leaders. Bradlaugh, Foote and Ross all had moderates and extremists at work within themselves. After exhaustive attempts to quantify the difference between different responses to religious belief, Dr Budd is driven to conclude that 'The answer is partly a question of individual personality, and partly a question of the kinds of explanation and allegiance which were available to each man, living where he did, when he did, and receiving the ideas he did.'[91]

Another way of expressing the division is to use the language of 'chapel' and 'mission'—a distinction of function arising out of how individuals saw themselves and their beliefs in relation to the world and their own needs. Within the 'chapel'—the local society—the emphasis would be on Secularism and denominational activity; in the 'mission' the emphasis would be on converting unregenerate Christians. Arthur Moss made this distinction between both the function and content of his indoor and outdoor lectures. G. W. Foote made the same point when he wrote in an early article on 'The Policy of Secularism', 'Our destructive or negative work really means proselytising.'[92] All the freethought leaders were aware that, in addition to this missionary activity, 'chapels' would have to be formed to build up the Secular faith once the religious one had been destroyed. The balance of emphasis depended on the local situation and the individual preferences of the members. Malcolm Quin had an easy religious upbringing; he never knew 'a dismal tyranny' of belief, and so never felt the need for aggresive atheism.[93] It is likely that second-generation freethinkers, like Owen Balmforth of Huddersfield, felt the same way. Men like this were inclined to be 'positive' Secularists. But for many others, their Christianity had meant a great deal to them; losing it was a dramatic experience which made them, at least at first, as eager to spread the gospel of freethought as they had once been to spread that of Christianity. Chapman Cohen told G. W. Foote.

in spite of your constant and unsparing attacks on Christianity you yet appear to regard it as something intrinsically great, something to be dreaded, and treated with the deference with which a medieval Saint treated Satan. You despise Christianity as much as I do, but you appear to be somewhat afraid of it. You have not the easy-going contempt for it that I have; and I think the difference is due to the fact that you once believed in it and I never did.[94]

In the Columbia University Bampton Lectures for 1966, A. MacIntyre made a similar point, contrasting 'the self-conscious ex-Christian atheist' who 'continues to ask systematically the questions to which traditional theism gave the answers', and 'the secularised unbeliever' who 'sees no point in affirming it in the first place'.[95] In this sense, most of the nineteenth-century freethinkers were of the first type, but, in so far as some, like Holyoake, were striving towards the truly secular second type, they could find themselves in conflict with the first.

*Notes*

1   See D. Tribe, *President Charles Bradlaugh, M.P.*; A. H. Nethercot, *The First Five Lives of Annie Besant*; and L. E. Grugel, *George Jacob Holyoake*.
2   G. J. Holyoake, *Bygones Worth Remembering*, 2 vols. (London, 1905), I, p. 30.
3   The details of Bradlaugh's private life are given in his daughter's account, H. B. Bonner and J. M. Robertson, *Charles Bradlaugh*; see also E. Royle, *The Bradlaugh Papers* (Wakefield, 1975), pp. i–x; and D. Tribe, *op. cit.*
4   *N.R.*, 22 October 1864; *A.J.*, 16 May 1891.
5   *F.*, 18 April 1915; see also the *Boston Advertiser*, quoted in *N.R.*, 16 November 1873.
6   H. M. Hyndman, *The Record of an Adventurous Life*, pp. 339–40.
7   *N.R.*, 25 July 1880.
8   *N.R.*, 26 June, 6 November 1887, 3 November 1889.
9   H. M., Hyndman, *op. cit.*, pp. 336–7; *Radical Leader*, 25 August 1888; G. W. Foote, *Reminiscences of Charles Bradlaugh* (London, 1891), pp. 9–10; *A.J.*, 10 July 1897.
10  S. Weintraub (ed.), *Shaw. An Autobiography, vol. 1 ( 1856–1898)* (London, 1970), p. 151; H. M., Hyndman, *op. cit.*, p. 340; R. G. Ingersoll to G. J. Holyoake, 20 July 1891, Holyoake papers, Co-operative Union, no.

3310.

11   *Bradlaugh and To-day* (London, 1933), pp. 33, 84; H. M. Hyndman, *op. cit.*, p. 337.

12   In addition to the biography by L. E. Grugel, *op. cit.*, see J. McCabe, *Life and Letters of George Jacob Holyoake*, 2 vols. (London, 1908); and Holyoake's two autobiographies, *Sixty Years of an Agitator's Life*, 2 vols. (London, 1892), and *Bygones Worth Remembering*.

13   *N.R.*, 9 April 1864, 21 March 1863, 14 May 1865; see also M. Quin, *Memoirs of a Positivist*, pp. 46–7.

14   *N.R.*, 1 July 1877, 24 April, 8 May 1881; *S.R.*, 14 May 1881; *F.*, 13 August 1882, 20 May 1883; K. Marx to F. Engels, 27 July 1866, quoted in R. Harrison, *Before the Socialists*, p. 170.

15   H. Snell, *Men, Movements and Myself*, p. 48.

16   See G. J. Holyoake, *In Memoriam: Austin Holyoake* (London, 1874), and Austin Holyoake, *Sick Room Thoughts* (London, 1874); also the entry in *Dictionary of Labour Biography*, vol. 1 (London, 1972).

17   *S.C.*, 1 September 1872; G. W. Foote, *Reminiscences of Charles Bradlaugh*, p. 6; see also *S.C.*, 24 February 1878; *N.R.*, 30 September 1866.

18   A. Besant, *An Autobiography*, p. 89; the principal sources for her life are this autobiography, and A. H. Nethercot, *op. cit.*

19   A. Besant, *op. cit.*, pp. 134–5; *N.R.*, 30 August 1874; C. M. Davies, *Mystic London* (London, 1875), pp. 92–9.

20   *N.R.*, 2 May 1875; C. Bradlaugh to Alice and Hypatia Bradlaugh [1874], B.L. no. 388.

21   *N.R.*, 17, 24 January 1875; *S.C.*, 28 February 1875.

22   G. B. Shaw, 'Mrs. Besant as a Fabian Socialist', in S. Weintraub, *op. cit.*, p. 139.

23   G. B. Shaw, 'Annie Besant and the "Secret Doctrine"', in S. Weintraub, *op. cit.*, p. 142.

24   W. E. Adams, *Memoirs of a Social Atom*, 2 vols. (London, 1903, reprinted New York, 1968), II, p. 405.

25   Thomas Scott to G. J. Holyoake, 12 September 1874, Holyoake papers, Co-operative Union, no. 2274; W. E. Adams, *op. cit.*, II, p. 406; *F.*, 4 July 1915.

26   *F.*, 23 May 1915.

27   The principal sources for Charles Watts's life are 'Saladin' [i.e. W. S. Ross], *Sketch of the Life and Character of Charles Watts* (London, n.d.), first published in *S.R.*, 26 August, 2 September 1882; *S.C.*, 21 April 1878; *F.*, 22 July 1894; *A.J.*, 24 February 1906; *L.G.*, March 1906; *F.*, 23 May 1915; *Labour Annual* (1899), p. 166; see also *Reasoner*, 26 September 1858; *N.R.*, 9, 16 April, 21 May, 12 November 1864, 29 April 1866; *S.R.*, 1 September 1877, 17 May 1879.

28   *S.R.*, 9 September 1882.

29   *N.R.*, 10, 17 April, 5 June 1870, 2 August 1872. For Kate Watts see *N.R.*, 12 February, 20 August, 24 September 1871; *S.R.*, 11 March, 1 September 1877; *L.G.*, September 1904. For Charles Albert Watts see F. J. Gould, *Pioneers of Johnson's Court* (London, 1929), p. 4.

30   Quoted in *S.R.*, 20 August 1881.

31 *S.R.*, 2 September 1882.

32 The principal sources for Foote are *S.C.*, 17 March 1878; *Republican*, April 1883; *F.*, 1 July 1883; *L.G.*, August 1895, November, December 1915; *F.*, 2 May, 31 October, 1, 7 November 1915.

33 *N.R.*, 1 June 1873.

34 *S.C.*, 17 March 1878; M. Quin, *op. cit.*, pp. 55–6; *L.G.*, December, August 1915.

35 *F.*, 2 March 1902, 25 October 1903, 7 November 1915; *L.G.*, December 1915.

36 *F.*, 11 March 1883; *S.R.*, 10 March 1883; *L.G.*, November 1915, *F.*, 31 October 1915; *Birmingham Weekly Post*, 23 November 1907; H. S. Salt, *Seventy Years among Savages* (London, 1921), pp. 208–9.

37 *S.R.*, 13 October 1877; *L.G.*, December 1915; *F.*, 31 October 1915.

38 The principal sources for Ross's life are *Biograph and Review*, January 1882; *S.R.*, 9, 16 September 1882; *L.G.*, April 1900; *A.J.*, 8 December 1906; *F.*, 9 December 1906.

39 *N.R.*, 21 March 1880.

40 *L.G.*, April 1900; *S.R.*, 16 September 1882.

41 *A.J.*, 14 October 1899, 24 May, 6, 13 December 1902, 8 October 1904, 3 March 1906; E. Pack, *The Trial and Imprisonment of J. W. Gott for Blasphemy* (Bradford, n.d. [1912]), pp. 135–8.

42 See G. A. Aldred, *No Traitor's Gait*, p. 90.

43 *N.R.*, 26 October 1890; *A.J.*, 11 September 1897; see also *S.C.*, 31 March 1878; *F.*, 1, 8 August 1897; *A.J.*, 16 October 1897; *F.*, 6 June, 4 July 1915; M. Quin, *op. cit.*, p. 53; K. Marx to L. Kugelmann, 13 July 1867, 12 December 1868; K. Marx to F. Engels, 20 June 1686—in K. Marx and F. Engels, *Werke*, (Berlin, 1965) vol. XXXI, p. 353, vol. XXXII, pp. 97, 582. Her full biography appears in the *Dictionary of Labour Biography*, V.

44 *F.*, 1 January 1893, 10 November 1906, 4 August, 3 November 1907; *L.G.*, December 1907; *F.*, 3 October 1915.

45 *Republican*, August 1883; *F.*, 5 August 1906, 1 August 1915; E. Pack, *op. cit.*, p. 134. For a full biography see *Australian Dictionary of Biography*, vol. VI.

46 *Republican*, February 1886; *F.*, 1 January, 24 September 1893; *Truth Seeker*, April 1896; *F.*, 27 November 1898, 25 August 1901; *L.G.*, September 1901.

47 *Republican*, May 1883; *Truth Seeker*, October 1896; E. Pack, *op. cit.*, pp. 146–7.

48 *F.*, 11 October 1903; 12 February 1928; F. J. Gould, *op. cit.*, p. 148.

49 *A.J.*, 14 May 1898; *F.*, 15 May 1898; also *N.R.*, 21 July 1872; *F.*, 25 March, 27 May, 26 August, 18 November 1883, 18 May 1884, 5 December 1886, 1 January, 5 November 1893; *Truth Seeker*, June 1896; *F.*, 8, 22 May 1898; *Reformer*, 15 May 1898; *F.*, 24 October 1915.

50 *N.R.*, 6 July, 17, 31 August, 5 October 1879; *Republican*, December 1881. The references to Shaw are from Y. Kapp, *Eleanor Marx*, vol. 1: *Family Life (1855–1883)* (London, 1972, reprinted 1979), p. 271, and A. H. Nethercot, *op. cit.*, p. 160. Kapp accuses Bradlaugh of cheating

Aveling over the Science School finances—Y. Kapp, *Eleanor Marx*, vol. 2: *The Crowded Years ( 1884–1898)* (London, 1976, reprinted 1979), pp. 205, 470—but a very different story is presented in the Bradlaugh papers—see E. B. Aveling to Charles Bradlaugh, 28 April 1880, 26 January 1882, 23 May, 11 July 1883, 29 July, 10, 11, 12, 22, 27 August, 25, 29 September, 1 October 1884, B.L. nos. 585, 586, 939, 1035, 1054, 1127, 1132, 1137, 1140, 1152, 1154, 1160, 1161, 1162, 1168; C. Bradlaugh to E. B. Aveling, [July], 9, 11, 12 August 1884, B. L. nos. 1128, 1131, 1135, 1136, 1139; E. B. Aveling to A. Besant, [July], 22 September 1884, B. L. nos. 1129, 1158; also E. B. Aveling to W. J. Birch, 26 July, 11 October 1883, 14 August 1884, B. L. nos. 1055, 1070, 1145; G. A. Gaskell to A. Besant, 8 August 1884, B. L. no. 1130; and M. Reed to E. B. Aveling, 24 September 1884, B. L. no. 1159. In these and other letters in the collection Aveling's indebtedness to Bradlaugh is made plain. See also the many I.O.U.s, receipts and prevaricating letters, some of them not dated.

51   J. F. C. Harrison, *A History of the Working Men's College, 1854–1954* (London, 1954), pp. 54, 58, 73, 81 [Sam, senior]; *Radical*, November 1884; *Truth Seeker*, February, November 1895; *Rochdale Observer*, 28 September, 2, 5 October 1895 [Sam, junior]; *N.R.*, 8 March 1874; *Republican*, May 1885; *F.*, 1 January 1893; *Truth Seeker*, March 1896; *F.*, 12, 19 December 1915; P. Fryer, *The Birth Controllers*, p. 173 [George].

52   *S.C.*, 19 March 1876, 11 August, 8 September 1878; *S.R.*, 27 July, 7 September 1878, 30 December 1882; *F.*, 1 January 1893; *Watts's L.G.*, September 1895; *Truth Seeker*, February 1896; *F.*, 12 January 1913, 11 January 1914, 14 March 1915, 15 August 1937.

53   *Reynold's Newspaper*, 6 March 1898; *F.*, 5 September 1915; 15 January 1933; F. J. Gould, *op. cit.*, pp. 31–2.

54   *Truth Seeker*, March 1895; *F.*, 19 February 1954; C. Cohen, *Almost an Autobiography* (London, 1940), *passim*.

55   Cf. S. Budd, *Varieties of Unbelief* (London, 1977), pp. 119–22.

56   C. B. Campbell, 'The Conceptualization of Irreligion' (1970), 'The Pattern of Irreligious Denominationalism in England' (1972), *Toward a Sociology of Irreligion* (London 1971); S. Budd, 'Militancy and Expediency—an Account of the Secular Movement in the Nineteenth Century' (1966), 'The British Humanist Movement, 1860–1966' (D.Phil. thesis, Oxford, 1968), *Varieties of Unbelief*.

57   See *F.*, 29 September 1901.

58   *Secularism, Scepticism, and Atheism. Verbatim report of the proceedings of a Two Nights' Public Debate between Messrs. G. J. Holyoake and C. Bradlaugh* (London, 1870).

59   *N.R.*, 20, 27 March, 24 April 1870; *A.J.*, 3 February 1906.

60   *N.R.*, 12 March 1882; *S.R.*, 18 March 1882; see also *S.R.*, 4 March, 8 April 1882.

61   C. R. Mackay, *The Life of Charles Bradlaugh, M.P.* (London, 1888), pp. 427–35.

62   *S.R.*, 8 October 1887, 4, 11, 18 February, 3, 10 March, 21 April, 9, 23 June, 14, 21, 28 July, 4 August, 8 September 1888; *A.J.*, 2, 30 March

1889, 10 May 1890, 28 March, 18 April 1891, 6 January 1894, 16 June 1906; *N.R.*, 26 February, 13 May, 3 June, 29 July 1888, 24 February 1889.

63   *S.R.*, 23 September 1882, 28 March 1885. For the boycotting of the branches see *N.R.*, 9 July 1882, 15 August 1886; *S.R.*, 18 April 1885, 21 August, 4, 11, 18, 25 September, 16 October 1886.
64   *F.*, 8 April 1894.
65   *F.*, 6 October 1895.
66   *F.*, 22 June 1902; G. A. Aldred, *op. cit.*, p. 223.
67   G. Payne to A. Besant, 5 November 1886, B.L. no. 1295; *Radical*, 15 August 1897.
86   E.g. *A.J.*, 1 December 1906.
69   *Secularist*, 4 March 1876.
70   E.g. *F.*, 21 May 1882, 24 February 1884.
71   *Our Corner*, January 1883; *N.R.*, 17 June 1888.
72   *Secularist*, 2 December 1876.
73   *Agnostic Annual* (1884), pp. 5–6; *Present Day*, August 1884; *F.*, 5 October 1884.
74   C. Bradlaugh, *A Plea for Atheism* (1864, 20th thousand, 1880), p. 4.
75   G. A. Aldred, *op. cit.*, p. 233.
76   *F.*, 14 August 1898.
77   *F.*, 5 October 1884; *L.G.*, December 1900; *F.*, 16, 30 December 1900, 6, 13, 20 January 1901, 19 January 1902; E. B. Bax, *Reminiscences and Reflexions of a mid and late Victorian* (London, 1918), pp. 190–5.
78   *S.R.*, 30 October 1880.
79   *S.R.*, 8 October 1881, 28 July, 7 April 1883.
80   *S.R.*, 27 September 1884.
81   *S.R.*, 18 October, 8 November 1884.
82   *S.R.*, 18 July 1885.
83   *S.C.*, 1 August 1872; *S.R.*, 31 March 1883; *F.*, 6 April 1890.
84   *S.R.*, 12 April 1879.
85   *F.*, 7 February 1909.
86   *N.R.*, 18 October 1868.
87   *F.*, 7 January 1883.
88   N. J. Demerath III and V. Thiessen, 'On Spitting against the Wind. Organisational Precariousness and American Irreligion', *American Journal of Sociology*, LXXI, no. 6 (May 1966), pp. 674–87.
89   E. Bittner, 'Radicalism and the Organisation of Radical Movements', *American Sociological Review*, XXVIII, no. 6 (December 1963), pp. 928–40.
90   C. B. Campbell, 'The Pattern of Irreligious Denominationalism in England'.
91   S. Budd, *Varieties of Unbelief*, p. 103.
92   *S.R.*, 6 September 1879.
93   M. Quin, *op. cit.*, pp. 28–9.
94   C. Cohen, *op. cit.*, pp. 109–10.
95   A. MacIntyre and P. Ricoeur, *The Religious Significance of Atheism* (New York and London, 1969), p. 15.

# VIII

# Members and their activities

## Members

Contemporaries were agreed that the Secularist movement in the nineteenth century attracted large numbers of working-class people; and, except when they were being derogatory, they also agreed that these people were from the more respectable portion of the working classes.[1] 'Freethought gains the élite of the working class,' said the *Freethinker* in 1888, and the *National Reformer* in 1892 claimed to be read by 'the pick of the working classes'. But towards the end of the century are there suggestions that the shopkeeper/poor clerk was becoming significant within the movement, especially in London—though, as Charles Booth pointed out, the lower middle classes and working classes consorted together 'in a free and friendly way'. *Justice* in 1890 claimed that Bradlaugh's 'strength has always lain among the Secularist small shopkeepers'. Bradlaugh denied this, but a police report in 1894 estimated that 'The class of persons who purchase "The Freethinker" and frequent [the] above meetings [i.e. at the Hall of Science and in the open air] is somewhat above that of the average mechanic and appear to be respectable. They are as a rule intelligent and studious. Many of them are clerks &c.' Stanton Coit's *Ethics* in 1902, without refutation, described the N.S.S. as 'the lower middle-class organisation of Freethinkers'.[2]

The most exhaustive analysis of biographies and obituaries given in the freethought press has been undertaken by Dr Susan Budd. Her analysis of the occupations of 263 Secularists, drawn from sources over the period 1852–1965, shows that some 40 per cent were what she classes semi-skilled or unskilled workers, 20 per cent skilled or craft workers, 20 per cent whilte-collar workers, and 15 per cent owners of small businesses, leaving 3 per cent rural workers and under 2 per cent of the professional classes.[3] This may well be true of Secularism as a whole, but obituary notices are a difficult source, and my own survey, limited to sources over the period 1865–1915, shows some differences.

The brief obituary notices which appear in the freethought press vary in quality: some local secretaries sent in the names of everyone who died; some sent in the names only of important people; most did not bother at all. The likelihood is that many of the names received were those of the men (and, very rarely, women) who were of standing within the local societies, who were best known, and who had contributed most to the local effort—not least because they had usually been on the scene longest. Most people who died within the period, obviously, were—with the exception of a few unfortunates—the more elderly among the membership. Secondly, what the local secretary wanted to put in the obituary notice is not usually what the historian wants to know. Some give very little, other than the date of death, age, and a eulogy on what thorough freethinkers they were. Only occasionally are we told about their place of birth, education, family, conversion to freethought, public life, or occupation. Even when supplemented with other sources, the picture does not become much clearer. Thirdly, the obituary notices and biographical sketches are often stereotyped: it was appropriate to say certain things in an obituary, and one does not know how far to believe what was written. Possibly an account of a freethought 'conversion' could become as conventional as that of a religious conversion.

Nevertheless, some conclusions may be derived from such sources, and an analysis of obituary notices is useful when taken in conjunction with the impressionistic evidence. Of 150 local members about whom some information is available,[4] the occupations of 97 are given, and these break down as in Table 1. Compared with Dr Budd's, these figures show a smaller proportion of semi-skilled and unskilled workers, and a larger number of men who ran their own businesses; but this seems quite a plausible picture of the *senior* membership of the societies. Many of these members, however, may have started out in more humble occupations. Fourteen people actually began, for example, as textile workers, though only four show up in the final figures. The others, with the exception of Tom Barclay of Leicester, who became a bottle-washer, had gone on to higher things—three stationers and a bookseller; a draper; a temperance hotel keeper; and two into the co-operative movement, one as a C.W.S. manager. Indeed, the only example of downward social mobility in any occupation is Willie Dyson of Barnsley, who had been a policeman but became a collier.[5]

The most noticeable gap in all these occupational figures is the rural one. Dr Budd found only seven people out of 263 who could be fitted into the rural category, as either farmers or labourers, and I

*Table 1 The occupations of Secularist members*

| | | |
|---|---|---|
| *Professional* | 3 | (3·1%) |
|   Medical | 1 | |
|   Accountant | 1 | |
|   Architect | 1 | |
| *Owners of own businesses* | 31 | (32·0%) |
|   Shopkeepers | 9 | |
|   Other businesses | 9 | |
|   Booksellers and newsagents | 11 | |
|   Inn and coffee-house keepers | 2 | |
| *White-collar workers* | 15 | (15·5%) |
|   Teachers | 1 | |
|   Clerical | 4 | |
|   Managers and supervisors | 4 | |
|   Journalists | 2 | |
|   Salesmen | 2 | |
|   Co-operative movement (management) | 1 | |
|   Trade union official | 1 | |
| *Craft and skilled workers* | 22 | (22·7%) |
|   Craftsmen (who may also have owned their own businesses) | 13 | |
|   Shoemakers | 3 | |
|   Printers, compositors, etc. | 4 | |
|   Other skilled workers | 2 | |
| *Semi-skilled and unskilled* | 25 | (25·8%) |
|   Factory employees | 2 | |
|   Weavers | 4 | |
|   Coal miners | 11 | |
|   Transport workers | 4 | |
|   Other semi-skilled | 1 | |
|   Unskilled | 3 | |

have found none who remained in the fields. Freethought was overwhelmingly a movement of workers in towns and industrial villages, not in agriculture—as the distribution of local societies confirms.

Other information to be derived from the sources is almost too sparse to be of any real significance. Dr Budd found ninety-one freethinkers whose former beliefs are given, of whom thirty-five had been Roman Catholics, and twenty-one Methodists, but only nine Church of England.[6] This probably reflects the nature of the twentieth-century sources, which were written for a movement increasingly aware that its main enemy was the Catholic Church. In a group of sixty-two (including leaders) which I have been able to identify for the period 1865–1915, fifteen were Church of England, ten were Methodists, seven were Roman Catholics and ten were Unitarians—not all of the latter having ceased to be Unitarians on becoming Secularists. The numbers are too small for much weight to be given to them, though there is evidence from both Huddersfield and York that there was an easy relationship between the local Secular Society and the local Unitarian chapel, while at Leicester the Gimson family was Unitarian, although the adult menfolk transferred to the Secular Hall.[7]

Of fifty-five members for whom past political involvement is given, two-thirds had been Owenites and one-third Chartists (there is some overlapping when individuals are given as both), and the experience of five went back to the days of Cobbett, Carlile and Hetherington; there were also, inevitably, survivors of 'Peterloo'. Of the thirty-six members for whom present political loyalty is given, six were primarily Co-operators, six trade unionists, nine radicals, ten socialists, and five anti-socialist individualists.[8] These figures are for avowed activities; most members would probably have had interests in several of these areas.

When one asks why these people adopted the religious views they did, Dr Budd has convincingly replied that a majority regarded reading the Bible and/or Thomas Paine as the most significant influence on their early lives and the shaking of their faith.[9] In addition the impact of lectures (especially by Bradlaugh), outdoor missions, and reactions to the Bradlaugh case were important, but no one was remembered as having become a Secularist as a result of the Knowlton trial even though N.S.S. reports claim that members were gained at this time. What the political details suggest is that the largest single influence on the membership was the legacy of Robert Owen. To have been an Owenite in the days of the war of Charles Southwell, G. J. Holyoake, Robert Cooper and Emma Martin, with the Christian apologists, John Brindley, Brewin Grant and Joseph Barker, was to have been a freethinker. The Secularist movement as formed by Holyoake was a continuation of the propagandist branch activity of the old Rational Society. The obituaries suggest that the Secular movement of the later nineteenth century still contained a central, ageing membership of committed Owenite freethinkers, on to whom had been grafted other radicals during the golden years of 1877–85. Those societies which were old and stable enough to provide sufficient entries to affect the figures were likely to be those which most closely reflected the 'hard core' Owenite membership.

The most striking fact about all these figures is that they refer almost entirely to men. As with the Churches, in which women were most attracted to the 'high' end of the spectrum, the freethought societies were most successful with womenfolk at the Ethical end of their spectrum. In the *Daily News* census of religious attendance in London in 1903, nine London Ethical Societies had total congregations of nearly 1,200 people, 42 per cent of whom were men, 39 per cent women and 19 per cent children.[10] No Secularist societies were as successful as this, and women members in most cases seem to have been the exceptions in a mainly male movement. At a Lancashire Secular Union conference in 1867 attended by about three hundred people, only about thirty were women. When Mrs Markland of Wigan died in 1887 the branch lost its only woman member. Whenever women were well represented in lecture audiences, this was a matter for comment. Those societies which were social 'chapels' as well as propagandist 'missions' usually had most success with the ladies (often the wives and daughters of male members), but even here the men continued to predominate. Leicester was able to get forty women to attend special meetings of the debating society addressed by Mrs Bradlaugh Bonner on women's topics, but the average proportion of women entered in the society's nomination book between 1885 and 1900 is only just over 20 per cent, about the same as for the female members of the Huddersfield Secular Society as listed in the *National Reformer* for the period 1877–80.[11] While the menfolk were Secularists, sometimes their women continued to attend church; only rarely do we find the reverse.[12] There were, of course, prominent women in the movement: Annie Besant, Harriet Law and Kate Watts; also Mary Sowden, Miss Thornton Smith, and Edith Vance, the N.S.S. general secretary from 1892 to 1927. Occasionally there were also leading local women: in 1871 the Leicester secretary was Deborah Ross, wife of her predecessor; and one of the Yorkshire district lecturers in 1890 was a woman.[13] Overall the evidence suggests that Dr Budd's conclusion derived from obituary notices, showing only 21 women out of 382 names, is too low,[14] but, even with the higher estimates indicated by the Leicester and Huddersfield examples, this was a small achievement for a movement which in theory proclaimed the equality of the sexes and denounced the Churches (which were in practice more successful) for their unequal treatment of women. The Bible was evidently to blame for blinding women to their own best interests.[15]

Dr Budd has also suggested a low level of family participation and a general failure to pass freethought commitment from one generation to the next.[16] Again, this is basically true, but should not be exaggerated. The Secularist movement was at its peak for too short a time for much impact to be made on the rather inadequate data available to the historian. Sons may well have gone off to join analagous movements long after Secularism had ceased to be an option available to them. Where a local society did last for a number of decades, some family participation does seem to have been present. The York Secular Society in 1879 contained fifteen members under their secretary, William Button: four of these members were women, all of them of the Button family.[17] There were several married couples in the Huddersfield society, where the Hopkinson family had both parents as staunch members, a son as society treasurer, and two daughters teaching in the Sunday school.[18] George Reddall's father took on the *Secular Chronicle* for a while after his son's death,[19] while Harriet Law was later helped to edit it by her daughter. A number of the obituary notices show Secularists to have been the children of Owenites. Nevertheless it is probably true to say that many members would have been first-generation freethinkers, like G. W. Foote, who asserted rather defensively.

Freethought at present is naturally sporadic. Why should you expect it to be otherwise? The Freethinker, or at least the open Freethinker, is an exceptional person. He must have some originality of mind, some independence of spirit, and some positive courage. Is it reasonable to expect such qualities to be hereditary?[20]

Where Secularism flourished as a social organisation, family ties and loyalties were present. Where, as Foote recognised, Secularism originated in individual circumstances and reactions, it was likely to remain a matter for the individual.

The quest for the 'typical' member of a freethought society is a difficult one, for the nature of the evidence is such as to describe in detail only the untypical. The impression which the short obituary notices give is of independently-minded, rugged, largely self-educated, argumentative and at times eccentric individualists. We may presume that they would have to be most of these things to survive long as Secularists.[21]

In his 'Random Recollections' Sydney Gimson recalls a number of the members of the Leicester society. One 'character' was Tom Barclay, who was unusual enough to write an autobiography. Barclay, who was born about 1852, was the son of Irish Catholic parents, had little childhood education apart from Sunday School, and worked in a ropewalk and in the hosiery trade when young. But he was, as Gimson recalled, 'essentially intellectual, with literary tastes and more than a little literary gift of his own'. He borrowed religious books and novels from the library, began attending Canon Vaughan's Working Men's College, taking the Society of Arts examinations in English, and the Science and Art Department examination in Botany, Physiography, and Physiology. Then he followed the University of Cambridge Extension examination in Political Economy. He read Darwin, Huxley, Tyndall, Spencer, Kant and Hegel, which set him on a road to freethought which he reached on reading Draper's *Conflict Between Religion and Science*. He also read Henry George and Ruskin, which began to make a socialist of him. He read the periodicals of freethought—shocking his mother with a *Freethinker* Bible cartoon—but found neither 'the polemics of Charles Bradlaugh, nor the erudition of John M. Robertson, nor the questionable sarcasms of G. W. Foote' half so satisfying as Ingersoll's works—'the masses could understand these'. Barclay, with his workmate, George Robson, was a member both of the Leicester Secular Society and, at various times, of the S.D.F., the Socialist League, the Anarchists and the I.L.P. His intellectual gifts, however, had in Gimson's words, 'always been greater than his practical common sense', and he ended his days a bottle-washer.[22]

Not all Secularists, of course, were quite so talented as Barclay, but there does appear some justification for the Secularists' claim that their members were above the average in their thoughtfulness and devotion to higher mental pursuits.[23]

*Numbers*

When the evangelical *Rock* reviewed W. Rossiter's article on 'Artisan Atheism' in the *Nineteenth Century*, it correctly pointed out that, whilst most atheists might be artisans, that did not mean that most artisans were atheists. In any survey of freethought membership, the historian cannot forget that 'The Old, Old Story that can bring men and women of all ages together and hold them there in rapt attention

is not yet effete nor disproved by a handful of noisy Secularists who
go from place to place making a great show with poor materials'.[24]
The Secularists recognised this for themselves, and sought
consolation in the unregenerate nature of the age and the unfairness
which gave the Churches advantages in propagandism, and they
then doubled their efforts to smash that Bible on which popular
credulity was based.[25] In fact, though they seldom realised it,
Christians and freethinkers were fighting the same battle—against
apathy; and often the freethinkers were as wont to look down on
religious revivalists pandering to the masses as Christians were to
deplore the vulgar techniques employed at freethought meetings.
What is clear is that the Churches were still being much more
successful in attracting adherents than were the freethought
societies.

How many people did the freethinkers manage to draw into their
orbit? This question is impossible to answer in any but an
impressionistic way. One lecture audience at the Hall of Science
could amount to over a thousand people. On the other hand, when
Sam Standring lectured at the Co-operative Hall, Pendlebury, on
'Christ and the Labour Party' in 1892, his audience of colliers voted
by fifty to six not to have any more such lectures in the hall.[26]
Though most of the thousand at the Hall of Science returned each
week for more, they were guaranteed a first-rate lecturer, which was
always a great incentive. Out in the provinces, Bradlaugh, Besant,
Watts or Foote could usually—though not always—fill a hall, but
they were not there to do it every week. Bradlaugh lamented in 1869:

When we look at the crowded and approving audiences assembled at the
recent Newcastle and Oldham lectures, and including, certainly a large
proportion of the *élite* of the working classes in the respective districts, it is a
matter for sincere regret that so many auditors are only brought together on
the occasion of similar lectures, and at other times remain as if utter
strangers to the movement.[27]

It would therefore be a most generous calculation which allowed the
Secularists' influence to extend to an audience of several hundred for
each of the 120 branches of the N.S.S. at its height, and even that
would yield a total of perhaps only 60,000.

When the question is narrowed from one of audience size to
membership, then a much smaller figure must be considered. We do
not know what the membership of the N.S.S. was. Bradlaugh's
Christian brother calculated from financial details that the
membership in 1884–85 was 'only' 18,327 with perhaps an
additional 6,000 too poor to pay a subscription, but he reached this

*Table 2 Estimated N.S.S. membership figures, 1875–1915*

| Year ending May | Subscription income £ s d | Approximate paid-up membership | New members | New branches |
|---|---|---|---|---|
| 1875 | | 300 [a] | | |
| 1876 | | 1,192 [b] | | |
| 1877 | | [2,000] [c] | | |
| 1878 | 90 16 5[d] | 1,362 | | |
| 1879 | | | 660 | 12 |
| 1880 | | [6,000] [e] | | |
| 1881 | | | 828 | 9 |
| 1882 | | | 1,304 | 12 |
| 1883 | 187 16 3½ | 2,817 | 1,883 | 17 |
| 1884 | 252 16 2 | 3,792 | 1,747 | 16 |
| 1885 | 189 13 10 | 2,845 | 1,367 | 8 |
| 1886 | 177 19 3 | 2,669 | 988 | 7 |
| 1887 | 126 16 1 | 1,902 | 505 | 6 |
| 1888 | 137 6 6 | 2,059 | 593 | 5 |
| 1889 | | | 492 | 5 |
| 1890 | 149 4 4 | 2,238 | 709 | 11 |
| 1891 | 116 7 2½ | 2,327 | 794 | 14 |
| 1892 | 130 4 9½ | 2,605 | 1,074 | 12 |
| 1893 | 95 16 3 | 1,916 | 784 | 6 |
| 1894 | 78 18 7½ | 1,579 | 433 | 4 |
| 1895 | 74 7 8½ | 1,488 | 300+ | 3 |
| 1896 | 57 11 8½ | 1,152 | | 11 [f] |
| 1897 | 48 11 6½ | 972 | | 2 |
| 1898 | 45 7 0 | 907 | 88 [f] | 1 |
| 1899 | 51 0 0 | 1,020 | 176 | 3 |
| 1900 | 36 14 6 | 735 | 94 | 2 |
| 1901 | 37 19 0 | 759 | 32 | 0 |
| 1902 | 23 12 6 | 472 | 29 | 2 |
| 1903 | 32 10 6 | 650 | 27 | 3 |
| 1904 | 26 11 0 | 531 | 43 | 2 |
| 1905 | 25 7 6 | 507 | 36 | 3 |
| 1906 | 27 11 6 | 551 | 60 | 10 |
| 1907 | | | 38 | 1 |
| 1908 | 24 10 0 | 490 | 147 | 4 |
| 1909 | 26 18 6 | 538 | 141 | 4 |
| 1910 | 37 12 6 | 752 | 172 | 6 |
| 1911 | 38 8 0 | 768 | 215 | 6 |
| 1912 | 38 12 6 | 772 | 62 | 0 |
| 1913 | 33 7 0 | 667 | 209 | 10 |
| 1914 | 44 9 4 | 889 | 79 | 1 |
| 1915 | 42 19 10 | 860 | 51 | 2 |

figure by dividing the maximum subscription of 4*s* a year into the
*total* income of the society for that year.[28] If one more correctly and
realistically takes the branch subscription of 1*s* 4*d* a year and the
income derived solely from subscriptions, then the figure for 1884–85
should be 2,845, plus an allowance for members too poor to pay.

The N.S.S. never published its membership figures. When
challenged to do so, Foote explained that 'Mr Bradlaugh never
reported the total membership of the Society, nor has Mr Foote done
so. It is difficult to calculate in the absence of a specific rule as to
arrears, and Mr Bradlaugh never attempted it.'[29] In effect this
meant that each year the total of new members could optimistically
be added on to the old, in the hope that those who had dropped out
were simply in arrears. Undoubtedly some were, and others were
excused their subscriptions on grounds of poverty, but even the most
optimistic formula will not produce the figure of 6,000 which Mrs
Besant gave the first International Congress in 1880. Calculated
strictly by subscriptions, the year of maximum membership was
1883–84, with 3,792.

Occasionally we are given the membership of an individual
branch, and only rarely is this in three figures. In 1878 the whole
Manchester and District Secular Union had only 190 members, and
in 1884 the North of England Secular Propaganda Association,
embracing societies from Leeds to Manchester, had only 498
members. The strong Huddersfield society had fifty-four enrolments
in the N.S.S. in 1879, and the weaker York society had fifteen. The
Hull branch in 1890 had forty-five paid-up members, and 'nearly
seventy' the following year. Finsbury in 1897, with thirty-three
members, was second only to Camberwell in London, and the West
Ham branch was restarted in 1899 with thirty-six. The Leicester

*Source.* Annual printed financial statements, and Conference Reports from
*N.R.* and *F.*
*Notes.* The branch rate of subscription was 1*s* 4*d* to 1890, then 6*d* to 1896,
then 1*s*, but the rate for 1891–96 has been calculated at the full individual
rate of 1*s*, as this gives some plausible continuity to the level of membership.

  *a N.R.*, 13 September 1880.
  *b Secularist*, 17 June 1876.
  *c* Subscriptions to the Giordano Bruno monument—*N.R.*, 27 May 1877.
  *d* N.S.S. Minute Book, May 1878.
  *e N.R.*, 5 September 1880.
  *f* New branches from 1896 and new members from 1898 are derived from
the N.S.S. Minute Books, and may not be complete.

society was exceptionally strong in 1900, when it had 206 members.[30] Even if all the new N.S.S. members in the 1880s were presumed to belong entirely to the new branches, the average branch size would be only a hundred and twenty. This would make the maximum size of the N.S.S. about 14,500. More realistically, the average branch size would probably be nearer half this. To double the number of paid-up members would therefore appear to be an adequate adjustment to make in establishing a total figure for N.S.S. membership.

The figures suggest that between a quarter and a half of the paid-up members in any one year would be new members and, although this would not necessarily makē for stability, it would give societies a larger circle of adherents than crude membership figures suggest. These would be the people who still felt that they belonged even though they no longer bothered with the formalities of membership, and they would still be among their former colleagues when Bradlaugh came to lecture. Only by including such people could Mrs Besant have found 6,000 members on the books in 1880.

### Activities

The local societies attempted to cater for their members in a comprehensive way. This was the 'chapel' aspect of their work. It necessarily involved smaller numbers than the most popular of the public lectures, but for those men and women who regarded themselves as belonging to the society, its 'chapel' life was one of the most important things about it.

As with the churches, 'chapel' life had two aspects—elevation and entertainment. The need for this former to be expressed in a quasi-religious manner seems to have been a peculiarity of British freethought.[31] Like the Owenites before them, the Secularists accumulated about themselves the whole paraphernalia of religious observance, often turning their halls and lecturers virtually into chapels and preachers, with the addition of music and singing. At first a number of societies used the 'old Social Hymn Book'—that is, the Owenite collection. A form of Secular burial service was written by Austin Holyoake and published in the *National Reformer* in November 1868, and a form for the Naming of Infants by Charles Watts appeared there the following month. These were reissued in 1875, along with a collection of hymns, by Watts and Annie Besant. They were given a savage review by James Thompson, the poet, in the *Secularist*. As Count Goblet d'Alviella said a few years later,

'Their manual embodies a considerable number of hymns, but apart from a few which are pretty freely suffused with the breath of Pantheism, these utilitarian lyrics are of so commonplace a character that in some cases they border on parody, not to say more in disparagement of them.'[32]

The desire for music was not limited to any one section of the Secularist movement, and in this respect 'militants' and 'non-militants', 'eliminationists' and 'substitutionists' alike shared in the 'denominational' aspect of freethought. The ideal Secular society, as outlined by Bradlaugh in an editorial note in the *National Reformer* in 1870, was supposed to provide a debating class, a singing class to train young men and women to sing choruses before and after lectures, a children's school, a social gathering or tea party at least once a month in inclement weather, and an outdoor excursion at least once a month in better weather. Austin Holyoake had already urged freethinkers to acquire halls in respectable places in good streets. The *National Reformer* was indeed 'chapel' building, though there were limits to what was tolerable: the Halifax branch was threatened with expulsion from the N.S.S. in 1878 when its new Institute was registered as a place of religious worship.[33]

The foremost advocate of music was John H. Tyson of Stalybridge, who was doubtless anxious to indulge his own tastes and talents in the movement. He used the *Secular Chronicle* in 1875 to float the idea of a 'Secular Church', making available to freethinkers 'the glories of harmony' and the heritage of the poets. There was even a proposal to write a secular libretto for *The Messiah*! The Stalybridge Secular Choir and its orchestra became quite a feature of Lancashire Secularism in the later 1870s: one lecturer at Stalybridge in 1876 found his address preceded by Mozart's *Gloria in excelsis Deo*—though the words had been changed. Tyson urged his fellow freethinkers to compete with the churches in attractiveness, and he was not alone in urging this. C. A. Watts was expressing a general sentiment when, in 1882, he called for more singing at meetings in order to attract women and children, who were, after all, the mainstay of the churches. And it was not only women who were put off by the rather barren nature of some freethought meetings: when Alice Bradlaugh played the piano before the morning lecture at the Hall of Science in 1869, this was welcomed as a relief from 'the cold logic, or hard facts, of the lectures'. Bradford in 1868 and Glasgow in 1887 were also reported to have music at lectures, and it was deliberately introduced by Foote at the Hall of Science as an additional attraction after Bradlaugh's death in 1891.[34]

Religious-style meetings can be distinguished from lecture meetings, according to Dr Budd, by the behaviour and expectations of the audience.[35] The member of an audience at a lecture will feel free to leave in the middle, to chat with his neighbour, to applaud and to smoke; the member of a congregation at a service will feel constrained to do none of these things—and the reluctance of many working men to accept these conventional constraints is one reason why the churches failed to attract many working men. Nevertheless, many Secularists were keen to turn their Sunday morning lectures into services, and some their Sunday evenings as well. On one occasion at the Leicester hall, Bradlaugh refused to begin his lecture until a man had put his pipe away.[36]

The well documented history of the Leicester society can give a rare glimpse into the life of a local Secular society. Admittedly Leicester was unusually successful, but occasional reports from other societies show that they also had the same aspirations and occasionally the same achievements. The religious impulse at Leicester was first imparted in the 1870s by a group of Positivists led by George Findley, a second-hand book seller. They were active in the society's Sunday school, and in March 1878 one of their number, Malcolm Quin, began the practice of giving a short reading before the commencement of the Sunday evening lecture. The following year they arranged for glee singing with piano and harmonium accompaniment. Once established in their new premises in 1881, the Leicester Secularists at last had a hall worthy of their aspirations. Though the Flemish Renaissance style is now rather dated, and its dimensions are dwarfed by new glass and concrete fabrications, the Leicester Secular Hall is still quite an impressive building. The main lecture hall was 66 ft by 31 ft and 30 ft high with a gallery, and the club room was 49 ft by 22 ft. There was also a library, refreshment rooms, a lecturer's house with a bookshop attached, and a spacious basement. Outside the hall the Secularists proclaimed their philosophy with busts of Socrates, Jesus, Voltaire, Paine and Owen, representing the five great critics of the orthodoxies of their age.[37]

The Sunday programme proposed for the new premises was a school in the morning, a 'Musical Service' in the afternoon, and a lecture in the evening. A Secular Hymn Book was issued in 1882, which the *National Reformer* criticised because it called Secularism 'a new religion', and a harmonium was bought the following year, when a new choirmaster was also appointed. Earlier we are told that the choir had been restricted to members and their families after reports of disorderly conduct at the choir soirée. On 15 September it was decided that no crying of literature was to be allowed 'to the audiences at the Sunday Services'. This terminology indicates the hybrid nature of what went on at the hall on Sundays.[38]

In addition to these 'services' and the Sunday school, which appears to have lapsed in the later 1880s and had to be revived in 1894, the society had other features which would have been familiar to the orthodox chapel-goer. The society records contain a Band of Hope certificate in connection with the Sunday school in the 1880s, and the annual report for 1899–1900 refers not only to the choir and Sunday school, but also to the women's meeting and sewing circle. Less orthodoxly, the Secularists started a swimming club and gymnasium in 1894, had an active amateur dramatic society, and, from 1885, a Sunday cricket club.[39]

Though the appeal of these latter was recreational, they also helped make an important point of principle. Drama represented the struggle of good and evil, expressed in Greek tragedy, Shakespeare, and the modern theatre of Shaw, Galsworthy and, later, Ibsen; performances were naturally on a Sunday. The cricketers also openly challenged Sabbatarian prejudices. In 1885 nine Leicester Secularists, wearing Bradlaugh's Northampton colours, played cricket on a Sunday and attracted a large crowd. Police came and took names and addresses. The following week the team was attacked by a mob who tore up the wickets and threw the ball in the river, whence it 'was rescued by a sensible dog'. Two years later a report showed some progress, for the Sunday cricket club was allowed to play for ninety minutes without molestation. 'We intend carrying on the campaign until we win the public of Leicester over to our views,' they announced; but Foote cuttingly commented, 'We should be glad to hear that the Leicester Secularists also intended to "carry on the campaign" by means of thorough-going Freethought lectures.'[40]

It is certainly true that, as Robert Forder complained after visiting the Leicester society in 1886, they behaved as if they had signed a peace treaty with the Christians,[41] but this is not to say that examples of what went on at Leicester could not also be found elsewhere, including the Old Street Hall of Science. Like Leicester, Huddersfield had its Ladies' Secular Sewing Class, as well as a thriving Sunday school.[42] There was a long tradition of drama in the freethought movement, going back to Charles Southwell, who was renowned for his performances as Othello and Shylock. Charles Watts and his wife Kate were enthusiasts for the stage, and Mrs Theodore Wright (formerly Mrs Austin Holyoake) even appeared professionally. The general standard was probably not very high, but it doubtless amused the Secularists and their friends.[43]

The most usual form of entertainment was the concert or the soirée. At a concert held at the end of February 1869 in aid of the Hall of Science Building Fund, Bradlaugh recited, Victor Le Lubez sang the *Marseillaise*, Edward Truelove played his flute, the three Misses Lowry sang sentimental songs, Messrs Giles and Adams sang comic ditties, Mr and Mrs Gilham performed a farce, Alice Bradlaugh played the piano while Hypatia sang, and other songs were sung by Jenny Odger, Mr Lester and Mrs Austin Holyoake. The public face of these Secularists could seem very humourless, but they knew how to enjoy themselves in the family atmosphere of their own communities. In 1878 Alice Bradlaugh started the London Secular Choral Union, director of music Herr Trouselle, who was also responsible for the choir at the Sunday evening 'services' organised at the South Place Chapel by the B.S.U. Regular quarterly entertainments were organised by the Choral Union for many years.[44]

Apart from such festivals, the annual events of the Christian calendar were also widely celebrated. Bradlaugh attended the Huddersfield Good Friday tea and entertainment with his wife and sister in 1867, and both the Huddersfield and Failsworth Secular Sunday schools celebrated Whitsuntide in the accustomed local manner with a 'walk'. Every year the Failsworth society held a New Year's Eve tea party; Leicester gave a 'poor people's dinner' on Christmas Day, for which they lifted their ban on smoking and drinking in the hall; and at the Bradlaugh Club and Institute in 1895 the ladies spent Christmas Eve fitting out the children of the neighbourhood with 'strong boots and warm clothing, and filling their arms with parcels of grocery and joints of meat', while on Boxing Night their hall was crowded for a 'dance, song and chat'. Other festivals were also celebrated: Leicester had its annual 'Chapel Anniversary', when (recalled Gimson) 'we always had many old friends gathered together and got a very good collection'; Huddersfield had its annual Sunday School anniversary. Many societies celebrated Paine's birthday on 29 January: in Huddersfield in 1875 Mr J. Miller gave 'a recitation given at a similar meeting in London, 51 years ago, (contained in Carlile's "Republican")'; while in 1890, at the West Ham branch, fifty children of members were entertained with food, music and a magic lantern show before being sent home with a printed memorial card to which Paine's portrait was fixed.[45]

Outings were a regular and popular feature of the annual programme of most societies. Sometimes business could be combined with pleasure, as in 1875 when the Manchester and District Secular Union went to the Manchester Aquarium for its quarterly conference. Occasionally there were problems, as when the London Secular Federation's outing to Brighton in 1889 had to be cancelled because the railway company refused to lay on a special train, and the Secularists had to go to Epping Forest instead. From 1893 there were also annual pilgrimages to Bradlaugh's grave at the Brookwood Necropolis. A great deal of emphasis was placed on the family at these entertainments: in 1882, for example, 250 children of London freethinkers met at the Hall of Science and travelled in six omnibus vans to Loughton in Epping Forest on Sunday, 20 August:

Arrived at the Robin Hood, the children partook of a hearty meal of lemonade, raspberryade, &c., *ad lib.* Donkey-riding, dances, and other sports followed. Tea was also provided, and after many games and some rambling through the forest, all drove home, merry as marriage bells, and thoroughly delighted with the day's excursion.

The only discordant note the whole day was sounded by a policeman who objected to their brass band playing the *Marseillaise* as they returned through Clapton.[46]

Leicester did not have a monopoly of Sunday sports for adults, either. Edward Aveling formed a 'Pioneer' Cricket Club in 1884, and the Camberwell branch had a 'Bruno' cricket club (named after the Renaissance 'martyr', Giordano Bruno) in 1889, which challenged other branches to matches. West Ham had fixtures against Bethnal Green in 1891. The 'Iconoclasts' cricket club in 1908 had its problems: four times the team lost the toss and the match, so they appealed for the aid of the Blessed Virgin, and won the next toss and the match by eight runs! As with many of the churches, which were inspiring sporting clubs at this time, the 'Iconoclasts' had to admit in 1913 that they were no longer able to restrict their membership to freethinkers. There was also a Queensberry Rowing and Athletic Club, which met for gymnastics at the Hall of Science in 1893, and, of course, the bicycle was not forgotten. A 'Holyoake' cycling club was formed in 1891 to secularise the Sabbath under the presidency of G. J. Holyoake; cycling missionaries, distributing tracts along the road, were also a feature of the new age.[47]

Finally, the atmosphere of Secularism is provided by E. D. Jerrold, writing in the *Weekly Dispatch* in 1879 after a visit to the Hall of Science: observing the audience, one discovers in a moment that this is more than a congregation or coterie; it is a club. Handshakes link all the eleven hundred. Their talk is of former meetings, of lectures here and celebrations there; I have heard one dapper Secularist—who looked like a flourishing broker's clerk but was really a hairdresser—beseech a pretty Atheist to give him 'the second waltz' next Thursday; and the invitations to tea that are exchanged in the lobbies as the meeting finally disperses argue a hearty and widespread hospitality.[48]

For such people Secularism was more than a dry list of weekly lectures, or a society riddled with bureaucratic factions; Secularism was a way of life which ministered to spiritual and social needs without appealing to supernatural agencies and beliefs.

The Old Adam was nevertheless present even in these regenerate congregations of the unfaithful. One of the most abiding themes in the records of the Leicester society and in reports of the Old Street society concerns the relationship between the 'chapel' and the 'club'. Not all activities were regarded as entirely innocent amusements.

Clubs were popular working-class institutions, and their spread was encouraged in the later nineteenth century by the Reverend Henry Solly's Club and Institute Union (founded 1862). Some Secular clubs were modelled on C.I.U. clubs, such as that at Birmingham in 1872, and they all faced the same problem—what the jubilee history of the C.I.U. called 'The Beer Problem'.[49] Though some Secularists favoured total abstention, most probably held the attitude adopted at Birmingham:

We are satisfied, from experience, that it is best to keep ale and the like for those members who use it; because when the public house incentive to drink is taken away, all are found to use it as moderately and harmlessly as tea and coffee.

This club, with its chess, draughts and dominoes, was admirable, forming as it did part of a balanced programme of Secularist and secular activities which also included Sunday lectures, a library, a dramatic club and music.[50] But all too often the club became the cuckoo in the Secularists' nest; and, particularly towards the end of the nineteenth century, freethinkers and political radicals alike were beginning to find that too many working men were interested in the club for its own sake, with its 'free and easy' entertainment, and no longer saw it as a mere relaxation from more intellectually demanding pursuits. There was indeed a running battle between the two aspects of society work both at Old Street and at Leicester, and by the later 1880s what had once been seen to be an inducement to men to join a Secular society and a convenient source of income had become a major problem for the freethought leaders.[51]

The club at the Old Street Hall of Science was first formed in March 1871 after the Middlesex magistrates had, for no apparent reason, refused to renew the hall's wine and beer licence. Within the first six weeks nearly 500 members were enrolled. The club's programme was of an 'improving' sort, and there was clearly nothing subversive about it under the watchful eye of its treasurer, Austin Holyoake. After two years this club seems to have failed, but was revived in January 1874 by G. W. Foote and Charles Watts to provide 'Intellectual culture, moral training, and judicious recreation'. Apart from a highly ambitious educational programme, nothing more sinister than draughts, chess and a reading room was promised, which may be why a different London Secular Club came into being at 149 Old Street in January 1875.[52]

A third attempt was made to get an official club started in August 1875, with Watts as president, Foote as vice-president, and Robert Owen Smith, the legal tenant of the hall, as secretary. Members who paid either a guinea a year of 3*s* a quarter were entitled to free admission to a social party each Sunday after the evening lecture, a quadrille party on Mondays and Saturdays, and classes for debating (Tuesdays), dancing (Wednesdays) and elocution (Thursdays). There was also a coffee room with bagatelle, chess, draughts, cards and newspapers, as well as a library. By January 1876 over a thousand members had joined.[53]

It was this club which, after the departure of Foote and Watts in 1876-77, was to cause the trouble as increasingly Smith ran it as a commercial venture not directly controlled by the N.S.S. Critics of Bradlaugh were all too ready, however, to associate the club with the N.S.S. to the embarrassment of the latter, and in vain the *Freethinker* pointed out that the N.S.S. had no control over what happened on Sunday evenings after the lectures. It was this unsavoury reputation the Hall of Science had acquired which convinced Mrs Bradlaugh Bonner that it could never be made an adequate memorial to her father.[54] Finally, in 1894, the club went too far when it arranged a professional boxing match at the Hall. The N.S.S. forced the club to withdraw its plans on threat of the N.S.S. disaffiliating from the club, which caused George Standring, the club's president, to resign his N.S.S. vice-presidency. The following year the club secretary, James Anderson, was expelled for saying that Foote had misused N.S.S. funds; Smith was also deprived of his N.S.S. vice-presidency; and the entire Finsbury branch withdrew in sympathy with Anderson. It is no surprise that Foote's later troubles over retaining the Hall of Science were mixed up with the fate of the club, or that its leaders were later to form the 'awkward squad' which set up the Freethought Federation.[55]

Supporters of the latter remained ardent champions of club life, and were the mainstay of the Bradlaugh Club and Institute at the Ball's Pond Road Secular Hall. In 1896 the *Jerusalem Star* was regretting that Camberwell audiences were simply left to disperse after lectures. The Camberwell secretary replied that he did not think a club would help the spread of Secularism, as the experience of the Lambeth, Peckham, and Ball's Pond branches, as well as of the Hall of Science itself, showed. Camberwell was right, for the same fate awaited the Bradlaugh Club. In 1900 Foote could report with self-satisfaction, 'Lecturing went on for a while on Sunday evenings, but it soon dropped, and the place sank into the usual type of London Club, where the Objects are full of principle and the mouths are full of beer.'[56]

At Leicester, where beer was also the problem, the society eventually triumphed over the club. The fortunes of each ebbed and flowed, and in 1893 a general meeting of members voted by twenty-three to twenty-one to close the public reading room and open the bar on Sunday lunchtimes. Sydney Gimson much regretted this decision, and in 1894 issued a circular in his capacity as president in which he nicely stated the objects and problems of a local society torn between propaganda and beer:

If our principles are worth anything, if our Society is worth keeping alive, we must show that we help to make better men and better women of those who come among us, and that young people brought up in connection with our place are stronger and better for our teaching. Ours should be an educational institution, where all could get good training mentally and, if possible, physically; morally connection with our Society should be an incentive to honest, independent and useful action . . .

We need a special vigilance to guard ourselves from lazily letting the pleasures of club and social life absorb all the energy that should be given to upholding the principles that we believe would make the world a far brighter and better place to live in.

In this spirit, F. J. Gould was appointed permanent organiser in 1899 and, after putting the society's archives in admirable order, he turned his attention to the club, which, he believed, had 'taken too big a share of the members' interest': all subscriptions were paid to the club, not the society; most members were recruited through the club, not by propagandist work; reliance on the club meant that Secularists could not appeal to respectability; it made the society just another working men's club. 'There are many intelligent people in the town who are of our way of thinking, but whose social habits do not incline them to Club life.'[57]

Finally, on 30 September 1902, the sale of alcoholic drinks in the club was abolished by forty-seven votes to thirty-six, at a calculated cost to the society of £100 a year—a fifth of its income. Sydney Gimson later wrote with the wisdom of hindsight, 'We soon settled down to quiet steady work again, but of course we found that teetotalism is no cure-all!'[58]

The people who frequented the Leicester and other clubs, however, should not all be seen as wickedly corrupt and immoral people. Tom Barclay lured his Roman Catholic mother and sisters into the Leicester club one night on the way home from seeing a performance of *The Mikado* at the theatre:

At the time the Secular Club had a bar open for the sale of alcoholic drinks to its members and their friends: Mr F. J. Gould had not yet come among us. My mother admired the grand place with its books and pictures and spacious tables, and thought the members very nice people.[59]

Neither should the opponents of the clubs be seen simply as moral kill-joys. Barclay himself recalled that he soon pulled out of any club which tagged 'and Literary Institute' after its name and then proceeded to ignore it. The freethinker was very much the sort of person who *would* stand out for a principle, even when this made him unpopular with the bulk of his fellow working men. Some of the strongest centres of working-class enlightenment were not public houses but Temperance Hotels, like Thornton's of Huddersfield or Laycock's of Bradford, 'where they drink tea and eat toast and talk with the volubility of a ladies' sewing circle'.[60]

## Notes

1  E.g. *Weekly Dispatch*, 8 June 1879; *Methodist Times*, 20 September 1888.
2  *F.*, 5 February 1888; *N. R.*, 31 January 1892; C Booth, *Life and Labour*, 1st series, vol. 1, p. 99; *N. R.*, 23 February 1890; Chief Inspector Melville's report, 23 October 1894, H. O. 45 10406/A46794 (8); *Secularist*, March 1902; see also *Secular Work*, May 1896.
3  S. Budd, 'The British Humanist Movement, 1860-1966', p. 476; *Varieties of Unbelief*, pp. 95-6.
4  These details refer to members, other than national leaders; the information comes mainly from the periodicals, principally obituary notices.
5  T. Barclay, *Memoirs and Medleys* (Leicester, 1934); *Truth Seeker*, September 1896.
6  S. Budd, *Varieties of Unbelief*, p. 97.

7   E. g. D. F. E. Sykes, *The History of Huddersfield* (Huddersfield, n. d.), p. 245 [Sykes contributed to the *Secularist*, but later moved away from the freethinkers]; *N. R.*, 27 January 1878; S. A. Gimson, 'Random Recollections', I, pp. 2-4, 6.

8   In a number of the obituaries several allegiances are given: I have in each case chosen the one which appears to have been the most important.

9   S. Budd, *op. cit.*, pp. 104-23, which is substantially the same as her earlier article, 'The Loss of Faith', *Past & Present*, no. 36 (April 1967), pp. 106-25.

10  R. Mudie-Smith, *The Religious Life of London* (London, 1904), pp. 48, 99, 111, 126, 166, 174, 236, 255; see also H. McLeod, *Class and Religion in the Late Victorian City* (London, 1974), pp. 30-1, 308.

11  *N. R.*, 28 July 1867, 23 October 1887; Leicester Secular Society, Scrapbook, September 1899; Nomination Book (1885-1901), Leicestershire C. R. O.

12  E. g. *F.*, 8 September 1895.

13  *N. R.*, 31 August 1890. There were also a number of women delegates to the annual conference, including Miss Annie Brown of North West London, who was also a director of the Secular Society Ltd, and Miss Kathleen B. Keogh of the same branch, who became N. S. S. assistant secretary and a vice-president in 1911.

14  S. Budd, *op. cit.*, pp. 94-5.

15  E. g. *S. C.*, 20 October 1878.

16  S. Budd, *loc. cit.*

17  *N. R.* (1879), *passim*.

18  *S. C.*, 16 December 1877.

19  *S. C.*, 24 October 1875.

20  *F.*, 10 September 1905.

21  E. g. 'Honest Tom', described by D. Fagan and E. Burgess, *Men of the Tideway* (London 1966), p. 138.

22  S. A. Gimson, 'Random Recollections', I, p. 34; T. Barclay, *op. cit.*, pp. 14-52.

23  E. g. the Lancashire Bradlaughite described by the Rev. W. Tuckwell, *Reminiscences of a Radical Parson* (London, 1905), pp. 176-7.

24  *Rock*, 29 July 1887; W. Rossiter, 'Artisan Atheism', *Nineteenth Century*, XXI, February 1887, pp. 262-72, XXII, July 1887, pp. 111-26.

25  E. g. Wheeler in *F.*, 4 January 1891.

26  *Anti-Infidel*, May 1892.

27  *N. R.*, 2 May 1869.

28  *Anti-Infidel*, July 1885.

29  *F.*, 20 November 1892. The N.S.S. Minutes, 25 November 1915, note that 'membership depended not as much upon subscription as upon declaration'.

30  *S. R.*, 7 September 1878; *N. R.*, 16, 23 November 1884; *F.*, 23 February 1890, 8 February 1891; *Secular Work*, February 1897; *F.*, 7 May 1899; Leicester Secular Society, Scrapbook, Annual Report (April 1900).

31  See the comment quoted in *S. R.*, 25 March 1877.

32 *N. R.*, 15 November, 20 December 1868, 19 December 1875; *Secularist*, 8 April 1876; Count Goblet d'Alviella, *The Contemporary Evolution of Religious Thought in England, America and India*, trans. J. Moden (London, 1885), pp. 151-2.

33 *N. R.*, 11 September 1870, 1 March 1868, 10 March, 7 April 1878; *S. R.*, 27 April 1878. Places of religious worship were exempted from the poor rate, and were preferentially treated under the anti-radical legislation of 57 Geo. III, c. 19.

34 *S. C.*, 17 January 1875; *N. R.*, 4 July 1875, 19 March 1876; *S. R.*, 25 March 1882; *N. R.*, 28 February 1869, 13 September 1868; *F.*, 6 November 1887, 5 July 1891. Bradlaugh and Wheeler also supported music to attract women and children—*N. R.*, 23 October 1870; *F.*, 9 August 1885.

35 S. Budd, 'The Humanist Societies', in B. R. Wilson (ed.), *Patterns of Sectarianism* (London, 1967), pp. 377-405, esp. pp. 384-6.

36 S. A. Gimson, 'Random Recollections', I, p. 17.

37 *Ibid.*, p. 19; Leicester Secular Society, Minute Book II, 13, 27 March 1878, 3 December 1879; F. J. Gould, *The History of Leicester Secular Society*, pp. 20-1.

38 Leicester Secular Society, Minute Book II, 30 March, 17, 24 April 1881, 23 March, 27 June 1882, 3 September, 1 October 1883, 15 September 1885; *N. R.*, 24 September 1882.

39 Leicester Secular Society, Minute Book III, 31 January 1894; Scrapbooks, *passim*.

40 S. A. Gimson, *op. cit.*, II, p. 1; *F.*, 14, 28 June, 12, 19 July 1885, 26 June 1887.

41 *N. R.*, 7 February 1886.

42 *N. R.*, 1 December 1878.

43 See James Thompson's description of a rehearsal for *Othello*, starring Charles and Kate Watts, Mrs Austin Hoyoake and G. W. Foote, in a letter to Susan Bradlaugh, 29 November 1874, quoted in *Our Corner*, September 1886.

44 *N. R.*, 7 March 1869, 4 August 1878, 27 July 1879; *S. R.*, 14 September, 5, 12 October 1878.

45 *N. R.*, 5 May, 23 June 1867; *F.*, 24 August 1902; *N. R.*, 12 January 1868; Leicester Secular Society, Minute Book II, 22 December 1884; *Jerusalem Star*, February 1896; S. A. Gimson, *op. cit.*, I, p. 39; *S. C.*, 7 February 1875; *N. R.*, 9 February 1890.

46 *S. C.*, 13 June 1875; *F.*, 30 June 1889, 6, 27 August 1882.

47 *N. R.*, 1 June 1884; *F.*, 13 June 1884, 19 May 1889, 5 July 1891, 12 July 1908, 27 April 1913; *N. R.*, 30 April, 19 March 1893.

48 *Weekly Dispatch*, 8 June 1879.

49 B. T. Hall, *Our Fifty Years* (London, 1912), pp. 177-92.

50 *S. C.*, 1 August 1872. The theory behind Radical Clubs is expressed in *International Herald*, 9 November 1872.

51 E. g. *N. R.*, 2 October 1887; *Radical*, July 1888, *F.*, 21 April 1889, 6 September 1896.

52 *N. R.*, 26 March, 21 May 1871, 4, 25 January, 22, 29 March, 5 April

1874, 10 January 1875. There was also a Ladies' Social and Progressive Club in 1872—*N. R.*, 24 November 1872.

53    *N. R.*, 20 June 1875, 2 January 1876.

54    C. R. Mackay, *Life of Charles Bradlaugh*, pp. 4-5; *Light of the World*, October 1891 (cutting in B. L. no. 2323); *F.*, 13 December 1891. Foote allowed a 'Free and Easy' after the Sunday evening lectures in 1892—*N. R.*, 28 February 1892.

55    N.S.S. Minute Book IV, 25, 30 October, 29 November, 21 December 1894, 21, 31 January, 3, 31 October 1895, 30 January 1896; *F.*, 10 November 1894, 9 February, 24 March, 14 April 1895.

56    *Jerusalem Star*, July, August 1896; *F.*, 18 February 1900.

57    Leicester Secular Society, Minute Book II, 24, 28 March, 24 November 1884; III, 8, 30 March, 7 April, 11 May, 1 June 1885, 14 May 1888, 26 July 1893, 31 January 1894; circular from Gould, November 1901, in Scrapbook I.

58    *Ibid.*, Scrapbook II; *F.*, 19 October 1902; S. A. Gimson, *op. cit.*, II, p. 8.

59    T. Barclay, *op. cit.*, p. 54.

60    *Ibid.*, pp. 62-3; *F.*, 7 July 1895. For another description of Laycock's see *Truth Seeker* July 1901; for Thornton's see *Huddersfield Daily Examiner*, 29 December 1875.

# IX

# Propaganda

Though individual Secularist societies might be tempted to become inward-looking, the most successful lived also by mission. This was maintained in three ways: by lectures, provided regionally or nationally, often in association with local societies; through the weekly or monthly periodicals issued by the leaders; and through occasional tracts, pamphlets and other publishing activities.

## Lectures

During the golden age of Secularism the branch structure of the N.S.S. was vitally important to its regular missionary work. As Arthur Moss realised in 1890, a galaxy of national orators was all very well, but success 'will depend very largely upon those who take official positions in the various Branches in London and the provinces. It will depend upon their enterprise, their tact and their wisdom in carrying on the work in their own particular district.'[1] This was often the weak link in the chain, and it was the main reason for the collapse of Secularism in the 1890s. Like all voluntary societies, the branches were dependent upon accidents of personality and the enthusiasm of the few. The following, from the secretary of the Leyton and Walthamstow branch, was a familiar story:

I am very sorry to say I have not succeeded in getting anything definite from our late members so can not see any chance of commencing operations in Walthamstow this summer. You see I was obliged to give up the Secretaryship and no one would take the position. That was what really caused the smash. When I tell you I am at work every evening till 9 o'clock you will see I had no time to do the work. I worked hard for two years to keep the thing going and at last had to give it up very reluctantly and there was not one among our members who would take it up, and now I get all kinds of excuses from them when I approach them about it. I cannot say how sorry I feel and how disgusted at their conduct.[2]

A lecture from a national leader would, of course, rally these members for the occasion, but, unless they could be brought together regularly as an *active* branch, little permanent good would be achieved.[3]

In the period of growth and success between 1866 and 1890 under Bradlaugh's leadership, this essential and reciprocal relationship worked well, with thriving societies, local initiatives, and a supply of lecturers. The object of all the regional unions, from the Lancashire Secular Union in the 1860s to the British Secular League of 1903, was to supply lecturers, particularly to the smaller centres of activity, and Bradlaugh's chief sanction against rebel societies was to withdraw the lecturers. When decline came in 1887, G. W. Foote attributed it to 'the want of good lecturers', and his new lecturing plan of 1890 was designed to supply them. In this plan he recognised that many branches were too poor to arrange their own lectures, and he therefore proposed that the Central Executive should do this for them on condition that half the profits of such lectures went back to the Executive. This scheme naturally appealed only to those branches which could not be sure of a profit, and so proved to be a constant drain on funds.[4]

In addition to regular and special lecturers, the Secularists also copied the revivalist techniques of the Churches. Camp meetings had long been popular among the freethinkers of the North, one of the biggest being at Castle Hill, Huddersfield, in July 1874, when between 15,000 and 25,000 people ('including some hundreds attracted by curiosity') gathered from as far afield as Newcastle, Nottingham and Liverpool to ratify Bradlaugh's revival of the N.S.S. after the collapse of the early 1870s. Towards the end of the century, G. W. Foote resorted to 'demonstrations', with large meetings addressed by a relay of top people. This was done at various open-air lecturing stations in London in the summer of 1900, and then at Birmingham Town Hall in October 1900.[5]

The reports of lectures and demonstrations carried by the periodicals of the movement usually emphasise their success. Occasionally, however, a report suggests that not even the national leaders could be guaranteed an audience on every occasion. Sometimes excuses were made: at Leeds in 1876, posters announcing Charles Cattell's lectures were put up only two days before, otherwise they would have been torn down, and as a result the audiences were thin; and Bradlaugh's small audiences in Sheffield in the summer of 1887 were attributed to the heat and the Jubilee excitement. The weather, or local holidays, was always a good stand-by, but sometimes there was no excuse. At Lanark in

1877, Bradlaugh was planned to give two political lectures: his afternoon audience comprised twenty-two people and, when only forty turned up at night, he refused to lecture. Annie Besant had 'extremely sparse' audiences at the Ball's Pond Road for a lecture on Thursday evenings on 'Histories of the Bible' in 1885, and she petulantly reprimanded the members through the *National Reformer*. Towards the end of his lecturing life Bradlaugh was beginning to lose his grip: he could only half-fill a hall in Sunderland, and attracted only a 'fair' audience at Huddersfield to hear a morning lecture on the Eight Hours Question, while his afternoon lecture drew even fewer people to hear about Theology. This is not to suggest that the halls were usually not filled, but that they were not always full. There was, as Foote recognised, a shortage of lecturers who could draw a 'paying' audience, and, with the increasing number of alternative amusements available to potential audiences, even the best lecturers were having problems by the end of the century.[6]

Nevertheless, much good was done by the lecturers over the years, and certainly much hard work was put in by them. In 24 days in 1871 Charles Watts travelled 1,400 miles, delivering twenty-seven lectures in twelve towns and villages, and holding two set debates.[7] Bradlaugh and Watts were joined in 1875 by Annie Besant; and Thomas Slater and Joseph Symes were appointed official N.S.S. lecturers two years later. At the height of the movement in 1883 there were no fewer than ten approved lecturers—Bradlaugh, Besant, Aveling, Hypatia Bradlaugh, Symes, Foote, Slater, Robert Forder, Arthur Moss and George Standring; W. W. Collins and Arthur Hunt were added the following year, and John M. Robertson made his first appearance in 1886. In 1883 Annie Besant proposed to the N.S.S. conference stringent educational qualifications for N.S.S. certificated lecturers, an indication that in the 1880s the N.S.S. was moving towards a denominational structure with a formal 'ministry'. The educational hurdle imposed was a considerable one: the diploma course fell into three parts, only graduates being totally exempted. Part 1 required proficiency in general literature, with Green's *Short History of the English People*, Buckle's *History of Civilisation* and Hamblin Smith's *English Grammar* as set books; those who had already passed the Oxford or Cambridge Senior Local Examination were exempted. Part 2 was on science, and required a study of either Darwin's works or Aveling's *The Students' Darwin*, Büchner's *Force and Matter* and Draper's *Conflict between Science and Religion*; or, alternatively, a South Kensington Advanced Stage pass in a science subject. Part 3 was on theology, and required a study of Paley's *Evidences of Christianity*, *The Freethinker's Text Book* by Bradlaugh and Besant, and W. K. Clifford's *Lectures and Essays*. The examiners were Edward Aveling, Charles and Hypatia Bradlaugh, Annie Besant and H. W. Lloyd Tanner of Oxford University. The idea of a diploma was still being adhered to in 1913, when a successful candidate needed a 66 per cent pass in Biblical Knowledge, Theology, and General Science and Evolution (as illustrated in Astronomy, Geology, Biology and Sociology).[8] How many of the lecturers were certificated is not clear, especially in the later period, but most were not. In 1891 the N.S.S. had only one full-time lecturer—Stanley Jones of Liverpool—and the following year only five 'special lecturers' were named—Forder, Moss, Harry Snell, William Heaford and Sam Standring, none of whom was full time. After the wholesale defection of lecturers in 1896, when seven names disappear from the list,[9] the N.S.S. was reduced to the services of Cohen, Heaford, Moss, Watts and Foote. With the dropping of Watts in 1902 and the addition of J. T. Lloyd the following year, these men were the mainstay of the N.S.S. lecturing force up to the First World War.

The conduct of lecture meetings varied enormously, according to the size of the hall, the nature of the audience and the topic of the lecture. The most popular freethought lectures appear to have been those 'destructive' of the Bible. There was great entertainment to be had in mocking the ridiculous, and cutting the intellectual pretensions of the clergy down to size. The lecturer was the hero; partisanship was everything. One moderate Secularist complained in 1886:

It seems to me that the sole object which the majority [of] Secularists care for is to sit listening to an hour's discourse [on] subjects such as 'Did Jesus Steal One or Two Donkeys?' and, if the lecturer can only give vent to an utterance which reflects upon the character of Christ, their delight seems unlimited, and the rafters ring again and again with their applause.[10]

Christians naturally shared this opinion, and suspected the lecturers of playing to their audiences. The *Sunday Times* reported on Foote at Shoreditch Town Hall in 1912:

He spoke with a certain rough humour, using colloquialisms freely and evidently taking pleasure in drawing the laughter of his audience. There was a suggestion that he was talking down to his hearers, for many of his 'points' were frankly childish.[11]

This sort of comment was sometimes, but not always, fair. Arthur

Moss recalled that Bradlaugh was 'a very industrious and careful lecturer . . . whenever he lectured he had a perfect library of books brought on to the platform, and he had them properly arranged, so that if any person asked questions he could at once refer to the passage and let them know exactly what they desired'. Bradlaugh himself lectured from very few notes: for a lecture on 'The Blasphemy Laws and their Results', delivered in Halifax in 1882, he carried only two sheets of paper, containing a series of single-word, or single-phrase, headings, under a hundred words in all. With these notes he would have held his audience captive for over an hour. Foote always lectured without any notes at all. Such lecturers warmed to their audiences and responded to them: their perorations were always the climax to an hour-long crescendo of argument and humour.[12]

The image of freethought was shaped by the impression which it created out of doors, especially in the metropolis, where several recognised lecturing places were generally frequented by all manner of religious, political and social groups. In an article entitled 'Sermons at Battersea' which appeared in *All the Year Round* in July 1870, the author found the open ground near Cheyne Walk, at the end of Battersea Bridge, occupied by 'a dozen or more groups of about twenty persons, in the centre of each of which, arms are seen going up and down, hammering, as it were, on the anvil of argument, or, rather, assertion'. This sort of scene was repeated in the London parks almost every Sunday throughout the summer months, with Christian missionaries and freethought lecturers indulging in a free market of ideas. Such outdoor work was often of a rougher nature than the indoor variety: there was less time for the niceties of debate and more need to attract a miscellaneous crowd and to subdue hecklers. For this reason some freethinkers were doubtful about the merits of outdoor advocacy, which attracted 'roughs and street loungers of questionable respectability'. Nevertheless, as Chapman Cohen wrote in 1897, 'The maintenance of a vigorous open-air crusade is in every way essential to our movement. It is the hardest, the least showy, but, I believe, the most important branch of our propaganda.' Many freethinkers, not least Bradlaugh and Cohen himself, were first attracted by outdoor lecturers.[13]

One merit of outdoor work was its relative spontaneity. Although formally organised plans of lectures were issued for the London area, there were relatively few expenses and much of the work seems to have been undertaken by ordinary branch members. During summer, when it was 'often difficult to induce people to enter close lecture-halls, especially when the platform is not occupied by a professional lecturer', the outdoor work was the only practicable form of propagandism. Foote's attempt to take over this work and organise it from the top in the 1890s, when increasingly it was the *only* propagandism undertaken, was one cause of the resentment felt among the London branches.[14]

During the peak years of the 1880s the N.S.S. had outdoor lectures during the summer months in about a dozen places in London. Though most of the national leaders began lecturing in the open, they gradually withdrew indoors as they got older, leaving the work to the younger men, or to a few local stalwarts. Amongst the latter was W. J. Ramsey, though in the 1860s much of the work was also carried by the humanitarian Deist, Joachim Kaspary, assisted by the aptly named Epenetus Earwaker. Other well known figures in London were John Fagan (1831-1904), who began the work in 1862, and from 1870 used to devote his evenings and Sundays to walking round every freethought and republican meeting selling the *National Reformer* and freethought publications; and also Fred Haslam, (1833-98), who was active from 1851 until his death. He had helped break down Hyde Park railings in 1866, and was a member of the International as well as a freethinker. By trade he was a mattress-maker who was under-employed and badly paid as a result of female labour in his trade, and he looked to his lecturing work to supplement his income.[15]

Chapman Cohen, who devoted his summers to open-air work in London and his winters to provincial tours, noted how 'In the provinces the halls usually form the chief strength of the movement, open-air lecturing being chiefly incidental, and having a secondary value; but here in London the positions are reversed, outdoor propaganda occupying the position of honor, and serving as the recruiting ground for the indoor attendances'.[16] This was generally true, though where there were no branches or no halls there was no alternative to the outdoors, and each provincial town usually had a place traditionally used by outdoor speakers, such as Woodhouse Moor in Leeds. The summer weather everywhere naturally drew people into the fresh air and offered opportunities to the outdoor lecturer.[17]

The most spectacular form of propagandism was the set debate, often extending over several nights, between the champions of freethought and Christianity. Sometimes the same individuals were concerned on more than one occasion, giving the impression that the

debates were collusively arranged to make money. In fact they were
genuine efforts, neither side being willing to concede that the other
would not be eventually converted. Scores of these debates were
conducted over the years on the merits or otherwise of Christianity
and freethought. Like modern football matches they offered
temporary excitement and entertainment (though both sides could
always claim to have won) and an opportunity for a little vandalism
on the part of a hooligan minority.[18]

The most familiar of these self-appointed champions of
Christianity was the Reverend Brewin Grant, who, as a young
theological student, had entered the lists against the Owenites, and
as a Congregationalist minister had organised a campaign against
the Secularists in the 1850s, thereby giving the new movement a
healthy start in life. He had first debated Secularism with Bradlaugh
at Sheffield in 1858, but in the 1860s he left the Congregationalists
and joined the Anglicans. He recommenced his anti-Secularist
career in the Sheffield area in 1867, and in 1870 debated with
Charles Watts at Mexborough. He met Bradlaugh twice thereafter,
and on both occasions the debate was broken off before the end.
They arranged to meet for six evenings in May and June 1874 at the
Bow and Bromley Institute to discuss 'The Relative Merits of
Secularism and Christianity', but on the fifth evening the owners of
the hall closed it, leaving Bradlaugh to deliver his speech in the Clay
Hall Tea Gardens while Grant simply went home. The following
year they met again, at the South Place Chapel on the question 'Is
Atheism, or is Christianity, the True Secular Gospel as Tending to
the Improvement and Happiness of Mankind in this Life, by Human
Efforts and Material Means?'. The fifth night again ended in
disaster, as the crowd walked out after Bradlaugh's speech,
knocking down poor Ramsey as he stood at the door.[19]

These set occasions for mental, and occasionally physical, conflict
retained their attractiveness even in the twilight of the twentieth
century. When Foote held a two-nights debate in Caxton Hall with
Dr J. A. Warschauer in 1911, 'The crush was almost more than the
stewards inside the Hall could cope with'.[20] Debate was also a
natural means by which radicals could air their own differences; not
only Bradlaugh and Holyoake within the Secularist movement, but
also Bradlaugh and Hyndman (1884), Foote and Besant (1887),
Corrie Grant and Besant (1887), and Frederick Millar and Besant
(1889) on the merits of Individualism and Socialism, which was *the*
question of the day for many people in the later 1880s.

*Publications*

There was a close connection between the oral and the written propaganda of the Secularists, but whereas the former made an immediate impact, the latter was essential in the process of consolidation. Furthermore, a lecture was an admirable occasion for the sale or distribution of literature, and so the two forms of propaganda went hand in hand.[21] Some freethinkers even advocated the use of the tract in preference to the lecture, for, unlike the lecture, the tract could 'be perused in quietude, re-read and pondered over'—though, of course, it could also be thrown away.[22] In fact many of Bradlaugh's lectures were subsequently written up for the *National Reformer* and for publication as tracts. Annie Besant adopted the same practice, though Foote never felt able to do so. Debates were also often published, week by week, in the periodicals as well as in pamphlet form. There were also a number of 'official publications': Bradlaugh and Besant produced a *Freethinker's Text Book* at the request of the Conference in 1875, and a series of N.S.S. tracts was begun the previous year. All the leaders turned out pamphlet after pamphlet in an effort to convince the believer of his error and the non-believer of his wisdom. The Secularist who visited any 'advanced' bookshop in the later nineteenth century would have been overwhelmed with choice—from Collins, Hume, Voltaire, d'Holbach and Paine through to the latest works of British and American authors.[23]

By far the most important of all this literature were the periodicals, which served the movement as lectures, tracts, conveyors of news, communications from leaders, advertisements and begging letters all rolled into one. When Annie Besant turned to freethought, it was a copy of the *National Reformer* which put her in touch with the N.S.S.; and when C. M. Davies began his tours of London heterodoxy, he first bought copies of the periodicals as a guide. The *Saturday Review* in 1866 did not find the various artisan newspapers 'pleasant reading', but among the artisans themselves they were in great demand. In 1875 the Nottingham Secular Society alone sold 2,386 copies of the *National Reformer* (i. e. nearly fifty a week) in addition to 2,301 *Secular Chronicles*, 1,466 miscellaneous tracts and 204 copies of debates. In 1876 the *National Reformer* was selling 500 copies in Leeds alone each week, whilst the first issue of the *Secular Review* sold over 400 in the district, three-quarters of which went after Bradlaugh's lectures in Heckmondwike and Shipley.[24] Even so, such sales need to be put into perspective: as W.

Cooke Taylor told the Social Science Association in 1867, 'I think we may almost place irreligious literature in the same category with immoral,' by which he meant that it held a small market on the fringe of the reading public.[25] Though there was to be a great expansion in the amount of freethought literature in the next two decades, this was to remain its position. As with lecture audiences, the machinery of the religious interest was far larger and obtained much greater success than anything the freethinkers could manage. Nevertheless, the periodicals of the freethought movement did succeed in making an impact out of all proportion to their size and their editors each developed special relationships with their readers which cannot be valued purely in terms of circulation figures. As Foote told his readers shortly before his death, in a survey of the *Freethinker* over the years:

The relations between the Editor of the *Freethinker* and its readers have never been those of an ordinary newspaper and its readers. They have been those of fellow-workers in a common cause. We were not writing to please purchasers but to inspire evangelists. The consequence has been that in the majority of cases the *Freethinker* has reached its clientele as a weekly message of encouragement and inspiration.[26]

For many people the *National Reformer* and the *Freethinker were* the Secularist movement, for they held it together.

*The National Reformer*

After resuming the editorship of the *National Reformer* in 1866, Bradlaugh built up both the paper and its circulation, transforming it into a high-class weekly review which provided sixteen foolscap pages for 2*d*. To break even, Bradlaugh needed a weekly sale of 4,000 copies, with a further 500 copies for a reasonable profit, and this he had achieved by 1872, doubling the 1867 circulation figure of 3,000. The circulation then seems to have followed the general health of the movement, reaching a peak during the blasphemy prosecutions of 1882-83, but declining in later 1880s as Bradlaugh travelled less and as the public excitement associated with his parliamentary struggle waned. After a brief revival under J. M. Robertson's editorship after Bradlaugh's death in 1891, the circulation stagnated and then fell below that necessary for survival. Robertson closed it down on 1 October 1893, and replaced it with a monthly *Free Review*, which at 1*s* appealed to a more select market. Mrs Bonner started her own 3*d* monthly, the *Reformer*, in March 1897 but it lasted only until the beginning of 1899.[27]

The staff of the paper changed much over the years, as did its contents and emphases, closely reflecting Bradlaugh's personal career as Reform League agitator, republican, birth-control-er, M.P. and politician. As he recognised in 1886:

> The *National Reformer* has, for this last twenty-six years, been a sort of personal diary in which those who cared had companionship in our life. This has identified it very much with the career of one man, but we trust not to the detriment of the cause in which that man's work has been done.[28]

In the late 1860s the leading contributors were Dr George Sexton ('Melampus'), J. P. Adams, Henry Atkinson, Charles Cattell and James Thompson ('B. V.'), whose poem, 'The City of Dreadful Night', was first published in the *National Reformer* in 1874.[29] Sexton fell from favour in 1871 when he joined the International, and then became a spiritualist; and Thompson quarrelled with Bradlaugh in 1875; but by this time Annie Besant was on the scene. She became sub-editor in place of Charles Watts in 1877, and in the same year the Bradlaugh girls also began to contribute articles and J. H. Levy ('Dialecticus'), who taught political economy at the City of London College, joined the staff as a regular contributor on politics, economics, ethics, psychology, philosophy and religion. With the addition of Edward Aveling in 1879, the *National Reformer* had a formidable team of highly qualified writers whose exceptionally able articles made the *Reformer* an outstanding publication. Increasingly, though, its pages were filled with detailed accounts of Bradlaugh's struggle and his lawsuits. For those who liked this sort of thing, it provided a gripping story, week by week (with supplements) relating the heroic struggle of light against darkness. In the 1880s the paper was distinctly more of a political and philosophical journal than before Bradlaugh's entry into Parliament. In 1884 the substitution of Robertson for Aveling maintained the intellectual calibre of the staff, but the break-up began in 1887, when Mrs Besant gave up her co-editorship; Levy retired in ill health in 1890; Mrs Besant ceased to contribute after Bradlaugh's death the following year. There was little now left of contemporary interest in the paper, and Robertson's decision to replace it with a review in 1893 was a logical consequence of the paper losing the N.S.S. news to Foote's *Freethinker* in 1890.

The format of the paper changed little, week by week, between 1866 and 1893, and the devoted reader was able to spend many happy hours on his twopence-worth of enlightenment. It is hard to escape the conclusion, though, that the contents cannot have been easy to read. There was much earnest, intellectual matter, but little

of humour and no concession to the sort of person who seems to have
thrived on the vulgarity of the outdoor lectures. Those who accused
Bradlaugh of being a merely 'negative' freethinker cannot have been
thinking of his paper. That so many people did read it is a
remarkable testimony to the intellectual abilities and appetites of
some Secularists, and possibly an indication that, by the 1880s, it
was appealing also to a middle-class readership.

*The Freethinker*
Foote started the *Freethinker* in the knowledge that the *National
Reformer* was rather heavy, and, though he gradually made it more
sober as he grew older, it never completely lost its delightful sense of
the ridiculous. As one correspondent wrote in 1881, 'Your paper has
acted like a good tonic to a sluggish and anaemic Freethought
literary system.'[30]

The policy of the *Freethinker*, from which Foote never wavered, was
to be an aggressive, anti-Christian organ. The style was deliberately
popular. Each week two columns, headed 'Acid Drops' and 'Sugar
Plums', contained snippets of anti-Christian and pro-freethinking
news respectively. As Foote explained, these headings were 'not
sublime phrases, but there is no harm in them. The public now-a-
days is in a great hurry, and you must attract its attention before you
can be heard.'[31]

The first issue, dated May 1881, was edited by Foote and sub-
edited by J. M. Wheeler. It ran as an eight-page foolscap monthly
until September, when it became a weekly, with 'Special' issues at
Christmas (1881-89) and in the summer (1884-86). The size was
increased to twelve pages in April 1889, and sixteen pages in
October 1891. Not till 1893 was the price put up to 2*d*. The general
appearance was not dissimilar from that of the *National Reformer*,
although the whole tone was much freer. In addition to the 'Acid
Drops' and 'Sugar Plums' there was a 'Profane Jokes' section, and,
above all, there was a weekly cartoon.

Foote may have got his idea for this from George Standring's
*Republican*, which carried political and social cartoons from June
1881, but it was an advertisement in *The Times*, asking for assistance
to suppress *La Bible Amusante*, which gave Foote the inspiration to
reproduce a weekly comic cartoon. The impact was astonishing. The
circulation of the *Freethinker* soared in 1882 to 10,000 a week.
Moderate freethinkers like Malcolm Quin were shocked, and
Christians shuddered with horror.[32] It was these cartoons which
were largely responsible for Foote's being prosecuted for blasphemy

in 1882, and they were dropped by Aveling during Foote's imprisonment, but they were resumed in 1884 and continued until 1889. Not all were from *La Bible Amusante*, and few were really funny: they were, rather, crude sketches of biblical scenes interpreted literally to show their inherent absurdity;[33] or satirical cartoons on some anti-clerical or freethought theme, occasionally with bitter social comment—as in the Christmas issue for 1882, in which the first cartoon depicted 'A Merry Christmas Inside and Out', showing a clerical banquet within and a starving family outside in the snow. Contrary to popular impression among historians, few showed characters with Jewish features and they were not anti-semitic. After much criticism, in 1888 Foote took the unusual step of submitting the continuance of these cartoons to a referendum of his readership: only 10 per cent of the subscribers replied, and Foote's conclusion from the complicated pattern of cross-voting was 'What the great bulk of [our readers] think is still a mystery'—though the number of votes cast shows the circulation of the *Freethinker* at this time to have been around 4,000, with an estimated readership of 12,000. Foote continued with the cartoons until March 1889, when he found that dropping them made no difference to his circulation.[34]

The enlargement of the *Freethinker* to twelve pages in 1889 signalled Foote's growing importance in the N.S.S., and from 1890, when he became president, his paper took over from the *National Reformer* as the principal organ of the movement. It now acquired some of the regular *National Reformer* features, especially its 'Guide to the Lecture Room', and, with sixteen pages from 1891, its circulation, which had dropped and then stagnated in the later 1880s, began to improve: during 1890-92 Foote claimed it had gone up by as much as 50 per cent, and a police report in 1894 put the circulation at 'about five to six thousand weekly, a large number of which are sent into the provinces'. The circulation, though, was never sufficient to cover costs, except in the very early days. The decline of Secularism hit the paper hard, and by 1908 Foote had reached the conclusion that he could no longer hope to reach a popular market.[35]

The *Freethinker* represented one aspect of Foote's character. The other, more serious, side also yearned for expression, and he occasionally tried to start a paper in which to develop his more constructive views. There had been the *Secularist* in 1876-77; then in January 1879 he began a short-lived 6d monthly called the *Liberal*, and in January 1883 he resumed it under the title *Progress*, which was edited by Aveling (assisted by Eleanor Marx) during Foote's imprisonment. Aveling made it a socialist paper, but under Foote it again became radical, and lasted until 1887. He had orginally hoped to reach the wider radical public, but in 1886 he had to admit he was reaching only freethinkers.[36] In 1888 he tried again, with the *Radical Leader*, which lasted less than a year, and in 1903 with the *Pioneer*, devoted to non-political questions but aimed at a wider audience than the *Freethinker*—it lasted only eighteen months. Foote had clearly found his *forte* with the *Freethinker*. As a non-socialist, and as a specialised journalist unwilling to enter the general market, Foote's appeal was strictly limited, although what he did write in the *Freethinker* is not without interest.

### *The Secular Review* and *The Agnostic Journal*

The third major freethought publication was the *Secular Review*, originally started by G. J. Holyoake in August 1876, and edited by Charles Watts from February 1877. A new series was started in June 1877, uniting the *Review* with Foote's *Secularist* under joint editorship, but this arrangement lasted only until February 1878. Watts then ran the paper on his own until 1882, when W. S. Ross joined him, and from August 1884 it became Ross's paper alone. He renamed it the *Agnostic Journal* in 1889, and it continued under that title until shortly after Ross's death in December 1906. Like the other freethought journals, its circulation reached a peak in 1883, when it began to pay its way for a short time, but Ross's widow disclosed at the end that her husband had always had to subsidise it.[37] Physically the paper resembled the *National Reformer* and the later *Freethinker*, with sixteen foolscap pages for 2*d* a week, and the contents were an amalgam of the *Reformer's* weight and the *Freethinker's* wit, though the style became increasingly eccentric under Ross's editorship. The paper's peculiar feature was an editorial column called 'At Random', described by one correspondent as 'a strange *mélange* of exact erudition, grim humour, blistering irony, fiery eloquence, stately poetry, tearful pathos, and rollicking fun'.[38] Here, and in The Wasp's 'Flings and Stings' column, the Bradlaughites were chided for their many sins.

### *Other papers*

These papers were joined from time to time by smaller papers. G. J. Holyoake could never keep out of print for long, though his various attempts to revive his *Reasoner*, and his monthly *Present Day* (1883-86), were egocentric productions of little importance. Another review of the 1880s, Annie Besant's *Our Corner*, was far more significant, beginning as an 'improving' family magazine in 1883, becoming more serious and political after 1885, and turning into a socialist magazine with literary features in 1886-87. It was never overtly Secularist, though many Secularists as well as socialists wrote for it, and, when Besant was busy with her trade union activities and the *Link* in 1888 the concluding numbers were written largely by Bradlaugh, Robertson, Mary Reed and G. B. Shaw.

Apart from this, the most important papers were the *Secular Chronicle* and a group of publications which came out independently of the N.S.S. in the 1890s.

The *Secular Chronicle* was the most successful local paper to be established by freethinkers in the Bradlaugh years. It was begun by George Reddalls, a young Birmingham printer, in 1872 as a quarto $\frac{1}{2}d$ monthly, later doubled in size to sixteen pages for $1d$. The main contributors at first were a group of Midland activists, including Thomas Evans, Francis Neale, Charles Cattell, and H. V. Mayer, who contributed a 'Facetiae for Freethinkers' column, modelled on the one light spot which Austin Holyoake ran in the *National Reformer*. After losing £50 on the first volume, the second was reduced to twelve pages, and brought out weekly from October 1874. It now gained an extensive circulation across the country and became a useful mouthpiece for the non-Bradlaughite party, but it still did not break even. When Reddalls died of typhoid in October 1875, aged only twenty-eight, his father sold it to Harriet Law, who reduced the price to $1d$ and extended its programme to cover a wide range of topics under the general headings of atheism, republicanism, women's rights and Owenite co-operation. Mrs Law's own background as a member of the International showed itself in July 1874, when she included a portrait of Marx with a brief biography—the earliest friendly recognition of Marx in the pages of a freethought paper; a month later she gave Marx column space to refute George Howell's 'History of the International' which had appeared in the *Nineteenth Century*, something no other editor would give him.[39] Another unusual feature of the paper was a 'Ladies', Page', 'appropriated to the advocacy of those political, social, and domestic matters that especially effect women, knowing as we do, that the world's progress will be accelerated a thousand fold by their emancipation'.[40] At the end of 1878 Mrs Law no longer felt able to support the paper, which she then handed over to a joint-stock company. The latter body never really made much progress, and the gallant little paper came to an end. Under Reddalls it had been sympathetic to Holyoake's view of Secularism; under Mrs Law it was strictly impartial, which meant in effect that the opponents of Bradlaugh looked to its columns for a free voice in the crisis of 1877.

The leading local paper of the 1890s was the *Truth Seeker*, which was produced in Bradford as a penny monthly by John Grange of the Bradford Secular Society, assisted by Aurelis B. Wakefield of Hipperholme, and later by J. W. Gott of Bradford. At first the paper was a sober little production of twelve quarto pages, devoting itself to both local and national freethought and carrying each week a photograph and biography of a freethought leader—no doubt to give it a regular sale. After the end of the third volume in April 1897, the history of the paper becomes somewhat uncertain, as no complete run has survived.[41] J. W. Gott became editor in January 1900, and he began the practice of publishing cartoons from the New York *Truth Seeker*. The paper now became the organ of Gott's personal campaigns. Pack's blasphemous 'Adam the Dust Man' first appeared in its columns in August 1903, and reports of the blasphemy campaigns were written up as 'Pack and the Police' in September. By 1905 the paper contained nothing but cartoons—twenty-one of them in eleven pages, with a final page of advertisements for Gott's clothing business.

Another freethought paper in this more light-hearted vein was W. J. Ramsey's *Jerusalem Star*, 'Being a reprint of a journal published before and after the Flood', edited by 'Le Vitty Cuss'. This ran from June 1895 to September 1896 and was a four-page penny monthly, the contents of which comprised almost entirely Old Testament stories reported as modern news: the first issue, for example, had a headline, 'Terrible Flood! Many thousands drowned. Heart rending scenes. Only ten people saved'. It was a good jest, though the *Freethinker* boycotted it, and the anonymous sender of one copy to the Home Office was clearly not amused. This was, as the *Agnostic Journal* said, 'lower' as opposed to 'higher' criticism.[42]

The *Jerusalem Star* gave some space to criticisms of the N. S. S., but far more bitter in its attacks on Foote was *Secular Work*: it too was a penny monthly, published for a year from May 1896, and it was used by George Standring and J. P. Gilmour to rally the opposition which was beginning to form into the Freethought Federation. It failed not least because the *Freethinker*, *Jerusalem Star* and *Truth Seeker* all refused to advertise it.[43] In February 1897 Standring launched a four-page 'casual publication, issued for gratuitous circulation' to test the market for a weekly publication. It was named the *Radical*, after the long-running monthly political paper which he had earlier edited under the successive titles of *Republican Chronicle* (1875-78),

*Republican* (1879-86) and *Radical* (1886-89). The experiment was not
entirely successful, but in 1898 he made another attempt with
*Reason*, a weekly ½d paper aimed at 'the mass of the people in our
movement' to serve the Freethought Federation.[44] Like the other
papers of the 1890s, it too was very short-lived. The times were past
when Secularism could support new papers and new organisations.
It was the N.S.S. and Foote's *Freethinker* that survived.

## Publishing

The work of publishing the propaganda of freethought was a whole
business in itself. As a result of the quarrel over the Knowlton
Pamphlet, Bradlaugh and Besant withdrew all N.S.S. business from
Watts and started their own Freethought Publishing Company at 28
Stonecutter Street under the management of W. J. Ramsey.
Business was brisk in the early 1880s, and the company expanded in
1882 to 63 Fleet Street, on the opposite corner of Bouverie Street to
Richard Carlile's old shop; and in 1884 Arthur Bonner (son of a
clergyman prominent in the Reform League), who was to marry
Hypatia Bradlaugh the following year, became manager of a
separate printing department. In 1885 the landlord of 63 Fleet Street
went bankrupt and, rather than risk expulsion, Bradlaugh and
Besant took up the full lease. The business came to an end shortly
before Bradlaugh's death when his partnership with Besant was
dissolved. Their interests had become too diverse. Arthur Bonner
continued as a printer, and the publishing went to Robert Forder,
who had been publisher at the old Stonecutter Street address since
1886.[45]

Foote's *Freethinker* was born at Stonecutter Street, which became
the home of his Progressive Publishing Company, managed by
Ramsey, after Bradlaugh had moved out to 63 Fleet Street. In 1885
Foote also began printing on his account. Previously he had owned
the type but the actual printing had been done on commission. This
made his work vulnerable, as when the authorities prevailed upon
the printer, E. W. Whittle, not to produce the *Freethinker* for 23 July
1882. In 1886 he moved the business to more spacious
accommodation at 14 Clerkenwell Green, Ramsey coming with him
to manage the printing works and handing the Stonecutter Street
shop over to Forder. Foote continued his own printing until 1894,
when he transferred it to C. A. Watts. In 1899 he launched a new
Freethought Publishing Company to give his work the benefit of
limited liability protection, but because the *Freethinker* never paid he

took it over again on his personal liability in 1908, transferring his other publishing to the Pioneer Press, which remained the N.S.S. publisher long after his death.[46]

The business at 17 Johnson's Court was continued by Charles Albert Watts after his father's emigration. Here he was able to make the biggest breakthrough of all in freethought publishing. By trade both he and his father were printers, unlike Bradlaugh, Besant and Foote, who were primarily journalists. Not only did this give the younger Watts entire control over the processes of production, it also made him a true professional in a business in which the others were amateurs. Whereas they never made a profit, C. A. Watts was a business man as well, able to combine the shrewd eye of the publisher with a genuine desire to advance the cause of freethought in which he had been brought up.

His first periodical publication was the *Agnostic Annual*, which began life as a 6*d* booklet, sixty-four pages long, in 1884; it became the *Agnostic Annual and Ethical Review*, to meet the changing times and market, in 1901, and the *R.P.A. Annual and Ethical Review* in 1908. For this work he secured the pens of leading figures of the day, including T. H. Huxley, who contributed to a symposium on Agnosticism in the first issue. This was respectable freethought indeed, and Watts's market was largely that towards which G. J. Holyoake had struggled, somewhat prematurely, in vain. Watts saw that a younger, better-educated generation was growing up, who could be reached through quality literature at a low price. His next venture into publishing came the following year when he began his *Literary Guide*, 'a Monthly Record and Review of Liberal and Advanced Publications', which gave his readers 'a complete record of the best liberal publications in this country and of the more important ones published in foreign countries', including, of course, his own.[47] From June 1893 he also commenced monthly supplements, each of which condensed the argument of some book into four pages. In this way the public could become acquainted with the works and ideas of Leslie Stephen, W. E. H. Lecky, T. H. Buckle, Herbert Spencer, J. G. Frazer, E. Haeckel, Winwood Reade, Ludwig Büchner, Grant Allen and Edward Carpenter, among others.

*The Rationalist Press Association (R.P.A.)*
The next logical step was for Watts to issue as many of these works as possible for himself, and here he developed one of the most important ideas in modern publishing. In 1890, at 17 Johnson's Court, a Propaganda Press Fund was launched with C. A. Watts as

secretary, 'To assist in securing the amendment of the law which sanctions the confiscation of property left for anti-theological purposes, and to promote the issuing, advertising, and circulation of publications devoted to Freethought and advanced Religious Reform'.[48] Apart from Watts, the leading members were Dr Richard Bithell, F. J. Gould, Frederick Millar, and G. J. Holyoake, who was to become chairman. Commencing with £100 and the remaining 700 copies of Bythell's *Agnostic Problems*, their first publication was a penny pamphlet by Frederick Millar on *Darwinism and Religious Thought*, which appeared in April 1891, followed in the same year by Samuel Laing's *Agnosticism and Immortality* and Amos Waters's *Humanity and Dogma*. In May 1893 the title of the organisation became the Rationalist Press Committee, and then the Rationalist Press Association, which was launched in 1899 with an appeal for £1,000. By now respectability was assured.[49]

The R.P.A. was, in effect, a subscription book club, with a minimum annual subscription of half a guinea (later reduced to 5*s*), and it was controlled by the votes of its members, initially at the rate of one vote for each half-guinea subscribed. By 1900 membership had already exceeded 100, in 1906 it passed the 1,000 mark and was well on the way to 3,000 by the outbreak of war in 1914. The total income, plus balance brought forward, in 1900 was £257; by 1914-15 it was £2,361, with an additional £468 due in legacies, and there was sufficient capital for £2,000 to be invested in War Loans and £1,000 to be lent to the Treasury.[50]

One of the earliest works to be published by the R.P.A., Joseph McCabe's translation of Ernst Haeckel's *Weltplätsel*—*The Riddle of the Universe*—was the kind of success of which publishers dream. Within a year the first 2,000 were nearly sold out. A favourable review by Robert Blatchford in the *Clarion* brought a flood of correspondence, both for and against the book, over the next two years, and the cheap reprint of *The Riddle* had sold 100,000 copies by 1905; by which time the R.P.A. sixpenny reprint series, which had commenced with an edition of Huxley's *Lectures and Essays* in 1902, had run to twenty volumes, selling three-quarters of a million copies. This breakthrough into the mass market illustrates Watts's genius. With a gift of £1,000 from George Anderson (which caused Foote to break with Charles Watts, senior), and an agreement with Macmillan to share their imprint, the R.P.A. had acquired both the means and the respectability to move into the world of conventional mass publishing. In 1905 the R.P.A. turned its attention also to platform propagandist work, and appealed for two thousand shillings for an R.P.A. van. The principal lecturers were J. M. Robertson, Joseph McCabe and Hypatia Bradlaugh Bonner. In 1911 Watts launched another new series, 'Pamphlets for the Million', which, offering up to twenty-four pages for $\frac{1}{2}d$ and up to sixty-four pages for $1d$ further penetrated the lower-middle-class market with freethought works. The series included such diverse authors as McCabe, Laing, Haeckel, Ingersoll, and Paine, whose *Age of Reason* cost $2d$ for 124 pages. The *Daily Mirror* in 1913 gave a portrait of the sort of person who was now buying freethought material: Helena Gunning had won the top L.C.C. Scholarship at the age of twelve, but after a further year's schooling had had to go out in 1901 as a nursery governess after passing her Oxford Local Examination in Religious Knowledge, English Grammar, Literature, and French. On her shelves this remarkable young woman had Paine's *Age of Reason*, Grant Allen's *Evolution of the Idea of God* (R.P.A. cheap reprint no. 7), and J. A. Farrer's *Paganism and Christianity* (R.P.A. cheap reprint no. 43). Freethought propaganda had indeed come a long way since the days of Bradlaugh, though the presence of Paine is a useful reminder that it was the method more than the content that had changed.[51]

## Content

In periodicals like the *National Reformer*, and in the increasing number of rationalist books and pamphlets made available by the R.P.A. the arguments advanced against religion were philosophical and scientific, based on an acquaintance with recent intellectual developments. In periodicals like the *Freethinker*, the ground was contested more narrowly on the authority of the Bible. The two levels of approach were seldom joined. On the lower level, the anti-intellectual approach was common to both the man in the freethought audience and the man in the pew: each stimulated and justified the other; and each regarded his more philosophical colleagues with mistrust as traitors yielding to the argument of the enemy. This is not to say that some serious members of a working-class audience were not capable of appreciating the finer points of the more sophisticated arguments, if presented in a palatable way,[52] but what most wanted was, above all, the Bible. Extreme Secularism, as the mirror image of extreme Protestantism, lived by the Bible—*homines unius libri*. The Ashton Secular Mutual Improvement Society in 1867 announced a programme which, out of context, could be taken for that of a Protestant Bible class:

Next Sunday we shall commence with reading and perusing the Bible, beginning with Genesis. Now is the time for lovers of knowledge to assemble together on a Sunday to instruct one another.[53]

Few freethinkers felt the need for anything else, and if they read any biblical criticism it was likely to be Paine's *Age of Reason*. William Kent surmised (perhaps unfairly) that this was all that John Burns had ever read on the subject—if he had read any of J. M. Robertson's works they 'would have taken him into realms beyond his depth, partly because they were outside his interests'; George Lansbury, as a boy in London, saw Bradlaugh many times, 'but I could not understand very much of what he was teaching'; Snowden heard Bradlaugh debate 'Has or is Man a Soul?' at Burnley in 1879, and found 'The subject was far too abstruse for my comprehension'; one effect of Huxley's *Essays* on Ben Tillet was 'to puzzle my ill-trained brains'. If these men had problems (one wonders if they ever coped with Marx!) then the ordinary working man certainly had them. The militants did not deny this, but argued that the mere destruction of the Bible was the beginning of free thought.[54]

The Bible therefore contained within it all that was necessary unto freethought salvation. 'Searching the Scriptures,' G. W. Foote proclaimed,

is the best cure for believing in the Scriptures. Many a man has been made a Freethinker by having his attention drawn to texts he never suspected. . . . There is 'rot' enough in the Bible to damn a thousand volumes. Some of it is unscientific, some of it is silly, and some of it is downright beastly. Anybody who put together such stuff nowadays, and called it God's Word, would be regarded as a lunatic or a criminal, and sent to the asylum or the gaol.[55]

The truth of the Bible indeed rested on its supernatural origins. When Bishop Wilberforce suggested a Revised Version at the Convocation of Canterbury in 1870, Bishop Wordsworth warned, 'Beware lest by altering the text of the authorised version of the Bible, you shake the faith of many.'[56] In a generation which began with *Essays and Reviews* (1860) and closed with Dean Farrar's *The Bible: its Meaning and Supremacy* (1897), the freethinkers could claim that the Christians were doing their work for them. The advent of 'Higher Criticism' seemed a justification of the freethought position. The conviction of the freethinkers was that, ultimately, Protestantism would lose its Bible and yield to freethought, leaving the final choice (in Ingersoll's words) between 'Rome or Reason'.[57] More perceptively, Cohen realised that 'Superstition with a plausible exterior is ever the more dangerous', and when the new ideas began to penetrate the most open of the Nonconformist

Bethels—R. J. Campbell's City Temple—the freethinkers' task did indeed become more difficult. William Kent's mother cannot have been the only one who 'rose to the New Theology like a fish to a tempting and long-looked-for bait.'[58]

Nevertheless, the mainstay of freethought propaganda remained biblical criticism of a variety which had been common in the first part of the nineteenth century. There is little difference between Robert Cooper's *The Holy Scriptures Analyzed* (first published in the late 1830s), and G. W. Foote's and W. P. Ball's *The Bible Handbook*(1888), which was designed for easy reference when a freethinker found himself in discussion with a Christian, and gave examples which illustrate the ways in which freethinkers throughout the nineteenth century attacked the Bible. There were lists of quotations, arranged under the headings: Bible Contradictions; Bible Absurdities; Atrocities; Unfulfilled Prophecies and Broken Promises; and Bible Immoralities, Indecencies and Obscenities—the later giving freethinkers adequate replies to Christians who applied such epithets to them.

Foote was himself far too acute to think that this was all there was to biblical criticism, and Bradlaugh seems to have indulged in it less in his writings than in his lectures, but the approach was felt to be justified by the attitudes of some Christians themselves.[59] Even when the *Guardian* had long accepted the fallibility of Scripture, the *Rock* was still standing by 'the Old Book'. Defences of Christianity in terms of biblical literalism and texts torn out of context demanded replies in kind.[60] Mr Gladstone provided the Secularists with many happy hours, first with his concern over the Gadarene Swine in controversy with Huxley, and later in controversy with Ingersoll in defence of 'The Impregnable Rock of Holy Scripture'. Mr Gladstone was indeed a man of the people—in fact, in not believing in the *literal* truth of Genesis, but only in its *inspiration*, he was well ahead of many—and he was not alone in his conservatism.[61] In 1892 a letter appeared in *The Times* which Ross hailed as a justification for his own onslaught on Scripture, entitled *God and His Book*. Signed by a number of prominent Anglicans, including bishops, deans archdeacons and canons as well as the lower clergy, it called for 'A Declaration on the Truth of Holy Scripture', in view of the way in which the Bible was under attack:

We therefore solemnly profess and declare our unfeigned belief in all the canonical Scriptures of the Old and New Testaments as handed down to us by the undivided Church in the original languages. We believe they are inspired by the Holy Ghost, that they are what they profess to be, that they mean what they say and that they declare incontrovertibly the actual historical truth in all records, both of past events and of the delivery of predictions to be thereafter fulfilled.[62]

As late as 1908, Joseph McCabe was able to find a clerical opponent to discuss with him the proposition 'That the agreement of the first chapter of Genesis with the accredited facts of modern science is such that its composition can only be accounted for as the result of supernatural knowledge'.[63]

Out on the streets such conservatism gave the freethinkers everything they could wish for. The clock had stood still. As Charles Booth's reporter on Peckham Rye noted of the Secularist speaker there on Unity Sunday:

The speaker lacked all reverence. It was a narrow Christianity that he attacked, and his criticisms of the Bible were of the old-fashioned type for which the doctrine of literal inspiration alone affords any excuse. But round him on neighbouring platforms were plenty of speakers whose views are sure to be met in this way, one, for example, on the Unity platform, who, holding up the Bible, said, 'I believe every word in this book; I believe in the cover too, for it keeps all the rest together.'[64]

The most important modification in the theological debate between the two halves of the nineteenth century lay in the manner of conducting the science versus religion controversy. Whereas earlier discussions had centred on the implications of geological discoveries for an understanding of Genesis, later discussions were concerned with the implications of the theory of evolution for the natural and spiritual history of Man. Darwin's name, despite himself, was at the heart of the matter. This is not to claim that the conflict between religion and science was inevitable, as the freethinkers thought. Huxley himself wrote in 1885, 'The antagonism of science is not to religion, but to the heathen survivals and bad philosophy under which religion herself is often well-nigh crushed.'[65] This implied the secularisation of science and a strict demarcation of legitimate fields of interest, theology being left to speculate upon those realms about which science could only be agnostic. However, given the traditional, all-embracing claims of theology, as exemplified most crudely in the continued defence of Genesis as consistent with modern science, there were many partisans prepared to defend and attack religion in terms of such warfare.

After the initial disquiet at Darwin's *Origin of Species*, the theological world was divided over whether and how far to accept the theory of evolution as expressed by Darwin, and there was no clear division of opinion between Christians and agnostics of the kind implied by the celebrated confrontation between Wilberforce and Huxley in 1860. What is clear, though, is that the less men understood about Darwin, the more they thought they knew. Lord Balfour's barber, who talked of 'the doctrine of evolution, Darwin and Huxley and the lot of them—hashed up somehow with the good time coming and the universal brotherhood, and I don't know what else',[66] was probably typical of many who listened to freethought lectures on Sundays. What men like this sensed, rather than understood, was that *something* momentous had happened even though, as Foote complained in 1885, Gladstone could continue to write as though Darwin had never lived.[67]

Something momentous had indeed happened. As Harriet Martineau wrote to G. J. Holyoake of the *Origin*

What a work it is!—overthrowing (if true) revealed religion on the one hand, and natural (as far as Final Causes and Design are concerned) on the other. The range and mass of knowledge take away one's breath.[68]

But Darwin was, surprisingly, taken up only slowly by the Secularists. Much of what they needed from him they had already from different sources. A materialist theory of the human mind had long been current: Robert Cooper's *Immortality of the Soul* (1852) was republished by Edward Truelove as late as 1887, when Foote regarded it still as 'among the best popular expositions of materialism made in this country'. The work of Darwin was, of course, noticed in the periodicals and referred to in lectures—Dr Sexton, for example, lectured at the Hall of Science on 20 April 1871 on Darwin's *Descent of Man*—but a full appreciation had to await the advent of Edward Aveling. His first named contribution to the *National Reformer* was a series entitled 'Darwin and his Views', which appeared in January, February and March 1879, with a further series from November 1879 to September 1880. After this amount of exposure, no freethinker could again claim to be ignorant of Darwin.[69]

The application of Darwinism to freethought, however, was indirect. Much of what passed for Darwinism was simply the evolution of Erasmus Darwin or Herbert Spencer. 'Social Darwinism' was a misnomer. Darwinian 'materialism' entered freethought by way of Germany, in the writings of Ludwig Büchner and Ernst Haekel, though Büchner's most famous works—*Force and Matter* (1855) and *Nature and Spirit* (1857)—both preceded the publication of Darwin's views.[70] As Edward Clodd wrote on the jubilee of Darwinism in 1908, it was really Huxley's *Evidences as to Man's Place in Nature* (1863) that marked out the battleground. Biology itself, and even theories of evolution in the animal kingdom, were compatible with theology; it was the new anthropology, concerned with the evolution of man, which was not.[71]

When freethinkers did use 'Darwinism' it was to attack the concept of the mind as a unique and non-physical characteristic of man. Büchner's essay *Mind in Animals* (1880) was almost immediately translated into English by Annie Besant. Alice Bradlaugh's only publication was a lecture on *Mind Considered as a Bodily Function*. In 1889 W. P. Ball in the *Freethinker* asked 'Can a non-intelligent cause produce an intelligent effect', in which he appealed to Darwin and Lamarck to explain why there was no need for Christians to look outside nature for the source of intelligence in man because 'The gradual evolution of intelligence has obviously been brought about by the struggle for existence and the survival of the fittest through innumerable generations.[72] The use of Darwin's theory of natural selection added greater sophistication to the argument about the nature of mind without changing it in any fundamental way, and, to an audience prepared to believe that science was truth, such theories appeared obviously true. Only a few warning voices were concerned lest freethinkers erect Darwinism into a new superstition to be accepted uncritically and unintelligently.[73]

Materialism went through a similar change during the nineteenth century.[74] Crude, mechanistic materialism, like evolution, had long been a part of the freethought inheritance, but Bradlaugh was one of the first popular lecturers to refine the concept away from the determinism of the Enlightenment towards the Monism of Spinoza's philosophy.[75] By the later nineteenth century this had become the standard position, though it is doubtful how many freethinkers really understood what Monism was. Its clearest exponent was probably Chapman Cohen, who outlined its kernel as 'the evolution of all existing past forms, and so on through an endless sequence, without the intrusion or co-operation of an external and independent force, at any stage of the process'.[76] That is, the traditional dualism of mind and matter was abolished, not in favour of matter, but in favour of one substance incorporating what had traditionally been called mind and what had traditionally been called matter. The great gospel of Monism, putting materialism upon a Darwinian basis, was Haeckel's *Riddle of the Universe*, which made its impact on England through the R.P.A. F. A. Ridley, who became president of the N.S.S. in 1951, thought that just as the Bradlaugh era of Secularism was characterised by politics, and the Foote era by the attack on the Bible, the Cohen era saw the development of materialism as the philosophy of atheism. Though this scarely does Bradlaugh justice, it is true that, as the Bible ceased to be important in the twentieth century, philosophical materialism became the principal ground for debate.[77]

Though the basic arguments in the nineteenth century were modified rather than changed, and though even the process of modification was slow and uncertain among many followers of Secularism, the periodicals do show an awareness of modern writings and ideas on religious subjects. Edward B. Tylor's *Primitive Culture* (1871) was regarded almost as highly as Darwin's works and, together with his study of the *Early History of Mankind* and his *Anthropology*, it was recommended by Foote to his readers in 1888. J. M. Wheeler was particularly interested in anthropology, and cited J. G. Frazer's *Golden Bough* in an article on *Yom Kippur* in 1892. Foote later described the *Golden Bough* as 'one of the half dozen really great books that a serious student of human affairs meets with in a lifetime'. Indeed, as Sidney Hartland explained in the *R.P.A. Annual* for 1913, the value of anthropology to the freethinker was that it could not be countered simply by a new gloss on a text of *Genesis*; instead it set the Judaeo-Christian view of man in a non-Christian context.[78]

The position of intellectual freethought in 1905 can be gauged from a list of 'The Hundred Best Books from the freethought point of view' which W. Mann published in the *Freethinker* in that year. Significantly there is only one work by Charles Bradlaugh in it—his notes on Genesis, a work of biblical scholarship using techniques of internal criticism, and not a particularly novel piece of work. In the section of the list on Evolution, Darwin is not represented, but Aveling's *Darwin Made Easy* is, along with Huxley, Tyndall, Winwood Reade and Spencer. The list on Atheism includes Hume, Feuerbach, Strauss, Büchner, Holyoake, Haeckel and Schopenhauer. Tyler, Spencer, Lubbock, Hume and Frazer are recommended on the Origin of Religion; Buckle, Lecky, Leslie Stephen, White, Draper and Gibbon among the Historians. The list is, not surprisingly, a mixture of old and new.[79] Some freethinkers would possibly have read some of these; few if any would have read all, though Thomas Alfred Jackson, a young socialist revolutionary of the Gott camp, shows what could be achieved. He was converted to freethought by reading G. H. Lewes's *History of Philosophy*; he then read Tolstoy, Blatchford and Huxley, followed by Marx, Engels, Spencer, Shaw, Bax, Nietzsche, Heine, Tyndall and Haeckel.[80] This was remarkable, but some among freethinkers of every generation were remarkable men.

*Notes*

1   *F.*, 4 January 1891.
2   F. R. Bird to Miss E. M. Vance, 24 March 1894, N.S.S., Organisation Committee, Minute Book.
3   E. g. at Birmingham in 1872—*S. C.*, 1 November 1872.
4   *F.*, 29 May 1887, 11 January 1891, 28 February 1897.
5   *N. R.*, 12 July 1874; *F.*, 28 October 1900.
6   *N. R.*, 13 February 1876, 26 June 1887, 18 March 1877, 26 April 1885, 5 October, 28 September 1890; *F.*, 1 January 1893, 23 February 1896.
7   *N. R.*, 23 April 1871.
8   *N. R.*, 23 September 1883; *F.*, 16 March 1913.
9   *Secular Work*, December 1896.
10  *S. R.*, 30 January 1886. The best collections of an eye-witness account of freethought meetings are by the Rev. C. M. Davies—*Heterodox London* (1874) and *Mystic London* (1875).
11  *Sunday Times*, 21 January 1912; see also *Birmingham Weekly Post*, 23 November 1907, and, for a similar complaint about Bradlaugh, the *Christian Evidence Journal*, August 1875.
12  *Bradlaugh and To-day*, p. 21; *F.*, 13 March 1887. Bradlaugh's notes for the lecture at Halifax in 1882 are in the possession of Mrs R. Corina.
13  *All the Year Round*, 16 July 1870; *S. C.*, 21 October 1877; *S. R.*, 28 June 1879; *F.*, 12 July 1896, 1 August 1897.
14  *F.*, May 1881; *Jerusalem Star*, September 1895.
15  *N. R.*, 23 May 1869; *S. C.*, 1 September 1872; *N. R.*, 4 February 1872; *F.*, 30 October 1904, 27 February 1898; *Secular Work*, November 1896.
16  *F.*, 1 August 1897.
17  E. g. Arthur Moss's lectures in the North East—*N. R.*, 17 August 1890, reprinted in E. Royle, *The Infidel Tradition*, pp. 111-14.
18  E. g. Mrs Besant at Hoyland in 1876—*N. R.*, 17 September 1876, reprinted in E. Royle, *op. cit.*, pp. 215-18.
19  E Royle, *Victorian Infidels*, pp. 203-6, 211; *N. R.*, 5 January 1868, 27 February 1870, 31 May, 28 June 1874, 4 July, 15 August 1875. Another 'champion' of Christianity was the Rev. A. J. Harrison, who debated with Bradlaugh in 1870, 1871 and 1872; with Watts in 1872; and with Foote in 1877.
20  *F.*, 9 April 1911.
21  E. g. *F.*, 13 October 1889; *S. R.*, 6 October 1877; *N. R.*, 6 August 1871.
22  *S. C.*, 21 October 1877.
23  *Catalogue of the Works sold by the Freethought Publishing Company*, November 1878, reprinted in J. Saville (ed.), *A Selection of the Political Pamphlets of Charles Bradlaugh* (New York, 1970); see also *F.*, 29 January 1899, 6 July

1901.

24  A. Besant, *An Autobiography*, p. 134; C. M. Davies, *Heterodox London*, II, p. 149; *Saturday Review*, 27 October 1866; *N. R.*, 9 January 1876; *S. R.*, 10 September 1876.

25  Quoted by Elie Reclus in an undated letter to G. J. Holyoake, Holyoake papers, Co-operative Union, no. 3797.

26  *F.*, 3 January 1915.

27  *N. R.*, 4 August 1867, 7 January 1872, 1 October 1893; *F.*, 15 October 1893, 10 December 1905; *N. R.*, 3, 10 September 1893.

28  *N. R.*, 3 January 1886.

29  *N. R.*, 22 March, 12, 26 April, 17 May 1874.

30  *F.*, 30 October 1881.

31  *F.*, May 1881.

32  *Republican*, May, June, July 1881; *F.*, 4 September 1881; *Republican*, May 1883; *F.*, 7 January 1883; M. Quin, *op. cit.*, pp. 68-9; T. Barclay, *op. cit.*, p. 48.

33  E.g. *F.*, 26 October 1884.

34  *F.*, 14 October 1888, 17-31 March 1889.

35  *F.*, 4 January, 25 October 1891, 21 February, 17 July, 18, 25 September 1892; Chief Inspector Melville's report, 23 October 1894, H. O. 45 10406/A 46794; *F.*, 25 March 1900, 6, 27 December 1903, 17 June 1906, 25 October 1908.

36  *F.*, 18 July 1886.

37  *S. R.*, 22 April 1882, 14 July 1883; *A. J.*, 23 February 1907.

38  *S. R.*, 17 April 1886.

39  *S. C.*, 7 July, 4 August 1878.

40  *S. C.*, 2 January 1876.

41  A. B. Wakefield's own set of the first three volumes is in the possession of Mrs R. Corina. There is then a gap before the British Library occasional copies begin with the second half of volume V (November 1898). The R.P.A. has some later issues beyond those held by the British Library, and the N.S.S. has a few odd copies. Percy Ward took over the paper briefly in the winter of 1901–02, when the paper was renamed the *Secularist*, but J. W. Gott continued it under its old title. The later copies are not dated.

42  *Jerusalem Star*, June 1895; H. O. 45 10406/A 46794 (9), 16 July 1895; *A. J.*, 28 December 1895.

43  *Secular Work*, June, October 1896.

44  *Reason*, 10 March 1898.

45  H. B. Bonner and J. M. Robertson, *op. cit.*, II, pp. 100-1. For Arthur Bonner see A. Bonner and C. B. Bonner, *Hypatia Bradlaugh Bonner* (London, 1942), pp. 41-2.

46  *F.*, 6 April 1884, 4 January 1885, 1 August, 5 September 1886, 22 April 1894, 16 July 1899, 13 September 1908.

47  *Watts's L. G.*, November 1885.

48  F. J. Gould, *Pioneers of Johnson's Court*, p. 12; see also A. G. Whyte, *The Story of the R. P. A., 1889-1949* (London, 1949).

49  *Watts's L. G.*, June, July 1890, April 1891; *A. J.*, 3 January 1891; *L. G.*,

February, July, August 1899; see also *Ethical World*, 29 July 1899. Samuel Laing was a former Senior Wrangler, lawyer and railway director; he was Liberal M. P. for Orkney and Shetland until 1886—*A. J.*, 3 September 1892, 14 August 1897.

50  Figures compiled from the Annual Reports as printed in the *L. G.* for March each year.

51  *Clarion*, 23 January 1903; *L. G.*, March 1905; A. G. Whyte, *op. cit.* pp. 52-6, 71, 74-6; *L. G.*, November 1905; G. S. Streatfield, 'The Challenge of Secularism', *London Quarterly Review*, CVI (4th series, vol. IX), January 1909, pp. 21-38, esp. pp. 27-8; *L. G.*, January 1913 (cover advertisement); *Daily Mirror*, 18 April 1913.

52  E. g. at Bethnal Green in 1890, according to Sam Standring—*N. R.*, 5 October 1890.

53  *N. R.*, 3 March 1867.

54  W. Kent, *John Burns, Labour's Lost Leader* (London, 1950), p. 300; *Bradlaugh and To-day*, p. 93; P. Snowden, *An Autobiography*, 2 vols. (London, 1934), I, pp. 43-4; B. Tillett, *Memories and Reflections* (London, 1931), p. 77. There may, of course, be an element of false modesty in these autobiographical recollections.

55  *F.*, 13 March 1887.

56  Quoted in W. O. Chadwick, *Victorian Church*, part II, 1860-1901 (London, 1970), p. 44.

57  E. g. Chilperic Edwards, *F.*, 26 February 1899; see also *N. R.*, 5, 19, 26 July 1885; *F.*, 26 July 1885, 30 April 1911, 4 January 1903; R. G. Ingersoll, *Rome or Reason: a reply to Cardinal Manning* (London, n.d.—first published in the *North American Review*, 1888).

58  *F.*, 5 January 1902; W. Kent, *The Testament of a Victorian Youth* (London, 1938), p. 177.

59  E. g. by Arthur Moss, *S. R.*, 9 August 1879.

60  See W. O. Chadwick, *op. cit.*, pp. 60-1, 64-5, 87, 408.

61  *F.*, 8 November 1885.

62  Quoted in *A. J.*, 3 January 1892.

63  *L. G.*, November 1908.

64  C. Booth, *Life and Labour*, 3rd series, III, pp. 187-8.

65  T. H. Huxley, 'The Interpreters of Genesis and the Interpreters of Nature', *Nineteenth Century* XVIII, nos. cv, cvi (November, December 1885), pp. 685-706, 849-60, esp. p. 860.

66  Quoted by D. Bowen, *The Idea of the Victorian Church* (Montreal, 1968), p. 156; see also J. Kent, *From Darwin to Blatchford* (London, 1966).

67  *F.*, 8 November 1885.

68  H. Martineau to G. J. Holyoake, n. d. [1859], Martineau papers, B. M. Add. Mss. 42, 726.

69  *F.*, 17 July 1887; *N. R.*, 23 April 1871, 19 January–2 March 1879, 16 November 1879–19 September 1880.

70  See J. Passmore, 'Darwin's Impact on British Metaphysics', *Victorian Studies*, III, no. 1 (September 1959), pp. 41-54.

71  *L. G.*, August 1908.

72  *F.*, 29 September 1889.

73 E. g. Constance F. Plumtre, 'The Progress of Liberty of Thought', *Agnostic Annual* (1898), pp. 6-9; R. F. Licorish, *F.*, 19 September 1915.
74 See B. Russell, *A. J.*, 13 December 1902.
75 E. Royle, *Victorian Infidels*, pp. 118-19; see, e. g., C. Bradlaugh, *Is there a God?* (1860), partly quoted in E. Royle, *The Infidel Tradition*, pp. 143-6.
76 *F.*, 1 December 1912. An idiosyncratic form of Monism, called 'Hylo Idealism', was developed in the *S. R.*—see 31 May 1884, and F. J. Gould's criticism of it, 22 November 1884.
77 *F.*, 11 February 1954.
78 *F.*, 8 January 1888, 20 October 1892, 5 July 1908; E. Sidney Hartland, 'The Debt of Free Thought to Anthropology', *R. P. A. Annual* (1913), pp. 3-14.
79 *F.*, 26 November 1905.
80 E. Pack, *The Trial and Imprisonment of J. W. Gott*, pp. 149-51.

X

# Finance

All this propagandist work in support of local societies, the N.S.S., periodicals and lecturers had to be paid for, and the burden fell on the ordinary members.. For a movement appealing primarily to the working classes, this could be enormous, even when on occasions a patron could be found to help out a society or an individual in difficulties.

Though not a rich movement, there often appeared to be money to spare in the pockets of the members: they were not of the very poor, and they could usually afford the little luxuries which being an active branch member involved. When E. Douglas Jerrold visited the Hall of Science in 1879, he wrote:

I notice that everybody has money to spare; that indulgence in Sunday newspapers and everyday tracts is universal. I hear of schemes of practical benevolence in which everybody seems to have joined with dime or ducat, and whereof the results are respectable, if they do not quite reach the proportions of Turkish Aid Funds and newspaper subcriptions for the relief of meritorious murderers. And it must be borne in mind that these audiences are not of that plump and pursy middle class that is supposed to furnish our national vertebrae; they are men of narrow means—men who are essentially mediocre in station, fortune and instruction.[1]

Thus while the member had to find only 1s 4d a year to join the N.S.S. (reduced to 6d in 1890, though raised to 1s in 1897), and only a further 2s 8d, 6d and 1s, respectively, for his local branch, he was likely to spend much more than this on his weekly freethought. For example, an active member at the Old Street Hall of Science would have paid 9d for a ticket to the Hall of Science tea party organised in February 1869; membership of the London Secular Choral Union would have cost him 3s 6d a quarter, while the concert seats cost between 1s and 3d each. The Hall of Science club subscription was 3s a quarter, and in 1881 the club reading room charged an extra 1s a year for newspapers. On top of this there was the admission charge for lectures—at least 1d—and there was his weekly 2d for his *National*

*Reformer.* If he wished to improve his mind at the Hall of Science Schools, he would have had to pay out at least 2s 6d to secure admission to each class, and more for a practical class with Dr Aveling. Then, if he still had money to spare, there were always innumerable appeals to be met. Being an active Secularist, especially if one's family were also Secularists, could be a relatively expensive commitment.[2]

Many of the leisure-time activities were designed to raise funds. The concert held at the Hall of Science in March 1869 yielded £10 for the building fund; and bazaars were also a favourite means of supporting local efforts. The Failsworth Secular Sunday School in 1879 held an Easter Bazaar which raised £141 3s 3d and left the organisers with another £80-worth of unsold goods, though by 1887 they had still paid off only £430 of the £730 debt on their new schools, opened in 1880. At a bazaar organised at the Hall of Science in 1870 to coincide with the annual N.S.S. conference, total takings amounted to £150 7s 11d, £133 15s of which was profit for the hall; a repeat bazaar the following year was not quite so successful, but still raised £51 1s 4d. Apart from subscriptions and social occasions, money could also be raised locally by lectures, especially if a national leader could be persuaded to come and give one for nothing. Bradlaugh reckoned he had given away £400 in this way between January 1883 and October 1884, and he requested not to be asked to give any more such lectures in future. At G. W. Foote's lectures at Manchester one Sunday in 1909, the collections were towards the cost of installing electric lighting in the Secular Hall. Northampton was not so lucky in 1897, for, having spent £20 on a magic lantern, they were disgusted when Charles Watts carried the entire collection away with him.[3]

Bradlaugh's system was usually to do just this. By taking the profits of a lecture instead of a fee, he was able to use the successful branches to subsidise the unsuccessful: it also kept the finance tightly in his own hands, though he carried all the risks at the expense of being thought to be making a fortune out of the movement. More usually, there was a fixed fee of half a guinea, a guinea or two guineas. By contrast, as the *Jerusalem Star* pointed out, Fabians and Socialists did not even charge their travelling expenses, which made them more popular than official Secularists with the poorer branches.[4]

Many of the lesser freethought lecturers worked freelance, often for whatever a collection might yield them. Fred Haslam worked for twenty years free of charge, 'but when I found others taking fees, I

thought it time I had a little for my services, but I have received little
more than would cover expenses. Sometimes I have received less
than a shilling,' he told a reporter from *Secular Work*. On one
occasion he was fined for taking a collection (actually, he 'shook
hands' at the gates) after a lecture in Hyde Park. In an attempt to
put London lecturing on a more secure footing in 1875, Messrs
Ramsey, Green and Forder formed a propagandist organisation
with the guarantee of 5s for each lecture delivered. Funds were
raised by a levy of 1s per annum on each branch, plus a public
appeal, and any profits yielded by the lectures. This was also the
idea behind Foote's 'new' lecturing scheme of 1891. Neither seems to
have been particularly successful. Bradlaugh's system was a special
N.S.S. Propagandist Fund for which donations were solicited to
assist recognised lecturers. There was never enough money to do all
that was required, even in the golden age, and in the 1890s all
Foote's schemes were crippled for lack of finance. Not only did
income from membership subscriptions fall catastrophically, from
£116 in 1891 to £37 in 1899–1900, but a credit balance of £218 on the
revenue account had become a deficit of £100 by 1899–1900, the
accounts first going into the red after the disastrous year of quarrels
in 1895–96. The dream of the treasurer was for a subscription
income augmented by donations which would meet all
requirements; for this he estimated he needed between £1,000 and
£1,500 a year, but even in the mid-1880s the total budget of the
N.S.S. had been under £500.[5]

The balance of requirements over income each year was met by
special funds and special appeals. In addition to the Special
Lecturing Fund, which financed N.S.S. lecturers, in 1870 Bradlaugh
launched a Shilling Fund to be used at his own discretion without
accounts. It was to be justified by Bradlaugh's success: the so-called
'President's fighting fund' to 'fight the bigots' was sufficiently
popular to silence Bradlaugh's critics. The appeal to finance the
legal cases arising out of the Knowlton Pamphlet prosecutions
reached nearly £1,300, enough to meet all the expenses. Nevertheless
in 1882 the *Secular Review* could object when 'coppers go to the
"fighting president," to be sunk in the fathomless sea of his never-
ending litigations'.[6]

Foote resorted to the Shilling Fund too, but with rather less
success and rather more criticism. He held special 'Shilling Months'
in 1893, raising £130 in January, but far less in July; in 1900 he
nominated the first week in October 'Shilling Week' for a Twentieth
Century Fund, like that launched by the Wesleyans. The 'week'

dragged on into December, but raised only £53.[7]

Poor branches had originally been excused payment of subscriptions to the central body, but it seems that many simply excused themselves. The secretary of the South Shields branch wrote to headquarters in February 1895 to request a £5 grant towards the cost of Cohen's six months of lectures in the town: between October and December the branch had lost only 30s, but in the second quarter bad weather had cut audiences and income. The N.S.S. general secretary wrote back to remind the branch that it was 30s in arrears with its subscriptions. The branch offered to pay the money a year late, 'at the same time, I am afraid, leaving this year's standing against us for the present'. Some branches simply resented paying and receiving no results. The Barnsley branch secretary complained in 1896 that 'all we have to do with the N.S.S. is to pay our members' fees, general and benevolent funds, special lecture and honorarium dues, and the deficits after Messrs Watts, Moss and Cohen's visits, and that's all'.[8]

The biggest single call on funds came if a society decided to acquire its own lecture hall, for which money was usually raised by issuing £1 shares in a joint-stock company. Attempts were made to do this at various times in Newcastle, Edinburgh, Leeds, Halifax, Oldham, Grimsby, West London, Camberwell, Derby, Leicester and Manchester, as well as at Old Street in London.[9] Some ventures, as in Leeds, Grimsby, Camberwell and Leicester, were successful; other attempts were still-born; some, like Foote's scheme to lease the Old Street Hall of Science in the early 1890s, were disastrously under-subscribed. The Leicester example illustrates what could be done, given strong local support and a considerable amount of local wealth.

The Leicester prospectus, issued in 1872, was for £5,000 to be raised in £5 shares. Half the 1,000 were immediately taken up by Josiah Gimson, the Secular Hall Company treasurer, who later took a further 165. John Sladen, the president, took sixty, and Michael Wright took forty. These men, together with Thomas Coltman (also forty) provided the bulk of the capital. The remaining 195 shares were held by thirty-eight people, no individual holding more than twenty. These lesser shareholders were mainly shopkeepers and skilled artisans. The danger with a joint-stock company was that the shareholders would gradually sell out, thus transferring control to some outside body. At Leicester the hall was preserved by the Gimsons. By 1904, 781 shares were held by six members of the Gimson family; fifty-seven by three members of the Wright family and the executors of a fourth; and eighty by the Sladen executors. The remaining eighty-two shares were held by only eight people and the executors of a further four, the only survivors of the original small shareholders being George Woodford, a mattress maker, with eighteen shares; John Thomas Boyd, the manager of a cotton warehouse, with six shares; and G. J. Holyoake, with seven.[10]

The other danger to a society with its own hall was that it would not be able to afford the upkeep. This happened at Rochdale in 1893, and almost happened at Camberwell in 1902 when the lecture audiences fell off during the Anglo-Boer War. In this case, Foote launched a £50 appeal, and the shareholders rejected a motion to sell the hall. At Leicester, the salvation of the society again was Josiah Gimson, who bequeathed £100 a year for ten years to support the society's work.[11]

As a relatively poor movement, both local and national organisations depended on men like Gimson when really large sums of money were needed. This, of course, put the freethought members in their power, for better or worse. The Edinburgh hall owed its existence to John Lees and W. A. Wilson, partners in a rope and twine manufacturing business, who advanced the money necessary for purchase. The Baskerville Hall in Birmingham cost £1,942, of which £1,440 was raised, including a loan from the Hall Building Society of £800, repayable over nine years. Daniel Baker, a wealthy steel-pen manufacturer, paid the balance as a donation; and the hall was given by Baker to Charles Watts in 1892, with the assistance of donations from, among others, George Anderson and the Marquis of Queensberry. The latter's sister, Lady Florence Dixie, was one of W. S. Ross's principal supporters, while George Anderson was the main prop of the N.S.S. in the 1890s, and afterwards of the R.P.A.[12]

Anderson, who died in 1913 at the age of ninety, was engineer and general manager of the Waterford Gas Company until his retirement in 1902. He had been brought up by his grandparents in Glasgow, was converted to freethought by Robert Owen's *Essays on the Formation of Character*, and had been actively involved in freethought ever since. Like many of the patrons of the movement, he was a self-made man.[13] In 1891 he joined Foote in a syndicate to lease the Hall of Science for a further twenty-eight years, and resigned from Mrs Bonner's rival scheme for a Memorial Hall because he thought it impracticable to look for a freehold site costing at least £10,000. Anderson did his best to help Foote raise the money to buy Robert Owen Smith's lease on the Hall of Science, and in 1893 he offered to give £300 if 3,000 shares were subscribed by the end of July, and when this did not happen he extended the offer six months on condition 4,000 shares were subscribed. His money was safe—only three other subscribers took over a hundred shares; most took fewer than ten, and such small subscribers could never reach the target. In 1900 he supported Foote's Twentieth Century Fund with a similar offer: £10 for every £100 subscribed up to a maximum of £8,000 for the purchase of a hall. He later increased his offer to £15,000 if the movement could match the figure. By now, though, he was beginning to doubt Foote's ability to manage money, and was being attracted instead to the plans of C. A. Watts. Foote suspected Charles Watts, senior, of working behind his back. In the end nothing came of the proposal, and freethought was never to have its equivalent of the Westminster Central Hall of the Wesleyans; but the R.P.A. did get £1,000 from Anderson.[14]

The heaviest financial burdens of all were borne by the leaders themselves. All were deeply in debt on account of the movement, and allegations that any of them profited by it seem totally unfounded. George Reddalls lost £1 a week on the *Secular Chronicle*, and the 'Guarantee Fund', though supported by a number of Midland leaders and society secretaries, yielded only £5 12s 6d in five months, while Reddalls lost £33. Harriet Law was said to have lost £1,000 in the three years she ran the paper.[15] Annie Besant lost by *Our Corner*, and Mrs Bonner by her *Reformer*.[16] J. W. Gott both supported the *Truth Seeker* out of his clothing business and employed boycotted freethinkers as salesmen, though he also relied upon the movement to given him trade in exchange.[17] The best the *Secular Review* ever did was to pay its way without paying its editors in 1883, and by 1891 Ross was so deep in debt that he had to appeal for help: £286 was subscribed, including £50 from Captain W. B. McTaggart (one of the paper's main contributors), £25 from the Marquis of Queensberry, £10 from Samuel Laing, and £5 from Huxley.[18]

Bradlaugh was saved from bankruptcy in 1869, after the failure of several of his dubious companies against which he had secured loans, solely by the patience of his creditors and timely loans from J. Mack and his father-in-law, Abraham Hooper; and when he had to break his American lecture tour in 1874 and then fight two election campaigns at Northampton, he was saved by a loan of 6,000 francs from Prince Jérome Napoleon.[19] Only a legacy of £2,500 from Henry Turberville in 1876 gave him anything like personal comfort and enabled him to move out of Turner Street and into St John's Wood. Even so, his personal debts in 1888 amounted to nearly another £2,500 when they were cleared by a public subscription. These later debts were incurred partly by lecturing at a loss—in 1881–83 he calculated he had held 150 meetings without profit and lost £600 on eight of them; and partly by litigation, which had cost him £400 in excess of public subscriptions. It was a tribute to Bradlaugh that the appeal in 1888 raised £2,491, including more than 6,000 penny donations from presumably poor men. Even so, in 1889 he had to borrow £400 on the security of legacy not yet received. Beyond this, the Freethought Publishing Company had been financed by the issue of debentures secured against the company, and when the partnership with Besant split up, Bradlaugh took upon himself the financial commitments of the company. This gave him liabilities nearly £6,000 in excess of assets, and when he died his creditors had to settle for 10s in the £1.[20]

G. W. Foote was in even worse trouble. In 1886 he lost about £700 when a fire damaged his premises, and the depression in freethought from the later 1880s meant that the weekly *Freethinker* was always a drain on resources. He also carried the risk and the losses involved in hiring various West London halls for Sunday lectures after the closure of the Hall of Science, and guaranteed Cohen's salary while he lectured in London in the summer of 1895.[21] He was kept going by loans from George Anderson, who, in 1895, suggested that the N.S.S. should pay its president an honorarium for his services. The Conference voted £100, but only £80 was paid in 1896, and when the sum fell to £25 in 1897 Foote killed it off. Meanwhile the Freethought Federation and *Secular Work* were attacking him for his continual begging and lack of leadership. George Standring alleged that he used £30 from the Benevolent Fund for general purposes, which the state of the General Fund makes all too likely. Finally, in 1899, when over £1,000 in debt on his printing account, Foote decided to form the Freethought Publishing Company to take the liabilities off his shoulders.[22] This brought further problems, for he proposed to issue 5,000 £1 shares, and to take 1,000 of them himself. This caused George Anderson, who was becoming tired of the tone of the *Freethinker* in contrast to the *Literary Guide*, to demand back his loans, even to the extent of taking Foote through the bankruptcy court. This he did, but Foote found another patron, a Mr Chancellor, who had already taken out 500 Freethought Publishing Company shares, and now bought up Foote's 1,000 to protect them. Foote then continued in business, all transactions being in his wife's name, until his discharge from bankruptcy in 1905.[23] The skies then began to clear, thanks to a group of friends led by J. W. de Caux, a Great Yarmouth J.P., who saw that Foote did receive an annual honorarium of around £300. By 1913 the Pioneer Press was breaking even, though Foote still had to subsidise the *Freethinker* out of his honorarium.[24]

Despite these grave financial embarrassments, the freethinkers always had to face the charge that they were lacking in charity. A favourite cry of Christian hecklers at outdoor meetings was 'Where's yer 'ospitals', implying that Christianity was true because it led to philanthropy, whereas freethought did not.[25] In vain did the freethinkers try to demonstrate that philanthropy had existed before Christianity. In fact, within their limited means, the freethinkers were philanthropic: a Thomas Paine birthday party was held in Birmingham in 1863 to raise funds for distressed Secularists in Lancashire, who were being denied Christian charity; Bradlaugh gave two lectures in Sheffield in 1864 on behalf of flood victims; and the damages he won in his various libel suits were always given to charity; in 1878 the Leeds Secularists ran their soup kitchen; and the Leicester society minutes record many instances of charitable giving.[26] For most Secularists, though, charity had to begin at home with their own benefit and friendly societies.

The General Secular Benevolent Society had been founded in 1860 and lasted until 1871, raising funds by arranging outings, soirées, and the like. It was then replaced by a Freethinkers' Benevolent Fund, created to help sick and indigent freethinkers: the subscription was 1*d* entrance and 1*d* a week. In 1879 this was wound up with a balance of £23 1*s* 2*d* and its work was transferred to the N.S.S. Benevolent Fund. During the 1880s this seems to have flourished: in 1886–87 seventy-five grants and four loans were made, amounting to nearly £100, but by 1895–96 this had been nearly halved and only fifteen branches were contributing to it, of which only Birmingham, Nottingham and Glasgow gave over £1.[27] Some branches or regions also had their own funds. The Lancashire Secular Union set up a Sick and Provident Society in 1867; the Northern (Newcastle) branch formed one in 1875; and Leicester, which was not in the N.S.S., began a sick club in 1886 which for 2*d* a week gave 6*s* a week benefit for eight weeks, and 3*s* for a further four weeks. In 1892 in Leicester, an additional Benevolent Fund gave sickness, accident, unemployment and strike or lock-out benefit for 2*d* a month.[28]

This level of activity did not, naturally, please everybody, and disgruntled freethinkers could always be found to claim that the movement had neglected them in their hour of need. Fred Haslam could always count on Bradlaugh for help, but he had got nothing from Foote after 1894, 'owing to Freethinkers' money going for other purposes', by which he probably meant the abortive Hall of Science scheme. In 1897 the Freethought Federation set up its own fund. Lapsed and hungry freethinkers could always sell their souls to Christians for a mess of pottage, and street-corner evangelists could then 'prove' the inhumanity of Secularism, however vigorously the fact was denied. Overall, though, the Secularists' record in matters of benevolence appears to have been as extensive as their limited means would allow, and certainly no disgrace to them.[29]

After the storms of the 1890s the Edwardian years were calmer, thanks largely to a scheme evolved by Foote to solve his financial problems by enabling bequests to be secured for freethought work. The problem was that blasphemy was against the law, and therefore any bequest for its dissemination could be declared null and void. This meant that if a freethinker left money to the N.S.S., or any other such body, the will had only to be challenged in the courts for the freethought movement to lose the money, either to the contestant or to the lawyers. The only way round the problem was for the money to be left personally to a freethinker for him to use for unspecified purposes, in the hope that he could be trusted to apply the money to freethought. Although some legacies were not contested, others were, costing the movement many thousands of pounds which it could ill spare. For example, when Jonas Spencer of Manchester died in 1885 and left £500 for the Secular Hall scheme there, his executors refused to pay the money over and the courts upheld them. On other occasions, prejudice against freethinkers might well have encouraged the courts to rule unfavourably in disputed will cases, as in 1875 when Bradlaugh inherited £20,000 from H. J. Blackmore (known as Henry Turberville, brother of the novelist, R. D. Blackmore). There were, in all, three wills, and Bradlaugh eventually received only £2,500. Ross was even less fortunate. He inherited £13,000 from Glegg Bullock in 1891, but there was an earlier will and Ross spent all the money trying to secure the inheritance. Bullock had been a patron of Ross before his death and had clearly intended him to have the money, but to leave the money to an atheist could be taken to signify an unsound mind, thus nullifying the will.[30]

In 1890, alongside the Propaganda Press Committee, a Liberty of Bequest Committee was formed under the chairmanship of G. J. Holyoake to agitate for a change in the law. The Committee's Civil and Religious Liberty Bill failed to make any progress in Parliament, though, and in 1896 Foote started his own 'Scheme for

Defeating the Blasphemy Laws'.[31] The idea was to set up a limited liability company which would be theologically neutral but which could give grants to subsidize freethought. Foote was confident that this would be legal, though his view rested on the slender legal grounds that, in his own blasphemy trial in 1883, Lord Chief Justice Coleridge had ruled that blasphemy lay in the manner and not just in the substance of the matter in question. This could be interpreted to mean that a freethinking body was not in itself illegal, provided it were legally dissociated from the manner in which the propagandist work was undertaken. Foote therefore proposed to create, quite distinct from the N.S.S., a company to be called the Secular Society Ltd, which he hoped would be able to receive bequests and then grant subsidies to the N.S.S. However, as G. J. Holyoake pointed out somewhat sceptically, the scheme would remain uncertain until tested in the courts. Nevertheless Foote was supremely confident and went ahead in 1898. A year later, C. A. Watts copied the idea for the R.P.A.[32]

The Secular Society Ltd was to promote freedom of publication, secularisation of the State by the abolition of all religious tests, the disestablishment of Christianity, secular education, liberty of bequest, the recognition of marriage as a wholly civil contract and the repeal of Sabbatarian legislation; and it was authorised to lease, rent or build premises, employ lecturers, writers and organisers, and publish books, pamphlets and periodicals. It was also authorised 'To assist, by votes of money or otherwise, other Societies or associated persons or individuals who are specially promoting any of the above objects'.[33]

This did indeed, as Foote claimed, contain 'all the essentials of Secularism', and some members of the N.S.S. began to fear that the Secular Society Ltd was a ruse by Foote to supersede the N.S.S. and to obtain independent financial control of the movement. Foote did not help matters by declaring:

Some apprehensive persons want to know what is to become of the N.S.S. if the incorporated society succeeds. I reply, that I don't know and don't care. If it succeeds, the Secular Society, Limited, will be really and practically the old N.S.S. with a legal status . . . For the rest, we may leave the result to natural selection. If the new organisation helps the old one, and both can live together in peace and co-operation—well and good. If the new organisation absorbs the old one by achieving its objects more efficiently—that is also well and good.[34]

This unsentimental attitude to the N.S.S. was tactless, though Foote was right. Henceforward, despite denials to the contrary, the

N.S.S. was subordinate to the Secular Society Ltd, which comprised only a small élite of N.S.S. supporters. In fact Bradlaugh had run the N.S.S. in a similar manner, by nominating vice-presidents who could swamp the branch delegates on the Executive, and by using the proxy votes of direct members to override those of the branches,[35] but this had not been quite so blatant. However, for once Foote's scheme worked, and was accepted with little protest once it proved him to have been right.

The total number of directors of the company, appointed at various times from 1898 to 1915, was only twenty-one, and, apart from the obvious leaders—Foote, Watts, Forder, Cohen, Moss, Lloyd—they included two builders, a corn chandler, a retired doctor, an insurance agent, a sanitary inspector, and a french-polisher—all men in comfortable circumstances, except possibly for the latter.[36] Between 1900, when the first legacy of £800 was received from W. J. Birch, a Liverpool commercial traveller, and 1914, the Secular Society Ltd was bequeathed eleven sums amounting to £5,514 18s 7d, most of which was spent either on the N.S.S. or on Foote personally. The first publication grant was in January 1899 to subsidise 8,000 copies of a pamphlet by Foote on the 'Peculiar People' for sale at N.S.S. branches at 2s a hundred, and in July 1899 the society took twenty shares in the Freethought Publishing Company. By the end of the first year of operations 143 members had joined the Society. Occasional grants were made thereafter to the N.S.S.; to various branches; for lecture campaigns by Watts, Cohen, Gould and others; and the West London lectures at the Athenaeum Hall, St James's Hall and elsewhere were now organised by the Society and not by Foote personally. Indeed, the minute books of the Secular Society Ltd are a record of most of the propagandist activity organised by Foote or the N.S.S. for the Edwardian years. The most regular subsidies were to the N.S.S. in the form of payment for offices and secretary shared by the two societies, and payments to Foote in his dual capacity as chairman of the Secular Society Ltd and president of the N.S.S. In 1900–02 he received £50 on each of these two accounts, and in 1903 the Freethought Publishing Company was given an interest-free loan of £100. Although the Secular Society Ltd did help other people—T. A. Jackson and J. W. Gott received £2 and £3 a week respectively to lecture and distribute literature in 1912—it is undoubtedly true, as many people suspected, that Foote was the individual to gain most by the scheme.[36]

The real test of the legality of it all came in 1914, when Elizabeth

Bowman, widow of Charles Bowman, died. The latter had died in 1908, leaving the residue of his estate to the Secular Society Ltd on the death of his wife, but the will was now contested by the next of kin on the grounds that the Secular Society Ltd was unlawful and contrary to public welfare (i.e. blasphemous). Mr Justice Joyce ruled in Chancery in April 1915 on the Society's behalf; the Bowman trustees then appealed, but their appeal was dismissed in July 1915, with the right of further appeal to the House of Lords. Finally, in May 1917, Lords Sumner, Parker and Buckmaster, with the Lord Chancellor dissenting, dismissed the Bowman appeal. At last, in January 1919, the Secular Society Ltd received capital and income from the Bowman bequest valued at £8,408—sufficient to carry Secularism into the inter-war period.[37]

*Notes*

1  *Weekly Dispatch*, 8 June 1879.
2  *N.R.*, 21 February 1869, 4 August 1878, 27 July 1879; *Republican*, February 1881.
3  *N.R.*, 7 March 1869; *S.R.*, 17 May 1879; *F.*, 13 March 1887; *N.R.*, 12 February, 24 September 1871, 5 October 1884; *F.*, 14 November 1909; *Secular Work*, January 1897.
4  *N.R.*, 26 March 1871; *Jerusalem Star*, October 1895. For N.S.S. rates under Foote see N.S.S., Organisation Committee, Minute Book, 26 October 1893, 18 March 1895.
5  *Secular Work*, November 1896, January 1897; *S.C.*, 28 November 1875; *F.*, 11 January 1891; N.S.S. Minute Books, copies of Annual Financial Statements; *F.*, 20 June 1897.
6  *N.R.*, 5 June 1870, 17 March 1878; *S.R.*, 10 June 1882.
7  *F.*, 24 December 1893, 7 October, 16 December 1900.
8  R. C. Chapman to Miss E. M. Vance, 18 February and 11 March 1895—letters in N.S.S. Minute Book IV; *Secular Work*, October 1896.
9  E.g. *N.R.*, 3 November 1872, 12, 19 October 1873 (Grimsby); and 18 January 1885 (Camberwell).
10  *N.R.*, 15 December 1872; Leicester Secular Society, Shareholders' Allotment Book, 1873–75; and Register of Members, Annual Lists, 1873–1904.
11  *F.*, 7 May 1893, 10 August 1902; *N.R.*, 6 January 1884.
12  *N.R.*, 3 June 1883, 5 October 1884; *S.R.*, 24 August 1878; *N.R.*, 24 January 1892. Lady Florence Dixie helped Ross both in her own name and as 'Izra'—*A.J.*, 18 November 1905, 6 January 1906.
13  *L.G.*, June 1902, September 1913; *F.*, 25 July, 1 August 1897.
14  *F.*, 20 September 1891, 7 August 1892, 8 October 1893, 12 August 1900, 24 March 1901; *L.G.*, September 1900, April 1901, January 1902.
15  *S.C.*, 1 July 1873, 1 October 1874, 6 June 1875; *F.*, 8 August 1897.
16  *N.R.*, 9 December 1888; *Reformer*, 15 October 1898.

17   *Truth Seeker*, 1 August 1903; *Labour Annual* (1900), p. 152; *Ethical World*, 26 February 1898.
18   *S.R.*, 14 July 1883; *A.J.*, 18 July, 1 August, *et seq.*, 1891.
19   H. B. Bonner and J. M. Robertson, *op. cit.*, I, pp. 299–303; D. Tribe, *President Charles Bradlaugh*, pp. 115–17, 152. Bradlaugh began to borrow from Abraham Hooper in 1865, and by February 1868 owed nearly £500; he began borrowing from J. Mack in November 1868. The loan from Jerome Napoleon came on 17 March 1874—see B.L. nos. 143, 144, 148, 149, 172, 173, 196, 198, 199, 200, 210, 211, 214, 216, 221, 224, 225, 230, 232, 374.
20   *N.R.*, 29 August, 10 October 1875; 13 August 1876, 11 November 1883, 26 August, 2, 16 September, 7, 28 October 1888, 22 February, 15 March, 5 April, 11 October 1891.
21   *F.*, 3 October 1886, 1 September, 6 October 1895, 1 March 1896.
22   *F.*, 7 July 1895, 11 April 1897; *Secular Work*, June 1896; *Radical*, 15 August 1897; *F.*, 15 May 1898, 16 July 1899.
23   *L.G.*, December 1902; *F.*, 7 July–4 August, 20, 27 October, 24 November 1901; 15 January 1905.
24   *F.*, 19 January 1908, 15 February 1914.
25   E.g. *F.*, 12 July 1896. The reference to hospitals was probably originally prompted by the annual Hospital Sunday collections made by the various denominations.
26   *Birmingham Daily Gazette*, 30, 31 January, 2 February 1863; H. B. Bonner and J. M. Robertson, *op. cit.*, I, pp. 216–19; *N.R.*, 17 February 1878; *S.R.*, 9 March 1878; Leicester Secular Society, Minute Books, *passim*, e.g. II, 17 March 1880, collection for Irish Relief Fund.
27   *N.R.*, 19 March 1871; *S.C.*, 1 February 1873, 17 August 1879; N.S.S. Minute Book IV, Financial Statements, 1886–87, 1895–96.
28   *N.R.*, 14 February 1869, 2 May 1875; F. J. Gould, *History of the Leicester Secular Society*, pp. 36–7.
29   *Secular Work*, November 1896; *F.*, 4 April 1886.
30   *N.R.*, 14 August 1887, 13 August 1876; *S.R.*, 18 July 1891.
31   *Watts's L.G.*, October 1890; *N.R.*, 18 January, 27 December 1891; *F.*, 30 August 1896.
32   *F.*, 19, 26 June 1898, 19 March 1905.
33   *F.*, 19 June 1898.
34   *F.*, 10 July 1898.
35   *Secularist*, 5 May 1877.
36   The Secular Society Ltd, Register of Directors, and Minutes of Directors; also *F.*, 4, 25 March 1900.
37   *F.*, 1, 22 November 1914, 25 April, 23 May, 25 July, 8, 15 August 1915; *Daily Telegraph*, 15 April, 31 July 1915 (cuttings in the Secular Society Ltd, Minute Books); *F.*, 20 May–24 June 1917; N.S.S. papers, Bowman box; summaries of bequests and lectures are on loose sheets in the Secular Society Ltd, Minute Book II.

# Part III
# Freethought and reform

# XI

# Republicanism and foreign affairs

'Although it is quite true that Freethinkers are not necessarily Radicals, it is an undoubted fact that the majority are so. Since the time of that great apostle of liberty, Thomas Paine, the questionings of arbitrary authority in all matters political and religious have gone together.' In these words J. M. Wheeler summed up in the *Freethinker* the political attitudes of his readers.' There were differences as to the degree of radicalism, but very few Secularists would not have regarded themselves as radicals, and, with more or less enthusiasm, voted for the Gladstonian Liberal party. And, as has been argued with respect to Bradlaugh's popularity in the North East,[2] the freethought leaders attracted more support with their popular radical politics than they did with their theological views. In studying Secularism the historian is concerned not only with an anti-religious movement to be interpreted as a point on the theological spectrum, but also with a political movement which was a part of the mainstream of the British liberal tradition.

Charles Bradlaugh's political philosophy was that of the architypal radical. He defined radicals as 'those men and women who maintain that every citizen should have: equal opportunity before the law; equal burden, duty, and right under the law, and (as included in these) equal representation in making the law and creating the government'. Radicals did not, on the other hand, 'claim an impossible dead-level equality for all mankind, but do claim that the law shall not heavily handicap any at starting; that it shall not erect barriers against the weakest—difficult if not impossible to surmount—or create unfair class distinctions to the detriment of the poorest'. They also 'desire to diminish the enormous and ever-increasing burden of taxation, and they desire to better apportion the fashion in which the fiscal burden now presses'.[3]

The individual political programmes advocated in the *National Reformer* and the *Freethinker* are all developments of these basic points. Their gospel was J. S. Mill's essay *On Liberty* (1859). Though in the 1870s Bradlaugh found some Conservative freethinkers, and religious radicals, who held aloof from him, he was able without difficulty to make the N.S.S. a powerful instrument for radicalism. Not till the mid-1880s did the political spectrum of freethought widen sufficiently to cause problems, with J. M. Robertson and Annie Besant tugging towards the positive liberty of the New Liberalism or socialism, while W. S. Ross pulled to the right with a Carlylean contempt for democracy. G. W. Foote was then left to try to hold together the pieces, which he could do only by unravelling that identification of freethought with radical politics which Bradlaugh had woven on the traditional pattern. At the same time, the Secularists were experiencing all the tensions of Liberalism in decline—pulling towards State socialism, or anarchic libertarian Individualism, and leaving many, including Foote, disillusioned, bewildered, and increasingly out of touch. A history of Secularist politics between 1866 and 1915 is a history of the climax and decline of the old style of radical politics.

Freethinkers were actively involved in the radical agitation which led up to the passing of the Reform Act in 1867. G. J. Holyoake and Charles Bradlaugh were both on the council of the Reform League,; Robert Cooper (d. 1868) was a founder of the Reform Union; and Harriet Law, who in June 1867 was elected to the general council of the International Working Men's Association, had been one of those to speak in Hyde Park in July 1866 after the crowd had pushed down the railings. Bradlaugh took an especially active part among the extremists in the League who forced the leadership to call the government's bluff in 1867 by holding a prohibited meeting in the Park on 6 May.[4] Dean Mansel was not alone in fearing in 1866 that a consequence of the Reform Bill would be the 'preponderating influence of secularism and infidelity'.[5] He need not have worried. Bradlaugh was even at this stage in his career more moderate than his opponents thought. He believed scrupulously in law and order: once in the Park on 6 May he refused to use force even to remove three gentlemen who happened to be sitting on the park bench from which he had intended to speak![6] In July 1868 he sent his Northampton election manifesto to Mr Gladstone for his approval, and wrote:

I trust 'ere long to be able in your presence to prove how little those who so often attack me, understand of my objects, or my mode of striving for them. I have refrained from thrusting myself upon your attention but believe me that, despite many wide differences of opinion between us, I look to you to stand first and leader in the great struggle in which only the first step has been taken.[7]

English radicalism was constitutional to the core, though the only people who knew this at the time were its opponents to the left, whose spokesman was Karl Marx.[8]

Immediately after the Hyde Park meeting Bradlaugh resigned from the council of the Reform League, as he feared its work would be damaged by association with his name—though Thomas Hughes later accused him of leaving after double-crossing the executive by playing the moderate in private and the extremist in public.[9] When the general election came in 1868, the extent to which the executive (especially the secretary, George Howell) had sold the League to the official Liberal party became apparent: no working men were returned to the new Parliament, and a bitter reaction set in which Bradlaugh was well placed to personify.[10] Dissatisfied radicals turned to new organisations and more extreme agitations.

The cry such radicals took up after 1868 was Republicanism, by which they meant a criticism not only of the monarchy, but also of the aristocracy, their land, and their political stronghold in the House of Lords. Beyond this, republicanism meant the representation in Parliament of working men by working men. The principal organisations set up to agitate for these ends were the Labour Representation League and the Land and Labour League.

The Labour Representation League, founded in September 1869, expressed the views of the moderates, including G. J. Holyoake, and it was in no sense an embryonic I.L.P. Its aim was merely to secure the election of working-class Liberals. Bradlaugh was nominated a member, but refused to join. To him it was 'a wire-pulling association, neither Whig, nor Tory, nor Radical, and too friendly with the Treasury department to please us'.[11] The Land and Labour League grew out of the Holborn branch of the National Reform League in October 1869. It included both Bradlaughite Secularists and old O'Brienites, who, with their distinctive views on land and currency reform, provided Marx with the most ideologically aggressive members in the International.[12]

*Land reform*

Land reform was to be a major issue among English reformers from the 1860s until the end of the century. As with the wider radical movement, there were several views as to the nature and extent of the reform needed, from the relative moderation of the Land Tenure Reform Association to the land nationalisation programme of the Land and Labour League. The moderates were heirs to the Anti-Corn Law League's attacks on the landed aristocracy. Richard Cobden had advocated land reform in his last major speech in 1864, and the issue had then been taken up by a number of journalists, academics, lawyers and politicians, including J. S. Mill, Henry Fawcett, Shaw Lefevre, Thorold Rogers and Locke King.[13] Bradlaugh was invited to the first meeting of the Land Tenure Reform Association, but not the second, while the more moderate Holyoake was an active member. Those Secularists who followed Bradlaugh had more affinity for the work of the Land and Labour League. In 1864 the freethinking journalist William Maccall had advocated in the *National Reformer* a National Land League, and a pamphlet by him on 'The Land and the People' was reprinted in the *National Reformer* in 1869. As was usual with Bradlaugh, his ideas were first worked out in lectures, and he turned his attention to the land question, which was 'now apparently being really taken up as the question of the day', when he lectured at the Mile End branch of the National Reform League in April 1869. By August he was delivering a regular lecture on 'The Land, the People and the Coming Struggle', which was published in the *National Reformer* during 1870 and appeared as a separate pamphlet in 1871. When the Land and Labour League was founded in October 1869, Bradlaugh and George Odger were the candidates for its presidency (which was put in abeyance to avoid a conflict), and the secretaries were Martin Boon and George Eccarius of the International. Despite the strong O'Brienite and Marxist representation on the League, Bradlaugh remained a leading member, and at the presidential election in 1870, when Patrick Hennessey was elected, Bradlaugh had only one vote fewer, and he remained on its general council until 1874, by which time it was moribund.[14]

Announcements of the Land and Labour League disappear from the *National Reformer* in May 1874, but the land question was kept before the public in the periodicals. The collapse of the agricultural labourers' strike in 1874 led Bradlaugh to urge the destruction of the land system as the only permanent way to solve their problems; and the Secularist *Northampton Radical* looked to the assimilation of the county and borough franchises to destroy both the Tories and the Church in the countryside. Charles Cattell argued in the *Secular Chronicle* that the basic problem with the British economy was that land for sporting purposes was left uncultivated, while the country had to import an increasing proportion of its requirements. All these were to be issues in the coming decade.[15]

The land issue really revived in 1879 with the importation of corn from America, which Joseph Symes hailed as the end of the landlords' power. Public interest, however, was not yet fully roused, and a lecture by Bradlaugh on 'The Land Question in England', delivered in Bradford in June 1879, was attended by only a small audience. In October, November and December a series of preliminary meetings was held at the Hall of Science to discuss reviving a national land agitation, and a land conference was called for 10 February 1880 at St James's Hall, with Bradlaugh as chairman. He now favoured peasant proprietorship rather than outright nationalisation, and invitations were not sent to the latter's supporters. Nevertheless James Murray and Dan Chatterton attended and put a motion for nationalisation, which was defeated. Bradlaugh's position was supported by Annie Besant and Edward Aveling. The Secularist organisation of the meeting had clearly triumphed, though Charles Watts was among those who felt that the programme had been pushed through unfairly by Bradlaugh.[16]

The outcome of conference was the Land Law Reform League, with Bradlaugh as president, and Robert Forder as secretary. The N.S.S. was affiliated to the League, and the N.S.S. stucture was used to recruit members. The only non-Secularists on the committee were Joseph Arch and the Reverend Stewart Headlam. The land nationalisers were not silenced by Bradlaugh's *coup*, however. Initially they comprised old followers of Ernest Jones, or O'Brienites like James and Charles Murray, but by the time the Land Nationalisation League was formed in 1882 their complexion had changed and the Secularists were again to the fore—Charles Watts, W. S. Ross and Herbert Burrows were on the provisional council, as indeed was the ubiquitous Headlam, but there were also socialists of the newer generation. In 1883 a juncture of the Social Democrats and the Land Nationalisation League produced the Land Reform Union, which in 1884 was captured by the followers of Henry George and turned into the English Land Restoration League.[17]

The publication of Henry George's *Progress and Poverty* in Britain in January 1881 was the most significant event in the revival of the land agitation, though the book arrived in an England already stirred by the Land Law Reform League, the agricultural depression, and Gladstone's proposals for a reform of the Irish land law. The first mention of *Progress and Poverty* in the *National Reformer* was a friendly review from an American correspondent which appeared in the first issue of 1881. By 1882 George's ideas were being criticised more fully. J. H. Levy pointed out how it was wrong to propose taxing land at its full value when part of that value belonged to the tenant, not the landlord—a principle recognised in the 1881 Irish Land Act. William Maccall attacked 'The Newest Panacea' and recalled the O'Brienite versions of land nationalisation instead. George's ideas nevertheless swept the country. In three years the English publishers of *Progress and Poverty* (Kegan Paul) had put 66,469 copies into circulation, and, with other editions, there were probably around 100,000 published, including 40,000 in a 6*d* edition.[18]

The exact method by which the land question was to be answered exercised the minds of many radical leaders and pot-house politicians. George's schemes initially entailed nationalisation without compensation, but the single land tax became increasingly important after 1884 and was dominant after 1888: the land was to be progressively transferred by taxation to the community, while rents would go to the State. The former Owenite biologist, A. R. Wallace, wanted nationalisation with compensation, as did the O'Brienites. Charles J. Garcia, writing in George Standring's *Republican*, wanted no compensation, and an attack not just on landlords but on all capitalists. Standring himself was not so extreme, and was still being influenced by Thorold Roger's exposition of the 'Norman Yoke'. Bradlaugh was the most conservative of all: he dismissed both 'land restoration' and the 'Norman Yoke' on the grounds that the people never had owned the land, and, if they had, it could never now be restored. He was attacked by Stewart Headlam for these views—it must have been a new experience for Bradlaugh to be attacked by a clergyman for not being extreme enough. Mrs Besant tried to persuade the Fabians that Bradlaugh's proposals for the compulsory purchase of land at its average productive value (which was nothing in the case of 'waste' lands) amounted to socialism, but Bradlaugh spoilt her case by denying it.[19]

By the mid-1880s, land reformers had polarised between the Land Law Reform League and the Land Nationalisation Society. As an M.P. Bradlaugh was in a position to try to introduce legislation to implement his proposals for the compulsory purchase of waste lands, but he withdrew his draft Bill in 1886 when it received very little support in the country. He tried again, but without success, in 1887 and 1888. Despite Ireland, and despite the plight of the Scottish crofters in the later 1880s, land reformers, like the Secularists themselves, were finding it difficult to make much impact on public opinion. The county franchise had been extended in 1884, and yet one of Bradlaugh's correspondents could write despondently from Biggleswade in 1887, 'It is almost singular how much more conservative the great body of agricultural labourers here have become within the past two years.' The whole of England was growing more conservative, and Liberal-radicalism was being pushed to the Celtic fringes of the United Kingdom.[20]

## Republicanism

In the tradition of Paine, Shelley and Carlile, Bradlaugh and his followers had little time for the royal family. Queen Victoria's main offence—an offence felt widely, even in the House of Commons—was her absence from public life in the decade following the death of the Prince Consort in 1861, but the focus of the attack was directed elsewhere, on the cost to the public of the whole parasitic family, its reputation in the previous century, and the behaviour of the Prince of Wales as particularised in the Mordaunt divorce case. It could have been no surprise that Queen Victoria had little sympathy for Bradlaugh in his later parliamentary struggle. She probably never saw the *National Reformer*, but his views were made quite explicit in his influential pamphlet *The Impeachment of the House of Brunswick*, first published in the *National Reformer* in 1871-72.[21]

The inspiration for the republican movement in England was two fold: its more extreme manifestations were stimulated by events on the Continent, but, as was so often the case with English radicalism, the timing was decided by the moderates, who took their lead from Parliament. In 1869 a meeting of the Poor People's Union at the Goswell Road Hall resulted in the formation of an International Republican Association (later, the International Democratic Association). 'Several of us,' reported the *National Reformer*, 'considering the growth of democracy since the old Chartist days in this country, and republicanism and socialism on the continent, felt the time had arrived for England to speak out, and keep pace with other nations . . .' The driving force came from economic depression (1,032,000 in receipt of relief in 1869), and the fall of the French Empire. On Good Friday 1870 the members of the Land and Labour League demonstrated on behalf of the unemployed, with scarlet sashes round their waists and carrying caps of liberty on poles. In September the collapse of France occurred, and in the same month a periodical named the *Republican* appeared with the motto (from October): 'Labour the source of all wealth: of the food, clothing, and lodging of the Nation: of the Rents of the Landlord, and of the Interest of the Monied-Lord'. Bradlaugh thought, 'This journal deserves support from advanced political workers.'[22]

Popular republicanism now spread rapidly. Public meetings were held in London at which Bradlaugh gave major speeches, and in Birmingham the veteran Secularist Charles Cattell called a meeting to form a republican club, with himself as president and George Reddalls as secretary. This initiative was rapidly imitated in Nottingham, Sheffield, Northampton, Newcastle, Jarrow and Middlesbrough. On 24 March the London Republican Club was inaugurated, and two days later the *National Reformer* was published with a separate section headed 'Republican Department'.[23]

During 1871 republican clubs were formed not only in association with Secularists but also by more extreme groups, and at a meeting held at the Eleusis Club, Chelsea, in April, the Universal Republican League was established.[24] The struggle for the soul of English republicanism now developed, with Bradlaugh the extreme atheist but relatively moderate radical on one side, and the *Republican*, the O'Brienites, the International Working Men's Association and Dr Marx on the other.

Bradlaugh was a thorough constitutionalist and an English patriot. Although prepared to support extremism overseas, he took a pride in the belief that England was different. Here, continental models of agitation were out of place, and he was determined to keep the agitation within the framework of the law. Even in 1867, when he had challenged the government's decision to close Hyde Park, he had done so on the grounds that people had a *legal* right to enter the Park. When republican clubs were being founded by Secularists in the spring of 1871, he cautioned them to be open and legal, and to keep clear of treason and sedition. On 22 March, at a meeting chaired by Odger to prepare a republican programme, 'Red flags and caps of liberty were displayed at the back of the platform'. Two days later at the Hall of Science the chairman, Austin Holyoake, 'trusted that all their proceedings would be characterised by a total absence of useless display—flaunting of banners and colours, caps of liberty, and drum beating...'. After further rebukes from the *National Reformer*, the *Republican* retorted on 1 May, 'Has it come to this, that "Refinement, which now fashioneth the world", has even reached the Devil himself.' G. J. Holyoake, whose own advocacy of refinement had alienated many Bradlaughites, may have been forgiven an ironic smile. In the same issue of the *Republican* a veteran

Chartist and Secularist from the West Midlands, H. V. Mayer, wrote deploring rowdyism, red flags and red caps at public meetings. He argued that demonstrations should be held on major occasions only, and that they 'must be conducted logically and decorously, and the less it has to do with red caps and red flags the better'. The reason why suggests a major factor in the shaping of English radicalism between 1850 and 1880—'I know how Chartism suffered from a similar policy, and I have no desire to see Republicanism share a similar fate.' A month later these views were supported by G. J. Holyoake, who entered the fray with a letter to the *Daily News* protesting at the unEnglish sentiments of the International (he was refering to Marx's *Civil War in France*). The *Republican* dismissed him as 'a senile busy body'. Shortly afterwards, George Odger broke with his fellow members of the International on the same issue, and then Bradlaugh launched a full attack on the International, supported by his fellow Secularist and Land and Labour League treasurer, Victor Le Lubez.[25]

The event which exaccerbated this bitter ideological and personal dispute was the Commune. The mainstream of the British radical movement had traditionally been sympathetic to Continental republican movements of all kinds—room had been found for socialists like Louis Blanc and Stanislaus Worcell as well as for non-socialists like Louis Kossuth and Joseph Mazzini. Opponents of the Second Empire had found many friends among the British radicals, but with the Commune those opponents were themselves murderously divided. Radicals such as Bradlaugh and Odger could not bring themselves to support the Communards.[26]

In his inaugural speech as president of the London Republican Club, Bradlaugh expressed his willingness to co-operate with all reform groups (even the moderate Land Tenure Reform Association), but he denounced J. Johnson, the secretary of the Universal Republican League, as either a madman or a spy for advocating physical force republicanism. He encouraged a Republican Club Organisation Committee at the Hall of Science to co-ordinate republican lectures throughout the country, to seize the initiative from the Universal Republican League, and he rejected the International as both foreign and unrepresentative—two of the heaviest charges in Bradlaugh's vocabulary. The International replied by claiming Bradlaugh had sold himself to the Tories; while Bradlaugh, in a lecture at the Hall of Science, attacked the International still further for its secrecy and for advocating class war by the defeated Communards: the struggle of proletariat and bourgeoisie might well be the issue in France, but in England the basic issue for Bradlaugh was the land.[27]

How much support Bradlaugh got, and how far his efforts can be taken as representative of Secularists, is not easy to tell. Through the *National Reformer* he was able to rally his faithful followers, and he appears to have carried with him nearly all the major leaders, both national and local. On the other hand, there was no really clear dividing line: Joachim Kaspary, who conducted open-air freethought lectures in London, was a member of the Universal Republican League, as was Victor Le Lubez, who was a close friend and supporter of Bradlaugh; but George Sexton, a principal writer for the *National Reformer*, left the Secularists in 1871 and joined the International.[28] One group of French refugees refused to accept £7 collected by Bradlaugh for them, but a crowded meeting of refugees shortly afterwards was persuaded by Le Lubez to pass a vote of confidence in Bradlaugh and to reject the International's attacks on him. The *New York World* thought of Bradlaugh as 'the coming Cromwell' and reported the London Republican Club as having 30,000 members. This was a gross exaggeration, for in January 1872 the membership reached only 250, but the impression of Bradlaugh's strength is an instructive one.[29]

The republican movement in the country owed less to the Commune than to the parliamentary agitation against the royal family. The first wave of protest began over the proposed £30,000 dowry for Princess Louise, in March 1871, and a second wave came with the proposed £15,000 allowance for Prince Arthur, in August. The lead was taken by G. O. Trevelyan, whose pamphlet *What does she do with it?* attacked the Civil List, and his fellow radical M.P.s, Charles Dilke, P. A. Taylor, Auberon Herbert and Henry Fawcett. They were able to get fifty-three votes for a reduction in Prince Arthur's proposed allowance, but only eleven Members opposed it altogether. Dilke made himself notorious, with republican speeches in Manchester and Newcastle; but a royalist reaction followed in 1872 when the Prince of Wales caught typhoid (which had killed his father). In the debate on the Civil List in 1872 Dilke and Herbert were supported only by Sir Wilfred Lawson and George Anderson. Respectable republicanism was dead.[30]

The fires lit at the popular level were less rapidly extinguished. The agitation of 1871 had produced about two-dozen republican societies in the provinces, while other groups had emerged in the intense, back-biting, sectarian world of the London political clubs. Amongst the leaders, Bradlaugh was now one of the most important.

With a final attack on his atheism in February 1872, the *Republican* breathed its last; and in September the *National Reformer* gleefully reported the dissolution of the London Council of the International. The provincial societies were so closely identified with freethought groups that Cattell had to remind Secularist republicans that one did not have to be a Secularist to be a republican, though 'many friends of the Republican movement are also working in the Secular cause'.[31]

In London, apart from the London Republican Club, the principal organisations and centres of potential opposition to Bradlaugh were the London Patriotic Society, with its premises on Clerkenwell Green, the Eleusis Club in Chelsea, and, for a brief time, the West End section of the International, meeting at the 'Sir Robert Peel', off Oxford Street. It was here, at the end of September 1872, that an Irish teacher of elocution named John De Morgan made his English début.[32]

Bradlaugh's aim was to co-ordinate all the diverse republican activities, and, one suspects, to seize the initiative after the collapse of the International. A meeting was called at the Hall of Science on 21 October, at which the British Republican Association was launched on the model of the London Corresponding Society of 1794. This seems to have made little impression, and the initiative next passed to the Universal Republican League, which called a Fenian amnesty demonstation in Hyde Park on 3 November. Some of the speakers were arrested, which temporarily united all the republicans—Hennessey, Bradlaugh, De Morgan, Charles Murray and George Odger (the last three named being among those prosecuted)—and a joint protest meeting was held on Clerkenwell Green. Bradlaugh then called a meeting of his British Republican Association at the Hall of Science, at which most of the London societies were represented, and made arrangements for a fully representative conference early in 1873. Meanwhile, in Sheffield, a delegate meeting of South Yorkshire republican clubs had met to establish a reform movement for universal suffrage, disestablishment of the Church, and repeal of the Game Laws, and they organised a national conference to meet in December 1872.[33]

The principal figure in the Sheffield movement appears to have been John De Morgan, about whose mental stability Bradlaugh was beginning to have grave doubts. Only six delegates went to the Sheffield conference (including Cattell, who immediately reported back to Bradlaugh), though they were claimed to represent twenty-two clubs. The organisation which ensued, the Republican

Brotherhood, had a strong Irish flavour. The London Republican Club immediately disowned the Brotherhood, and when Cattell, Reddalls and six others refused to serve on its ten-man executive it was doomed to insignificance. The London societies met again early in the new year, and in May held their own conference in Birmingham, at which the National Republican League was formed. Its first act was to send Bradlaugh to Spain to convey greetings to the successful Spanish republican leader, Castellar.[34]

The National Republican League went some way towards uniting the various republican societies which had grown up since 1871, and, with the collapse of the N.S.S. after Bradlaugh's withdrawal in 1871, provincial republicanism in effect took over the Secularist structure. The League was primarily a Bradlaughite organisation, and it did nothing to satisfy Bradlaugh's critics in the London clubs. The West End section of the International refused to recognise the Birmingham conference because the programme ignored 'all important questions of a *true social character*'; while the *International Herald* found Bradlaugh far too conservative. The Universal Republican League accused the council of the National Republican League of expressing, without a quorum, views contrary to those of both itself and the Eleusis Club; but the fact was that the secretary, G. W. Foote, could not get a quorum for the council meetings. Without the excitement of 1870 and 1871, the republican movement was dying.[35] A useful boost was given by the impending marriage of the Duke of Edinburgh, which meant an increased annuity of £10,000 a year, against which Bradlaugh called a protest meeting in Hyde Park, but the general crisis of confidence in the royal family was over, so far as most people were concerned. Bradlaugh went off to lecture in America, and the republicans gave no lead in the 1874 general election campaign. The truth was that, with the N.S.S., the National Republican League and the Land and Labour League all inactive, popular radicalism was as feeble as the Gladstonian Liberalism which the enfranchised public decisively rejected at the polls in 1874.[36]

Deserted by its parliamentary and middle-class supporters, only a remnant of popular republicanism survived in the London clubs and freethought societies. The 'Republican Department' of the *National Reformer* disappeared after 20 September 1874, but the following April George Standring began a little paper entitled the *Republican Chronicle* in which to advocate republicanism without reference to theology, and to draw all republicans together in an attack on the Church, the Financial Interest, Intemperance, the Land Laws, and the prevailing distribution of political power. Standring, like Bradlaugh, was a constitutional republican, whose motto was 'Ballots, not Bullets', and he was prepared to work for change in public opinion over a generation. He believed that any attempt to hasten the coming of the republic would simply provoke a monarchical reaction. In the event, that reaction was to come anyway.[37]

The first line of attack, as in 1871, was against the royal family. Petitions were got up in 1875 to oppose a grant of £142,000 to the Prince of Wales on the occasion of his visit to India, until details of his private income and debts were published. A meeting was held in Hyde Park, chaired by Charles Watts, in July 1875, and the following year Annie Besant arranged petitions to oppose any further grants to royalty until their finances had been made public. With 102,937 signatures, these petitions demonstrated the depth of popular feeling among radicals; they were presented by the two working-class M.P.s, Burt and Macdonald, and greeted with laughter by the House.[38]

The Royal Titles Bill gave another slight encouragement in 1876, but there was little permanent sign of popular enthusiasm for the cause.[39] Standring was forced to admit, 'The torpor in which Republicans as a body are steeped continues to be as profound as ever,' and he decided he would have to work through less advanced movements in the hope that they might eventually lead to a republic. The new strategy was also advocated by Charles Cattell, who saw the main hope to lie in the education of the people to be republicans—avoiding Cromwell's error of a republic without any republican citizens. Cattell looked to the new Radical Clubs, which were being founded in the 1880s, to keep Liberals up to the mark until the day came when there would be only Tories and Radicals. The moderates, however, received a setback in 1881 with the assassinations of Alexander II, President Garfield, and Burke and Cavendish in Phoenix Park: this was not the way in which Englishmen were to conduct their affairs. In October 1881 Standring held a meeting at the Hall of Science to re-form the London Republican Club, but only seventy or eighty people came. They set up a new Republican League which was to agitate for the repeal of the Act of Settlement, to consolidate republican activities, to educate citizens as republicans, and to promote allied social and political movements. Prince Leopold's marriage in 1882 then helped revive the campaign for an end to all grants to royalty while their finances remained a secret. Small republican groups were gathered by Aurelis Wakefield in Hipperholme, J. F. Rayner in Southampton and John Lees in Edinburgh, where there were sixty-two members, but, although such activities were nominally independent of freethought, they were in fact entirely dependent on Secularists.[40]

On the occasion of Prince Leopold's marriage, W. S. Ross wrote an article on 'The Rattle and the Ring' in which he bitterly castigated

the German king-factory, which factory seems to have a monopoly of turning out microcephalous mediocrities with an inimitable blend of insatiable cupidity. Each of these Hanover trinkets, including the elderly invisible one, have a crack on the top of their heads suited for the dropping in of half-crowns, and millions of half-crowns are dropped into their cranial crack even by starving wretches who cannot get bread.[41]

Unfortunately for the republicans, this latter observation was all too true: Watts's compositors refused to set up 'The Rattle and the Ring' for the *Secular Review*, and the work had to be done by Watts himself, assisted by his son, Ross, and 'The Wasp'. Insulting the royal family was no longer popular.[42]

The Republican League staggered on a little longer, with branches in Halifax, Edinburgh (where J. M. Robertson was now active), and South Shields, but in 1884 Standring had to hark back to the earlier period for material, republishing an article from the *National Reformer* of 1869 and Dilke's speech on royalty of 1871. Grants to Princess Beatrice and the Prince of Wales's eldest son in 1885 made little impression on the public, and Standring now conceded, 'we do not know at this moment of a single Republican organisation in the United Kingdom', and in 1886 he changed the name of his paper from the *Republican* to the *Radical*.[43] Only one republican candidate had fought the 1885 general election—at Hull—and he had come bottom of the poll. Significantly, perhaps, Standring forgot to count Bradlaugh, though he was one, and in 1889 was pressing in the adjournment debate against grants to the Prince of Wales's children.[44]

The 1887 Jubilee demonstrated how unpopular republicanism had become. As Foote said to Wheeler at the time, 'Here is something that threatens to swamp us all.' 'It was,' he recalled, 'a splendid display of militarism. Nothing else in the life of England was represented. It was the Widow of Windsor and her Army and Navy.' He was right. The 'retreat from Reason' was about to begin: the period of Liberal supremacy was over; the N.S.S. was in decline; imperialism was the new creed of the day. In 1889 the *Radical* drew back on its freethought basis and introduced articles specially for

Secularists; but in September Standring had to bring it to a close after fourteen years of fruitless journalism.[45] Thereafter republicanism rumbled on in the *National Reformer* and *Freethinker*, rarely finding an opportunity for overt expression. The Prince of Wales continued to be an asset to republican propagandists; and the Jubilee of 1897 and the death of Queen Victoria both provided Foote with events on which to pass some sound, commonsense comments, while the rest of the nation wallowed in sentimentality—though the N.S.S. was realistic enough to rent out seats in the office window for the Jubilee procession in 1897.[46]

The most apt summary of this history of failure came from the pen of J. Ramsay MacDonald, writing in the Ethical journal, *Democracy*, in 1901:

In the 'seventies the throne seemed to be tottering. The *Impeachment of the House of Brunswick* was selling by the thousand; the Queen and the Prince of Wales had no hold upon the popular mind; there was a spirit of democratic independence abroad; the common man believed in the common man. That has gone.[47]

He did not say why. In 1910 even Chapman Cohen in the *Freethinker* had some good to say of Edward VII. He had, after all, behaved as a constitutional monarch—unlike his mother; he had worked for international understanding and peace; and his deathbed thoughts had not been of his Maker, but whether his horse, Witch of the Air, had won at Kempton![48]

*The aristocracy*

Part of the republican programme was for the abolition of the House of Lords. The delay to the 1884 Franchise Bill in the Lords occasioned a protest meeting in Hyde Park and a further one in St James's Hall, at which Bradlaugh was one of the speakers. The reaction was both customary and ineffective. The different leaders had their own ideas about what to do with Their Lordships. Wheeler wanted not abolition but reform, including the creation of life peers, the restriction of the power of veto to one session only, and, of course, the replacement of the bishops by lay peers. Bradlaugh, in theory at least, wanted total abolition, but in practice was prepared to settle for reform rather than revolution.[49] In November 1884 the N.S.S. affiliated to the League for the Abolition of the Hereditary Chamber, with Besant and Foote as its representatives on the general council. In a new agitation brought about by the Lords' rejection of Home Rule in 1893, the N.S.S.

again had two representatives (Foote and Moss) 'on account of its size and formidability'—a rare acknowledgement of the central importance of the N.S.S., even at this late date, in radical agitations. The usual demonstration was held in Hyde Park, with Moss, Foote and Edith Vance of the N.S.S. among the speakers, but all was in vain. Not until the next crisis in 1909–10 were the Lords' powers finally curtailed.[50]

Another aspect of the republican war against the aristocracy was Bradlaugh's attack on perpetual pensions, which were for many noble families what the Civil List was for the monarchy—the Churchill family pension alone was worth £4,000 a year. In 1880 Secular societies were warned to prepare petitions ready for a parliamentary initiative by Bradlaugh in 1881. By April, 943 petitions had been presented with 269,151 signatures, but Bradlaugh was unable to move for a Select Committee as he was not allowed to take his seat. When finally accepted in 1886, his first act was to give notice of a Question on perpetual pensions, but his attempt to move for a Select Committee was frustrated by the curtailment of private members' time during the Second Reading of the Home Rule Bill. The Select Committee was, however, appointed by the Conservative administration in 1887, and Bradlaugh's motion for a full enquiry was accepted by the House the following year. The government then rejected the Select Committee's recommendations and simply decided to continue the practice of commutation at twenty-seven years' purchase. An attempt the following year to reverse this decision failed by 205 to 264 votes. The issue had nevertheless been raised, and the Secularists doubtless gained a little from association with the campaign against what radicals widely regarded as a system of 'outdoor relief' for the aristocracy.[51]

### Ireland

The most blatant example of landlordism and English Imperialism was in Ireland, and the Secularists, like most radicals, had strong feelings about English government there. Bradlaugh sympathised with the aims of the Fenians but not their methods. Ever since serving in the British army in Ireland as a young man he had felt strongly on behalf of the Irish. In March 1867 the Fenians, Kelly and Cluseret, had met in Bradlaugh's house to draft their manifesto, with which he helped them although he did not agree with all the points it contained. Then, after the arrest of the Fenians in Manchester in September, he seconded the proposal at a public meeting on Clerkenwell Green for a memorial to the government on behalf of the prisoners; but when forty people were killed in an attempt to release the prisoners in December, Bradlaugh had nothing but condemnation for the violence.[52]

These events stirred him to take up the Irish question. In October 1867 he published 'A Plea for Ireland' in the *National Reformer*, followed by 'The Irish Question' in January 1868. His policy at this time was to advocate justice and land reform for Ireland, not Home Rule, though in 1871 he opened the columns of the *National Reformer* to a discussion of Isaac Butt's Home Rule proposals. In 1880 he, Besant and Levy were all supporters of Gladstone's policy, attributing the need for the arrest of Land Leaguers to the legacy of the Tory government, but opposed to any measure of coercion which went beyond the existing law. Bradlaugh supported the 'Clôture' brought on by Irish obstructionism in Parliament, but he led the unsuccessful opposition to the Coercion Bill. Charles Watts in the *Secular Review* expressed similar views: whilst recognising the justice of the Irish case, he was opposed to the separation of Ireland from England, and thought the Irish wrong not to give Gladstone's Land Act a fair trial. The remedy, he characteristically added, lay in educating the peasantry to emancipate them 'from slavish obedience to the authority of priests'. The Irish did not always reciprocate these expressions of support: the Irish M.P.s played an important part in keeping Bradlaugh out of the House of Commons; while the journal of the Land League complained that 'the morals and the mental health of Ireland are assailed from England in the most dangerous and insidious fashion every week' when the *Freethinker* was sold in Dublin.[53]

The Secularist leaders seem generally to have supported Irish self-government but opposed complete Home Rule. Holyoake and Robertson, no less than Bradlaugh, Besant and Watts, held this view; but when Gladstone declared for Home Rule in 1885 they reluctantly fell into line. Bradlaugh recognised that it was eighteen years too late to implement Isaac Butt's limited proposals, and his advice to Secularists in April 1886 was 'to stand firmly by Mr Gladstone in granting self-government to Ireland'. At a mass meeting at St James's Hall on 22 April, chaired by Labouchere, all the London branches of the N.S.S., except Bermondsey and East London, gave their support. What disturbed Secularists, as it disturbed many other Liberals, about the proposals was what Foote called 'Mr Gladstone's Irish Stew': as Annie Besant pointed out, the abandonment of any provision for Irish Members at Westminster would either reduce Ireland to colonial status or make it virtually independent; neither was desirable, and she favoured the federal solution. George Standring also thought a federal solution, with local self-government, the only practical way of maintaining fraternity between north and south in Ireland, though he was willing to support Gladstone in the general election campaign of 1886. Foote, though, went so far as to agree with Chamberlain in support of local self-government. He reminded his readers that 'there is little doubt the desire of the priests is that Home Rule shall mean Rome Rule', and he added a cartoon of a Catholic priest riding on the back of a pig. The Belfast riots in the summer of 1886 underlined Foote's belief that the Irish difficulty was fundamentally a religious one.[54]

By 1890 Foote and Wheeler had changed their minds about Home Rule, if not about the Church. They now argued that the Home Rule struggle was perpetuating the influence of the priesthood, which would wane once Home Rule had been granted. During the 1890s the Ulster question replaced the Catholic question in the minds of the readers of the *Freethinker*, though religious divisions penetrated even the Ulster branch of the N.S.S., with W. M. Knox, the branch secretary, criticising Protestants and Catholics alike, while John Kennedy supported the Unionists, who, he said, comprised 'the whole Protestant population of every sect, which forms a large majority in the six counties of the plantation, with a few Catholics who have anything to lose'. Both Foote, and Robertson in the *National Reformer*, were inclined to agree with Knox, and condemned Orangemen as much as Catholics.[55] Despite occasional voices against Home Rule, usually on anti-Catholic rather than Unionist grounds, the Secularists seem to have settled by 1893 for a federal solution to the Irish problem. Sympathy for the majority of the Irish people proved greater than anti-Catholicism throughout the period 1866–1915, and in the end it was the intolerance of the Protestant minority that came in for most criticism. In 1914 Foote reminded Edward Carson, 'It was not God, but Great Britain, that made the Protestant the upper dog in the Irish fight.'[56]

## The Eastern Question

The Eastern Question aroused deep feelings among radicals, whose anti-Russian sentiments were strongly expressed in both 1876 and 1878, and the freethinkers, felt no special attraction to a Christian cause and were cool towards Russia throughout. If they showed any bias at all, it was towards the Turk. Bradlaugh, Foote, Mrs Law and Watts all condemned the Bulgarian Horrors, but unlike Mr Gladstone they refused to take a partisan viewpoint, blaming the conflict on the religious bigotry of both sides. Foote wrote in his *Secularist*, 'Let us strive to procure justice for the Sclavonic provinces, but let us not do Mohammedanism injustice or attempt to resolve the Eastern Question into a religious war.' One correspondent thought Gladstone deserved praise for taking his stand on the broad ground of humanity, but Theodore Wright was probably more typical in urging freethinkers to see that humanity was the victim of both sides. Bradlaugh was not in favour of the extension of Russian power into Turkey, but was not prepared for a war to prevent it. The most outspoken anti-Russian and anti-Gladstonian views came in prose and verse from William Maccall, writing in the *Secular Chronicle* after the fall of Plevna in 1877: he castigated freethinkers, humanitarians and Liberals who had rejoiced in the victories of Holy Russia, and he suspected a European plot to dismember Turkey similar to that which a century before had led to the partitions of Poland.[57]

In 1878 the freethinkers continued in the main to advocate peace. Bradlaugh's foreign policy was opposition to war with Russia; the adoption of a neutral position between the Russian and Turkish despotisms; opposition to the acquisition of territory by Britain, in Egypt or elsewhere (in 1876 he had opposed the purchase of Suez Canal shares); and opposition to any increase in military or naval expenditure. He also thought that misgovernment by Britain, not Russian aggression, was the major threat to India, and that for anyone to encourage war at a time of trade depression was wicked. He was prominent in the peace demonstrations held in Hyde Park on 24 February and 10 March, at which Tory mobs attacked the demonstrators and were dubbed 'Jingoes' by Holyoake in one of his letters to the *Daily News*. Most freethinkers were opposed to Tory policies on principle, and eventually found themselves, if not in agreement with, then at least in alliance with, Liberal opinion. Throughout the Eastern crises of 1876–78, though, they had maintained the unpopular point of view.[58]

G. W. Foote adopted a similar position in 1896, when Dr John Clifford and the Reverend Hugh Price Hughes and their 'Nonconformist Conscience' were calling for England to fight Turkey in defence of the Armenian Christians. This was Gladstone's last great campaign, and Foote and Wheeler were as little impressed in 1896 as they had been in 1876. Foote wondered whether

Christians in Britain would be so upset if the Armenians were butchering the Turks, and Wheeler wondered what the British would think if the Turks questioned their treatment of the Irish, or of the Matabele in South Africa. In 1912 Foote was again pro-Turkish, arguing that the Christians had overall shown themselves to be more intolerant than the Mohammedans.[59]

## Africa

The same anti-Christian viewpoint informed freethought opinions of British policy in Africa, which again were both coolly rational and unpopular. The heroic, and notoriously Christian, General Gordon received no sympathy whatever in 1885, and Foote's *Freethinker* had a cartoon showing the death of Gordon, entitled 'The Mahdi Answers Prayer'.[60]

In South Africa, the Secularists were opposed to British imperialism. In 1881 the N.S.S. protested at the annexation of the Boer republics and urged branches to write to their local newspapers. In 1899 Chamberlain was compared with the anti-Dreyfusards in France, while Ramsden Balmforth of Huddersfield, now in Cape Town, put the blame on both Chamberlain and Milner.[61]

The issues in the second Anglo-Boer War were, however, more confused than in the first, and the freethinkers adopted several different positions. On the one side, Joseph Symes in Australia had become an imperialist, anxious for Britain to maintain its authority to safeguard the Empire. On the other side, the West Ham branch wanted the N.S.S. to issue a circular in favour of the Boers, as in 1881. In the middle, Foote could support neither, and he and Watts favoured arbitration. The sight of two 'Christian' nations in armed conflict was a source of bitter amusement, and a cartoon appeared in the *Truth Seeker* showing John Bull and Paul Kruger fighting around the Cross of Faith.[62] General Secularist feeling may have been pro-Boer: at Leicester, during the Secular bazaar in 1900, portraits of Baden Powell, Roberts, French and White had to be covered over with those of Owen, Paine, Holyoake and Mazzini because they were greeted with groans.[63] Foote as ever adopted the most intellectually subtle position. To begin with he recognised with heavy irony that Kruger was a true Christian of the Cromwellian type, though he warned that God would not protect the Boers against the guns of the British Empire. He also recognised the genuine grievances of the Outlanders, but urged the British not to 'rush into the frightful crime of an avoidable war'. Once war had broken out, he deplored the attempt to blame it on Chamberlain, but attributed it both to the British government and people over twenty years, and to the growing ambitions of Kruger and the Boers over the same period. However, he was stirred by the relief of Mafeking: Baden Powell's courage and victory from the position of under-dog touched even Foote's sense of pride, as well as disproving the Boers' claim to have God on their side. This touch of patriotism aside, it would be fair to describe the position adopted by the Secularists in 1900 as officially neutral, but with an inclination towards the Boers among the rank and file.[64]

## *India and the Far East*

India, next to Ireland, was the country most frequently used to exemplify the results of British imperial policy. At the Hall of Science in 1872 Bradlaugh 'commenced a new subject', namely 'How we have treated India', drawing largely on W. M. Torrens's book *Empire in Asia*, but it was Annie Besant, with a long series of articles on India and Afghanistan in the *National Reformer* in 1878 and 1879, who really introduced the topic to the Secularists. Thereafter both Bradlaugh and Besant were keenly interested in the East, and as an M.P. Bradlaugh began to specialise in Indian affairs, culminating in his triumphant visit to the Indian National Congress in December 1889.[65] His championing of native rights led him to be accepted as unofficial 'Member for India' in the tradition of Henry Fawcett and John Bright, and in 1889 he moved an amendment introducing the elective principle into the India Councils Bill, but this Bill, and one of Bradlaugh's own, were both lost at the end of the 1890 session. Through her conversion to Theosophy, Annie Besant, of course, long continued her interest in India, but only W. S. Ross of the other Secularist leaders showed much sympathy with her new views.[66]

The attraction of the East was, nevertheless, undoubtedly a strong one, providing an instance of another religious culture different from and (it was believed) superior to that of the arrogant Christian West.[67] Predictably, therefore, Foote had little sympathy for the Christians in China in 1900; he poured scorn on Christian alarm at the 'Yellow Peril' in 1904; and he took satisfaction in the victory of Japan over Russia in 1905: 'If a Heathen nation can beat a Christian nation in war, and also outshine it in moral as well as intellectual comparison, what will be the fate of Christian pretensions?' he asked.[68] One can only wonder what he would have said of Pearl Harbour—and Hiroshima.

## Peace and war

The freethinkers were, at heart, men of peace, if not outright pacifists. War was to them irrational, and any pleasure they took in exposing Christian hypocrisy on the subject was poor compensation for the horror of war itself. From 1877, when William Heaford argued strongly in favour of the Courts of International Arbitration, to the outbreak of the First World War, the leaders of Secularism associated themselves with the cause of peace. The peace movement, however, was dominated by Christians, and so in 1910 the freethinkers set up their own Peace Society, appealing to Secularists, Positivists, Humanitarians and members of the Ethical societies, with Mrs Bradlaugh Bonner as chairman and J. M. Robertson as president. Beyond passing a resolution opposing compulsory military training in schools, and standing out against any form of conscription, there was little the Peace Society could do.[69] Foote watched rearmament with realistic fatalism: unless nations could agree to arbitration, 'Any country that keeps an army (or navy) at all, is bound in common sense to keep it as strong as is thought necessary,' he argued in 1906; and in 1909 he accepted the rearmament of the navy as 'a necessary evil' but 'no more to be worshipped than the bolts and bars that secure our houses by night'. He thought it ironic that the first 'Dreadnought' should be launched by the wife of the Archbishop of Canterbury.[70]

With the war approaching in 1914 his fatalism grew more pronounced, as all the dreams of his rational youth faded away: 'No, the millennium of peace, fraternity, and happiness is not coming yet. But blessed is he who works for it knowing he will never see it,' he wrote in May, not long before his death. When war did come, he maintained a remarkable sense of proportion, refusing to join in the general condemnation of Germany, and instead insisting that all who had joined in the armaments race had been responsible for the war. He was struck by the irony of Christian nations at war with each other while the 'unspeakable' Turk looked on.[71]

The reaction of a local Secular society to the war is given in Sydney Gimson's recollections of the Leicester society. Convinced that war was inevitable, some members were determined to ensure British success, and enlisted at once; some were lukewarm; some were pacifists and became conscientious objectors when conscription was introduced. A few members left because of the unpatriotic talk of others. Most held together, worked for victory, and shared in the hospitality arranged for refugees from Belgium.[72]

The war broke the International Freethought organisation: Haeckel, the darling of the Rationalists in 1900, blamed the British for the war, as did Paul Carus, the editor of the German-owned *Open Court* periodical of Chicago. Foote considered all sides at fault, though the Germans bore more than an equal share of the blame. When the first major Zeppelin raid came over London in October 1915, killing fifty-six people and wounding 114 others, Chapman Cohen spoke out against retaliatory bombing. The advocacy of reason was to be continued even in the depths of war.[73]

*Notes*

1  *F.*, 3 February 1884; see also C. Watts, *S.R.*, 9 February 1884.
2  See above, pp. 64–6.
3  C. Bradlaugh, 'The Radical Programme', *N.R.*, 26 April, 3, 10 May 1885.
4  *N.R.*, 29 July 1866, 12 May 1867.
5  Quoted in R. Harrison, *Before the Socialists*, p. 115.
6  *Daily Telegraph*, 7 May 1867.
7  C. Bradlaugh to W. E. Gladstone, 18 July 1868, Gladstone papers, B.M. Add. Mss. 44, 111, f. 68.
8  For Marx's view of Bradlaugh in the 1870s see K. Marx to C. Longuet, 4 January 1881, K. Marx and F. Engels, *Werke* (Berlin, 1967), vol. 35, p. 147.
9  G. Howell to C. Bradlaugh, 10 May 1867, B.L. no. 151; and the correspondence between Bradlaugh, Howell, Hughes and Beales, 4 May–18 June 1872, B.L. nos. 253 ff.
10  F. M. Leventhall, *Respectable Radical*, pp. 93–143.
11  *N.R.*, 10 July 1870.
12  R. Harrison, *op. cit.*, pp. 215–20. The O'Brienites were the followers of J. Bronterre O'Brien (d. 1864), a leading socialist campaigner of the 1830s and the 'schoolmaster' of Chartism.
13  H. J. Perkin, 'Land Reform and Class Conflict in Victorian Britain', in J. Butt and I. F. Clarke (eds.), *The Victorians and Social Protest* (Newton Abbot, 1973), pp. 177–217, esp. pp. 195–8.
14  *N.R.*, 29 August 1869, 23 January 1864, 14 March, 4 April 1869, 13, 20 November 1870, 15 January 1871; R. Harrison, *op. cit.*, pp. 219–20. The Land and Labour League also took up the matter of the Game Laws, and P. A. Taylor's Anti-Game Law League was commended to Secularists in *N.R.*, 11 August, 29 December 1872.
15  *N.R.*, 9 September 1874; *Northampton Radical*, 11 November 1874; *S.C.*, 1 July 1874; see also *Secularist*, 11 November 1876; *S.R.*, 27 September 1879, 7, 14, 21 February 1880. Robert Forder was one of those arrested

in John De Morgan's 'liberation' of Plumstead Common in 1876 *S.C.*, 23 July 1876; *S.R.*, 3 September 1876.

16 *N.R.*, 27, 13 July, 19 October, 23 November, 14 December 1879; *S.R.*, 7, 14, 21 February 1880; *Republican*, March 1880.

17 *N.R.*, 29 February, 7 March, 9 May 1880; *Republican*, June 1880, November 1882; E. P. Lawrence, *Henry George in the British Isles* (East Lansing, Mich., 1957), pp. 32–4.

18 *N.R.*, 2 January 1881, 17 September 1882; *Republican*, February 1883; E. P. Lawrence, *op. cit.*, pp. 34–7.

19 *Ibid.*, pp. 51–60; *Republican*, October 1884, September 1883; *N.R.*, 15 March 1885; *Church Reformer*, 15 April 1885; *Progress*, July 1886.

20 *Our Corner*, March 1886; *N.R.*, 2 May 1886, 10 July 1887, 13 May 1888; James Long to C. Bradlaugh, 2 July 1887, B.L. no. 1383; R. Douglas. 'God gave the land to the people', in A. J. A. Morris (ed.), *Edwardian Radicalism, 1900–1914* (London, 1974), pp. 148–61.

21 *N.R.*, 6 March 1870, 23 July 1871 – 1 September 1872. For an example of abuse of the Prince of Wales see 'Royal Patronage of Idiocy', *N.R.*, 23 April 1871.

22 *N.R.*, 4 July 1869, 4 December 1870; R. Harrison, *op. cit.*, pp. 227–8. For the Poor People's Union see *N.R.*, 6 June 1869.

23 *N.R.*, 15, 22 January, 26 February, 26 March 1871.

24 *Republican*, 15 May 1871.

25 *N.R.*, 22 January, 26 February, 2 April 1871; *Republican*, 1 May, 15 July, 1 August 1871; H. Collins and C. Abramsky, *Karl Marx and the British Labour Movement* (London, 1965), pp. 236–9.

26 For Bradlaugh's work on behalf of the Provisional Government see the letters from Charles Tissot, 18 September, 10, 13, 24 October 1870, 4 February 1871—B.L. nos. 217–20, 227–8; *N.R.*, 11 January 1871; *Republican*, 1 July 1871.

27 *Ibid.*, 1 August 1871; *N.R.*, 2 July, 24 September, 8 October, 12 November, 3 December 1871.

28 *N.R.*, 10 December 1871; *Republican*, 15 May 1871; *N.R.*, 15 September 1872; *International Herald*, 13 April 1873.

29 *Eastern Post*, 16, 23 December 1871, quoted in Y. Kapp, *Eleanor Marx*, vol. 1, p. 141; *N.R.*, 24 December 1871; *Eastern Post*, 21 October 1871, quoted in R. Harrison, *op. cit.*, p. 233; *N.R.*, 28 January 1872.

30 N. J. Gossman, 'Republicanism in Nineteenth Century England', *International Review of Social History*, VII (1962), pp. 47–60, esp. pp. 51–3; R. Jenkins, *Sir Charles Dilke* (London, 1958, revised ed. 1965, Fontana ed. 1968), pp. 68–72.

31 *N.R.*, 15 September, 6 October 1872.

32 *N.R.*, 17, 24, 31 March, 25 August 1872 [Patriotic Society]; 27 February 1870; *Radical Leader*, 4 August 1888 [Eleusis Club]; *N.R.*, 13 October 1872 [I.W.M.A. West End Section]. For De Morgan see S. St. Clair, *Sketch of the Life and Labours of John De Morgan* (Leeds, 1880); also *International Herald*, 16 March, 15, 29 June, 12 October 1872; *N.R.*, 1 September, 27 October 1872.

33 *N.R.*, 27 October, 3, 10, 17 November, 1 December 1872. The initiative

in south Yorkshire came from Barnsley, where the power-loom weavers were locked out for demanding an advance in wages, and were supported by the Leeds Section of the I.W.M.A. The Barnsley secretary was Thomas Kelly—*International Herald*, 28 September, 5, 12, 19, 26 October 1872.

34   *N.R.*, 8 December 1872; *International Herald*, 7, 14, 21 December 1872, 4 January 1873; *N.R.*, 15 December 1872, 12, 26 January, 2 February 1873; *International Herald*, 22 February 1873; *S.C.*, February, March 1873; *N.R.*, 18 May, 1–22 June 1873. The *International Herald* kept up its criticisms of Bradlaugh and his wing of the movement throughout the spring and summer of 1873. For a less than flattering account of Bradlaugh in Spain, see *International Herald*, 30 August 1873.

35   *N.R.*, 6, 27 April, 3, 10 August 1873; for opposition to Bradlaugh see *International Herald*, 8, 15, 22 March, 10, 24, 31 May, 7 June, 5 July, 2, 9 August 1873.

36   *N.R.*, 3, 10 August 1873, 8 February, 22 March 1874.

37   *Republican Chronicle*, April, May 1875. For the political tradition of the London Clubs see C. Booth, *Life and Labour*, series I, vol. 1, p. 99.

38   *N.R.*, 16 May, 25 July 1875, 25 June 1876.

39   *N.R.* 9 April 1876; *S.C.*, 16 June 1878.

40   *Republican*, January 1880, February, April, November, December 1881, February, May, July, December 1882.

41   *S.R.*, 1, 8 February 1882; see a similarly phrased passage in *S.R.*, 7 January 1882.

42   *S.R.*, 11 March 1882.

43   *Republican*, April, June, November 1883, January, March, April 1884, February, May 1885, August 1886.

44   *Ibid.*, January 1886; *N.R.*, 4 August 1889.

45   *N.R.*, 9 January 1887; *F.*, 5 June 1887; *Radical*, February, April 1887, January 1889; *N.R.*, 6 October 1889.

46   *N.R.*, 9 July 1893; *F.*, 23 May, 6 June 1897, 3 February 1901.

47   *Democracy*, 23 February 1901.

48   *F.*, 15 May 1910.

49   *Republican*, August, September 1884; *N.R.*, 17 August 1884; *Our Corner*, September 1884; *N.R.*, 14, 21 September 1884.

50   *N.R.*, 7 December 1884; *F.*, 29 October 1893, 2 September 1894, 5 December 1909.

51   *F.*, 25 May 1884; *N.R.*, 28 November, 5, 12 December 1880, 30 January, 6, 20 February, 13, 20 March, 3, 17 April, 1 May 1881, 31 January, 21 March, 23 May, 5 September 1886, 1 April, 26 August 1888, 26 May 1889.

52   H. B. Bonner and J. M. Robertson, *Charles Bradlaugh*, I, pp. 33–4, 252–62; *N.R.*, 24 November, 22 December 1867.

53   *N.R.*, 20 October 1867, 19, 26 January 1868, 26 November 1871, 28 January 1872, 4 May 1873, 14, 28 November 1880, 30 January, 13 February 1881; *S.R.*, 29 October 1881, 17 June 1882; W. Arnstein, 'Parnell and the Bradlaugh Case', *Irish Historical Studies*, XIII no. 51 (March 1963), pp. 212–35; *F.*, 9 July 1882.

54  *S.R.*, 12 November 1881; *Our Corner*, October, November 1883; *N.R.*, 27 December 1885, 3 January, 18 April, 2 May 1886; *F.*, 20 June 1886; *Our Corner*, June 1886; *Republican*, June, July 1886; *F.*, 31 January, 20 June, 22 August 1886.
55  *F.*, 6, 13 April 1890, 10 May 1891, 26 June, 10 July 1892.
56  *N.R.*, 14 August, 10 July 1892, 19 February 1893; *F.*, 19 July 1914.
57  *S.C.*, 10 September 1876; *N.R.*, 24 September, 29 October, 5 November 1876; *Secularist*, 9, 16, 23 September 1876; *N.R.*, 3 December 1876; *S.C.*, 30 December 1877; see also *S.C.*, 16 September 1877.
58  *N.R.*, 9, 16 January, 27 February 1876, 6 January, 24 February, 10 March 1878; *Daily News*, 13 March 1878; see also *S.R.*, 11 May 1878.
59  *F.*, 25 October 1896, 17 November 1912. For Foote's attitude towards Greeks and Turks in Crete see *F.*, 28 February 1897.
60  *F.*, 15, 22 February 1885.
61  *N.R.*, 6 March 1881; *Republican*, March 1881; *F.*, 17 September 1899; *Ethical World*, 2 December 1899. Ramsden Balmforth was the brother of Owen Balmforth, the Huddersfield Secularist.
62  *F.*, 29 October 1899, 4 March 1900; *Truth Seeker*, January 1900; *F.*, 11, 18 February, 4 March 1900; N.S.S. Minute Book IV, 22 February 1900. Symes also advanced the view that the British would treat the blacks better than the Boers had done.
63  *F.*, 30 September 1900. Sydney Gimson recalled that most of the Leicester Secular Society members were 'Pro-Boers', and several protest meetings were held in their hall, one addressed by J. M. Robertson on 6 January 1901, with lantern slides, on the British concentration camps. Robertson had been out to South Africa as a reporter for the *Morning Leader*—S. A. Gimson, 'Random Recollections', II, pp. 9–11.
64  *F.*, 3 September, 29 October, 5, 12 November 1899, 27 May 1900.
65  *N.R.*, 3, 10 March 1872, 10 November–22 December 1878, 14, 21 December 1879, 25 November 1883, 6 February 1887, 4 August 1889, 26 January 1890. See also the correspondence in the Bradlaugh papers (N.S.S.) concerning the Burma ruby mines (1887), and Bradlaugh's visit to the Indian National Congress (1889).
66  *N.R.*, 30 March, 10 August 1890; *A.J.*, 29 July, 5 August 1905.
67  E.g. J. M. Wheeler on Buddhism, *F.*, 20 August 1882.
68  *F.*, 29 July, 7 October 1900, 4 September 1904, 21 May 1905.
69  *S.C.*, 30 September 1877; *F.*, 13, 20 November 1910, 18 February 1912, 23 February 1913.
70  *F.*, 5 August 1906, 25 July 1909, 22 January 1911.
71  *F.*, 3 May, 9, 16, 23 August 1914.
72  S. A. Gimson, *op. cit.*, II, pp. 30–1.
73  *L.G.*, May 1915; *F.*, 7 March, 24 October 1915; see also N.S.S. Minute Book IV, 27 August 1914.

# XII

# Liberalism, labour and socialism

## Liberalism

In foreign and domestic policies alike, there was little to distinguish the freethinkers from the rest of the radical wing of the Liberal party, except in so far as religion entered directly into consideration, or when an anti-religious moral could be hung on a political story.

In the 1860s Mr Gladstone appeared to symbolise all that was bright in the radicals' future: believing him 'to be the most able and honest statesman whom the people have on their side', Bradlaugh was expressing a view commonly held in 1867[1] Gladstone's first Ministry was, of course, something of a disappointment to working men, and calls were made in the *Secular Chronicle* for the direct representation of labour. Speaking at a conference held in Birmingham Town Hall in 1872, George Reddalls advocated a working-class electoral fund to support candidates against intransigent Liberals; and in 1875 Charles Cattell and 'Civis Mundi' both returned to the subject in a discussion in the *Secular Chronicle*.[2] Nevertheless, such was the radicals' detestation of Toryism, and particularly of Beaconsfield's foreign policy, that this opposition to certain aspects of the Liberal party never developed into a complete attack on the party, and Mr Gladstone's personal standing remained high. By late 1876 M. C. O'Byrne was demanding in the *Secular Chronicle* that Mr Gladstone should resume the leadership of the Liberals, a theme echoed in the *Secular Review* by Charles Watts a few months later.[3] The Liberal victory of 1880 was hailed as a new dawn. With pardonable exaggeration, G. J. Holyoake spoke the prevalent mood in the *Secular Review*:

The dead days of the Tory rule are over. Progress has been dead for six years. Political life has been suspended. The enterprise of industry has been arrested. The savings of the people are wasted. Public debt was increasing. All is changed now. The Liberal benches of Parliament are crowded with new members bent on prosecuting the interests of justice and progress. The political atmosphere is fresh and sweet once more. England is like a new country. Men greet each other in the streets as though a great calamity had been arrested or a great plague swept away. This is the meaning of the recent revolution.[4]

This was before the outbreak of the Bradlaugh case, Irish coercion, and the bombardment of Alexandria. Within a couple of years a distinct split in Secularist attitudes emerged. To some of the older leaders Gladstone could still do little wrong, and the defects of his Ministry could be blamed on the Whigs. This was the line taken by Bradlaugh, Levy and Besant in the *National Reformer*. On the other hand there was increasing pressure from other leaders for radicals and labour to reassert themselves independently of the Liberals. In 1883, W. S. Ross went furthest in suggesting that Secularists should contest elections as Secularists rather than as radicals, but most freethinkers were thinking in terms of participation in a new radicalism. Following the example of the French radicals, Foote called in 1884 for a new Radical party; and J. M. Wheeler told freethinkers not to waste their votes on inconsistent Liberals in the coming election.[5]

In all this, Mr Gladstone's personal reputation was undiminished. The enemies of the people were the Whigs, and, surprisingly, 'Brummagem Liberalism' led by Chamberlain, which Foote described as 'the politics of middle-class Dissent'. Gladstone had, according to George Standring, been led astray 'by usurers, stock-jobbers and military adventurers'. Standring, like a number of other Secularists, was later to turn in his disillusionment to socialism. Many others, though, continued to adhere to the principles of Liberalism, and both Bradlaugh and Foote gave a clear lead in this latter direction. In an article in *Our Corner* on 'Mr Gladstone, Lord Salisbury, and Lord Hartington', Bradlaugh had no difficulty in deciding which he preferred. All the leaders of freethought were agreed that, whatever the failures of Liberalism had been, the only good thing that could be said for Toryism was that it might produce a genuinely radical reaction in the country.[6]

By the end of the decade the mood had changed. Not only was Mr Gladstone's religion out of date, but even as a politician he was now seen to have 'held Radicalism in check by his unquestionable ascendancy and the glamour of his personality'. 'He was certainly not a thinker in any proper meaning of the word,' added Foote on Gladstone's death; 'He was rarely five minutes in advance of the average man on any great question.'[7] The man who did think ahead, Chamberlain, had gone over to the Conservatives, as Charles Cattell had prophesied as early as 1874.[8] The other great radical, to whom many freethinkers looked, was Charles Dilke, but he had been broken by 'Mrs Grundy' in 1886.[9] Liberalism was increasingly identified with Nonconformity, which soured relations between it and the Secularists. J. M. Robertson argued that Nonconformity had now lost its cutting edge; it had ceased to be thinking and critical; the new radical impulse within Liberalism would have to come from freethought. This he attempted to provide in the pages of the *National Reformer*, in two carefully argued articles entitled 'A Sketch of a System of Politics'. He also took a prominent part in the movement towards the 'New Liberalism' which reached fruition in 1906.[10] But Secularism was too weak to be an effective political force within Liberalism in the twentieth century; by the Edwardian years it had been reduced to a pressure group on the fringes of the political world.

No other prominent Secularist, apart from Bradlaugh, was elected to Parliament until Robertson was returned for Tyneside in 1906, although active agnostics like Samuel Laing and John Morley were M.P.s and rose to high positions, as did John Burns, who had attended the Battersea branch of the N.S.S. in the 1880s. Secularists were nevertheless actively involved in radical politics at both national and local level. This was particularly true of the 1880s, when radicalism emerged as a strong political force. Charles Watts considered standing at Hull in the 1880 general election, but withdrew to avoid splitting the Liberal vote; G. J. Holyoake unsuccessfully sought the Liberal nomination at Leicester in 1884; and Foote came forward in 1885 at Walworth, failing to secure nomination by only a narrow margin.[11] Annie Besant argued that the strong radicalism of the 1880s had been created by the persistent lecturing work of the N.S.S. during the previous four years, and, with the Bradlaugh case to focus people's attention for the next six years, the N.S.S. continued to be a central feature in the organisation of radical opinion in the country, exerting an influence far beyond the narrow confines of freethought. As the parliamentary reform agitation reached a climax in the summer of 1884, it was often local Secularists who, inspired by Bradlaugh, organised the demonstrations.[12] From 1885, though, reaction appeared to be setting in. The 'caucus' system, by which the Liberal party was now controlled, was seen to be working against the radicals, and particularly against working-class candidates. In the *National Reformer* Levy called for proportional representation; while Foote feared that the new single-member constituencies would 'vestrify' politics and give all power to the caucus. He considered 'politics will be seriously debased unless the Second Ballot and the Payment of

Members are inserted in the constitution'.[13]

The setback of 1885 and the shock of defeat at the polls in 1886, especially marked in London, stirred the radicals to new organisation. The old borough of Marylebone returned four Liberals and five Conservatives in 1885, and as a result the various radical clubs, including the North West, West Central and Paddington branches of the N.S.S., formed the 'Combined Political Committee, Federated Clubs and Associations, Marylebone', to agitate for a complete radical programme, including a large measure of Secularist reforms. On 24 March 1886, at a conference at the Hall of Science, the radicals of London came together in the Metropolitan Radical Federation, with a programme of adult suffrage, a shorter residential qualification, compulsory registration of voters, the second ballot, the payment of M.P.s and election expenses, shorter Parliaments, compulsory secular and free education, the abolition of the hereditary principle in legislation, reform of the land laws, separation of Church and State, and a reform of local government, including Home Rule for Ireland. The Federation, which survived into the twentieth century, was prominent for less than ten years: it was built on the London clubs, many of which were Secularist origin, and its decline and that of freethought were two sides of the same coin. The N.S.S. was an affiliated member, and G. W. Foote was actively involved in its propaganda. At the first annual dinner, though, a significant split occurred which divided Bradlaugh from Foote. The latter wanted the radicals to remain independent of any other party; the former wanted the M.R.F. to unite with the Liberals to attack all upholders of privilege. In the event, Bradlaugh's view was to triumph and, after the reform of local government in London, the strength of Secularists and radicals alike was sunk in the Progressive cause.[14]

In general in the 1890s, not only was freethought contracting, but it was also retreating from a direct involvement in politics. Its programme was increasingly restricted to reforms of particular interest to Secularists—the abolition of the oath, repeal of the blasphemy laws and the Sunday observance laws, compulsory non-religious education in all schools receiving public funds, abolition of all chaplaincies paid for out of the public purse, compulsory civil marriage and easier divorce, and repeal of all laws exempting churches, Church schools and other such buildings from taxation. This programme, set out by the Lancashire and Yorkshire Secular Federation in 1892, accurately reflects what most freethinkers were coming to feel the main purpose of their movement to be. Neo-

Malthusianism, peace and republicanism still figured in Mrs Bradlaugh Bonner's progamme in the *Reformer* in 1897, but under Foote the N.S.S. turned away from such causes, even though they had been of central importance to Bradlaugh in the 1880s.[15]

There were several reasons for this shift in emphasis. Partly, the number of political opinions within freethought was increasing. No longer were there merely degrees of radicalism; now there was socialism and even Conservatism as well. A number of the agnostic contributors to the *Secular Review*, Captain W. B. McTaggart, William Maccall and Joseph Ellis ('Philip Dawson') were all described as 'Conservatives' in 1888. In 1890 C. A. Watts was advising Foote to avoid all party politics, and the Belfast branch in 1894 urged the N.S.S. to end its subscriptions 'to the Metropolitan Radical Federation, the League for the Abolition of the House of Lords or any other political organisation'. By 1900 Foote was putting his faith in a free press, not the election of representatives. He saw the task of freethinkers as to mould public opinion, not to indulge in politics: 'We would rather be a force than a register—a cause than the most conspicuous effect.'[16]

This was putting a brave face on the failure of Secularism to retain the position of political importance it had occupied in the early 1880s, but it was also an indication of a change within Liberalism itself. Not only Ross, but also Foote, was beginning to have doubts about democracy. The older generation of radicals was growing disillusioned with the Liberal society it had fought for.[17]

*Liberty and libertarianism*

J. H. Levy, whose ideas were second only to Bradlaugh's in the *National Reformer*, was a typical example of the older generation of freethinkers. In a critical but generous portrait of him Belfort Bax wrote that Levy

used to pride himself on being an ultra-individualist. While holding in the main most of the planks of the old political Radicalism, his gospel always remained Mill's "Essay on Liberty." His hatred of all State action, other than that of the barest and most necessary police regulation, was an obsession with him. His political faith might be summed up in the phrase *laisser faire à outrance*. Yet, ... Levy was a scrupulously tolerant person, always ready to give his opponents a fair hearing, who regarded free discussion as the first of the rights of man.[18]

The same could have been written of Bradlaugh, Watts, Foote or Holyoake, and their mistrust of the state was a deeply held prejudice among many working-class radicals.[19] In criticism of Mrs Besant in 1888, Foote asserted the creed of every Liberal: 'Freethought must be personal. My brain is my castle, my conscience is my sanctuary. No one has a right there but I'; but he went on, more controversially,

Mrs Besant says that this brutal usurpation of the majority is 'in accordance with the principles of Democracy.' Not as I understand them. If Democracy meant that, I should be against Democracy. I regard Freethought as primarily above all forms of government and all social institutions.[20]

The older generation had assumed that Liberalism, Individualism and Democracy were compatible. The younger generation of Liberals, following the cue of J. S. Mill himself, began to have doubts. Such Liberalism could develop in the direction of anarchism or 'faddism', or, indeed, anti-democratic élitism, protected from outright authoritarianism only by a desire to restrain all majorities and minorities alike, including their own.

Freethought was always likely to attract the eccentric and the individualist, as G. W. Foote discovered as editor of the *Freethinker*:

Editing a Freethought paper is a dreadful business. It brings one into contact with many half-baked people who have little recipes for hastening the millennium; with ambitious versifiers who think it a disgrace to journalism that their productions are not instantly inserted; with discontented ladies and gentlemen who fancy that a heterodox paper is the proper vehicle for every species of complaint, and with a multitude of other loves too numerous to mention and too diverse to classify.[21]

Among the issues discussed in the freethought press were temperance, capital punishment, spelling reform, vegetarianism, anti-vivisection and anti-vaccination. On temperance, Robertson was prepared to support the local veto, together with free trade in drink, but Foote detected in the United Kingdom Alliance 'the impulse, deeply rooted in our nature, which impels us to mould all humanity according to the pattern of our own desires'. The argument for compulsory abstinence was akin to prohibiting shaving to stop other people cutting their throats; it 'would mean the tyranny of a few over the many, and would compel society to live according to the needs of weaklings and fools'. Behind Harcourt's Local Veto Bill of 1895 he saw the dark shadow of the 'Nonconformist Conscience'.[22]

Capital punishment the freethinkers were generally opposed to, though Foote doubted whether it was really humane or desirable either to lock a murderer up for life, or to let him loose again on society.[23] Reformed spelling ('honor', 'Labor', etc.) was used in both the *National Reformer* and the *Freethinker*. Only a minority seem to have taken vegetarianism seriously—G. W. Foote once declared, 'I am a vegetarian myself, but I like a little meat with it'[24]—but vivisection aroused great passions. In his study of the subject R. D. French has seen the anti-vivisection movement as characterised by a reaction on the part of religious and literary men against the advance of scientific naturalism. This ought to put the freethinkers firmly in the pro-vivisection camp, against such reactionary sentimentalists as Cardinal Manning and Lord Shaftesbury. In fact, it did not. Annie Besant's initial position was that of the pro-vivisection scientist (though in 1892 she recanted), and some Secularists justified research on live animals in terms of the benefits it offered in treating humans. G. W. Foote, on the other hand, perhaps falling into the 'literary' category, was opposed to vivisection, and was a close friend of Henry Salt of the Humanitarian League. In 1895 and 1904 he gave formal lectures to the League on 'The Rights of Men and the Rights of Animals' and 'The Kinship of Life', in which he argued that evolution had shown the animals to be our relatives if not quite our brothers, and that the principle of utility required the minimisation of *all* pain. One of the practical objects of the N.S.S. under his presidency was 'An extension of the moral law to animals, so as to secure them humane and legal protection against cruelty'.[25]

The compulsory vaccination laws probably aroused greater feeling than any other Victorian health legislation, except possibly the Contagious Diseases Acts. Bradlaugh became interested in the subject in the 1860s, and sat on the Royal Commission appointed in 1889. In 1877 the *Secular Chronicle* urged its readers to protest against 'that unnecessary and mischievous interference with the right of private judgment—Compulsory Vaccination'; and George Bone, secretary of the Walworth Freethought Institute, was also secretary of the South London Anti-Vaccination League. The *National Reformer* contained sympathetic reports of cases in which opponents of vaccination had been fined, and J. M. Robertson estimated that nine-tenths of the readership of the *National Reformer* were opposed to compulsory vaccination. Bradlaugh himself never published his views, but his daughter said that he was an anti-vaccinator; and in the columns of the *National Reformer* Levy went so far as to claim that the Infectious Diseases Notification Bill of 1889 amounted to a Bill to allow the compulsory imprisonment in hospital of innocent people. One of the few Secularists to support vaccination was Charles Drysdale, a doctor, who believed the vaccination process could be made safer and more acceptable. To Foote, the law requiring compulsory vaccination was 'an assumption of medical infallibility . . . almost as absurd as the pretensions of the priest'. He was appalled that a father whose child had died after vaccination could be imprisoned for not having his other children vaccinated. Compulsory vaccination in these circumstances was 'one more instance of the outrages upon personal liberty which show what a farce it is to boast about our land of freedom'.[26] George Weir, one of J. W. Gott's blasphemous lecturers, spent a week in gaol in Glasgow for refusing to have his child vaccinated. He was secretary of the Leeds branch of the Anti-Vaccination League, and helped defend several parents in court charged with the same offence. John Benson, the Leeds N.S.S. branch newsagent, had the distinction of being the first man in Leeds to be sent to Armley gaol under the vaccination laws. When Aurelis Wakefield was converted to freethought, 'He also took an active part in political controversy, and supported temperance views, though not holding the total abstinence ideal; and later became a prominent anti-vaccinist, a cremationist, a Republican, Malthusian, and Liberationist, and also an advocate of Co-operation'.[27]

Such a collection of interests came naturally to a freethinker. At times Liberalism could easily move over into libertarianism. J. Greevz Fisher, the Leeds leader, offered himself as a 'Liberty candidate' for East Bradford in 1892 on a programme of 'voluntary taxation, no compulsory education, liberty for Ireland with no government, the abolition of professional monopolies, and female freedom'. With the exception of the latter item, very little of this programme was supported by any of the other freethinkers. J. M. Robertson called it 'Anarchism without dynamite'.[28] Foote was accused on one occasion of clinging 'with a faith child-like in its simplicity, to the despotism of *Government* and *Law*'. Such complaints normally came from that northern group based on the Bradford *Truth Seeker*, where socialism, anarchism and libertarianism received considerable support once Gott had taken charge of the paper—though one does not know quite how seriously to take men like Malfew Seklew, who called his personal philosophy 'Atheogism', which he defined as 'the economics of Socialism, the politics of Anarchism, the common sense of science, the class consciousness of the S.D.F. and the self-consciousness of the disillusioned Ego, freed from social, sexual, political, moral, and religious superstitions and sophisms'.[29] At the other extreme, a fanatical adherence to the principles of liberty led some freethinkers

into the Liberty and Property Defence League. Fredrick Millar, a
leading member of the League, was also a principal contributor to
the *Agnostic Journal*, and even G. J. Holyoake joined in the 1890s,
under the impression that it offered 'self-defensive individualism',
though George Standring was being a little more perceptive when he
said, 'The Liberty and Property defenders deprecate State
interference, not in the interests of a generous and enlightened
individualism, but as a possible means of obstructing the spirit of
reform.'[30]

Both these extremes were a far cry from the sober, serious and
moderate discussions on politics and society which took place in the
*National Reformer*, the *Freethinker* and the *Secular Review*. On the one
hand, with Levy, who edited the journal of the Personal Rights
Association, Bradlaugh, Foote, Watts, Holyoake and the rest were
strong upholders of individual liberty, but on the other they were
political realists and sought not the abolition of the State, but a
utilitarian balance between the claims of the State and of the
individual, along the lines of Mill's essay *On Liberty*.[31] Steering a
middle way between libertarians and socialists, Charles Watts
argued the classic case for representative democracy:

The liberty of the individual consists in his being master of his own actions
in so far as his conduct is consistent with the laws of his country and the
welfare of the community. While the liberty of the people in general consists
in their being governed by laws of their own making or adoption.

Applied to social questions, this meant 'that, in pursing our own
good in our own way, we should strive not to unnecessarily damage
the interests of others'. For him, this meant opposition to all but
moral force, and co-operative rather than State socialism. With J. S.
Mill, Watts mistrusted a blind faith in the majority, especially when
that majority was under the sway of religion: majority decisions
were not automatically right, and minorities, right or wrong, had
just as important a part to play in human progress as majorities.[32]
With regard to the violent anarchists who so troubled the 1890s,
Foote was clear that violence was wrong (including the legitimised
violence of the State against those anarchists who had thought, but
not actually acted out, their violence). However, he recognised that
once the anarchists had struck, as in Barcelona in 1897, there must
be sufficient State power to maintain the equal claims of all men to
freedom against the aggression of individuals claiming too much
freedom for themselves. For Foote, as for generations of Liberals, the
State's essential function was as policeman, safeguarding liberty and

maximising it.[33]

## Social Darwinism

As a group of men and women who put their faith in science and individualism, the freethinkers were peculiarly exposed to those Social Darwinist ideas which became so fashionable in the later nineteenth century, and which, particularly as developed by the younger freethought leaders, came dangerously near to negating the very liberalism upon which they prided themselves. Nothing could illustrate better the élitist implications of Liberalism when democracy and liberty appeared to beckon down different paths.

This is not to say that every freethinker, even when a Liberal individualist, was prepared to accept the whole of Herbert Spencer's work uncritically. Those who took his politics were most likely to be old Liberals like J. H. Levy, G. J. Holyoake and Bradlaugh. On the other hand, Chapman Cohen was critical of Spencer's static and atomised view of society, and was echoing a view more widely accepted at the end of the nineteenth century, when he argued that the individual and the State were two aspects of the one organism, each dependent on the other. Spencer's political thought, however, was not always connected logically with his social thought, and it was this latter which began to captivate those men whose intellectual apparatus was developed after the 1860s.[34]

The language of biology—evolution, race, inheritance—was unavoidable in political and social discussions, and not all of it should be taken to imply acceptance of a rigorous Social Darwinism. However, in discussions about neo-Malthusianism and socialism, Social Darwinism became central.

The theory of evolution itself had no moral or political connotations, and could as easily lead to A. R. Wallace's socialism as to Herbert Spencer's individualism, depending on the inclinations of those who came to biology for a justification of their prior political theories.[35] All sides seem to have agreed that the future of the race was in peril, but they differed widely in the conclusions they drew. Most of the Secularist leaders, except Ross, thought natural competition and birth control compatible, and that to limit the population would be beneficial; Ross thought that 'Knowltonism' 'would be unconformable with physical law because it would not involve the conditions compatible with the Survival of the Fittest'. Paradoxically, socialist neo-Malthusians, like Besant and George Standring, were optimistic that the example of voluntary restraint on the part of the middle-classes would influence the poor to reduce their own fertility without compulsion; more conservatively-minded Secularists, like Charles Drysdale, wanted the State compulsorily to determine who should be born, to safeguard the quality of the population.[36]

The anti-socialist implications of evolution were exploited by both W. P. Ball and G. W. Foote in defence of individualism. Foote was what J. M. Robertson called a biological fatalist.[37] This became apparent in the third night of his debate on socialism with Mrs Besant in 1887. With G. B. Shaw in the chair, he informed his audience:

You remove competition, and you remove parental responsibility for offspring. The feeding of the children will be done by the State if the parents are unable to do it, and what would be result? (A Voice: 'Enough to eat'.) The result will be—(dissent)—. . . You would have to do one of two things. Either you would have to weed out the utterly incapable—the semi-idiotic, the scrofulous, the consumptive, and all those whom a sensible doctor would declare unfit to procreate—and sternly forbid them to do so. Otherwise you would have a perennial supply of the unfit, who would all flourish; whereas, under the present competitive system, notwithstanding our hospitals, our charities, and our workhouses, they gradually get eliminated, because the odds are against them from the very beginning. (Cheers, and cries of 'No, no'.)[38]

Not only is this a surprising statement, in view both of Foote's suspicion of medical experts (with reference to vaccination[39]), and of his keenness to promote international arbitration to control the struggle between nations; but it is also surprising in its illiberal and inhumanitarian complacency. What is missing here is that sense of compassion which usually distinguished the freethinkers' attitudes towards the poor.[40]

### The labour movement and freethought

The identification of the whole of the working poor with the labour élite, and the assumption that what was possible for the élite was possible for all, lay behind much of the freethinkers' attitude towards labour questions, including their ready adoption of some of the crudities of Social Darwinism.[41]

As radicals, freethinkers supported the political representation of labour, and as individualists they supported the economic freedom of labour. Given the class nature of British politics in the early twentieth century, Foote looked forward to a hundred representatives of labour in the House of Commons, which would do nothing but good, labour not only gaining in power but also in responsibility.[42] This concept of a Labour party was not that of the socialists, though such non-doctrinaire Lib-Labism was the political ideal which was widely accepted by many members of the two largest sections of the labour movement in the nineteenth century—the co-operative and the trade union movements, with both of which freethinkers were actively concerned.

The co-operative movement shared a common ancestry with Secularism in the Owenite movement of the 1830s and 1840s. G. J. Holyoake was a prominent advocate of both, and many local freethought societies (not least that at Rochdale) had in their early days been closely associated with the beginnings of co-operation in their localities.[43] As the co-operative movement grew, however, it moved further away from its idealistic origins; those who retained the greatest commitment to the co-operative vision were an unholy alliance of Christian Socialists and freethinkers. Such people were advocates of producers' as well as of consumers' co-operation, and, despite the failure of co-operative schemes after the collapse of the economic boom of 1873, they continued to offer co-operative production or co-partnership as a *via media* between the two unpalatable extremes of private capitalism and State capitalism.[44] In 1875, for example, Charles Cattell was urging that capital from consumers' stores and from trade unions be used to finance co-operative production, thus ending the master–servant relationship, strikes and lock-outs; he even foresaw the time when co-operation would supersede the trade unions themselves.[45] The conservative possibilities of co-operation did not go unnoticed, and by the 1880s what had started as a radical way of reconstructing the economy had been twisted into a palatable method of fending off the ogre of State socialism.

The attitude of many radicals to the trade union movement was ambivalent. To most it was a regrettable evil made necessary by capitalism, but inappropriate in a co-operative economy. Old Owenites like Holyoake believed this; but other individualists were not prepared to view the unions even in this light. In a debate at the Co-operative Hall, Ardwick (Manchester), in 1867, Thomas Evans, a Secularist lecturer, argued that trade unions represented a monopoly of labour inimical to true freedom, and this fear of the despotism of the unions was far from uncommon. In 1877 Annie Besant debated with Alexander Macdonald, the miners' leader, whether it was right for the miners to lower output in order to protect themselves during the depression; she thought not. In 1902

Holyoake wrote to *The Times*, deploring the tyranny of the unions over the men, which he hoped would be changed after the Taff Vale decision.[46] Nevertheless, freethinkers were also deeply concerned about and involved in trade union affairs, though their general attitude was probably closer to that of Henry Broadhurst than to that of Tom Mann. Bradlaugh's close connection with the miners' unions is well known, as is Annie Besant's involvement as a socialist in the match girls' strike of 1888 and the dock strike the following year. G. W. Foote also spoke at trade union demonstrations; and in 1893-94 the N.S.S. gave a guinea to the miners' lock-out fund—a gesture of support, if nothing else.[47]

In the 1880s two issues arose which drew out the distinctions between many radicals and many, though not all, trade unionists; and both cost Bradlaugh some personal support. On the question of the eight-hour day, Bradlaugh was opposed to legislation to prevent men working longer if they wished. Debating the subject with Hyndman in 1890, he argued

> Some worker may desire to see his children better clad and better fed, with opportunities for more enjoyment—(hear, hear)—and he may specially exert himself, while he thinks he is well and strong, to make provision for the future and to exercise that thrift which is so much sneered at. (Cheers.) (A voice: 'Thrift on 18 bob a week? Bosh!') Yes, thrift is bosh in the words of those opposing me, but it is the life and soul of our country, it is that which has made it what it is.[48]

In both 1889 and 1890 he opposed Cunninghame Graham's Eight Hour Bill. The Northumberland miners may have been exceptional in continuing to support Bradlaugh after this, but they did so on grounds other than his: some coal heavers feared the Bill would *increase* their hours of working *to* eight a day.[49] The other issue was the new Employers' Liability Bill, to extend the provisions of the 1880 Act. Bradlaugh sat on the Select Committee in 1886, where he argued that a workman ought to be free to contract out if he wished. The unions, including the conservative Broadhurst, realised that employers would put pressure on their men to contract out, and so wanted compulsion. It was his attitude towards the Employers' Liability Bill which, in 1889, led *Justice* to call Bradlaugh, rather unfairly, 'the greatest enemy of labor in the House of Commons', and which cost him the support of the Miners' Conference in 1890.[50]

Bradlaugh, Holyoake and Foote should not, however, be taken as wholly representative in this matter. Just as the labour movement itself was much divided between old and new, radical and socialist, skilled and unskilled, so the Secularist movement contained many shades of opinion. Bradlaugh's views were influential, but there was an increasing gap between them and those of a number of his followers in the country. The division between Bradlaugh and Besant in the 1880s represents an important fissure in the old radicalism. Local freethinkers were active trade unionists, and they found membership of the N.S.S. perfectly compatible with actions which Bradlaugh or Foote almost weekly spoke out against. The N.S.S. branches contained trade unionists like William Woodhall, for twenty years a local official of the South Brancepeth lodge of the Durham Miners' Union, serving as secretary, delegate and president; or Joseph Brown, secretary of the North East Secular Federation, whose father was secretary of the tailors' society in Durham, and who himself was founder and president of the Durham branch of the Amalgamated Society of Engineers. Successively in Durham, Sunderland and Newcastle he gained a reputation as a labour activitist. During one strike he was blacked by all the employers in Newcastle, but was reinstated as a condition insisted on by the men when the strike ended. He was leader of the great 1886 strike at Armstrong's works, founder of the local Eight-Hours League, and a delegate to his union's district committee, representing his branch at the T.U.C. in 1892. This man was a Liberal, as opposed to socialism as Bradlaugh himself, but he was able to speak for labour in a way which was foreign to much of the national leadership of the freethought movement.[51]

Increasingly one senses that the leadership was growing apart from labour and out of touch with its own members. This was not entirely the leaders' own fault. Their ideals had long been radical in a political sense, and in intellectual terms they still were; but what was radical for one generation could become conservative in the next. Holyoake, and to a lesser extent Bradlaugh and Watts, had once been a social radical; and Bradlaugh was a true radical of the mid-century political type; but Foote was a Liberal, half-way to becoming a twentieth-century Conservative of the extreme *laisser-faire* type, although he remained committed intellectually and emotionally to the left. The decision by Foote to abandon Bradlaugh's overt radicalism, and to concentrate instead on narrower freethought issues, was made necessary by the fact that politically and socially the world was changing. While some freethinkers could hold on to Foote's individualism, others were seeing in socialism a new policy and a new cause. The dilemma of Liberalism between 1885 and 1915, and the reasons why it lost the support of labour and the traditional 'left' to the new forces of socialism, can be explored through the history of freethought in these years, as the N.S.S. was itself undermined from within and without by men and women who could no longer find the old solutions adequate to answer the problems of a rapidly changing world.

## Secularism and socialism

Socialism, both Marxist and otherwise, was a new factor in British radicalism in the 1880s. Whereas Bradlaugh had been able to weather the attacks of the Marxist republicans of the early 1870s, a decade later it was the Secularists who were to be put under pressure by critics more revolutionary than themselves.[52]

The dividing line between socialists and radicals was not always so clear-cut as that between the views of H. M. Hyndman and J. H. Levy, for example, or Besant and Foote. To Sam Standring, writing in 1880, 'Socialism may be said to be the groans of downtrodden people yearning for a share of liberty and justice which belong by natural right to all humanity.'[53] By this standard, Bradlaugh should be recognised as a socialist, which plainly he was not. Not even land nationalisation was a touchstone for distinguishing between the two schools. Yet contemporaries were well aware of what socialism was, and what 'socialistic' measures were.

Bradlaugh's campaign to enter Parliament in the early 1880s was, of course, a cause to appeal to radicals and socialists alike, as was Foote's imprisonment for blasphemy, but by 1884 the cracks between the two were becoming too deep to be papered over in this way. Socialists were asking for measures of social and economic reform; the radicals talked of political and legal rights, apparently more concerned with abstractions than with the immediate exploitation of the poor.

The debate about radicalism and socialism, however, took place not between Secularist and socialist societies, but within Secularism itself, before there were many socialist societies in existence. The Secularist organisation thus contributed towards the spread of socialism, despite the personal views of the leaders. In 1896 there was only one socialist on the N.S.S. Executive, though perhaps as many as half the members at that time may have been socialists.[54] Socialism was, for example, discussed by the moderate B.S.U. in 1878 and 1879, and a radical programme was put forward by 'W.P.' in the *National Reformer* in 1880, which included such socialist measures as old-age pensions, sick and disablement pay, free medical care, and State employment for the unemployed. Though the weight of articles by Levy was intended to counteract such views, his articles in turn were subjected to discussion and criticism by 'S.S.' [Standring?] and J. L. Joynes, while the *Secular Review* was open to E. Belfort Bax to put forward 'A defence of Scientific Socialism'.[55] Though the readers of freethought journals were left in no doubt as to where their editors and leaders stood, each freethinker was appropriately left to make up his own mind. In this sense, Secularism was positively helpful to the spread of the new socialism.

In February 1884 Bradlaugh devoted his Sunday morning lectures at the Hall of Science to what had undoubtedly become the question of the day: 'Will Socialism help the English people?' At the first lecture, on 'What is Socialism?', 'strong opposition was urged by foreigners'. Bradlaugh's thesis was that native socialism had declined in England after the 1850s when Britain became the 'workshop of the world', but that the recession of the past ten years had revived interest. This new socialism, however, was a poor amalgam of the philosophic socialism of Germany, the bourgeois-hating socialism of France, and the anarchism of Southern Europe. Its nature was summed up in the closing sentences of the Communist Manifesto, which Bradlaugh deplored.[56]

These views sparked off a fierce debate in the pages of the freethought press, and led H. M. Hyndman to meet Bradlaugh at St James's Hall on 17 April 1884 to debate the question which Bradlaugh had posed. Contemporary reports agree that Bradlaugh was the more effective debater. In the *National Reformer* Annie Besant identified most of the socialists in the audience as Germans, and thought Hyndman 'very shallow in his knowledge of the history of English working class movements'. She was right. The English working class had been radical, not socialist, and in 1884 Bradlaugh was still its most popular and representative leader. But J. Benny, an old Owenite, was probably also right when he observed that Bradlaugh had won 'more by the art of talking than the art of reasoning', for if Bradlaugh had won the battle, then Hyndman was to win the war.[57]

The Sunday following the debate, 20 April, William Heaford reviewed the controversy at the Battersea branch and spoke in favour of socialism, encountering 'strong opposition'; at Paddington C. R. Drysdale attacked socialism, and faced some opposition. The Battersea branch became the centre of the socialist attack, and the discussion was continued on 27 April and 4 May. The debate was now under discussion across the country. On 4 May it was considered in Dewsbury, Bolton and Glasgow, and on 4 and 11 May in Newcastle. Aveling lectured on socialism at the Hall of Science on 25 May, and H. H. Champion appeared at Battersea on the same day to explain 'The aims and objects of the Democratic Federation'. On 8 June Stewart Headlam came to Battersea with a lecture on 'Christian Socialism'. On 25 May Glasgow had another lecture on socialism (from J. Bruce Glasier), followed in the evening by a soirée in memory of Owen and Mill—a pleasant reminder that Glasgow's was an Eclectic Society. At the South Place Chapel, Hyndman lectured on Scientific Socialism and was opposed by Annie Besant, who on 9 June at West Ham lectured on 'Social Reform, not Socialism.' On another occasion she was at South Place to defend Bradlaugh against Rabbinowitz (a Russian Pole), Kitz (a violent German), Shaw (who called himself 'a loafer') and Abraham (a foreign Jew). All Annie's prejudices were showing in her *National Reformer* report. In Edinburgh young John Robertson called a meeting to discuss the debate at which he defended socialism against the branch's capitalist patron, John Lees. Robertson then went on to conduct an argument in the *National Reformer* with Levy, who had criticised Robertson's report of the debate which had been published in *Progress*.[58]

By the middle of June the first 5,000 copies of the debate were 'nearly exhausted', and a second printing had been ordered. Gimson of Leicester recalled, 'almost all Secularists were Individualists of the Radical Individualist type which was influenced by John Stuart Mill and Herbert Spencer and Charles Bradlaugh', but his society provided an open platform for all the social and political ideas current at the time. Already on 16 January 1884 Hyndman had been to the Leicester society to lecture on 'Constructive Socialism', followed on 23 January by William Morris on 'Art and Socialism', which was afterwards published by Larner Sugden (the Leek Secularist and architect of the Leicester Secular Hall), who was a disciple of Morris. Here, in a society the president of which was a follower of Auberon Herbert socialism was given a free reign.[59]

One of the first converts at the Battersea branch was a young engineer, John Burns, who already had a reputation as a radical speaker on Clapham Common and in Battersea Park. He had been a keen Bradlaughite, sitting in his local 'parliament' as member for Northampton. On 9 November, he lectured at the Battersea Secular Society on 'Poverty: its effects, causes and remedies'. Another engineer in the audience, who had missed the original debate, was

Tom Mann, who joined the Battersea branch of the Social
Democratic Federation which Burns formed in May 1885. In
Nottingham, as in Leicester, the local N.S.S. branch was hospitable
to socialist lecturers, including William Morris, though here young
Harry Snell was converted not by the speakers but by reading the
original debate for himself. He was also helped in his change of views
by the conversion of the greatest Bradlaughite of them all—Mrs
Annie Besant.[60]

After Aveling's departure from the N.S.S., Annie Besant recruited
John Robertson to replace him on the *National Reformer*, and under
his influence she began to moderate her opposition to socialism.
Robertson did not agree with Hyndman, State monopoly or
revolution, but he did think socialism was an ideal to be approached
by piecemeal reform. Annie was convinced, and on 21 January 1885
attended a meeting of the London Dialectical Society at which G. B.
Shaw was to defend socialism. To his surprise, she announced her
conversion to his views and asked to join the Fabian Society.[61] She
developed her new creed in a series of articles on 'The Evolution of
Society', which appeared in her magazine, *Our Corner*, from July to
October 1885. Reviewing these in the *Freethinker*, Foote noted she
was now 'a full-blown Socialist: a rapid conversion begun and
completed (to all appearance) since the Bradlaugh–Hyndman
debate'. The lines of division were therefore drawn right through the
Secularist leadership: Foote and Levy against Robertson and
Besant, with Bradlaugh unhappily on the anti-Besant side.[62]
Personal animosity added to the political division between Besant
and Foote. In the same issue of *Progress* as Robertson's review of the
debate Foote had argued that socialist attacks on capital were
playing into the hands of Tory democracy and threatening the
nationalisation of the land agitation, which (unlike socialism) was a
practical campaign.[63] Mrs Besant's apostasy was too much for him
and his young colleague, W. P. Ball, and they made an all-out attack
on her. Reviewing her articles on 'Modern Socialism' in *Our Corner*,
Foote wrote:

A pinched stomach is bad enough, but there are worse things to anyone with
a sense of human dignity. A full trough is dearly paid for at the price of
being a pig. In a democratic age there is a natural thirst for greater equality,
and the levelling of human conditions is to some extent desirable. Levelling
up is a slow process, which irks impatient spirits, but it is a sure one.
Levelling down is a swifter process, and that is the aim of Socialism.[64]

Bradlaugh's *National Reformer* review of the same work was more
moderately phrased, but amounted to the same thing. W. P. Ball

devoted a thirty-six page pamphlet to an attack both on *Mrs Besant's Socialism* and on Mrs Besant herself. In reply, two members of the Ball's Pond Road branch refused to take the *Freethinker* so long as Ball was connected with it, and a letter from Ball, which was refused insertion in the *National Reformer*, appeared disguised as an advertisement for the pamphlet in the *Freethinker*. Foote and Besant argued the merits of socialism in *Progress*, and in February 1887 they held a formal debate at the Hall of Science. With such exposure, Secularists cannot have avoided a thorough knowledge of the case for as well as against socialism.[65]

Annie Besant's appeal as a socialist lay in her skills as a writer, lecturer and organiser, and in her moderation. Rather than join the S.D.F., she threw her energies into the Fabian Society, and did what she could to take Secularists and Liberals there with her. In February 1886 she persuaded the Fabians to extend their organisation and form provincial branches to carry out propagandist work, and shortly afterwards she herself started branches in Edinburgh and Deptford. In January she had dropped the section on puzzles and amusements from *Our Corner*, and from March she substituted a section for 'The Fabian Society and Socialist Notes'. She became one of the seven-member Fabian Society executive, and organised a conference at South Place on 9, 10 and 11 June for which she persuaded Bradlaugh, as well as Robertson, to read a paper. Her hopes were for a united front of Radicals, Socialists, and Socialist Reformers, but Foote pointed out that the Metropolitan Radical Federation was already available for this purpose.[66]

Despite personal friendship, the Bradlaugh–Besant partnership began to break up in 1887: he refused once to accept her resignation as co-editor of the *National Reformer*, but when she offered it again in October 1887 he accepted it. During the spring and summer they had conducted a written debate in the columns of *Our Corner*, in which Bradlaugh defined socialism as communism, and thought Besant oversimplified the motives and position of capitalists; Besant on the other hand thought Bradlaugh off-target, his attacks being appropriate to Anarchists and Utopian Socialists but not to Scientific Socialists, and she suggested he had not really faced up to the inevitability of two classes under capitalism. He in turn could not understand how individual private property could survive under socialism; she tried to suggest that Bradlaugh was, in effect, already practically a socialist. He was not.[67]

What divided the two sides was the willingness of some socialists to contemplate violence. George Standring could not see how 'the wanton spoliation of innocent tradesmen' on 'Black Monday', 1886, could possibly lead to a permanent improvement in the condition of the people, and Foote objected the following year to the planned socialist disturbances in St Paul's cathedral. The events of 'Bloody Sunday' (13 November 1887) in Trafalgar Square, however, raised the different issue of the right of public meeting, and this brought radicals and socialists together again.[68]

The best chance of bringing the two sides together had always rested with Annie Besant and the Fabians.[69] After Bloody Sunday she began working with W. T. Stead of the *Pall Mall Gazette* in the Law and Liberty League, and together in 1888 they issued a halfpenny weekly called the *Link* 'so to organise Friends of the Commonwealth as to place all those who are ready to stand in the breach when the interests of the poor are endangered, or when any grave wrong is about to be done, in communication with each other': their most celebrated campaign was on behalf of the Bryant & May match girls in 1888, though the only mention of this celebrated event in the *National Reformer* was a report copied from *The Times* in July 1888. Perhaps Secularists were expected to buy the *Link* for themselves.[70]

By the late 1880s socialist ideas had infiltrated many Secularist societies. At Leicester, where the lecturers ranged from Wordsworth Donisthorpe and Frederick Millar of the Liberty and Property Defence League, J. H. Levy and Auberon Herbert, through to the Fabian essayists, Stewart Headlam and Eleanor Marx Aveling, Sydney Gimson recalled how 'Among our members and in our audiences the discussion of Individualism and Socialism went on furiously and, though I was on the other side, I must admit that Socialism was rapidly gaining converts'. At West Ham in the general election of 1892, the South Essex Secular Society declared in favour of Joseph Leicester, who supported secular education, but the majority of members voted for Keir Hardie, 'the Labor, Radical and Home Rule Candidate'. George Standring, who had originally opposed the socialists, moved towards the Fabians, and in 1892 urged Secularists, to co-operate with them; and in the *National Reformer*, with Bradlaugh and Levy gone, Robertson too was advocating moderately socialistic measures, though he did not like Engels's uncritical use of the word 'bourgeoisie' in the English context. Among the Wednesday lectures at the Hall of Science in 1893, during October and November, were Agnes Henry on 'Woman's Position under Anarchy'; Tom McCarthy, secretary of the Dockers' Union, on 'The Dockers' Difficulty'; and Pete Curran on 'The Relation of Freethought to Socialism'.[71]

Foote thought there was no such relationship. He realised that the strength of the N.S.S. still lay in the non-socialists, who would leave if the N.S.S. declared for socialism. By concentrating on the destruction of the Christian superstition as 'the indispensable preliminary to all wise and desirable reform' he hoped to keep the movement together. True socialists, however, held that the ideological foundation of society was capitalism, not Christianity, and by refusing to attack this Foote was declaring the N.S.S. to be, *ipso facto*, anti-socialist. It was this attitude which led socialists within the N.S.S. gradually to leave. Harry Snell went in about 1895, 'not because of any fundamental change of opinion, but because its leadership was then individualist in character'. Though the rebel Freethought Federation was not a socialist body, many of those attracted to it, including Standring, were socialists. The *Jerusalem Star* urged Secularists not to be hostile to socialists, and *Secular Work* wanted freethinkers once more to become involved in politics: writing of the 1896 N.S.S. conference, 'The Laird' thought

> It is quite certain that unless Secularism becomes an active influence in the life of the common people, voicing their aspirations and hopes and championing their rights, it will speedily perish or be left high and dry on the lumber-shelf of forgotten ideas. . . . one must note with regret the almost total estrangement that exists between the N.S.S. and the problems of our social life, burning as they are for solution. . . . I firmly believe, after attending many Conferences and coming into contact with a great number of the N.S.S. members from all parts of the country, that the vast majority are Socialists. There is, therefore, nothing to hinder the N.S.S. from adopting the only known remedy for the social disease, except the apathy of its members and the diffidence of its leaders. We are a rapidly decreasing Society and look like rusting out. If we are to die, let us at least die fighting.

In the July issue he returned to the subject, with the opinion that, if the N.S.S. had taken up socialism in the 1890s as Bradlaugh had taken up republicanism in the 1870s, the N.S.S. could have done the work now being done by the I.L.P.[72]

He was right, except in two points. Firstly, he underestimated the number of Secularists who were still non-socialists.[73] Even the Freethought Federation did not feel able to declare for socialism—a decision which Snell felt kept 'genuine Socialists' out.[74] Secondly, whilst it was true that, as the Camberwell branch argued in 1902 when they let their hall monthly to the S.D.F., many members of the S.D.F. were freethinkers and so the connection with socialism was of benefit to the Secularists, the socialist movement remained much wider than freethought.[75] Just as Secularism could unite individualists and socialists against religion, so socialism united freethinkers and Christians against capitalism. The idea that a man could be a reformer *and* a Christian was largely beyond the comprehension not only of G. W. Foote and those who thought like him, but also of some of the more extreme socialists like J, W. Gott within the freethought ranks. The N.S.S. could have become the I.L.P. only at the price of forgoing its distinctive emphasis on the primacy of freethought. Stanley Jones, writing in the *Truth Seeker*, feared that this was already happening with individual members. Whichever way Foote had led the Secularists he would have lost, and so, whatever the pressures from the International movement (which was largely socialist), from Stanton Coit writing in the journals of the Ethical movement, or from socialists within the N.S.S., Foote could not—even had he wished to—afford to come off the political fence and declare for socialism.[76] Unfortunately, though, 'The Laird' was right in that he could not afford not to, either.

### Freethought, socialism and Christianity

The only ground on which Foote could fight the socialists, without losing the support of freethinking socialists, was religion, and he exploited it to the full. The attitudes of working men to the Church varied enormously, but it is generally true to say that, while they may not have grown more friendly towards it during the later nineteenth century, they had become less hostile, while the Church appeared to be adopting a more sympathetic attitude towards them.[77] The London leaders of the S.D.F. and some of the Fabians may well have been agnostics or atheists, but the I.L.P. and the labour movement in the country were not, as Blatchford, Hyndman and others pointed out.[78] Even when there was open opposition to traditional Christianity, it could take the religious form of John Trevor's Labour Churches.[79] As J. R. MacDonald realised, 'the Socialist, full of the reforming zeal of his creed, finds in the ethics of the Gospels a marvellous support for his economic and political proposals', although he had little support from the institutional Church.[80] MacDonald himself was active in the Ethical movement with Stanton Coit, and other labour leaders had similarly diverse experiences. Though Ben Tillet, Will Thorne and John Burns had little inclination to religion, Arthur Henderson was, and Philip Snowden had been, an active Methodist, and Tom Mann and Keir

Hardie both worked closely with Christians who were prepared to share their ideals.[81]

To Secularists this looked like folly, hypocrisy, or all that could be expected of socialism. Frederick Millar, as an out-and-out individualist, argued that Christianity and socialism went together as inevitably as freethought and Individualism. In Foote's eyes, Tom Mann was an expedient hypocrite who knew that the man in search of votes must please the religious majority. The greatest criticisms, though, were reserved for the arch-apostate, Keir Hardie, whose parents had been active Secularists in Glasgow, and regular readers of the *Freethinker*. For Hardie to turn to Christianity, and then use it to support his socialism against Liberalism, was only to add insult to injury.[82]

The principal contact between Secularism and socialism appeared to be made in the columns of the *Clarion*, following Blatchford's review of Haeckel's *Riddle of the Universe* in January 1903. For the next twenty-one months the merits and de-merits of Christianity were discussed in the paper, and circulated to a much wider audience in Blatchford's *God and my Neighbour* (December 1903) and George Haw's *The Religious Doubts of Democracy* (July 1904).[83] But, though this showed that interest in theological argument was far from dead, it also underlined the failure of Secularists to hold that particular field for themselves. Blatchford was an agnostic, reacting against the social attitude of the Church; he was not a thorough going freethinker of the Secularist type, and by 1907 his brief flirtation with atheism was over. The *Truth Seeker* reported in 1906 how Blatchford, 'speaking before 5,000 people in Bradford, almost burst a blood vessel in denouncing the *Truth Seeker*. Was it jealousy, or does he now regret having written "God and my Neighbour"?', the reporter wondered.[84]

The Bradford *Truth Seeker* represented most vociferously that small group of freethinkers for whom the N.S.S. was not socialist enough, and the socialists not atheistic enough. In London their views were put by Guy Aldred, who withdrew from *Justice* in 1906 in protest at the shallow independence of the Labour party in Parliament and the attitude adopted by the editor, Harry Quelch, towards religion. Aldred was outraged that socialists could consider their duty done once they had exposed those aspects of Christianity which directly threatened labour. Christianity was an entire system, which was fundamentally opposed to labour. Those who claimed to be both Christians and socialists, or who did not see the necessity for destroying all religion, had a 'sorry ignorance of the economics of

Marx and the teaching of history'. He was also horrified as a freethinker at the indoctrination of children which was taking place in the socialist Sunday schools.[85]

The Bradford group, led by J. W. Gott, used the columns of the *Truth Seeker* to flay all who fell short of their revolutionary socialist and atheistic programme. They caused not only Blatchford to strain his blood vessels, but Hardie's *Labour Leader* to refuse any further advertisements for Gott's clothing business. In Malfew Secklew's opinion, the S.D.F. had begun as pioneers but were now 'progressive mugwumps', and the leaders of the I.L.P. 'had injected Jesusism into the movement, and the virus drove the more healthy away'. About 1909 Gott and his friends formed the Freethought Socialist League, 'to combat the strong effort now being made by many Christians to "nobble" the Socialist Movement, and to use Socialism to save their dying creed'. The League's supporters feared that Christianity would destroy the Labour movement, just as earlier it had destroyed Chartism, radicalism and early socialism.[86]

This was an extreme version of a widely held opinion amongst freethinkers. It led a few socialists, like A.J.M., writing in Standring's *Reason* in 1898, to leave the Fabian Society and to concentrate on freethought; more often, though, the pull of socialism appears to have been stronger than the distaste for religion. In 1907 thirty-one Bradford Secularists, all of whom were socialists, mostly in the S.D.F., complained about Foote's attacks on Keir Hardie's religious statements. Presumably these men had not been drawn to Gott, or they would scarcely have defended Hardie, but they were clearly equally unimpressed by Foote.[87] Hardie's mixture of socialism and Sermon on the Mount had won, and the days of Secularism as the principal movement on the political left were over.

*Notes*

1  *N. R.*, 30 July 1865, reprinted in E. Royle, *The Infidel Tradition*, pp. 166–8; H. B. Bonner and J. M. Robertson, *Charles Bradlaugh*, I, p. 244.

2  *S. C.*, 1 January 1873, 18, 25 April 1875.

3  *N. R.*, 7 December 1873; *S. C.*, 17 December 1876; *S. R.*, 20 May 1877.

4  *S. R.*, 8 May 1880.

5  *N. R.*, 16 January 1881, 5 February 1882; *S. R.*, 3 November, 15 December 1883; *Progress*, April, May 1884; *F.*, 3 February 1884.

6  *F.*, 16 November 1884; *Republican*, March 1885 *Our Corner*, July 1886; *F.*, 3, 17 August 1884.

7  *F.*, 18 March 1894, 29 May 1898.

8  Cattell, who was himself a Birmingham man, had written in 1874:

'Republicans would do well to remember that persons of wealth and position are generally on the side of monopoly. In this particular case Mr Chamberlain is one of a number of wealthy men in England whose whole life has been spent in a manufacturing interest founded on the principle of "the old school". Moreover, it should be observed that he is comparatively a young man, and may as likely go over to the Conservative side, as he grows older, as to the other side.—*N. R.* 25 October 1874.

9   *Republican*, March 1886.

10  *Free Review* September 1895; *N. R.*, 31 May, 7 June 1891.

11  *S. R.*, 6 March 1880; G. J. Holyoake, *Sixty Years*, II, pp. 255–7; *F.*, 21 January 1885.

12  *N. R.*, 25 April 1880, 26 October 1884.

13  *N. R.*, 22 February–15 March 1885; *Progress*, August 1885; see also *Radical*, September 1886.

14  *N. R.*, 17 January 1886; *Republican*, April 1886; *Radical*, December 1886, February 1887.

15  *F.*, 4 December 1892; *Reformer*, 15 March 1897.

16  *S. R.*, 13 March 1886, 15 December 1888; *Watts's L. G.*, April 1890; N.S.S. Minute Book IV, 25 October 1894; *F.*, 7 October 1900.

17  When F. J. Gould was defeated in the 1907 municipal elections in Leicester, G. W. Foote sent him a postcard: 'Such is the beauty of politics, and the steadiness of democracy. I am afraid that the Deity called "Votes" is as great a fraud as any other in the Pantheon.'—Leicester S. S., Press Cuttings, vol. IV.

18  E. B. Bax, *Reminiscences*, pp. 229-30.

19  E. g. Bradlaugh—*N. R.*, 27 April 1884, 8 January 1888.

20  *F.*, 22 April 1888.

21  *F.*, 4 June 1882.

22  *N. R.*, 16 April 1893, 12, 26 May 1872; *F.*, 17 September 1882, 4, 11 August 1895.

23  *Radical Leader*, 11 August 1888.

24  *F.*, 13 March 1904.

25  R. D. French, *Anti-vivisection and Medical Science in Victorian Society* (Princeton, 1975), pp. 346-72; *F.*, 9 October 1881; *A. J.*, 23 April, 7 May 1892; *F.*, 1 March 1896, 6, 13 March 1904. French appears to underestimate the scientific opposition to some of the unnecessary cruelties involved in vivisection.

26  *S. C.*, 2 June 1878; *N.R.*, 23 April 1893; *Reformer*, 15 January 1898; *N. R.*, 4 August 1889, 26 April 1885; *F.*, 15 June 1884.

27  *Truth Seeker*, XIII, 'Special No.' [1907]; E. Pack, *The Trial and Imprisonment of J. W. Gott*, pp. 147-9; *F.*, 1 May 1898; *Truth Seeker*, April 1895.

28  *N. R.*, 26 June 1892.

29  *Truth Seeker*, September 1900, January 1903.

30  N. Soldon, '*Laissez-faire* as Dogma: the Liberty and Property Defence League, 1882-1914', and E. Bristow, 'Profit-sharing, Socialism and Labour Unrest', in K. D. Brown (ed.), *Essays in Anti-Labour History*

(London 1974), pp. 208-33, 262-89. The Holyoake quotation is from Bristow, pp. 271-2; *A. J.*, 3 August 1889; *Radical*, February 1887.

31  *Personal Rights: a monthly journal of Freedom and Justice*, January 1893; Oswald Dawson, *Personal Rights and Sexual Wrongs* (London, 1897), pp. 1-30. For a defence of Mill against J. F. Stephen see G. W. Foote, *N. R.*, 2, 16, 30 November 1873.
32  *F.*, 16 September, 8, 15 April 1894, 28 June 1896.
33  *F.*, 17 December 1893, 15 August 1897.
34  *F.*, 23 February, 16, 23 March, 6, 20 April 1902; D Wiltshire, *The Social and Political Thought of Herbert Spencer* (Oxford,1978), pp. 239-42.
35  R. M. Young, 'The Impact of Darwin', in A. Symondson (ed.), *The Victorian Crisis of Faith* (London, 1970), pp. 29-31.
36  *S. R.*, 24 June 1882; *Is Socialism Sound? Verbatim Report of a Four Nights' Debate between Annie Besant and G. W. Foote* (London, 1887), pp. 97-8; *Malthusian*, 15 August 1909; *Progress*, December 1884.
37  W. P. Ball, *Mrs Besant's Socialism* (London, 1886), p. 33; J. M. Robertson, *A History of Freethought*, p. 338.
38  *Is Socialism Sound?*, p. 90.
39  See above, p. 225.
40  Compare the attitude in this extract with that in Foote's article on 'The Unemployed,' *Progress*, November 1887.
41  E. g. the attitude taken by Bradlaugh in his debate with Hyndman, *Will Socialism Benefit the English People?* (London, 1884), pp. 16-18, partly reprinted in E. Royle, *Radical Politics, 1790-1900* (London, 1971), p. 128; or that taken by Foote, *Progress*, April 1886.
42  *Pioneer*, March 1903; see also the comments on the Barnard Castle bye-election, *ibid.*, August 1903.
43  This was commented on in *N. R.*, 12 March 1876.
44  See P. N. Backstrom, *Christian Socialism and Co-operation in Victorian England* (London, 1974); also E. Bristow, *op. cit.*; *N. R.*, 22 February 1885.
45  *Republican Chronicle,* June 1875.
46  *N. R.*, 22 January 1888, 3 March 1867, 23 December 1877, 20 January, 24 February 1878; *Secularist*, April 1902.
47  *Our Corner*, October 1887; *F.*, 30 August 1885; N.S.S. Minute Book, IV, Financial Statement, 1893-94.
48  *Eight Hours Movement. Verbatim Report of Debate between Mr H. M. Hyndman and Mr C. Bradlaugh* (London, 1890), p. 31
49  *N. R.*, 17 March 1889, 2, 23 March 1890; see also 31 March, 14 April, 5 May 1889.
50  *N. R.*, 5 May 1889, 20 April 1890, 1 February 1891.
51  *F.*, 26 November, 7 May 1893.
52  The impact of socialism is noted by T. Okey, *A Basketful of Memories* (London, 1930), pp. 61-2.
53  *Republican,* June 1880.
54  *Secular Work,* July 1896. The one socialist was William Heaford.
55  *S. R.*, 21 December 1878, 25 January 1879; *N. R.*, 31 October 1880– 20 March 1881, 5–26 November, 31 December 1882, 7 January, 4

February– 25 March 1883; *S. R.*, 31 March 1883.

56  *N. R.*, 13 January, 10, 17 February 1884; *Our Corner* March 1884.
57  *N. R.*, 27 April 1884, reprinted in E. Royle, *The Infidel Tradition*, pp. 174-8; J. Benny, *Benny on Bradlaugh and Hyndman* (London, 1884), p. 2. See also *Pall Mall Gazette*, 18 April 1884; *Republican*, May 1884; H. M. Hyndman, *Record of an Adventurous Life*, p. 339.
58  *N. R.*, 27 April, 4, 11 May 1884; also weekly lecture notices in *N. R.*, and *S. R.*, May 1884; *Republican*, June 1884; *N. R.*, 15 June– 27 July 1884; *Progress*, June 1884.
59  *N. R.*, 15 June 1884; S. A. Gimson, 'Random Recollections', I, pp. 20-3; see also T. Barclay, *Memoirs*, pp. 67-9.
60  W. Kent, *John Burns*, p. 17; *N. R.*, 16 November 1884; D. Torr, *Tom Mann and his Times* (London, 1956), p. 86; H. Snell, *Men, Movements and Myself*, pp. 55-7.
61  *Progress*, June 1884; A. H. Nethercot, *First Five Lives of Annie Besant*, p. 231.
62  *F.*, 4 October 1885; *N. R.*, 12 February– 20 September 1885, 14 March 1886.
63  *Progress*, June 1884.
64  *Ibid.*, June 1886.
65  *N. R.*, 6 June 1886; W. P. Ball, *op. cit.*, p. 24; *F.*, 27 June 1886; *Progress*, July 1886; *N. R.*, 13 February– 6 March 1887.
66  *Our Corner*, March, April, June, July 1886; *N. R.*, 6 June 1886; *F.*, 23 May 1886.
67  *N. R.*, 23 October 1887; *Our Corner*, March, April, June 1887.
68  *Republican*, March 1886; *F.*, 6 March 1887; for 'Bloody Sunday' see below, pp. 286–7.
69  E. g. Annie Besant supported Bradlaugh against socialist criticisms in 1886, and voted with the rest of the English delegation against the identification of freethought with socialism at the International Congress in 1887— *N. R.*, 21 March 1886; *F.*, 18 September 1887.
70  *N. R.*, 12 February 1888; *Our Corner*, July, August 1888; *N. R.*, 22 July 1888.
71  S. A. Gimson, *op. cit.*, I, p. 25; *N. R.*, 3 July 1892; *F.*, 17 January 1892; *N. R.*, 4 December 1892; N.S.S., Organisation Committee, Minute Book, list of lectures at back of volume.
72  *F.*, 3 February 1895; H. Snell, *op. cit.*, p. 156; *Jerusalem Star*, October 1895; *Secular Work*, June, July 1896.
73  *Ibid.*, November, December 1896.
74  *Ibid.*, September 1896.
75  *F.*, 30 November 1902.
76  *Truth Seeker*, November 1896; *F.*, 14 October 1900; *Democracy*, 13 April 1901; *Radical*, February 1897.
77  J. M. Ludlow and L. Jones, *Progress of the Working Class, 1832-1867* (London, 1867), p. 281; R. A. Bray, *Labour and the Churches* (London, 1912), pp. 21-2.
78  R. Blatchford, *My Eighty Years* (London, 1931), p. 199; C Tsuzuki, *H. M. Hyndman and British Socialism* (Oxford, 1961), p. 101; P.

Thompson, *Socialists, Liberals and Labour*, pp. 125-6, 234; A. M. McBriar, *Fabian Socialism and English Politics* (Cambridge, 1962), p. 147.

79  J. Trevor, *My Quest for God* (London, 1897), p. 237.

80  J. R. Macdonald, *Socialism* (London,1907), pp. 99-103; see also S. Yeo, 'A New Life: the Religion of Socialism in Britain, 1883-1896', *History Workshop Journal*, no. 4 (autumn, 1977), pp. 5-56.

81  B. Tillett, *Memories*, pp. 77-8; W. Thorne, *My Life's Battles* (London [1925]), p. 55; W. Kent, *John Burns*, pp. 298-300; E. A. Jenkins, *From Foundry to Foreign Office: the Romantic Life Story of the Rt Hon Arthur Henderson, M. P.* (London, 1933), pp. 256-7; C. Cross, *Philip Snowden* (London, 1966), pp. 4-5; T. Mann, *Memoirs* (London 1923, reprinted 1967), pp. 7-8, 85-97; *F.*, 18 November 1900. See also E. Royle, *Radical Politics*, pp. 81-4, 130.

82  *A. J.*, 2 November 1889; *F.*, 29 November 1891, 15 October 1893, 20 November 1892, 15 April, 9 September 1906.

83  *Clarion*, 23 January, 13 February 1903– 28 October 1904.

84  *F.*, 7 July, 22 December 1907; *Truth Seeker*, March 1906.

85  *A. J.*, 18 August 1906; see also G. A. Aldred, *No Traitor's Gait*.

86  *Truth Seeker*, January 1903, January–March 1907, undated issue [1909?]; *Labour Leader*, 6 December 1907.

87  *Reason*, 27 March 1898; *F.*, 27 January 1907.

XIII

# Women, sex and birth control

*Female emancipation*

The freethought movement made no distinctions as to sex in its organisation, and indeed numbered some distinguished female advocates of women's rights among its leaders over the years, from the days of Frances Wright, Eliza Sharples Carlile and Emma Martin to those of Harriet Law and Annie Besant. This was also true of the movement in America, where Elizabeth Cady Stanton and Helen Gardener were freethinkers and feminists; and France, where Maria Desraimes, president of the French Anti-Clerical Congress in 1881, was a prominent writer in support of the claims of women.[1] The principles of freethought upheld the equal treatment of both sexes. If an argument were advanced against female emancipation, it was likely to be empirically based on the apparently conservative and religious nature of the sex, though this in itself led most radicals and freethinkers to double their efforts to free women from that subordinate position in which they were placed by education, custom, and the law of the land.

As radicals, the freethinkers took part in the general campaign for the political emancipation of women, and Secularist journals were among the first to advocate the cause openly. In 1869 the *National Reformer* urged Secularist societies to work for the amelioration of the laws relating to married women, and the female suffrage; and the first leading article in the first issue of the *Republican Chronicle* in 1875 argued the extension of the vote to women on the grounds that all were subject to the same laws. Under Harriet Law's editorship the *Secular Chronicle* became more concerned with women's issues, and Mrs Law was especially angered by the backwardness of English women compared with their socialist sisters in Germany.[2]

Education was seen to be at the root of the matter, and equal opportunity to education was regarded as the *sine qua non* of female emancipation. In a powerfully argued series of articles on 'The Education and Position of Women' in the *Secular Review* in 1879, Kate Watts saw the educated woman not only as an asset in the home and to her husband, but also as a person in her own right, capable of earning her own living, marrying at leisure, or if need be not marrying at all without having to fear the alternative of the life of a spinster in a sweatshop. Kate Watts was herself a fine example of a freethought girl brought up in this fashion, and her argument for education expressed the classic radical position.[3]

Kate Watts's great rival, Annie Besant, opened her public career with a lecture on 'The Political Status of Woman', in which she blamed religious influences for the bondage of her sex, but once a socialist she turned to economic explanations: only socialists advocated 'absolute economical independence for women', she asserted in 1887, with complete disregard for what radicals like Kate Watts had been saying a decade earlier.[4] In fact both radicals and socialists supported such equality, often in oppostion to working-class opinion as expressed in the trade union movement. The Mines Regulation Bill of 1886, which was designed to prevent women doing surface work in the coal industry, was opposed by Donisthorpe's Liberty and Property Defence League, Levy's Personal Rights Association, and Charles Bradlaugh, who came into conflict with the Durham miners over the issue. The socialist argument for equal pay was put in the *Truth Seeker* in 1907 as one against the unfair competition of women for men's jobs, the surest way to appeal to the male-dominated trade union interest.[5]

Paradoxically, women's subjects received greater coverage in the *National Reformer* in 1890s under Robertson's editorship than in the 1880s under Besant's. An article on 'Women's Suffrage in England', by Bradlaugh himself, appeared there shortly before his death, and a number of contributions were supplied by Mary Reed, who was one of the women to rise in the Secularist movement by way of an education at the Hall of Science schools in the 1880s. Robertson devoted a leader in 1893 to the advocacy of female suffrage.[6]

The suffragettes of Edwardian England, though, did not find favour with G. W. Foote. In his eyes, it was the negation of freethought for women to break up W. R. Cremer's Peace and Arbitration meeting in November 1906 as a retaliation for his speaking in the House of Commons against women's suffrage.[7] The following year Foote argued perceptively

that the right of public meeting is far more important than the suffrage. Despots have put up with votes. They have always hated public meetings. Why don't the ladies think a bit? It really wouldn't do them any harm. Why should they try to be bigger fools than the men?[8]

And in 1912 he took the logic of equality to its extreme when he condemned the release of Mrs Pankhurst and Mrs Pethick Lawrence when they went on hunger strike: he was unhappy at the development of discriminatory 'justice', which penalised unpopular causes such as his own but treated others with leniency.[9] In a rare outburst of class language, he wrote on the same theme in 1913:

Is it not time to say that the 'militant' Suffragette movement is a middle and upper-class movement, and is therefore rather privileged than otherwise? Had it been a working-class movement the Government would have been far less embarrassed by its prisoners. It would have put their food within their reach and said, 'There you are; eat it or not, as you please. There are plenty of cemeteries.'

—which is what the government had said to Irish republican prisoners on hunger strike. Foote was not advocating this (that was left to Shaw in a letter to *The Times*); he would rather all prisoners had been treated humanely, but for some to be so and not others simply made the position of those others more hopeless. Foote had been in prison for his views, and felt he could speak with some authority.[10]

Women's suffrage presented the Secularists with a dilemma similar to that created by socialism. As Foote argued, a mental platform was not like a wooden one: the more planks added to the latter, the more people could climb on to it; but the wider the mental one, the fewer people could accept it.[11] So, although he was personally sympathetic to a non-violent agitation for women's suffrage, he opposed the N.S.S. supporting it officially. Clearly many freethinkers disagreed. The N.S.S. conference in 1909 passed over a resolution in favour of adult suffrage from the Liverpool branch, much to the disappointment of the national secretary, Edith Vance. At the 1913 conference the West Ham delegate, Miss Hypatia Pankhurst, moved a resolution from her branch for the equalisation of the legal status of men and women (already an N.S.S. object) by universal suffrage. The conference expressed 'substantial agreement' but, after a discussion, passed on without a vote.[12]

The *Freethinker*'s cup of wrath against militant suffragettes overflowed in 1914 when a women's church was proposed at Wallasey. In the 'Acid Drops' column, now probably written by Cohen, it was suggested that the east window should depict 'the blazoned figure of St Jael with the little hammer, the patron saint of very advanced ladies'.[13]

That women should be captivated by religion was one of the more unpleasant facts of freethought life. Indeed, W. S. Ross, who was the only major freethought leader to oppose women's suffrage, did so on the grounds that it 'would be to play disastrously into the hands of the priesthood', and he created a fictional character, Janet Smith, who embodied all the empty-headed foolishness of the ordinary woman.[14] Foote was a little more optimistic: he thought that the first consequence of giving women the vote would be to set back political progress and so strengthen the orthodox faith and the Established Church, but that with true liberation women would eventually become radical.[15]

As with most freethought arguments about politics, religion was found to be at the heart of the trouble. When Arthur Moss heard Miss Caroline Biggs speak on 'Why are Women Deprived of the Suffrage?' in 1878, he was moved to write to the *Secular Chronicle* with his own answer, of which Mrs Law doubtless approved:

While Christians retain the Bible, and believe in it, women will always be kept in subjection. The Secularist has acknowledged the equality of women with men; and the aggressive spirit of Secularism must knock down the Christian barrier, and give women a better and higher freedom than they have ever yet had.[16]

This was a very common argument, and the *Freethinker* did its best to ridicule the masculine bias of the Bible. After reviewing the story of the fall of man at the hands of woman, and the Church's consequent attitude towards women, Foote asked, 'Why is this story so insulting to women?' and answered, 'Because men wrote it.' He suggested that the next revision of the Bible should be undertaken by men *and* women, which might produce a truly revised version. W. P. Ball even tried revising the Bible story for himself, with women dominant instead of men: thus he imagined St Paulina's injunction for 'the man to learn in silence with all subjection'! More seriously, in 1886 J. M. Wheeler discussed the emergence of the worship of the Virgin and the appearance of Female Christs to fill the void left in an exclusively male orthodoxy; and it is interesting to note that a woman writing in the *Anti-Infidel*, attempting to refute Foote's claim that the Bible degraded women, referred to the revelation of the Bride of the Apocalypse, on which Joanna Southcott and other Female Christs based their fantasies.[17]

At the same time as such articles were appearing in the *Freethinker*, Elizabeth Cady Stanton in America was deciding to collect and comment on all biblical references to the position of women. She received little support from her fellows in the National Women's

Suffrage Association, except from Helen Gardener, who had already made a start on St Paul's epistles. Not till 1895, though, was Part I of the *Woman's Bible* ready for publication, followed by Part II in 1898. Whether Mrs Stanton knew of the *Freethinker* articles is uncertain, though she was acquainted with the English movement and had visited England in 1882.[18] Foote was certainly aware of what was happening in America, and in 1885 he reprinted Ingersoll's introduction to Helen Gardener's *Men, Women and Gods*, in which Ingersoll had uttered the widely believed dictum, 'The parasite of woman is the priest'.[19]

As usual, the most ferocious material came from the pen of Ross, who throughout 1887 and 1888 ran a series of articles in the *Secular Review* on 'Christianity and Women', subsequently published as *Woman: her glory, her shame and her God*. There were several women contributors to the *Agnostic Journal*, including Lady Florence Dixie; Victoria Woodhull Martin and Tennessee Clafin (Lady Cook), the terrible sisters of the American women's movement; and Elizabeth Cady Stanton herself.[20]

But, despite all this propaganda on behalf of women the truth was that only a small minority of them was ever actually attracted to freethought. With the exception of the Ethical movement, which, according to the secretary, Zona Vallance, contained 'a very large proportion' of women as members, freethought organisations were dominated by men.[21]

*Sex and legitimation*

Throughout the nineteenth century, movements which attacked Christian theology were assumed to be immoral, for morality rested on the Bible. The whole point of Secularism in Holyoake's eyes was that it provided a secular basis for morality and enabled freethinkers to maintain conventionally decent standards of respectability without supernatural sanctions.[22] Most freethinkers were eminently respectable—even austere—but the tag of immorality was hard to remove. One reason for this was the association of freethought with birth control, from which it was thought to be not far to free love. Bradlaugh and Besant refuted this charge, and Ross threw up his hands in horror; but every movement attracts its extremists, and there was just a hint of smoke to suggest a flicker, if not a flame, of truth in the charge. Freethought did, after all, challenge conventional wisdom in most areas of life, and sometimes the dividing line between liberty and libertarianism was a narrow one.

Attitudes towards prostitution provide one example. The freethought leaders did not approve of prostitution, but in refusing to accept traditional moral judgements about prostitutes they could be thought to be condoning the practice. The Contagious Diseases Acts proved extremely difficult, and many a freethinker must have brought out the felicific calculus of his utilitarian ethical system, as W. H. Ashurst did in a letter to G. J. Holyoake in 1870:

I began by being in favour of the Acts, as tending to diminish hereditary disease incidental upon unwise sexual intercourse; tho' I always feared the placing of power in the hands of the police over the liberty of women. I am now a decided repealer—quite convinced that the moral harm of the continuance of the acts far outweighs any physical good (the physical good in the long run seems, at best, questionable) they can produce. In fact, the Acts *must go*.[23]

In the *Elements of Social Science* George Drysdale disapproved of the C. D. Acts for their injustice to women, but otherwise his views on sex were quite shocking.[24] In a chapter on the 'Evils of Abstinence' he argued that young people of both sexes would be helped to better health and happiness by 'moderate indulgence in sexual intercourse'. 'Complete sexual abstinence', he went on, 'is in every case an evil, and more especially so in the years immediately after puberty.'[25] It was these views, and Bradlaugh's approval of the book, which disrupted Secularism in 1861, when Bradlaugh quarrelled with practically every other leader in the movement; and much of the opposition to the Knowlton Pamphlet was, one suspects, really levelled at Drysdale's work. The prosecution in 1877 tried to suggest that Knowlton advocated pre-marital sexual intercourse. He did not, but Drysdale did.

Prostitution became a topic for widespread discussion again in 1885, following W. T. Stead's revelations about 'White Slavery' in the *Pall Mall Gazette*. Foote was generally hostile to Stead's approach: it smacked of the 'pharisaicmadness' which was also being directed against Sir Charles Dilke. Those who wished to defend public morality, he argued, should not be circulating the Bible.[26] Stead's campaign against prostitution was wrong because it was aimed at symptoms, not causes: it would merely make prostitution worse by driving it into obscurity. In the pages of Foote's *Progress*, Aveling explained the socialist remedy, which lay in the abolition of the class system; and Foote himself, in attacking Mrs Ormiston Chant's purity crusade against prostitution in the music halls in 1894, drove home a similar message, that 'A woman is forced into prostitution by economical causes'. Whether they blamed the

Bible, or the economic system, or both, the freethinkers were decided opponents of the religious moralists, and friends of the poor prostitutes.[27]

The most shocking thing about Drysdale's *Elements* was that it had first been published in 1854 (when it was called *Physical, Sexual and Natural Religion*). Forty years later such an open discussion of sexual matters would have caused less of a stir, though it would, no doubt, have drawn unfavourable comment from some quarters. For, in the 1890s, Victorian respectability and morality were under attack from such people as Havelock Ellis, G. B. Shaw, Hardy, Whitman, Ibsen, Carpenter and Grant Allen.[28] The freethought leaders, as in most matters, tried to steer a moderate course, though they must have felt in the 1890s that the current of the 'new hedonism' was running against them. Foote informed his correspondents in 1892 that 'Secularism is committed to no public declaration on the subject of marriage. Most Secularists believe in marriage as a civil institution, which should be tempered by a rational law of divorce.' The following year Foote found himself in the unusual position of defending conventionality against a noble lord when Queensberry advocated plural marriages.[29]

The new views were most clearly expressed by Grant Allen in a *Fortnightly Review* article entitled 'The New Hedonism', published in March 1894. In this article he adopted the motto 'Self-development is greater than self-sacrifice' to describe the new libertarian mood:

It is our duty to think as far as we can think; to get rid of all dogmas, preconceptions and prejudices; to make sure we are not tied by false fears or vague terms; to examine all faiths, all beliefs, all fancies, all shibboleths, political, religious, social, moral ... We should each of us arrive at a consistent theory of the universe for ourselves, and of our own place in it.[30]

This was, of course, a view which all liberals, old and new, would have happily endorsed; but the conclusions reached when the old asceticism was replaced by the new hedonism were uncomfortable ones for old puritans of Bradlaugh's generation.

When he came discuss sexual matters, Grant Allen held out the vision of a new relationship based not on religious marriage, but on mutually responsible decisions made by consenting adults—responsible to each other, to their children and to the race. The unfit would not breed; the fittest would not be condemned to celibacy. Lucy Stewart, writing in the *Adult* in 1897, argued with perfect consistency that freethinkers ought to support free love on the utilitarian grounds that it would maximise happiness, since with birth control there would be no need to worry about producing unwanted children. In 1906 'Ajax junior' in the *Agnostic Journal* also advocated free love as the logical conclusion of Secularism.[31]

The expression of such views must have seemed like the realisation of a nightmare to those Secularists who had spent a lifetime refuting these very ideas when Christians had accused them of holding them. They were mainly expressed in a monthly periodical called *The Adult, the journal of sex*, published from June 1897 and edited, first by George Bedborough, and then by Henry Seymour, both of whom were Secularists. Of the more conventional freethought papers, the *Agnostic Journal* and the Bradford *Truth Seeker* appear to have been most open to the new ideas. The libertarian anarchy of Grant Allen sums up much of the philosophy behind Gott's group; and Ross, who loved to shock, was very much influenced by Queensberry and his sister, Lady Florence Dixie, who shared many of the views expressed in Allen's article.[32]

Charles Watts, on the other hand, was anxious that the consequences of a little free thinking should not be held to be synonymous with Secularism, and he did not want to be 'held responsible for all the theories which, in the exercise of their Freethought, some speakers constantly expound to their hearers'. Divorce was as far as Watts was prepared to go, and Foote of all people was driven to criticise the 'fanaticism of small minorities'. Defending marriage against Grant Allen's novel, *The Woman Who Did*, Hardy's *Jude the Obscure*, and the writings of Edward Carpenter, W. M. Salter argued in the *Ethical World* that the production of children was a social act and so a man must be made legally responsible by marriage for the maintenance of his woman and their children.[33] The libertarians would not have disagreed with this, but they hated the legal compulsion provided by marriage. Instead, their concern for the children of a non-legal union gave rise to an organisation called the Legitimation League, which was closely associated with the *Adult*.

The League was formed in Leeds in January 1893 by Wordsworth Donisthorpe (president), Oswald Dawson (secretary) and J. Greevz Fisher (vice-president). At first the ties between the League and official Secularism were close: its object—to secure legal rights for illegitimate children—seemed a harmless one. But when Oswald Dawson began to advocate free love, even such lovers of liberty as Frederick Millar and J. H. Levy were alienated. Gradually the League became more extreme. In 1895 it admitted that its purpose was to register cohabitation without marriage, and by 1897 free love was being openly advocated in the *Adult*. At this point the *Freethinker* parted company with the League's aims, and Arthur and Hypatia Bonner refused to include the Legitimation League in their *Directory of Reform Societies*.[34]

The move to an extreme position on sexual relations coincided with the ascendancy of Bedborough and his wife as secretary and treasurer of the League, but Bedborough's career was brought to a sudden termination in 1898 when he was prosecuted for selling a copy of Havelock Ellis's *Sexual Inversion*. The *Adult* was taken over by Henry Seymour, who, as a mere freethinker, anarchist and socialist, proved rather more to Foote's taste, but when Bedborough capitulated at his trial and pleaded guilty, the *Adult* and the League were brought to an end. Free love was to be an item more of the extreme socialist than extreme Secularist programme, though it was practised by some exponents of both, such as Guy Aldred.[35]

For most Secularists, even at the end of the nineteenth century, sexual irregularities were something to be avoided: they were reformers, not revolutionaries, in morals as in politics. Only in his advocacy of birth control was Bradlaugh prepared to challenge the conventional sexual *mores* of the Victorian Englishman.

*Birth control*

Birth control would emancipate women from the fear and bondage of child-bearing; it would brighten the home not overcrowded with hungry children; and it would put the new woman at the centre of the campaign for the new, emancipated and healthy society, building a better future for the race. To prevent women obtaining the knowledge necessary to achieve all this was seen as a crime against them and against humanity.

The freethinkers had long published pamphlets on birth control, almost all of which were aimed at women; but, between Richard Carlile's *Every Woman's Book* (1826) and Bradlaugh's espousal of Drysdale's *Elements of Social Science* (1861), there was little direct association between freethought and birth control. Bradlaugh's decision to make this link in 1861, when he and George Drysdale formed the Malthusian League, marked a new departure both for freethought and birth control. In the 1860s he not only associated freethought with contraception, but also identified contraception in the public mind with atheism and Malthusian economics, In fact, very little was said about the methods to be used to prevent conceptions: in such pamphlets as *Jesus, Shelley and Malthus* (1861),

*Poverty and its Effects on the Political Condition of the People* (1863), *Labour's Prayer* (1865) and *Why do Men Starve?* (1865), as well as in his lectures for the Malthusian League, Bradlaugh concentrated entirely on what was later to become known as 'Neo-Malthusianism', offering the prevention of conceptions as the means for securing an end to the otherwise inevitable poverty of the lower classes.[36]

As Drysdale pointed out,[37] the main opposition to contraceptive knowledge came from men who thought only fear of pregnancy kept their wives from adopting the same loose sexual morality as themselves, so, as long as the propaganda was confined to accepted political economy, it appears to have been little noticed or interfered with. Even Knowlton's pamphlet and Drysdale's book were circulated freely and neither at this stage was a best-seller. Prejudice, however, lay close beneath the surface. In 1868 Lord Amberley, who had read the *Elements* in 1864 at the suggestion of his tutor, James Laurie, agreed to chair a Dialectical Society discussion on 'Over Population and Public Health'. Bradlaugh, Charles Drysdale, and Laurie were also present. A few innocuous remarks by Amberley, to the effect that he hoped doctors would discuss methods of checking births, were attacked by the *British Medical Journal* and the *Medical Times and Gazette* in August, and then taken up by the Tories and churchmen of South Devon, which Amberley contested as a Liberal in the 1868 general election. By the time Amberley's views reached the press, he had been turned into an advocate of infanticide, abortion, and all manner of unnatural crimes.[38]

The principal opposition to Bradlaugh at this time came from within his own movement, from John Maughan and G. J. Holyoake (but not from Austin, who wrote a neo-Malthusian pamphlet, *Large or Small Families*, in 1870); and also from those socialist extremists who were already condemning Bradlaugh's moderate republicanism. In 1872 Fredrick Riddle, secretary to the Land and Labour League, wrote in the *International Herald*

We utterly deny that population has anything to do with the poverty of the working classes, which we maintain is solely due to the defective and unjust arrangements of society, which give the produce of industry to idlers.[39]

Seen in the light of this opposition to birth control propaganda from both freethinkers and socialists, Charles Watts's decision in 1876 not to defend a pamphlet of which he happened to be the publisher looks perfectly reasonable, and the Bradlaugh and Besant decision to defend the Knowlton Pamphlet seems but one more example of the way in which Bradlaugh was prepared to use the freethought movement to promote and defend his own personal campaigns. Nevertheless, as described in Chapter 2, he and Mrs Besant went ahead and after dividing Secularism, managed to carry the bulk of the membership with them.[40]

The importance of this trial for the dissemination of birth-control propaganda is a matter of some dispute. The general opinion, as put forward by Norman Himes in 1936, was that 'The Bradlaugh–Besant trial went far to make legal the *general*, free distribution of contraceptive knowledge', and had a significant effect on fertility levels. Marie Stopes, on the contrary, always maintained that birth-control ideas 'were surely and rapidly making their way and supplying the earnest demand of a thoughtful public for information and instruction in this theme, when a bombshell was hurled into the world of progress by the Besant and Bradlaugh"championing of the cause" which led to the famous trial of 1877 for obscenity'. Far from helping the cause, by defending a pamphlet which had never needed defending until Henry Cook added some indecent illustrations Bradlaugh and Besant had identified it with atheism and thrown genuine birth-control efforts into disrepute.[41] This is rather extreme, but it is a view with more truth about it than Bradlaugh's defenders have often allowed.

More recently, historians such as J. A. Banks, D. V. Glass and P. Fryer have all drawn attention to other factors affecting the downward demographic trend which coincided with the aftermath of the Knowlton trial, and the differential fall in female fertility amongst different sections of the workforce suggests that economic motivation, coupled with some knowledge of how to limit fertility, was the key factor, and this was leading to a reduced birth rate among female textiles workers *before* the Knowlton trial. Dr A McLaren has further emphasised the amount of birth-control information, some of it of rather a crude kind, which was available early in the nineteenth century.[42]

Nevertheless, the one indisputable fact about the 1877 trial is that it did vastly increase the publicity given to birth-control arguments, which may have contributed to the falling birth rate among the lower classes. Most newspapers gave detailed reports of the trial itself, and some local Liberal and Independent papers were even sympathetic, though only *Reynolds'* of the national press was favourable. Between 1834 and 1876 about 42,000 copies of the *Fruits of Philosophy* were sold; between the trial and August 1881, 185,000 copies were sold, most of them within a year, and counting pirated editions the total number of copies sold amounted to over a quarter of a million. The *Elements of Social Science*, which had sold about 20,000 copies before 1877, had sold 37,000 by 1880 53,000 by 1885 100,000 by 1914. Annie Besant's *Law of Population*, which appeared in the *National Reformer*, 7 October to 4 November 1877, and was then expanded as a pamphlet to replace Knowlton, had sold 175,000 copies when she withdrew it in 1891. All together probably a million pamphlets on birth control were put into circulation between 1877 and 1891.[43]

As a consequence of the Knowlton trial, Annie Besant suggested that supporters of birth control should revive Bradlaugh's Malthusian League, which seems to have lapsed in the late 1860s. Preliminary meetings were held at the Hall of Science on 6 and 17 July 1877, after which a constitution was drawn up. The objects of the League were 'To agitate for the abolition of all penalities on the public discussion of the Population Question' and 'To spread among the people, by all practical means, a knowledge of the law of population, of its consequences, and of its bearing upon human conduct and morals'.[44]

The second object did not include teaching how to prevent conceptions, and in fact amounted only to an exposition of the Malthusian economic system. The dominance of this, to the exclusion of much else, reflected the influence of Dr Charles Drysdale (brother of the author of the *Elements*), who was elected president. The first object was probably of more concern to freethinkers, and suggests Bradlaugh's hand. At first the League was very much a Secularist organisation. Among the founders were Bradlaugh, Besant, Touzeau Parris and his wife, W. H. Reynolds, and Edward Truelove—all prominent N.S.S. members.[45] Most of the practical propagandist work was undertaken by Secularists, either working with the League or, more often, as individuals looking to the N.S.S. as well as the League for support. W. H. Reynolds, who succeeded Annie Besant as secretary, wrote and published birth-control leaflets on his own account, which he then distributed through the Secularist network and by post. At his suggestion, George Standring wrote *The Malthusian Hand Book* in 1893, which had a 'steady, although not large' circulation until 1895, when a suggestion from Julia Dawson in her women's section of the *Clarion* led Reynolds to offer it for sale at half-price through the *Clarion*: 5,000 copies were sold at 4*d* each during the next few weeks.[46] Standring had first lectured for the League in Glasgow in

1881, and continued to do so until the First World War; other lecturers included Arthur Moss, William Heaford, Mary Sowden, Miss Thornton Smith, and Edward Calvert—all active freethought lecturers. Not till 1913 did the League itself organise an open-air propaganda mission, and then all the speakers were Secularists—they were probably the only members qualified for street-corner work.[47]

Marie Stopes claimed that the publication and spread of contraceptive information has never been illegal in Britain.[48] In a narrow sense this is true, but those who wished to prosecute the purveyors of what many still regarded as obnoxious and dangerous information could do so in two ways: firstly, they could prevent the spread of contraceptive information through the post, using the Post Office Protection Act of 1884 (and earlier, similar legislation); and secondly they could attempt to demonstrate that the work concerned was 'obscene' as defined by Lord Cockburn in 1868 (Hicklin's case). Here Cockburn had ruled that obscenity was not that which was repulsive, filthy, loathsome or lewd, but that which was calculated to deprave or corrupt.[49] At the Knowlton trial, Cockburn had found the *Fruits of Philosophy* obscene in this sense, but because no new trial had been ordered after Bradlaugh's successful appeal in 1878, no legal precedent was set to clarifiy the status of works of this sort until 1889. Then, after W. W. Collins had been convicted in New South Wales of selling Besant's *Law of Population*, the Supreme Court reversed the judgement by two decisions to one, the senior judge, Sir William Windeyer, resolutely commending the work.[50] It was still possible, though, for a prosecution to claim that any given piece of contraceptive advice was calculated to deprave and corrupt.[51]

G. W. Foote's attitude to birth control, as to much else, was that he was sympathetic but did not want publicly to associate the N.S.S. with it or discuss it in the *Freethinker*. He was anxious that the N.S.S. should not be blamed for actions such as that of the one-time secretary of the Finsbury branch, who was convicted to eighteen months for adultery with his wife's younger sister, which he commited in the belief that this was necessary to his health.[52] A debate was conducted in the *Agnostic Journal* as to whether or not the *Freethinker* ought to be carrying advertisements for contraceptive literature and appliances, and whether the literature should be sold at freethought meetings. Ross was, of course, opposed to all such Knowltonian 'filth', but both Robertson's *National Reformer* and Foote's *Freethinker* regularly advertised works like J. R. Holmes's *Theory and Practice of Neo-Malthusianism*, H. A. Allbutt's *Wife's*

*Handbook*, and T. R. Allinson's *A Book for Married Women*, as well as W. J. Rendall's quinine pessaries. As usual, though, the limit was reached and surpassed by J. W. Gott, who advertised in the *Truth Seeker* not only the works by Allison and Holmes, the *Elements of Social Science* and Dr E. B. Foote's *Home Cyclopedia*, but also such salaciously named books as Allen Laidlaw's *Sexual Love: What it is and What it isn't*, and Mrs Alice B. Stockham's *Tokology* ('a book for Women only') and its sequal, *Karezza* ('The Ethics of Marriage').[53]

For much of the late nineteenth century, neo-Malthusianism was associated with individualism and social conservatism. The socialist counter-argument, advanced in 1872 by Frederick Riddle, was never lost. In 1877, in the wake of the Bradlaugh–Besant trial, the controversy about the nature of poverty raged like a preview of that which followed the Bradlaugh–Hyndman debate in 1884, and it was revived as part of that later controversy. The members of the Malthusian League occupied an anomalous position in all this: some, like Besant and Standring, became socialists, without shedding their neo-Malthusianism; others, like Dysdale, favoured the extreme eugenic argument for social management, at a time when most eugenicists were opposed to birth control. The picture could become very confused.[54]

What is clear is that Bradlaugh had, for better or worse, confirmed the public prejudice that atheism was immoral. Part of his legacy to Foote was a movement to which very definite images were attached. The N.S.S. was clearly associated not with Holyoake's respectable and morally conservative brand of Secularism, but with Malthusian economic and political ideas which scarcely fitted it to become part of the new labour movement. They did, however, when shorn of their cruder Malthusian features, fit the N.S.S. to become a twentieth-century pressure group with a progressive approach to sexual questions, beyond anything that Bradlaugh, Foote and their generations would have dared—or desired—to see.[55]

*Notes*

*1* *F.*, 11 November 1906; *Labour Annual* (1899); *F.* 18 February 1894.

2 *N. R.*, 16 May 1869; *Republican Chronicle*, April 1875; *S. C.*, 2 January 1876, 31 March 1878. Richard Pankhurst, a Manchester Secularist lawyer, was active in both the Reform Union and its offshoot, the National Society for Women's Suffrage, which successfully agitated for female suffrage in the Isle of Man in 1880—*Republican*, January 1881; *N. R.*, 14 November 1880.

3  *S. R.*, 27 September, 4, 18 October 1879.
4  C. M. Davies, *Mystic London*, pp. 96, 99; *Our Corner*, August 1887; *Is Socialism Sound?*, p. 109.
5  N. Soldon, 'Laissez-faire as Dogma: the Liberty and Property Defence League', *loc. cit.*, pp. 215–16; *N. R.*, 20 February 1887; *Truth Seeker*, n. d. [1907].
6  *N. R.*, 18 January 1891, 13 April 1890, 26 March 1893.
7  *F.*, 25 November 1906.
8  *F.*, 26 May 1907; see also 20 July 1913.
9  *F.*, 7 July 1912.
10  *F.*, 29 June, 27 July 1913.
11  *F.*, 11 November 1906.
12  *F.*, 13 June 1909; 25 May 1913. For Hypatia Pankhurst see *F.*, 2, 16 March 1913.
13  *F.*, 29 March 1914; the reference is to *Judges* IV, v. 21.
14  *S. R.*, 8 October 1887.
15  *F.*, 9 December 1888.
16  *S. R.*, 20 October 1878.
17  *S. R.*, 1 July 1882; *F.*, 30 August 1885, 30 October 1887, 4 March 1888, 12 September 1886; *Anti-Infidel*, June 1892; see also *F.*, 19, 26 September 1886.
18  E. C. Stanton, *Eighty Years and More* (1898; reprinted New York, 1971), pp. 389-93, 452-3, 356-7, 360-1, 369.
19  *F.*, 29 November 1885; see also an article by Helen Gardener, reprinted from the New York *Truth Seeker Annual*—*F.*, 3 February 1895.
20  *S. R.*, 1 January 1887–26 May 1888; *A. J.*, 4 December 1897 (Martin and Cook); 4 January–1 February 1902 (Stanton); 27 May, 3 June 1905 (Dixie); see also Josephine K. Henry, 'A Woman gives her Reasons for not attending Church', 5 May 1900. For the Clafin sisters see M. Legge, 'Two noble women, nobly planned', *Modern Review*, April 1893; and V. Clafin Woodhull, *Life Sketches* (n.d. [1881]).
21  *Ethics*, 24 December 1904, issued as a pamphlet, *The Ethical Movement and Women* (January 1905).
22  E. g. G. J. Holyoake, *The Origin and Nature of Secularism* (London, 1896).
23  W. H. Ashhurst to G. J. Holyoake, 1 November 1870, Holyoake papers, Co-operative Union, no. 1984.
24  [G. Dysdale], *The Elements of Social Science* (1854, 27th ed., enlarged, London, 1889), pp. 266, 271.
25  *Ibid.*, pp. 80-6.
26  *F.*, 19, 26 July, 23 August 1885.
27  *F.*, 18 October 1885; *Progress*, September 1885; *F.*, 28 October 1894.
28  P. T. Cominos, 'Late Victorian Sexual Respectability and the Social System', *International Review of Social History*, VIII (1963), pp. 18-48, 216-50; S. Pierson, 'Edward Carpenter, Prophet of a Socialist Millennium', *Victorian Studies*, XIII (March 1970), pp. 301-18.
29  *F.*, 3 April 1892, 26 February 1893.
30  *Fortnightly Review*, LV, no. cccxxvii (March 1894), pp. 377-92, esp. pp. 379, 381.

31  *Ibid.*, p. 392; *Adult*, October 1897; *A. J.*, 20, 27 January 1906.

32  Ross described the *Adult* as 'a little monthly journal . . . which discusses the sex relations as conservedly as you would discuss the subject of shirt buttons or broad beans.'—*A. J.*, 23 October 1897.

33  *F.*, 30 May 1897, 13 March, 3 April 1898; *Adult*, April 1898; *Ethical World*, 8 January 1898.

34  *N. R.*, 4 June, 13, 27 August, 10, 17 September 1893; O. Dawson, *Bar Sinister and Licit Love* (London, 1895), pp. 21-55, 236-51, 258-307; *F.*, 30 May, 6 June 1897; O. Dawson, *Personal Rights*, pp. i–iv, 1; *Adult*, 6 January 1898.

35  See below, pp. 276–7.

36  N. E. Himes, *Medical History of Contraception* (London, 1936), pp. 236-7. The terms 'contraception' and 'birth control' are of the twentieth century, but they are used here for the sake of simplicity.

37  G. Drysdale, *op. cit.*, p. 349.

38  P. Fryer, *The Birth Controllers*, pp. 123-31; J. A. Banks, *Prosperity and Parenthood* (London, 1954), pp. 146-9.

39  *International Herald*, 16 November 1872.

40  See above, pp. 12–19.

41  N. E Himes, *op. cit.*, p. 243; M. C. Stopes, *The Early Days of Birth Control* (1922, 3rd ed. London, 1923), pp. 1–2, 18–19, 22; see also M. C. Stopes, *Contraception* (1923, 4th ed. London, 1934), pp. 304-6.

42  J. A. Banks and O. Banks, 'The Bradlaugh–Besant Trial and the English Newspapers', *Population Studies*, VIII, no. 1 (July 1954), pp. 22-34; D. V. Glass, *Population Polices and Movements in Europe* (1940, reprinted London, 1967), pp. 57-9; P. Fryer, *op. cit.*, pp. 175-9; A. McLaren, *Birth Control in Nineteenth-century England* (London, 1978), pp. 219-20

43  J. A. and O. Banks, *loc. cit.*; *N. R.*, 22 September 1878; N. E. Himes, *op. cit.*, pp. 231, 234-4, 250; D. V. Glass, *op. cit.*, pp. 40-1.

44  *N. R.*, 15, 22 July, 5 August 1877. The history of the Malthusian League is told in a series of articles by George Standring—*Malthusian*, 15 August 1909, 15 March 1914, 15 June, 15 September 1919; and by C. V. Drysdale, *ibid.*, 15 February, 15 June 1913, 6 June 1914, 15 May 1921. I have not had the opportunity of seeing R. Ledbetter, *A History of the Malthusian League, 1877-1927* (Columbus, Ohio, 1976)

45  *Malthusian*, 15 August 1909.

46  *Ibid.*, 15 March 1914; P Fryer, *op. cit.*, pp. 256-7.

47  *Malthusian*, 15 September 1919, 15 February 1913; P. Fryer, *op. cit.*, pp. 235-40. A. McLaren, *op. cit.*, pp. 107-13, appears to me to underestimate this aspect of the League.

48  M. C. Stopes, *Contraception*, pp. 309, 351.

49  J. C. Smith and B. Hogan, *Criminal Law* (3rd ed., London, 1973), pp. 562, 569-70.

50  *F.*, 3 February 1889; M. C. Stopes, *op. cit.*, p. 353.

51  See below, pp. 275–6.

52  *F.*, 10 July 1892; *A. J.*, 14 May 1892.

53  *A. J.*, 1892, *passim*; for examples of advertisements see *N. R.*, 15 March

1891; *F.*, 23 June 1889, 11 September 1892; *Truth Seeker* advertisement, n. d. (from Bradford Public Library).

54   *S. R.*, 3 November 1877; *Church Reformer*, 15 September 1884; *Secular Work*, July 1896; *Our Corner*, June 1886; *Republican*, January 1886, C. R. Drysdale, 'State Remedy for Poverty', *Progress*, December 1884, pp. 272-7.

55   See D. Tribe, *100 Years of Freethought* (London, 1967), pp. 200-25.

XIV

# Public opinion and the law

*The press and public opinion*

The bulk of the London press had little time for the freethinkers, and
only the local Liberal press was willing to give reasonably fair
reports, and then, principally, only of their political activities. Even
the leaders suffered: Foote's rôle in latter-day radicalism is seriously
underestimated by press reports which ignore his speeches, or even
his presence, at meetings in which he played a prominent part; and
Bradlaugh was still complaining in the later 1880s that the London
press was ignoring much of what he did and said, even in
Parliament.[1]

By selective reporting the press was able to perpetuate the image
of the atheist as immoral, drunken and dangerous. The attempt by
freethinkers to project a different image in their own press was
frustrated by difficulties of circulation: papers had to be ordered and
could not simply be bought over the counter. Sometimes a
newsagent would refuse to supply a paper at all: W. H. Smith would
not handle the *National Reformer* for many years, and would not
supply the *Freethinker*, even as a special order, until 1906; in
Scotland, Menzies' were refusing to handle the *Freethinker* in 1883,
and again in 1902.[2] Parcels of literature sent out by the freethinkers'
own wholesale publishers were liable to be seized by the Post
Office;[3] local freethought booksellers could be closed down by
market or municipal authorities on a number of pretexts;[4] and
freethought papers could be excluded from public libraries.[5]

Though this attempt to expunge popular freethought from the
records is inconvenient for the historian, it was probably the best
policy that opponents could adopt. By ignoring the existence of
freethought, and denying it publicity, they deprived the freethinkers
of their most potent weapon. Fortunately for the latter, however,
there were many people who were only too anxious to suppress
freethought by less subtle means.

A variety of ways was open to those who wished to defeat the
infidel. There was the time-honoured method of pressure from

employers. The secretary of the Manchester Secular Society lost his job and his house in 1891, after an anonymous letter had been sent to his employer, and this was the second time it had happened to him.[6] Lecturers could also be harrassed, and were frequently the victims of mob violence, as Mrs Besant found at Hoyland in 1876.[7] Contracts for the hire of lecture halls could be broken with impunity, as happened in Liverpool in 1867, when the local secretary, George Cowan, failed in a breach of contract case against Milbourn, the hall proprietor.[8] Libel was a good way of discrediting freethinkers. Several leaders were dogged by the 'Watch Story', according to which they were said to have proved the non-existence of God by challenging Him to strike them dead within three minutes.[9] Individual freethinkers could be subjected to all manner of petty prejudice, insult and inconvenience, especially in matters concerned with death.[10] In 1886 Canon Fergie of the Church Pastoral Aid Society published the story of how Isaac Mulrooney, an infidel miner from Wigan, had been struck dead for cursing the Virgin Mary. Bradlaugh and a group of local Secularists looked into this, contacted Mulrooney's sister, and not only showed the story to be false, but also turned up the fact that Mulrooney was not an atheist but an Orangeman.[11] There was a rare and fortuitous glimmer of light when the House of Commons in 1880 accepted an amendment to the Burials Bill which legalised silent secular funerals in burial grounds.[12]

The exact state of public opinion at any one time is hard to measure. G. J. Holyoake was apt to think that things were much better in the 1860s than they had been in the 1840s; Bradlaugh thought in 1890 that there had been great improvements since 1860. Both were right, but they were in part recording only their personal experience. Holyoake had won respect when Bradlaugh was still hated and feared; Bradlaugh had won respect (largely for political reasons, thought Foote), but when opponents had stopped abusing the *National Reformer* they still detested the *Freethinker*.[13] Both Holyoake and Bradlaugh believed in progress, but progress could be irregular and unsure. Recognition of some individuals, or even some societies, did not imply recognition of all; and advances gained could be lost. J. S. Mill had warned in his essay *On Liberty* that 'where there is the strong permanent leaven of intolerance in the feelings of a people, which at all times abides in the middle classes of this country, it needs but little to provoke them into actively persecuting those whom they have never ceased to think proper objects of persecution'.[14] The freethinkers knew to their cost how persistent this undercurrent was. Bradlaugh himself, writing in 1887, saw a generation free from persecution in the mid-Victorian period, after the Chartist and blasphemy trials of the 1840s, but a new period of reaction beginning in 1882 with Foote's trial.[15] Seen from a wider viewpoint, the reaction seems to have set in rather earlier, in 1877 with the Knowlton trial. Together with the Bradlaugh case and the *Freethinker* trials, this ushered in both a new period of aggression towards freethought, and a golden age of Secularism in reply. Thereafter, with fluctuations, the level of prosecution and persecution remained higher than it had before 1877, rising to a new peak in the years immediately preceding the First World War, with further blasphemy prosecutions and Harold Begbie's Purity Crusade.[16] This pattern is not exclusive to Secularism. The mid-1880s were a time of Irish and socialist unrest, and unemployment; and the years 1912-14 saw renewed industrial and suffragette violence. The same pattern of ebb and flow is apparent also in other countries: in Germany, Bismarck wooed the Liberals in the 1870s and the Catholics in the 1880s; in France, the republican triumphs of Gambetta were followed by the dark days of the Dreyfus case. In America the reaction set in somewhat earlier, in 1873 with the Comstock Law, under which in ten years there were 700 arrests and 333 sentences, the victims including leading freethinkers, E. B. Foote and D. M. Bennett.[17]

In Britain the law held several threats, both civil and criminal, which could be exploited against the offending infidel. In 1866, at the start of the period under review, there were laws against blasphemy and obscenity, as well as the remnants of the Taxes on Knowledge which required sureties to be deposited against the commission of libels; trusts and contracts for illegal (i. e. blasphemous) purposes were void; non-believers had no standing in the courts as prosecutors, witnesses or jurymen, and were not allowed to substitute a secular affirmation for the oath. Other Acts and local bye-laws threatened Sunday lectures, Sunday collections, and outdoor meetings in public places. The freethinker was circumscribed by the law, and only the reluctance of prosecutors to come forward, or the courts to convict, could safeguard them. In 1915, at the end of the period, some of these laws, relating to affirmations and sureties, had been substantially changed; others, relating to public meetings, obscenity and blasphemy, had been modified. But sufficient remained for the liberties of the British still to depend, as in Mill's day, on the uncertain tolerance of public opinion.

## The Taxes on Knowledge

The sureties system was soon disposed of. This system had been allowed to lapse, but was revived in 1867 against Joseph Collet's *International Courier*, which was shortly to become the official organ of the International Working Men's Association.[18] Following his part in the Hyde Park meeting in 1867, Bradlaugh too was summoned to pay sureties for the *National Reformer* under the Blasphemous and Seditious Libels Act of 1819 and later Acts of the reign of William IV.[19] As Bradlaugh pointed out, his £400 surety could be forfeit every week, and he refused to pay. He was prosecuted before the Court of the Exchequer in June 1868, but the case was then not pursued. To Bradlaugh's indignation, however, it was revived by the new Liberal admistration in January 1869, but Bradlaugh then dragged out the legal procedures until April, when the government offered a *stet processus*, pending legislation to repeal the relevant sections of the Acts. This was done in June 1869, and the last of the *a priori* restrictions on the press were lifted.[20]

## Civil rights

The matter of the oath and secular affirmations was also advanced in the late 1860s, and almost entirely dealt with in Bradlaugh's Oaths Act of 1888. The Affirmations Act of 1855 had permitted those with religious objections to the oath to make an affirmation instead. Those with non-religious objections to the oath could not affirm, and the oath of those who did not believe in religious sanctions was not recognised as binding—they were outlaws.[21] In practice, magistrates used discretion. In March 1865 Edward Truelove's evidence in a case before the Clerkenwell magistrates was not accepted because he was not competent to witness; but later at Bow Street he was allowed to take the oath. In 1868 at Bow Street he was not recognised and allowed to affirm under the 1855 Act. But several times he was rejected for jury service because he could not make an acceptable oath.[22] In a case involving Bradlaugh and a debtor named De Rin in 1867, concerning bills of exchange, Bradlaugh was allowed to affirm, but Austin Holyoake, who was about to be entered as bail under oath, was objected to by the defence for De Rin. Meanwhile the N.S.S. was gathering support for Denman's Evidence Bill, which became law in 1869. This still did not help Bradlaugh against De Rin, for the Act did not apply to affidavits (or to jurymen, or Scotland). The De Rin case went before a court of error for Bradlaugh to demonstrate that the bills of exchange in the dispute had been issued in England, but his affidavit was not acceptable. A Further Amendment Act (1870) was needed to put that right.[23]

Despite these Acts, the problem of jury service still remained. Secularists were frequently called, and then rejected in the courts at considerable inconvenience to themselves. As Foote pointed out, when this happened to him in 1887, this amounted to imprisonment, for if a juryman left court without being discharged, and was then called, he would be fined.[24] Even where changes had been made by the Acts, some magistrates continued to ignore them, as Thomas Lennard found in 1875 when the magistrate, a Mr Woolrych, at the Westminister Police Court refused his application to affirm under the 1870 Act because there was 'a higher authority than the law'; the N.S.S. took legal action, and the magistrate then conceded.[25] But despite the victory in Woolrych *ex parte* Lennard the difficulty persisted. In a debt case in York in 1882, Roe, the plaintiff, was non-suited, and again the N.S.S. had to take up the case and obtain a fresh hearing at which he was allowed to affirm. This illegal, inconsistent and confused administration of the law, of which the *National Reformer* reported many examples over the years, illustrates the incompetence and malicious prejudice of a number of English magistrates.[26] As late as 1913 a magistrate was refusing affirmation to a Secularist who had refused the oath, and the N.S.S. had to apply for a writ of *mandamus* to compel the magistrate to hear the case.[27] Bradlaugh's Act of 1888 allowed jurymen to affirm, but this again was sometimes ignored. In 1915 Henry Cowell, a member of the N.S.S. Executive, was dimissed after affirming, when the prosecution objected to him.[28] The trouble with Bradlaugh's Act was that affirmation was allowed only when grounds were given why the oath was not acceptable. The freethinker still had to make public confession of his unbelief before he could take advantage of the Act, and this still exposed him to ridicule and prejudice; and the Christian who simply preferred to affirm, but had no objection to the oath, was still excluded also.[29]

The primary purpose of Bradlaugh's Oaths Act of 1888 was, naturally, to apply the Evidence Amendment Acts of 1869 and 1870 to Parliament itself, and was the triumphant outcome of his long parliamentary struggle. After the strife of the years 1880-86 the outcome was an anti-climax. Alfred Webb, M.P. for Waterford (West), was the first Member to use the Act, on 6 March 1890, and at the first new Parliament after the passing of the Act, in 1892, over forty Members affirmed.[30]

## The Bradlaugh case and public opinion

Bradlaugh's parliamentary struggle was itself not only a matter of law, but also of public opinion. The House of Commons could have acted in 1880 as it did in 1886, and simply admitted Bradlaugh on oath from the beginning. The fact that it did not can be explained in several ways, emphasising the religious, political, moral and personal aspects of the case. What the Bradlaugh case illustrates is a state of mind, both in the House and in the country.

Bradlaugh was unable to believe that his opponents in Parliament were motivated by religious beliefs, and assumed that they were using religion for political ends. The 'Fourth Party'—Wolff, Churchill, Gorst and Balfour—were out to wreck the Liberal government's legislation, and, led by Wolff, they determined to waste as much time as possible. As George Standring wrote in the *Republican*, '"The Oath" is a subterfuge: the battle to be fought is really independent of it.' This was probably true, and was widely believed by Liberals as well as radicals, but the members of the Fourth Party also had strong religious backgrounds. Wolff's parents had met at Exeter Hall, centre of the Evangelical world, and had named their son after Henry Drummond, one of the founders of the Irvingite Church; Tory politics and the defence of the Church of England were alike to him. The same was true of Churchill: his father was a strict Sabbatarian, who had also opposed the admission of Jews to Parliament in 1848 and 1857; but, although Lord Randolph had been known to defend the Church of England before 1880, Sir Henry Lucy sceptically observed how 'This controversy about Mr Bradlaugh has stirred in him hitherto unsuspected depths of religious feelings'. Gorst had a better-known record of voting to uphold the Church of England, having made his maiden speech in 1866 against the abolition of Church rates, and having voted against Irish disestablishment in 1868. Balfour, whose Christian views were liberal to the point of unorthodoxy, significantly did not speak against Bradlaugh, though he voted with the others. Newdegate also was a man of strong Protestant feeling, who since the 1840s had been assiduous in his parliamentary duties and had 'acquired the *soubriquet* of "the Watchdog of the Constitution"', from the indefatigable spirit he has displayed in combatting all innovations likely to interfere with the established order and principles of either

Church or State'.[31]

The clearest case in which religion was believed to be of major importance in the opposition to Bradlaugh was that of the Irish. In 1880 fifty-six of the 103 Irish M.P.s were Roman Catholics, and the rest, following Parnell's example, knew that Irish political interests required the goodwill of the Catholic Church. In the crucial division on the Affirmation Bill in 1883, in which the margin of defeat was only three votes, Land Leaguers and Tories had crowded into the voting lobby together, the Irish voting sixty-nine to three against affirmation.[32]

Secularists were not surprised to find the might of the Catholic Church against them; they could expect nothing better of Cardinal Manning. But the force of general English opinion was almost as hostile. This was in part political—Harcourt was defeated at the Oxford bye-election by a Tory who tarred him with the Bradlaugh brush, though no Liberal could have hated Bradlaugh more than Harcourt—but it arose mainly from much deeper wells of English opinion, represented by such Protestant evangelical missionaries as Thomas Barber and Henry Varley. These men were not in themselves typical, but they spoke the fears and prejudices of many people. This fear was not of atheism itself—which was admittedly bad enough—but of an atheist in Parliament who was, at the same time, a popular republican demagogue who had insulted the royal family, and, above all, the publisher of the 'obscene' Knowlton Pamphlet. As Leslie Stephen wrote in the *Fortnightly Review* in 1880, the 'honest, stupid part of the church-going public feels that it has been insulted and is simply anxious to revenge itself upon the insulter'.[33] Tyler and O'Donnell inside the House of Commons, as well as Barber and Varley, used the Knowlton Pamphlet in their efforts to keep Bradlaugh out. Varley's sixteen page pamphlet, *Mr Bradlaugh shown to be Utterly Unfit to Represent any English Constituency. An Appeal to the Men of England* (27 February, 1882), contained four pages on Bradlaugh's blasphemous views, and seven on the *Fruits of Philosophy*, the *Elements of Social Science* and other birth-control works. It also had appended to it two verses from Mrs Besant's *English Marseillaise*, contrasted with the wording of the oath of allegiance.

To understand the mentality of the opposition, the historian must take seriously the assertion made by the anti-Bradlaughite pamphleteer, Thomas Barber, in *Ought Charles Bradlaugh to be an M.P.?*: 'there is as much difference between *religion* and *politics* as there is between *religion* and *morality*, and that is merely none at all'.[34] Attempts by historians to separate religion, morality and politics in their analyses of the opposition to Bradlaugh go against the structure of Victorian thought. It may well be that D. C. Lathbury, writing in the *Fortnightly Review* in 1881, was right when he said that opposition 'was evoked not so much by the fact that Mr Bradlaugh happened to be an atheist, as by the fact that the atheist happened to be Mr Bradlaugh', but one may doubt how many people, even in the sophisticated House of Commons, really paused to make this distinction.[35] Although atheism was indeed accepted as a private philosophy, even by anti-Bradlaugh pamphleteers, *any* avowed atheist was a different matter. The Marquis of Queensberry, who made no secret of his views, was rejected by his fellow Scottish peers in 1880; but, when Lord Byron (son of the poet) wished to take his seat without the oath, a Bill of Indemnity was rushed through both Houses, without comment, on 16 July 1880—right in the middle of the Bradlaugh storm.[36]

Bradlaugh was the personification of all that most God-fearing, Queen-loving, morally upright English gentlemen feared. What is remarkable is the amount of support he did receive in these circumstances, and this was almost entirely because, as with the Knowlton Pamphlet, he was able to divert the main issue to one of abstract liberal principle. He appealed to that other aspect of the Victorian Englishman's character, a respect for the constitution and love of fair play. Far from Bradlaugh being the aggressor who was subverting the foundations of the constitution—which many Tories undoubtedly believed him to be—he was able to pose as the injured party, denied his right and obstructed in his duty to represent his constituents. Coupled with a popular radical groundswell of opinion, which itself cared little in principle for either Church or Queen, this liberal sentiment in the end triumphed.

The acceptance of Bradlaugh in 1886 was on these terms. The Oaths Act was carried in 1888 with the support of many Tories and Christians, including Lord Randolph Churchill and Archbishop Benson, but British public opinion had still not taken atheism to its heart. Wise politicians had come to see that Gladstone had been right that the Bradlaugh case was 'doing tenfold more for atheism than his taking the oath on his own responsibility could possibly do'. The propertied classes were also coming to see that the Bradlaugh who opposed Hyndman's socialism was no real threat to the constitution of the country: E. Belfort Bax later wrote, 'on his coming down firmly on the side of the sanctity of the existing economic and social order and of private property in the means of production, they willingly forgave or at least condoned'. But when

Bradlaugh was accepted politically, contempt was still shown for freethought. Public opinion and the legal system of England were still directed against atheists, restricting their freedom to meet and to promulgate their views.[37]

## Profanity, obscenity and blasphemy

The laws against blasphemy evolved out of the old heresy laws after the destruction of the ecclesiastical courts during the period of the Commonwealth in the mid-seventeenth century. By what right the common-law courts assumed the responsibility for ensuring that the laity kept their faith is not clear, and the precedent on which the common law was based—Lord Chief Justice Hale's verdict in R. v. Taylor (1676)—is historically dubious, there being no contemporary report of Hale's ruling. In Hale's eyes, blasphemy was an extension of sedition, and therefore punishable in the secular courts; and in the eighteenth century the law was clearly applied on the precedent of R. v. Taylor. The terms 'blasphemy', 'sedition' and 'obscenity' were virtually interchangeable, being distinguished according to the object of the libel; blasphemy and obscenity were particularly difficult to separate, as in the case against John Wilkes in 1769, and in the nineteenth and twentieth centuries the two remained identified in both the legal and the public mind.[38]

The statutes in defence of Christianity were little used by the nineteenth century, and the Blasphemy Act of 9 and 10 Will. III, c. 35, was never actually applied. Its importance was that it defined blasphemy as a crime for the purpose of other Acts and the common law. Thus bequests for the propagation of views defined in the Act as blasphemous were *ipso facto* void, and contracts, such as that for the hire of the hall agreed between Cowan and Milbourn in Liverpool in 1867, were unenforceable because they were for illegal purposes. In addition to statutes and common-law precedents dealing specifically with blasphemy, there were a number of other statutes, precedents and local bye-laws which could be used to silence blasphemous speakers and writers, among others. Particularly effective was the Town Police Clauses Act of 1847, which allowed a £20 fine for obstruction in a public place by 'cart, carriage, sledge, truck or barrow, or any animal or other means'. 'Other means' was sometimes taken (as in Horner v. Cadman, 1886) to include making a speech in the highway, causing a crowd to assemble.[39]

The tendency in the nineteenth century was for a distinction to be made in the law of blasphemous libel between the 'manner' and the 'substance' of the alleged blasphemy. The distinction was never made explicit, though, as in all the cases the 'manner' was not thought to be such as would lead to a verdict other than guilty. The distinction was a very difficult one to make, as J. S. Mill pointed out in the *Westminster Review* in 1824, especially 'when the act itself is offensive to those who sit in judgement upon the manner of its performance'. The only recognition—and then only semi-official—of the distinction between 'manner' and 'substance' as a defence was its acceptance by the legal authority *Starkie* in 1830. Erskine nevertheless followed *Starkie* in his charge to the grand jury at Newcastle in 1840, as did the Royal Commission on Criminal Law in 1841. The only judge to accept *Starkie* was Mr Justice Coleridge in Pooley's case (1857), in which the prosecution was conducted by his son, the later Lord Chief Justice Coleridge.[40]

There were no prosecutions for blasphemy between Pooley's case in 1857 and the *Freethinker* cases in 1882-83, but other, milder, prosecutions did occur, and in 1876 the Secularists mounted a campaign for the repeal of the blasphemy laws, the N.S.S. executive sending G. J. Holyoake to take advice from J. F. Stephen.[41]

In 1881, after Georg Most, a German opponent of Bismarck living in London, had been arrested for an article published in his paper, *Freiheit*, George Standring wrote of Sir William Harcourt that 'England has a Home Secretary with the education of a Tory and the mental qualification of an unpaid magistrate'.[42] The Home Office records for the early 1880s bear out at least the first part of this statement. Only the restraining hands of his legal advisers, particularly Sir Henry James, the Attorney General, kept the Home Secretary from complete folly.

By January 1882 several parties were eager for the *Freethinker* to be prosecuted. Henry Varley tried to link Bradlaugh's name with the paper in January, and M.P.s began to ask questions in the House.[43] On 9 May Sir Richard Cross sent the *Freethinker* for 30 April to the Home Office, but Harcourt held himself back. Then Sir Henry Tyler acted and saved the Home Office the trouble. Harcourt was clearly sorry not to be involved, and he asked Sir Henry James whether he could not simply seize copies of the *Freethinker*. James was opposed to prosecution, because the evil of publicity would be worse than leaving the paper alone. Harcourt noted confidentially, 'I do not at all concur in this opinion but I will wait till the pending prosecution is decided.' James must have been relieved, and a comment he made in December, on being sent the Christmas issue of the *Freethinker* by Sir Thomas Nelson of the City of London, throws an instructive light on his attitude to the Tyler prosecution—'The difficulty I see about prosecuting is that we should be harnessing ourselves on to Tyler and Co$^y$·—a position not to be desired.' Sir Thomas Nelson had asked whether the illustration on page 7 of the Christmas *Freethinker* ('Moses getting a back view') could be prosecuted under the Obscene Publications Act, 1857. The answer was that the cartoon was blasphemous, not obscene: 'It is very possible however that the two questions may get mixed up especially in the mind of the Lord Mayor.' The City went ahead with a common-law prosecution for blasphemy, and Harcourt was delighted.[44]

The wisdom of the lawyers, and the folly of Sir Henry Tyler, Sir Thomas Nelson and Sir William Harcourt, were brought out by the effects of the *Freethinker* trials on sections of public opinion. The attempt by Tyler to implicate Bradlaugh was a miserable failure, and a far wider public than sympathised with the cartoons was moved to support Foote in the cause of a free press. The year of the trials, 1883, was the year of the peak of N.S.S. success. Many new members were attracted, and radicals of all complexions, of middle- as well as working-class backgrounds, and liberal intellectuals all rallied to Foote's support.[45] Petitions poured into the Home Office from all parts of the country, signed by clergymen, like the Reverend J. Llewellyn Davies and Stopford A. Brooke; Dissenting ministers, including the president of the Congregational Union and the president of the Baptist Union; newspaper editors, like R. H. Hutton of the *Spectator* and F. H. Hill of the *Daily News*; writers and intellectuals, like Herbert Spencer, Leslie Stephen, Francis Galton, G. J. Romanes, T. H. Huxley, John Tyndall and Henry Sidgwick; magistrates, like W. White (mayor of Birmingham), George Dixon, R. Chamberlain and J. Chamberlain; artists, like George Du Maurier and John Collier; M.P.s, like P. A. Taylor, E. Lyulph Stanley and C. Maclaren.[46] Harcourt was unmoved. He refused to change either the status of the prisoners or their sentences, and told the House of Commons that Foote's blasphemy had been indecent and obscene, even though Coleridge had specifically stated that it was not, during the Queen's Bench trial. The prisoners suffered the full rigours of the new 'reformed' prison system (including the 'healthy' plank bed) for their full terms. They were released to heroes' welcomes.[47]

The indictment in the Old Bailey trial was drawn up in terms of the strict interpretation of the law, and this was how Mr Justice North directed the jury. The Queen's Bench indictment was drawn up after the form of *Starkie*, and it was in this sense that Coleridge

summed up. In following no firm legal precedents, other than that
set by his father in 1857, he confirmed the tendency since *Starkie* for
the law to become more moderate: 'if the decencies of controversy
are observed, even the fundamentals of religion may be attacked
without the writer being guilty of blasphemy'.[48]

This judgement caused great confusion, and was greeted with
mixed feelings. On the one hand it was a distinctly liberal
interpretation, and worthy of a man admired by some Christians
and freethinkers alike as a humane and liberal Christian. Foote was
grateful for this, and regarded Coleridge's reinterpretation of the law
as a major triumph. Whether this was really justified at the time is
not clear. Coleridge did not think his judgement was significantly
new, and was surprised at the stir it caused. The failure to proceed
with a new trial may have been because Foote was already in gaol
for a similar offence, not because of the way Coleridge had summed
up.[49] J. F. Stephen, as a conservative and as a freethinker, disliked
the whole business. He believed, as did Holyoake, that the best way
to secure the repeal of a bad law was to enforce it: to make the law
less bad was to reduce the chances of destroying it. In his *History of
the Criminal Law* (1883) and in the *Fortnightly Review* (March 1884) he
argued strongly that Coleridge's ruling, however desirable in itself,
was bad law and dangerous. Whereas in his *Digest of Criminal Law*
(1877) he had given Mr Justice Coleridge's opinion in Pooley's case
as the most recent interpretation of the law, in the 1883 and 1887
editions of the *Digest* he rejected this moderate interpretation all
together. Subsequent editions of the *Digest* gave both interpretations,
but not until 1950 was the entry recast to accept fully Coleridge's
1883 interpretation.[50]

An Association for the Repeal of the Blasphemy Laws was formed
in May 1883, by the Reverend William Sharman, a Unitarian
minister from Foote's home town of Plymouth. Protest meetings
were held and petitions arranged as the radicals joined with
Headlam's Guild of St Matthew to campaign for repeal. Influential
support was gained, and in 1886 a repeal Bill was introduced in the
House of Commons by Professor Courtney Kenny of Cambridge
University.[51] Kenny's Bill failed, but was reintroduced in 1887. It
proposed to embody Coleridge's ruling and to extend protection to
all faiths on the model of the Indian Code; it did not, therefore,
propose so much to repeal as replace the blasphemy laws, and was
unacceptable to many Secularists. Again the Bill was not carried,
and when modified and reintroduced in 1888 it still lacked support,
both parliamentary and popular.[52] Whereas in 1883 the N.S.S. had

been thriving and blasphemy had been an issue of the day, five years later not even Bradlaugh could persuade the N.S.S. membership to whip up public opinion and petition for the Bill. The following year Bradlaugh introduced his own Bill, which did prompt seventy-one petitions with 6,630 signatures, but it was defeated by 141 to 46l. Further attempts were made in 1890, 1894, 1914, 1922, 1924, 1930 and 1936, but not till 1969 was the Act of 9 and 10 Will. III swept away, together with other obsolete legislation.[53]

Throughout the remaining years of the nineteenth century, and into the first quarter of the twentieth, the laws against blasphemy were used with increasing frequency, and the Home Office kept a watchful eye on the *Freethinker*. Foote thought he was protected by Coleridge's ruling, but in fact the Home Office was deterred only by the knowledge that to prosecute would be to publicise the *Freethinker* and to give Foote what he wanted. Left to himself, Harcourt would have prosecuted, though his successors, Cross and Childers, would not.[54]

The most vulnerable people were local freethinkers, especially booksellers who could usually be quietly and effectively dealt with under local bye-laws or even by the mere threat of prosecution. This happened, for instance, in Scotland in 1885 when an old Owenite bookseller, Robert Ferguson, was sentenced to fourteen days under the Glasgow Police Act of 1866 on a charge of selling profane illustrations (in the *Freethinker*). The matter went to the Appeal Court, where it was dropped, but the implied threat of the action was enough to damage the circulation of the *Freethinker*. In Edinburgh, George Weir was twice threatened by the police for lecturing, and this was sufficient for his landlord to turn him out of his shop.[55]

During the 1890s the Home Office was again asked to prosecute the *Freethinker* and Ramsey's *Jerusalem Star*, but the advice remained not to give them undue publicity.[56] The question was also raised as to whether the *Jerusalem Star* was obscene, which it was not, but other freethinkers were beginning to run into trouble because their publications might be thought obscene, especially as birth control, obscenity, freethought and blasphemy seemed inextricably mixed.

As Marie Stopes was to argue, the effect of the Bradlaugh–Besant trial was to confirm this confusion in the public mind.[57] The first 'victim' after Edward Truelove's imprisonment in 1878 was Dr Henry A. Allbutt, a Leeds Secularist who published a highly popular *Wife's Handbook* in 1884 or 1885. It reached a second and third edition in 1886, an eleventh in 1889, and a forty-fifth by 1913;

by 1929 it had sold half a million copies. Allbutt himself was never actually prosecuted for obscenity, but the Leeds Vigilance Association reported him to his professional associations, and he was struck off the register of the General Medical Council. His sin had been not so much to advocate birth control as to advocate it at sixpence, and to advertise his own products in the book.[58] Those who sold Allbutt's book, however, were liable to be prosecuted, as happened to Joseph Williamson in Gainsborough in 1886.[59]

In 1891 there were three cases before the courts for the sale of 'obscene' birth-control literature, involving S. C. Branch of Bath, whose case was dismissed by the magistrates;[60] H. S. Young at Bow Street, who was fined £30 for breach of the Post Office Act;[61] and Henry and Caroline Loader of Newcastle. The latter were not Secularists, but their case was taken up by local freethinkers when Henry Loader spent a month in gaol for selling the *Wife's Handbook* and the *Fruits of Philosophy*.[62] There were also prosecutions against J. R. Holmes's *Theory and Practice of Neo-malthusianism*, at Barnsley in 1892, and at Stanley in 1910, when a Secularist named James White went to gaol rather than pay a £20 fine, and died there.[63]

Birth-control literature was not the only thing to be prosecuted for obscenity in these years. In 1889 Vizetelly, the English publisher of Zola's works, was prosecuted at the instance of W. T. Stead's Vigilance Society and sentenced to three months in gaol. *Madame Bovary* was also suppressed, and Foote wondered why the Bible was not added to the list.[64]

The worlds of blasphemy and obscenity met in the activities of the Legitimation League, the *Adult*, and the misleadingly named Watford University Press. The latter, owned by Dr Rowland De Villiers, was a spurious company, but did publish serious works of an 'advanced' nature. De Villiers took over Robertson's *Free Review* in 1897 and continued it as *The University Magazine and Free Review*; he also published works by Robertson, Walter M. Gallichan ('Geoffrey Mortimer' of the *Literary Guide*, and 'M. Secundus' of the *National Reformer*), and other Secularist writers. The trouble began when the police took an interest in the anarchist connections of the Legitimation League, for, at the same time, a complaint was being lodged against the Watford University Press for publishing Havelock Ellis's *Sexual Inversion*, Part I of his *Studies in the Psychology of Sex*.[65] The police decided to strike at Bedborough, possibly as much to destroy the Legitimation League as the University Press, for they did not prosecute the printer of *Sexual Inversion* (who was Arthur Bonner), nor De Villiers, nor Ellis himself.[66] The arrest of Bedborough in June

1898 rallied all sorts of radicals, socialists, freethinkers and progressive intellectuals, and united the generations in protest. Henry Seymour founded a Free Press Defence Committee, the members of which included Grant Allen, G. B. Shaw, Edward Carpenter, Hyndman, Foote, Frank Podmore, W. M. Thompson, Truelove, Holyoake, Robertson and Herbert Burrows.[67] William Platt, who was also a member, had written an article on free speech for the *Adult* just before the arrest of Bedborough in which he passionately advocated an end the sexual exploitation of women, and asserted:

It is time someone in England started a crusade against the faddists who will insist on discussing and disturbing present day proprieties. . . . We badly want a narrow-minded, smug, canting, hypocritical, chapel-going, lecherous, middle-class humbug . . . to come forward in this matter.[68]

Detective John Sweeney, who led the plot to arrest Bedborough, did not quite fit the bill, but the Bedborough trial did promise to give Platt what he wanted. The 'New Morality' itself was on trial, as well as the whole question of how liberal the late Victorian age really was. Despite the initial upsurge of interest, the answer was most disappointing. The police raided Bedborough's premises, and the indictment included not only Ellis's *Sexual Inversion*, but also Oswald Dawson's *The Outcome of Legitimation*, and eleven articles from the *Adult*. At the October assizes Bedborough pleaded guilty and was bound over in the sum of £100, having secretly agreed with the police to end the Legitimation League.[69] The police were now free to suppress Havelock Ellis's work and the other publications of the University Press, obscene or not.[70] The nineteenth century thus closed with a rout for the defenders of free publication and free speech. This failure in itself emphasises the key role which the Secularists had played in the campaigns of the century. Foote doubtless spoke for many when he wrote that the free thinkers had been let down by the free lovers; and Bedborough himself admitted, 'I am a coward and I reverence more than ever the Bradlaughs and the Footes who have conquered where I have succumbed.' The fact was that English public opinion was not yet ready to make advances without martyrs to spur it along.[71]

The freethinkers were still prepared to be martyred in the campaign against the blasphemy laws, and the new century was to provide several opportunities when J. W. Gott, Ernest Pack and their associates refused to be daunted by the majesty of the English law. The war broke out in Leeds in 1903, when, in October, the police made a concerted attack on freethinkers and socialists who were speaking and selling literature without authorisation on Woodhouse Moor on Sundays. Gott, Pack and George Weir were each arrested and fined small amounts on several occasions, but public opinion at this stage was not wholly sympathetic to the police. The *Leeds Daily News* thought that individual policemen were vindictively picking on the freethinkers, and gave the example of one officer who was 'determined to push the law to its furthest limit against a body of men he considers dangerous'. The fact that the stipendiary magistrate did not impose maximum fines suggests that he shared this view.[72]

The Home Office files show that in 1902 Gott's *Truth Seeker* was beginning to cause concern. The Reverend D. W. Weir of Hulme, Manchester, had already warned John Heywood, one of the biggest distributors of newspapers in Manchester, not to handle the *Truth Seeker*, and he wanted the Home Office to stop the circulation of 'this most obscene and blasphemous paper'. The Chief Constable of Bradford wanted to know if an article in the issue for September 1902, 'Waiting for the Crown', was seditious because it imagined the Prince of Wales waiting for Edward VII to die. The Treasury Solicitor advised against anything which would attract attention to the *Truth Seeker*, but the Metropolitan Police Office thought that the Chief Constable should proceed without involving the Home Office. The *Truth Seeker* contained advertisements for Dr T. R. Allinson's birth-control literature, which had been prosecuted in March 1901, as well as the Watford University Press list, and the Metropolitan Police would certainly have themselves initiated a prosecution had the paper been published in London and not Bradford. The Home Office remained set against any prosecution, though, and the Bradford Chief Constable followed this advice.[73]

The Leeds police were not so careful, and in October 1903 decided to prosecute Pack, Gott and Weir for a cartoon which appeared in the current issue of the *Truth Seeker*. This cartoon ('The Great Prize Fight') had originally appeared in the *Freethinker* for 29 January 1888, and was reproduced without Foote's permission. The stipendiary magistrate was again inclined to favour the Secularists, and threw out the prosecution because the police had failed to mark correctly their copies of the *Truth Seeker*. Overall, the police had emerged from the episode as intolerant, heavy-handed and incompetent. The Home Office's advice to be discreet was vindicated. The only consequence of the case was that it discredited Gott and Pack in Foote's eyes; Pack's N.S.S. subscription was refuscd, and he was excluded from the 1904 conference.[74]

A new series of blasphemy prosecutions began in 1908. Harry Boulter was charged with delivering blasphemous lectures at Highbury fields in London. The prosecution was initiated by the Commissioner of Police on a warrant issued to Chief Inspector Jenkins, a Wesleyan local preacher. The N.S.S. organised the defence, although Boulter was not an N.S.S. member, and Atherley Jones (son of Ernest Jones) was retained. Boulter was found guilty, but conditionally discharged. This renewal of the blasphemy laws again stirred the radical section of public opinion, and Horatio Bottomley asked a question in the House of Commons. Foote's conclusion from this case was that his Secular Society Ltd was safe, for Mr Justice Phillimore's summing-up confirmed Coleridge's interpretation of the law.[75] Later in the same year Joseph Bates, a young Boston compositor who had been lecturing on atheism in the market place, was assaulted by a pious hooligan called Batchelor. Bates took out a summons, but the case fell through when Batchelor failed to attend. Immediately the defence counsel prosecuted Bates for obstruction, and he was fined 5*s* plus costs, but did not pay and was gaoled in Lincoln for fourteen days. Since other speakers in the market place had not been prosecuted, this action, like those in Leeds in 1903, looked like the selective use of the law to suppress freethought. Bates had not been an N.S.S. member, but now, helped by his local branch, he began lecturing more widely on atheism, financed by the Secular Society Ltd after losing his job on account of his views.[76] Boulter also remained active, and was imprisoned for a month in June 1909 for violating his earlier pledge for good behaviour. By trade he was a tailor, and his business was severly damaged by his notoriety, but in 1909 he was able to sell 3,259 *Freethinkers* at public meetings, so the cause benefited by his activities even if he did not.[77] The year 1909 also saw renewed censorship at a higher level, with the attack on Shaw's *Blanco Posnet*.

In 1911 the Leeds police renewed their campaign. T. W. Stewart ('Dr Nikola') had arrived in Leeds in July, and had been holding outdoor meetings which attracted up to a thousand people. He was charged with using 'highly blasphemous expressions', such as 'God is not fit company for a respectable man like me'. Gott was also prosecuted, for selling at the meetings a blasphemous pamphlet entitled *Rib Ticklers or Questions for Parsons*, which contained a short, anti-clerical poem and four pages of short and rather weak jokes of the 'Is it true . . . That when David saw Bathsheba bathing herself he thought he would like to bath Sheba?' variety. Gott was sentenced at the assizes to four months for blasphemy, and Stewart to three. Thereafter the *Rib Ticklers* continued to be published, in a slightly expurgated form, with Gott and 'Dr Nikola' in prison uniform on the cover.[79]

The revival of the blasphemy laws aroused strong public feeling in the press; the R.P.A. prepared a petition against the blasphemy laws; J. M. Robertson privately approached McKenna, the Home Secretary; and Charles Leach, Liberal M.P. for Colne Valley, wrote to McKenna that 'There is deep feeling in my division about these two prisoners. Can you in any way mitigate their punishment?' The answer was negative.[80] A meeting held at South Place in January 1912, chaired by Headlam, was supported by W. T. Stead; the Labour M.P.s MacDonald, Lansbury and Greenwood; Mrs Bonner, Henry Snell, F. J. Gould, Chapmen Cohen and G. W. Foote.[81] Only when Gott's wife died of a stroke in February 1912 was the Home Secretary moved to compassion, and he ordered the immediate release of Gott.[82] By now a move to repeal the blasphemy laws was well under way in the country. Harry Boulter had again been arrested in November 1911 and sentenced to three months for causing a breach of the peace. The case was over so quickly that no one had time to protest, and this fact drew W. T. Stead even closer to his old adversary, G. W. Foote, in their determination to fight such indiscriminate and illiberal police action.[83]

In Leeds, Thomas Jackson was sentenced to a maximum of fourteen days under the Town Police Clauses Act for profanity in April 1912; in October he was fined 10*s* by the sympathetic stipendiary magistrate for using intemperate language when a hundred and fifty university students tried to break up one of his meetings; and in December he was again sentenced to fourteen days for starting an address in Victoria Square, Leeds, with the words 'The God of this anti-infidel crusade is a mean, contemptible, cowardly, bloodthirsty old monster'.[84] In May 1912 the Nottingham branch of the N.S.S. went to Ilkeston for an open-air meeting. Two of their members—D. C. Muirhead, who took the chair, and Frederick Chasty, who was the speaker —were charged under the Town Police Clauses Act and sentenced to seven and fourteen days respectively.[85] In July 1912 Stephen Edward Bullock, an ill educated youth of nineteen, was arrested at Rotherham for a blasphemous lecture and sentenced to three months at Leeds assizes. The Bullock case underlined the weakness of the Coleridge distinction between 'manner' and 'substance'. As Foote said, 'Bullock used the language of his class. Everybody knows what it is, and that it means nothing.'

This echoed what J. F. Stephen had written in the *Fortnightly Review* in 1884: 'You cannot in practice send a man to gaol for not writing like a scholar and a gentleman when he is neither one nor the other, and when he is writing on a subject which excites him strongly.' Apparently in 1912 one could.[86]

Occasionally small advances were made. Councillor Sydney Gimson succeeded in persuading Leicester Council in 1912 to drop profanity as an offence in the bye-laws; and in Leeds, after the stipendiary magistrate had dismissed yet another case against Pack, the Leeds N.S.S. branch was given a permit to sell literature on Woodhouse Moor.[87] Stephen Bullock, who was lecturing in Barnsley, was even taken into protective custody by the police on one occasion when he was mobbed trying to speak from an orange box on Market Hill.[88] T. W. Stewart was twice summoned for using profane expressions in Walsall, and twice the charge was dismissed. This drew large crowds for a set debate between Stewart and H. C. Orchard, and Stewart had to be given police protection. All this might suggest that popular opinion had become less tolerant than the police and magistrates by 1913; but the pattern appears to have varied locally. On 26 and 27 September 1913 Stewart delivered blasphemous lectures at Wolverhampton, while his wife distributed their catalogue of birth-control materials to the crowd. He was committed to the assizes on both blasphemy and obscenity charges; he appeared before Mr Justice Coleridge (son of the former Lord Chief Justice) and was acquitted of obscenity but convicted of blasphemy.[89]

In 1912 a new National Committee for the Repeal of the Blasphemy Laws had been constituted by the N.S.S., R.P.A., Union of Ethical Societies, and the British and Foreign Unitarian Society. A Blasphemy Laws (Amendment) Bill was introduced in 1913 by R. D. Holt on the centenary of the relief of the Unitarians from the Blasphemy Act.[90] Petitions poured into the Home Office in support of Stewart and the Blasphemy Bill. The Home Secretary made a thorough investigation into Stewart's case, as the press was claiming that Stewart had been convicted partly on the obscenity charge for which he had acquitted.[91] Coleridge's explanation was that Stewart's meetings had been called primarily for the distribution of birth-control literature and that, whilst this was not illegal, 'the fact that "blasphemy" is used to push such a trade is a very material point in estimating the *bona fides* or otherwise of the blasphemer'.[92]

In other words, the 'manner' aspect of blasphemy was to be interpreted in the light of the presumed 'intent' of the accused. This was accepted by the Attorney General, Sir John Simon, in a memorandum on the blasphemy laws which he prepared for the debate on the Blasphemy Bill. Simon's recommendation to the Home Secretary was that all blasphemy statutes, except the Metropolitan Police Act (1839) and the Town Police Clauses Act (1847), should be abolished. Instead a Bill should be introduced to amend the common law 'to provide that verbal or written publications to be deemed blasphemous or obscene only if they contain obscene or indecent matter'. It is extremely likely that, had the government found time in 1914, these changes would have been made. The petitions on behalf of Gott and Stewart in 1911–1914 were signed by people far outside the usual circle of Secularism, including a number of M.P.s and fellows of Oxford and Cambridge colleges. The correspondence columns of the *Manchester Guardian* in December 1913–January 1914 gave the mattter a full airing, the bulk of the letters being opposed to the blasphemy laws; and a very respectably patronised meeting was held in Exeter Hall in March 1914, with G. H. Radford, M.P., in the chair.[93]

Repeal was not to be. The Blasphemy Bill failed to reach a second reading in 1913; when it was reintroduced in 1914, Mr Asquith informed a deputation that the measure had the support of himself, the Home Secretary and the Attorney General, but he was unable to give it any government time. This spelt the end of it; the crime of blasphemy survived.[94]

Gott, who had been a witty and attractive character, appears to have become more embittered after the death of his wife, and he was determined to flout the hated laws which defended the religion he despised. He was sentenced to fourteen days' hard labour for profanity at Birkenhead in November 1916, and served six weeks for blasphemy for selling the *Rib Ticklers* in Birmingham in 1917. In 1918 he was sentenced to two months at Westminster Police Court for exhibiting a poster contrary to the Defence of the Realm Act, and in November 1921 he was charged with obstruction for selling the *Rib Ticklers* and a birth-control paper, the *Liberator*, in Stratford Broadway, West Ham. The charge was then increased to blasphemy, and in December he appeared at the Old Bailey before Mr Justice Avory, and was sentenced to nine months' hard labour, the severest sentence since Foote's conviction in 1883. Despite medical evidence that Gott was seriously ill, he was made to serve his full sentence, and died shortly after his release in 1922.[95]

During these years much had been achieved. Foote's Secular Society Ltd was finally recognised in 1917, when the House of Lords established that Lord Chief Justice Coleridge's intrepretation of the law was the right one.[96] Though many of the lesser campaigns were in themselves not the best advertisements for freethought—and were distasteful to Foote himself—they nevertheless did help to feed a more respectable public opinion with arguments in principle against the laws controlling freedom of speech, and they forced the Home Office to concede two important points. The first was that minor and obscure violations of public taste were best ignored;[97] the second was that 'intent' was relevant in determining the guilt of the accused.[98] After Gott's case in 1921, though, there were no more successful prosecutions for blasphemy for over fifty-five years, and when the Blasphemy Act was repealed in 1969 the legal authorities were confident that the blasphemy laws were dead—their remaining function of safeguarding the peace being provided for by other legislation, notably the Town Police Clauses Act. Indeed, a major argument against the repeal of the blasphemy laws was that they were already dead.[99] In 1977 the latter-day successors to Mrs Ormiston Chant and Mr Harold Begbie succeeded in reopening this closed chapter with a case against *Gay News* on account of a possibly obscene poem on Christ, which therefore came within the scope of the blasphemy laws. Unaware of the views developed at the Home Office between 1907 and 1914, the courts ignored both the obscurity of the periodical and the intent of the author, and upheld a rigid interpretation of the law as it had been set out in 1883 and confirmed in 1917.[100]

Even so, the historian can see permanent gains in the period 1886-1915. Although there were more blasphemy prosecutions in the period after 1883 than before, public opinion was in general changing. By 1914 both the Home Office and the Bench (with a few exceptions) were inclined to be liberal; so too was the professional magistracy, if Leeds is a fair example. The strongest resistance to new ideas came from the unpaid magistracy and the police. Both still acted at times with blatant prejudice, and the law gave the latter considerable freedom, under the pretext of obscenity or public nuisance, to act as uncontrolled censors of what could be circulated and said. This division reflected a wider split in the public at large. By 1914 most 'educated' opinion was prepared to tolerate even men like Gott and Stewart. Freedom of speech was judged worth a little blasphemy and obscenity. Popular opinion, however, could still be fanatically hostile to a freethought speaker. A Christian mob was still a possibility in Britain in the years leading up to the First World War.

*Public meetings*

Apart from the blasphemy and public nuisance laws, freedom of speech could also be curtailed by laws restricting the right of public meeting. In effect, this is how the Town Police Clauses Act was used, and there are numerous examples of the application of this and similar legislation to public meetings in the period 1866-1915. Campaigning for the right to meet and speak was an integral part of the Secularists' activities, both as freethinkers and as radicals.

Firstly there were laws restricting indoor meetings, particularly on Sundays. A general prohibition on taking money at the doors of lecture halls had been part of the Corresponding Societies Act of 1799, and had been used against the Owenites in the 1840s, but this was repealed along with the sureties system in 1869.[101] The principal Act still in force was the Sunday Reformation Act of 1781 (21 Geo. III, c. 49), but this was widely believed to have been modified by a decision of the Court of Common Pleas in 1868, which opened the way for Sunday lectures by the National Sunday League.[102] This advance was threatened in 1878 by the Codification Bill, which, among other things, was proposing to re-enact the 1781 Act, which had defined a 'disorderly house' as *any* room or hall 'used for public entertainment or amusement, or for publicly debating on any subject whatsoever, upon any part of the Lord's day called Sunday, and to which persons shall be admitted by the payment of money, or by tickets sold for money'. All manner of radical groups recognised the threat which this implied, but the Bill was never in fact carried into law.[103] Nevertheless, 21 Geo. III, c. 49, remained on the statute book, and the Secularists had to be wary of maliciously intended prosecutions aimed at closing down their meetings.[104] On occasions, debating was prohibited after lectures, and admission charges were dropped to avoid a prosecution, but when local groups were threatened at Portsmouth (1892), Hull (1893) and Liverpool (1898) Foote went to the rescue, deliberately flouting the law and calling his opponents' bluff.[105]

The easiest method of preventing a public meeting was open violence. Occasionally the law upheld the rights of Secularists, but more often it was they who were charged with being the cause of a breach of the peace. It was this partiality in the administration of the law, as much as the law itself, which freethinkers were determined to fight.[106]

The situation appears to have grown worse from the mid-1880s, when socialists, and sometimes even the Salvation Army, were victims of legal prejudice in the same way as the Secularists. Herbert Burrows was fined 40s for lecturing for the S.D.F. one Sunday morning in the East India Road, although the Salvation Army met there with impunity on Sunday evenings. This brought support for the S.D.F. from all the radical clubs. In 1886 the police attacked meetings in Bell Street, off the Edgware Road, although other street preaching went untouched. Several socialists were fined, including William Morris, and one went to gaol for two months. In 1888 Christians petitioned the Metropolitan Board of Works to stop blasphemous lectures in Victoria Park; and all lecturers were banned on Camberwell Green after complaints about the freethinkers.[107]

The law with regard to street processions was as difficult as any in this area of free speech. The standard Home Office advice between 1862 and 1882 was that processions were not illegal, but should be prevented if likely to lead to a breach of the peace. After a case involving the Salvation Army in 1882 (Beatty *v.* Gillibanks) the advice was that, unless local Acts and bye-laws provided to the contrary, processionists must be allowed to go ahead, and should be afforded police protection, the attackers being charged with breach of the peace. The problem with the law of obstruction was that all traffic to some extent obstructed the public highway, and so the courts had to decide what constituted an improper use of the highway.[108] Such discretion in interpreting the law gave the police and magistrates power, and put unpopular groups—Secularists, socialists and Salvationists—at a disadvantage.

The problem with meetings in public parks and open spaces other than the highway was slightly different. As on Woodhouse Moor in Leeds, nothing could be sold in the London parks under the control of the L.C.C. without permission. Foote's *Bible Romances* was banned for many years. The L.C.C. had a system of licensing *bona fide* organisations, and the N.S.S. London branches were licensed from 1909, but in 1912 the renewal of licences was refused to several extremist groups, and Secularists were among those summonsed. This tightening of the regulations was seen as a political act on the part of the Moderate majority on the council, and, after protests, the licences were again restored the following year.[109]

The right of public meeting was challenged in various ways in every community,[110] but the two set pieces in the radicals' struggle were Hyde Park and Trafalgar Square, where the issue was complicated by popular myths about 'traditional' rights.

The royal parks, including Hyde Park, were private parks in

which the police had no authority, except under the Board of Works.
Meetings in the parks were subject only to Park Regulations. There
had been problems over the use of Hyde Park for meetings
throughout the century, and all mass meetings in the Park were
banned after the Garibaldi riots of 1862. In 1866 the Reform League
crowd had broken into the Park after the leadership had moved on
elsewhere, but in 1867 the Executive had deliberately challenged the
right of the authorities to close the Park. To restrict the activities of
agitators after this, new Park Regulations were put forward in 1872,
but they were not subsequently approved by Parliament, and the
right of meetings in the Park was then generally held to have been
conceded.[111]

Trafalgar Square was more difficult. The problem was not only
that the Square could be deemed a public thoroughfare, but that
under 57 Geo. III, c. 19, s. 28, no public meeting of more than fifty
people could be held within a mile of Westminster during the sitting
of Parliament. Bradlaugh believed that this ban referred only to
meetings assembled to petition Parliament, and he held a republican
meeting in the Square on 31 July 1871 in defiance of the police.[112]
The problem really became serious in the 1880s, when the socialists
were organising mass meetings of the unemployed in London.
Whatever their political differences with the S.D.F., the Secularists
joined them in defending the right to meet in the Square.[113] Tension
mounted in October 1887 as police and crowds clashed in both
Trafalgar Square and Hyde Park, and the gates of the Park were
closed. On 2 November the Metropolitan Radical Federation
planned a meeting in Trafalgar Square to protest at the
government's Irish policy and to demand the release of William
O'Brien. The Home Secretary was believed to have said that *bona fide*
political meetings were allowed in the Square, but on 9 November
the Metropolitan Commissioner of Police, Sir Charles Warren,
banned all meetings there. The M.R.F. nevertheless went ahead,
and on 13 November—'Bloody Sunday'—the authorities clashed
with the demonstrators in a fashion which entered into the folk
mythology of radical protest. The following Monday nine men were
sentenced to between one and six months' hard labour on
unsupported police evidence, and others were fined. W. T. Stead
started a Law and Liberty Defence Association (later, the Law and
Liberty League) to pay all the fines; two M.P.s, Cunninghame
Graham and John Burns, were among those arrested.[114]

The events of Bloody Sunday emphasised the growing split
between Secularism, as personified by Bradlaugh, and socialism,

with which Mrs Besant was now identified. Bradlaugh was horrified at a breakdown in public order such as he had feared since the late 1860s. In his excessive regard for the law he had supported the meeting because it was, in his opinion, a perfectly legal one, but he deplored the way it had got out of hand. He was lecturing in the provinces on 13 November, and had nothing to do with the events of the day. One suspects he was rather thankful. Annie Besant on the other hand was the dashing heroine of the hour, and it was her publicity afterwards which made Bloody Sunday an event to remember. Her *The Police and the Public* sold 100,000 copies in a few days, and stirred up bitter feelings towards the police. The funeral of Alfred Linnell, who died from injuries probably received in the police charge, was turned into a ritual of propaganda. John Dimmick, who died as he tried to help one of the 130 injured people, was buried quietly by his relatives. William B. Curner, a Secularist who died from his injuries after fourteen days in gaol, went unnoticed. All this was to Bradlaugh a waste, brought on as he had long feared by irresponsible agitators playing into the hands of the police.[115]

A meeting held at the London Patriotic Club on 16 November decided what to do next. A protest was planned for 20 November: Mrs Ashton Dilke proposed it be held in Hyde Park; G. W. Foote and a majority supported her. Annie Besant proposed that they should return to Trafalgar Square; Edward and Eleanor Marx Aveling supported her. When, according to George Standring's *Radical*, they saw that they were in a minority, 'Lady Macbeth Aveling' 'turned to Edward, D. Sc., and hissed "C-o-w-a-r-d-s!" between her teeth'. Nothing could more clearly sum up the Secularists' dislike of an agitator who urged others on to violence than Standring's pet name for Eleanor Marx; and nothing could sum up more clearly his contempt for the pretentious Aveling.[116]

The main outcome of the Trafalgar Square affair was Stead's Law and Liberty League, which embraced forty-six societies. Bradlaugh, however, did not like it, and so the N.S.S. was withdrawn in February 1888. Annie Besant, on the contrary, was a League organiser and editor of its paper, the *Link*, and withdrew from the *National Reformer* to give herself more time for it.[117] Bradlaugh preferred to defend the right to meet from his position in Parliament, which he did steadfastly and to some effect, but many radicals thought he had deserted them and joined the respectable. Foote also found himself in the minority. At a delegate meeting called to decide future action, his M.R.F. resolution to wait until after the next general election was defeated by ninety-two votes to thirty-seven votes, and a Law and Liberty League resolution calling for another meeting in Trafalgar Square was carried by a huge majority. Annie Besant was clearly the only Secularist leader still in touch with popular radical feeling.[118]

The lesson to be learned by the Secularists from this history of the years 1866 to 1915 was a difficult one, for in many ways things had not progressed. In 1912, with blasphemy prosecutions and the L.C.C. ban on outdoor meetings in London, the future looked as black as it had at any time since 1866. Despite some improvements in educated public opinion, the easy faith in liberal progress had been shattered. What was especially disturbing was that, since the 1880s, the freethinkers had been in retreat on all fronts. Not only were they weaker as an organisation, but they seemed to be further than ever from converting the mass of public opinion to their side. As the hopes for Liberalism and Liberty faded at home and abroad, democracy itself appeared to have failed. In dark mood in 1910, Foote wrote:

The censorship does not become more difficult under democracy. It becomes easier. What right have cranks and freaks to quarrel with the people's representatives acting for the people's good? Must not the rule of the majority prevail? And if Town and County Councils undertake functions to which they were never elected, and usurp authority to decide practically what people shall hear and read—by refusing the use of halls to advanced propagandists and shutting advanced books and papers from municipal libraries and reading rooms—the public utter no complaint, for this policy reflects their own prejudices and timidities. The result is that a censorship is developing against new ideas in every direction. Government by the mob, or its agents, is extending over the whole field of intellectual and moral activity; and the friends of liberty and progress will have to make a desperate effort to free themselves if they wish to escape being smothered to death.[119]

He was, perhaps, exaggerating in 1910, and forgetting the vast improvements that had occured by concentrating too much on his own problems. But, given twentieth-century experience of 'democratic' totalitarianism, one cannot help thinking that a liberal society might best be judged by its treatment of 'cranks and freaks'. J. S. Mill's essay *On Liberty* was both perceptive and prophetic.

*Notes*

1  *F.*, 31 October 1909; *N.R.*, 2 January 1887, 6 July 1890. For a general lament on the bias of the press see Francis Neale, *F.*, 4 September 1898.
2  *F.*,30 June 1889; *N.R.*, 1 March 1868; *F.*, 20 September 1903, 2 September 1906, 4, 11 March 1883, 3 August 1902.
3  E.g. *N.R.*, 21 October 1877.
4  E.g. *F.*, May 1881.
5  E.g. at West Ham, *F.*, 26 February, 12, 19 March 1899, 26 February 1911; at Camberwell, *F.*, 14, 21 February, 14 March, 11, 25 April 1909, 27 March 1910. In 1892 a local Secularist offered York Public Library twenty volumes of the *Secular Review* and *Agnostic Journal*, and a regular current weekly copy for the reading room, but the offer was refused—*A.J.*, 17, 24 December 1892. Manchester Public Library was wise enough to keep its weekly copies of the *National Reformer*, and consequently has a complete and valuable file—*N.R.*, 1 April 1883.
6  *F.*, 26 July 1891; see also Arthur Moss's case, *N.R.*, 13 May, 24 June 1888, 3, 24 March 1889.
7  *N.R.*, 17 September 1876; see also reports of mobs in Victoria Park disrupting Cohen's lectures—*F.*, 10, 17 April, 29 May, 3 July 1892.
8  *N.R.*, 27 January 1867; C. Bradlaugh, *The Laws relating to Blasphemy and Heresy* (London, 1878), p. 27. For other examples, at Huddersfield, Mirfield and Merthyr, see H. B. Bonner and J. M. Robertson, *Charles Bradlaugh*, I, pp. 241-7, 294-8; *N.R.*, 2 December 1866, 27 November 1870, 13 August, 22 January 1871.
9  H. B. Bonner and J. M. Robertson, *op. cit.*, II, pp. 63-81.
10  E. g. the Bolton tombstone case—*S.C.*, 19 March 1876; *Secularist*, 26 February, 18 March, 15 April 1876; for prejudice at a funeral, see *N.R.*, 7 March 1869.
11  *N.R.*, 9 January 1887, and letters in B.L., 20-26 December 1886, nos. 1317–24.
12  *S.R.*, 21 August 1880.
13  *N.R.*, 17 December 1864, 30 November 1890; *F.*, 1 November 1885, 9 October 1881.
14  Quoted in E. Royle, *Infidel Tradition*, pp. 208-9.
15  *N.R.*, 13 November 1887.
16  *F.*, 30 November 1913.
17  For the American struggle see P. Fryer, *The Birth Controllers*, pp. 117-18, 193-6, 201-19; *Adult*, March, April 1898; *Republican*, October 1880.
18  S. Coltham, 'English Working Class Newspapers in 1867', *Victorian Studies*, XIII (December 1969), pp. 159-80, esp. pp. 175-6.
19  The Acts were 60 Geo. III, c. 9, 1 Will. IV, c. 73, and 7 Will. IV, c. 76.
20  *N.R.*, 3, 10, 24 May, 21 June, 5 July, 29 November 1868, 24 January, 7 February, 18, 25 April, 2 May, 27 June 1869; C. D. Collet, *History of the Taxes on Knowledge*, 2 vols. (London, 1899), II, pp. 174-6.
21  E. Royle, *Victorian Infidels*, pp. 266-72.

22  *N.R.*, 29 March 1868.
23  *N.R.*, 22 December 1867, 25 October, 6 December 1868, 16 May, 19 December 1869, 23, 30 January, 6 March 1870.
24  *F.*, 20 March 1887; also *N.R.*, 4 August 1878, 8, 15 November, 5 September 1886.
25  *N.R.*, 24 January, 7 February, 16 May 1875.
26  *N.R.*, 9 April 1882; for a case at West Hartlepool Police Court, 1880, see H.O. 45  9597/96131.
27  *F.*, 7 December 1913.
28  *F.*, 8–29 August 1915.
29  *N.R.*, 24 June–29 July, 19 August–2 September, 18, 25 November, 9 December 1888; *F.*, 15 July, 25 November 1888; *N.R.*, 23 December 1888. Bradlaugh's Act was 51 & 52 Vict., c. 46.
30  *N.R.*, 16 March 1890, 14 August 1892.
31  *Republican*, July 1880; R. E. Quinault, 'The Fourth Party and the Conservative Opposition to Bradlaugh, 1880-1888', *English Historical Review*, XCI, no. 359 (April 1976), pp. 315-40; H. W. Lucy, *A Diary of Two Parliaments*, pp. 46-8; *The Biograph and Review* (1880), p. 294 (for Newdegate).
32  W. L. Arnstein, *The Bradlaugh Case*, pp. 210-24; see also Arnstein's earlier articles, 'The Bradlaugh Case: a Reappraisal', *Journal of the History of Ideas*, XVIII, no. 2 (April 1957), pp. 254-69, and 'Parnell and the Bradlaugh Case', *Irish Historical Studies*, XIII, no. 51 (March 1963), pp. 212-35.
33  *Fortnightly Review*, 1 August 1881, quoted by J. Rich, 'The Bradlaugh Case: Religion, Respectability and Politics', *Australian Journal of Politics and History*, XXI, no. 2 (August 1975), pp. 38-51.
34  Thomas Barber, *Ought Charles Bradlaugh to be an M.P.?* [1877?], p. 28.
35  *Fortnightly Review*, 1 December 1881, quoted by J. Rich. *loc. cit.*, p. 39.
36  B.W.N., *Shall Atheism Force on us an Alteration of our Laws?* (London, 1883); *S.R.*, 24 April 1880; *N.R.*, 25 July 1880.
37  J. Rich, *loc. cit.*, pp. 44-51; J. M. Robertson, 'Gladstone and Rationalism', *R.P.A. Annual* (1911), pp. 51-9; E. B. Bax, *Reminiscences*, p. 37; *F.*, 1 November 1885.
38  John Macdonell, 'Blasphemy and the Common Law', *Fortnightly Review*, n.s., XXXIII (January–June 1883), pp. 776-89; G. D. Nokes, *A History of the Crime of Blasphemy* (London, 1928), pp. 66-78.
39  Smith and Hogan, *Criminal Law*, pp. 609-26.
40  *Westminster Review*, July 1824, quoted in N.S.S. pamphlet *Laws against Religious Liberty* (London, 1892), pp. 4-5; H. Jephson, *The Platform: its Rise and Progress*, 2 vols. (London, 1892), II, p. 290; J. F. Stephen, *History of Criminal Law*, 3 vols. (London, 1883) II, pp. 470 ff.; and 'The Law on Blasphemy and Blasphemous Libel', *Fortnightly Review*, XXXV, no. ccvii (March 1884), pp. 289-318, esp. p. 314; W. A. Hunter, *The Past and Present of the Heresy Laws* (London, 1878).
41  *S.C.*, 23 July 1876. See the example of a prosecution for profanity in 1874 under a bye-law in Shrewsbury–*N.R.*, 12, 19 April 1974.
42  *Republican*, May, June 1881.

43   G.W. Foote, 'Prisoner for Blasphemy', *Progress,* July 1884–December 1885; *F.,* 19 February 1882.
44   H.O. 45 9536/49902, nos. 71 (9 May 1882), 79 (28 August, 2 September 1882), 79a (23 December 1882, 2 February 1883).
45   E.g. *F.,* 18 March 1883, 9 August 1885; and see above, pp. 32–4.
46   H.O. 144 114/A25454, nos. 34, 37, 52, 69, 75, 86, 106, 113, 125, 127, 206, 258.
47   *F.,* 20 July, 2 March 1884; *N.R.,* 2 March 1884.
48   G.D. Nokes, *op. cit.,* p. 98.
49   *N.R.,* 1 April 1877; H. B. Bonner, *Penalties upon Opinion* (3rd ed., London 1934), p. 105.
50   *Fortnightly Review,* XXXV, no. ccvii (March 1884), p. 315; J. F. Stephen, *Digest of Criminal Law* (London, 1877), p. 97; (1883), p. 108; (1887), p. 110; (1926), p. 160; (1950), p. 163. As a consequence the law remained confused: Richard Pankhurst brought a libel action against one Thompson in 1885, and, to secure damages, had to show that the words attributed to him were blasphemous. The lower court followed Coleridge and found for Thompson, but in the Appeal Court Baron Huddleston followed Stephen and found for Pankhurst—H. B. Bonner, *Penalties,* pp. 109-12.
51   *N.R.,* 27 May, 22 July, 5 August 1883, 25 May 1884, 4, 11, 18 April 1886; *F.,* 18 March, 22 July 1883; *Church Reformer,* 15 June, 15 August 1883.
52   *N.R.,* 6, 13 March, 27 February 1887, 22 April 1888.
53   *N.R.,* 14, 21 April 1889, 29 June 1890; *F.,* 10 March 1889, 13 May 1894; D. Tribe, *100 Years of Freethought,* pp. 231-2.
54   *F.,* 27 September 1885; H. O. 45 9536/49902, no. 79 (23 August 1882); H.O. 144 114/A25454, nos. 495 (13 July 1885), 496 (23 July 1885), 503 (12 May 1886), 506 (31 August 1886). The *Freethinker* was considered for prosecution as late as 1908—H.O. 45 10406/A 46794, nos. 12, 13 (4 January–1 March 1908).
55   *F.,* 25 October, 1, 22 November 1885, 31 January, 14 February 1886, 11, 25 September 1887, 5 February, 11 March 1888; *N.R.,* 29 November 1885, 14 February 1886. There were also complaints about the *Freethinker* in Edinburgh—H.O. 45 10406/A 46794, no. 1 (30 March 1887).
56   H.O. 45 10406/A46794, no. 8 (5 October 1894), no. 9 (16 July 1895).
57   See above, p. 256.
58   N. E. Himes, *op. cit.* pp. 251-6; P. Fryer, *op. cit.* 169-72; D. V. Glass, *op. cit.,* p. 41; J. A. Banks, *op. cit.,* pp. 155-62; F. H. Amphlett Micklewright, 'The Rise and Decline of English Neo-Malthusianism', *Population Studies,* XV, no. 1 (July 1961), pp. 32-51, esp. pp. 46-8; *F.,* 10 April 1887; *Radical,* December 1887; *N.R.,* 4 December 1887.
59   *Radical,* November 1886; *Malthusian,* 15 August 1909; P. Fryer, *op. cit.,* p. 174.
60   *N.R.,* 22, 29 November, 13 December 1891. Branch had sold twelve copies of Ida Ellis's *Essentials of Conception and How to Prevent it.*
61   *N.R.,* 18 October, 1, 8, 29 November 1891; *F.,* 29 November 1891;

P. Fryer, *op. cit.*, p.172; D V.Glass, *op. cit.*, pp.34-5. Young had posted a pamphlet, *Some Reasons for Advocating the Prudential Limitation of Families*, and a condom.

62   *N.R.*, 3, 10, 17, 31 January, 28 February, 17, 24 April 1892; *F.*, 17 January, 1 May 1892; P. Fryer, *op. cit.* , p. 172. Loader had the alternative of a £100 fine, but the prosecution had ruined his business and so he chose the prison sentence instead.

63   *N.R.*, 4 September 1892; *F.*, 18 December 1910; *P. Fryer, op. cit.*, pp. 235-6.

64   *F.*, 9 June 1889; *N.R.*, 23 June, 14 July 1889.

65   *University Magazine*, X, 1 August 1898; A. Calder-Marshall, *Lewd, Blasphemous and Obscene* (London, 1972), pp. 208-10.

66   *F.*, 19 June 1898; *A. J.*, 11 June 1898. De Villiers accused Bonner of collaborating with the police—*F.*, 4, 11 February 1900. Bedborough's real name was Higgs; De Villiers's was George Ferdinand Springmühl von Weissenfeld—A. Calder-Marshall, *op. cit.*, pp. 220, 223.

67   *Labour Annual* (1899), p. 80.

68   *Adult*, July 1898. It is significant that, although Platt had in mind the Vizetelly, Dreyfus and Moses Harman cases (the latter in Chicago), he made no reference to the Oscar Wilde case, which was not taken up by any of the freethought press.

69   *Adult*, October, December 1898; A. Calder-Marshall, *op. cit.*, pp. 218-19.

70   *F.*, 7 January, 10 February 1900; H.O. 45 9989/X78852, no. 3 (18 December 1899). The whole complicated story is told in A. Calder-Marshall, *op. cit.*, pp. 221-7.

71   *F.*, 6 November, 11 December 1898.

72   *F.*, 25 October, 8, 15, 22 November 1903; *Truth Seeker*, September, November, December 1903; E. Pack, *Pack and the Police* [1903], and *A 'Blasphemer' on 'Blasphemy'* (Bradford [1903]).

73   H.O. 45 10406/A46794, nos. 10, 11 (8 September–27 December 1902).

74   *F.*, 6, 20 December 1903; *A. J.*, 28 May 1904.

75   *F.*, 29 December 1907, 5, 19 January, 9, 16, 23 February, 1, 8, 22 March 1908.

76   *F.*, 11 October 1908, 11, 25 April 1909.

77   *F.*, 13, 20 June, 4 July, 1, 8 August 1909, 2 January 1910.

78   F., 29 August 1909.

79   H.O. 45 10665/216120, no. 6 (10 December 1911); *F.*, 3 September, 1 October, 26 November, 10, 17 December 1911; T. A. Jackson, *God and Gott* (Bradford n. d.), pp. 3-4; *Rib Ticklers, or Questions for Parsons* (n.d.).

80   H.O. 45 10665/216120, nos. 6, 11, 12, 26 (10 December 1911–10 January 1912).

81   *F.*, 21 January 1912.

82   *F.*, 25 February 1912.

83   *F.*, 7 April, 19, 26 November 1912.

84   *F.*, 28 April, 5 May, 27 October, 3 November 1912, 12 January 1913.

85   *F.*, 19 May, 2 June 1912.
86   *F.*, 28 July, 4, 11 August 1912; *Fortnightly Review*, XXV, no. ccvii (March 1884), p. 315.
87   *F.*, 10 November 1912; 13, 27 July, 3, 10 August, 7 September 1913.
88   *F.*, 20 April 1913.
89   *F.*, 5, 12 October, 30 November 1913; H.O. 45 10665/216120, no. 55 (26, 27 September 1913).
90   *F.*, 7 July 1912, 25 May 1913; *L.G.*, July 1913, May 1914.
91   E.g. *Reynolds'* and the *Daily News—F.*, 11 January 1914.
92   H.O. 45 10665/216120, nos. 59 (8 December 1913), 63 (17 December 1913).
93   *Ibid.*, no. 86 (1914); *L.G.*, January, February, April 1914; *Manchester Guardian*, December 1913–January 1914, *passim*; *F.*, 29 March 1914; see also E. Pack, *The Trial and Imprisonment of J. W. Gott*, pp. 118-22.
94   *F.*, 5 April 1914; *L.G.*, May 1914.
95   T. A. Jackson, *op. cit.*, pp. 2-3; *F.*, 4, 18, 25 December 1921, 1, 8, 29 January, 5, 12 February, 11 June, 5, 12, 19 November 1922. In 1916, at Birmingham, Gott had been defended by Norman Birkett, and was convicted on a retrial after the first jury had divided seven to five in favour of an acquittal.
96   *Bowman* v. *The Secular Society Ltd*; see above, pp. 188–9.
97   Herbert Gladstone summed up his policy in 1908 in response to a proposal from the Commissioner of Police for the prosecution of the *Freethinker*, 22 December 1907: he made 'a clear distinction between the case of a man who shouts blasphemy in the streets where it must fall on unwilling ears and a person who writes what is blasphemous in a publication of a small circulation, mainly among people who would not be shocked at its language. Again if a prosecution for blasphemy resulted in any trivial penalty it would only give a welcome advertisement to the offender, who would be held up as a victim of persecution.'—H.O. 45 10406/A 46794, no. 13 (1 March 1908).
98   H.O. 45 10665/216120, no. 59 (8 December 1913)
99   Smith and Hogan, *Criminal Law*, pp. 609-25.
100  There is a convenient summary of this case in *New Humanist*, May–August 1977; for the appeal hearings see *Weekly Law Reports*, 11 August 1978, pp. 404-23, and 9 March 1979, pp. 281-315.
101  E. Royle, *Victorian Infidels*, pp. 66-7. The Acts were 39 Geo. III, c. 79, and 57 Geo. III, c. 19, as amended by 9 and 10 Vict., c. 33—*Reasoner*, 26 November 1846; C. D. Collet, *op. cit.*, II, p. 175.
102  The test case was *Baxter* v. *Langley—N.R.*, 5 July, 29 November 1868.
103  *S.C.*, 23 June 1878; *N.R.*, 30 June, 7 July 1878, 27 April, 4 May 1879. The Bill was lost in the House of Commons in 1880. Another feature of the Codification Bill was that it embodied *Starkie* on blasphemy, and thus anticipated Coleridge's ruling in 1883. No one seems to have noticed this at the time, although it was referred to by the Attorney General in 1914—H.O. 45 10665/216120 (86).
104  Religious congregations were exempted, under the Toleration Act, from 21 Geo. III, c. 49, but all Protestant preachers had to swear belief

in the Scriptures, which Secularist lectures were understandably reluctant to do, though Chartists and Owenites before them had done so—E. Royle, *op. cit.*, p. 68; *N.R.*, 21 April 1878.

105   *F.*, 11, 18, 25 December 1892, 12 February, 12 March 1893, 2 October 1898. Foote was not averse to using the law himself: in 1905, when prosecuted for breach of contract over the hiring of the Atheneum Hall for Sunday lectures, he pleaded that, as the lectures were against the law, the contract was not valid. The plea was accepted, but Foote had then to be especially careful not to be caught in breach of 21 Geo. III, c. 49. One subterfuge was to allow free admission, with limited free standing inside the hall, but to charge for seats. *F.*, 23, 30 April 1905.

106   E.g. *N.R.*, 9, 16 July 1871, 17 September, 8 October, 19 November 1876; *S.C.*, 11 August 1878. But Arthur Moss was given police protection in Hyde Park in 1882—*F.*, 10, 17 September 1882.

107   *N.R.*, 20 September, 4 October 1885; *Our Corner*, August, September, October 1886; *F.*, 29 April, 6, 13, 20 May 1888. The Salvation Army also suffered—see *F.*, 3 June 1888.

108   H.O. 45 10332/136764; see also H.O. 45 9682/A48160 (1 August 1890).

109   *F.*, 13 February 1910, 28 July, 25 August, 1, 8 September, 20 October 1912, 15 June, 10 August 1913.

110   An attempt was made to stop meetings at the Mound, Princes Street, Edinburgh, but this was ruled illegal unless a breach of the peace were threatened—*F.*, 9 February 1913.

111   H.O. 45 9645/A 36331; *N.R.*, 21 May 1864, 29 July 1866, 12 May 1867, 3, 10, 17 March, 24 November, 8 December 1872, 26 January, 16 February, 9 March 1873. But in 1877 the Metropolitan Board of Works was given powers to prohibit public speeches in open spaces under its control—*N.R.*, 5 October 1879.

112   *N.R.*, 6 August 1871.

113   *Progress*, March 1886; *N.R.*, 4 September 1887.

114   *Our Corner*, November, December 1887; *Radical*, December 1887; *N.R.*, 11 December 1887.

115   *N.R.*, 27 November 1887; *Our Corner*, December 1887, January, February, April 1888; *N.R.*, 15 January 1888. See also G. B. Shaw, 'The Fabian Society. What it has Done', in S. Weintraub (ed.), *Shaw*, I, pp. 150-1.

116   *Radical*, December 1887; for Standring's attitude to Aveling see also *ibid.*, May 1888.

117   *Our Corner*, February, March 1888; *N.R.*, 5 February 1888.

118   *N.R.*, 19 February, 11 March, 25 November 1888; *Our Corner*, May, October 1888; *Radical*, April 1889. In 1892 Asquith decided that Trafalgar Square could be used, but only on Saturday afternoons, Sundays and bank holidays, and only after official notification had been given—*F.*, 30 October 1892.

119   *F.*, 20 February 1910.

XV

# Christianity and
# freethought

*The popular image*

The Christian reaction to freethought was in part determined by the
Church's own problems and fears, and in part by the propagandist
efforts of the Secularists, which were often given an importance out
of all proportion to their size. Certain Christian groups needed the
'Infidel', just as certain freethought groups needed the
'fundamentalist' Christian. They fed off images of each other.[1]

The Victorian Church was a highly successful institution.
Between the middle of the century and the 1880s or later, its mission
was in most places keeping pace with the expansion in population;
everywhere were signs of growth, affluence and confidence. Yet the
Church appeared to be threatened on two counts. Firstly, it was no
closer to reaching the mass of working men in 1900 than it had been
in 1850. Quite apart from Darwin, and the spread of intellectually
respectable agnosticism, there was a sense of mass infidelity among
the dangerous classes which chilled many hearts. Secularist
agitators were easy scapegoats for this failure. Secondly, traditional
Christian theology was under attack from new ideas, particularly
developments in science and historical scholarship. Liberals within
the Church were seen as the major scapegoats here.[2]

In the Secularists' image of the Church, a clear distinction was
made between the Church of England and the Nonconformists. The
former was identified with political oppression, and freethinkers
were able to exploit a great reservoir of radical and anti-clerical
popular feeling. The Nonconformists, particularly after about 1880,
were identified with moral oppression. This was less easy to exploit,
for Nonconformity, radicalism and freethought had much in
common, but with the development of the 'Nonconformist
Conscience' the Secularists were handed some easy ammunition.[3]

For the most part, Christians and freethinkers were on the same
side, though they seldom recognised the fact. They were the ones
who thought theology mattered enough to be argued about. A
majority of the working class remained indifferent to the claims of

Christianity and Secularism alike. Foote frankly recognised in 1912
what the true position was. Commenting on a Sabbatarian speech in
which the Archbishop of Canterbury had called the British people
'A Christian people', he wrote:

It is simply Christian impudence to call the inhabitants of England 'a
Christian people'. Three-fourths of these alleged Christian people never
darken church or chapel doors. They are not Freethinkers, of course, but
they are not Christians. They are indifferentists. Talk about 'God' and
'Christ' and 'Heaven' and 'Hell' has ceased to interest them. They do not
yearn for 'Salvation', which is the be-all_and end-all of Christianity. All they
want is to be better off in this world. And they are wise in their way,
although it is to be wished that they took the problems of existence more
seriously, and threw more of their weight into the crusade against the
enemies of liberty and progress.

The reporters in Mudie Smith's survey of religious attendance in
London reached similar conclusions.[4]

This was an admission of failure, though Foote would have liked
to suggest it was the next best thing to success; but he was
exaggerating the weakness of the Churches outside London.
Residual religious feelings were still strong; religious mobs could
still be directed at freethinkers; people continued to participate in
the folk cults of the Church. Many people still sent their children to
Sunday school, even if, as in Ben Tillett's case, it was only because
mothers (and fathers) wanted their Sunday afternoon nap.
Indifferentism may have been growing by the end of the century, to
the detriment of Christian and Secularist alike, but powerful
passions could still be aroused—often among the same people—by
either side. Anti-clericalism was, as ever, a warmly felt emotion
which could easily be brought to the boil, and anti-Sabbatarian
feelings were, if anything, growing stronger towards the end of the
century.[5] Freethinkers were not slow to publicise incidents which
would inflame such passions. The biggest handicap carried by the
Church of England was its Establishment. As *Reynolds' Newspaper* put
it in 1880:

The State Church is one of those aristocratic and venerable institutions that
must not be meddled with. To maintain it intact is one of the articles of the
Tory creed. The parson stands on the same hallowed ground as the
partridge and the pheasant.[6]

This sentiment was taken up in 1886 by Foote, commenting on the
Church Congress debate on the 'Church in the Rural Districts':

The parson is hand-in-glove with the squire, he looks down with ill-
concealed contempt on the serfs of the soil, and the Church is merely a

Conservative Caucus for the election of men who will trample on the rights of labor and defend every species of privilege.[7]

Though this was almost certainly unfair to most country clergymen, it was probably an accurate reflection of the popular image.

## Sunday legislation

The older style of freethought response to Sunday was to compete with the Churches on their own ground. Increasingly, though, as public opinion began to change, the movement grew for creating a purely secular 'Continental' Sunday, with Sunday concerts and Sunday cricket. The Leicester Secularists showed that both approaches were compatible, but G. W. Foote began to fear that too much entertainment on Sundays would 'draw off a lot of strength from our party'. Nothing could more clearly illustrate the common ground shared by Christians and their opponents, even in the midst of conflict.[8]

Two pressure groups were formed, each with strong Secularist support, to change the Victorian Sunday. The first was the National Sunday League, founded in 1856 by a Secularist, R. M. Morrell, who remained secretary until 1880. The League pioneered Sunday lectures at St Martin's Hall and other centres in London and the provinces, and campaigned against the restrictions on Sunday entertainments imposed by the Act of 1781. Bradlaugh kept apart from the League, for fear of damaging it, but Annie Besant was a vice-president.[9] The other organisation was the Free Sunday Society, founded to support P. A. Taylor's opposition to Thomas Hughes's Sunday Trading Bill in 1872. The Secularists took a leading part in this, aiming to show that Sunday legislation was, in fact, aimed only at the poor.[10] During the course of the later nineteenth century some Sabbatarian attitudes were relaxed, while others stiffened. By 1906 the Metropolitan Police had reached a *modus vivendi* with costermongers trading on Sundays; and at Newcastle a Town Meeting resolved to keep Sundays as a time for worship, rest *and recreation*. But Arthur Moss was unable to persuade Camberwell vestry to hold its elections on Sundays; the *Daily Telegraph* and the *Daily Mail* gave up their Sunday editions; and in 1911 the Rhondda Council closed all licenced lecture halls and theatres on Sundays, which not only deprived the N.S.S. of its weekly lecture but prevented striking miners from holding Sunday concerts to raise funds. The English—still less the Welsh—Sabbath had not moved far towards the Continental Sunday by 1914.[11]

*The Christian reaction*

Christian reactions to freethought and Secularism varied
enormously. Amongst many Christians one can detect a growing
appreciation of the Secularist position. Atheism was ceasing to be
quite the terrible thing it had been in the 1830s and 1840s.[12] Honest
doubt had arrived, and Secularism had become a serious topic.
Christians were beginning to ask themselves what was wrong with
the Church, rather than simply assuming that it was the Secularists
who must be wrong. This development was largely the result of a
growing liberalism within the Church itself, and sympathy for the
Secularists often coincided with a distaste for the Calvinism of the
Evangelicals. The *Church Times* in 1892, for example, thought 'The
crude theories of inspiration upheld so strenuously by the
Bibliolaters are responsible for many misconceptions of the Catholic
truth.' Tolerance for the views of others had become the new rule of
the day. 'It may be doubted,' continued the *Church Times*, 'whether
any man's belief is wholly composed of falsehood. We need then to
be able to pick out the truth that he holds, and lead him on to the
further truths that are wrapped up in it.'[13] This was the spirit of the
new generation of liberal catholics who produced *Lux Mundi* in 1890.
Foote could react to this sort of view only by himself adopting the
conservative Evangelical position, and accusing the authors of *Lux
Mundi* of heresy.[14]

The Broadchurchmanship of Dean Stanley and the High-
churchmanship of Father Ignatius did much to smooth relations
between Christians and freethinkers in the 1870s. Father Ignatius
even lectured at the Hall of Science in November 1872, with Austin
Holyoake in the chair, and was invited back the following month
and again in the spring of 1873. He gave the income from his lectures
to the Hall of Science building fund.[15] Annie Besant always
respected both Dean Stanley and Edward Pusey,[16] but the least-
expected tribute was paid by Foote to J. H. Newman, shortly before
the latter's death in 1890: Newman was 'the only Catholic dignitary
for whom we have very much respect, and we have spent many an
hour over his exquisite pages'. Newman had refused to sign a
petition against the admission of Bradlaugh to Parliament on the
grounds that, because the House of Commons had already admitted
Jews, it had lost its Christian character. This detachment Foote
contrasted with the active anti-Bradlaughite position adopted by
Cardinal Manning.[17]

The Christian who, more than any other, helped to build a bridge of understanding between Christianity and Secularism was the Reverend Stewart D. Headlam, founder of the Guild of St Matthew. Headlam became interested in Secularism in the early 1870s when, as a young curate, he had trouble with the Secularist questionings of the older lads in his Sunday-school class. Rather than simply dismissing these ideas, Headlam began to attend at the Hall of Science. On his first visit he heard Mrs Law denounce priests. That was a start. But on 4 April 1875, having heard Bradlaugh speak on 'Slavery in America', he was moved to write to a friend, 'how much nearer to the Kingdom of Heaven are these men in the Hall of Science than the followers of Moody and Sankey!' In 1876 Headlam took charge of the N.S.S. petition against the blasphemy laws, and thereafter could be relied upon to work with and support a number of Secularist causes.[18]

On St Matthew's Day, 1877, he started a guild at St Matthew's Church, Bethnal Green, where he had been a curate since 1873. The first avowed object of this Guild of St Matthew was 'To get rid, by every possible means, of the existing prejudices, especially on the part of "Secularists", against the Church—her Sacraments and Doctrines: and to endeavour to justify *God* to the People'. This Guild, which became a general one after Headlam's departure from Bethnal Green in 1878, was never very large—about a hundred members in 1884, a third of whom were clergymen—but it made a considerable impact on both Secularism and the Church.[19] Headlam in effect became unpaid chaplain to the Hall of Science, and was the obligatory clergyman on the management committee of the Hall of Science schools, thereby enabling them to obtain a South Kensington grant. During the great campaigns, Headlam did not hold back. On hearing the Knowlton trial verdict in 1877, he wrote to Bradlaugh expressing shock and offering help. When Bradlaugh was locked in the Clock Tower on 23–24 June 1880, Headlam characteristically sent his telegram of condolence in the name of Christ. In 1883 the Guild of St Matthew petitioned Parliament for the Affirmation Bill, for the repeal of the blasphemy laws, and for the release of Foote, Ramsey and Kemp. Both Headlam and Frederick Verinder, the Guild secretary, were on the executive of the National Association for the Repeal of the Blasphemy Laws. During 1882-83 Headlam lectured at the Battersea branch and at Leicester, and he took the Ball's Pond Road Secular Hall for a course of lectures in November and December 1883. After 1884 he increasingly turned his attention to socialism, but he never lost his interest in the Secularists and their work.[20]

Critics of Headlam could say that he achieved very little. Secularists accepted him as an individual, not as a representative of the Church.[21] They may well have been right. Headlam was never more than a curate—not even that after 1882—and he was at loggerheads with his bishop. He was scarcely the best person to reconcile anyone to anything: he seemed deliberately to go out of his way to adopt causes which would upset his fellow Christians—not only Secularism and then socialism, but theatres, music halls, dancers and the disgraced Oscar Wilde.[22]

Yet Headlam was not quite alone in the Church. He was himself a disciple of F. D. Maurice, and Maurice's influence was growing. The Christian Socialism of the 1850s, with its emphasis on co-operation with working men, had inspired Headlam long before he read Henry George and began to adopt the later kind of socialism. Through the Working Men's College, Maurice had influenced Secularists like Sam Standring and his father, and Christians like W. M. Rossiter, whose *Nineteenth Century* article on 'Artisan Atheism', published in February 1877, presented such a fair picture of freethought in London.[23] The Guild of St Matthew helped focus this wider trend in the 1880s. In 1880 and 1881 the Church Congress devoted some time to discussing Secularism, and on each occasion the papers and discussions were marked by considerable restraint. In 1880 the discussion was started off by the Reverend J. E. Symes, one of the earliest members of the Guild of St Matthew, and in 1881 Canon H. C. Shuttleworth was a speaker. More significant than the views of such obvious sympathisers were those of the Reverend Randall T. Davidson, chaplain and son-in-law to Archbishop Tait, and later Archbishop of Canterbury himself, who led off the 1881 discussion. He was not a member of the Guild, nor approved of much of what it did, but in the context of Secularism he commended its work. Other examples of sympathy for the Guild are to be found elsewhere, as in the 1881 Hulsean Lectures, delivered in Cambridge by the Reverend Joseph Foxley. The tide was clearly turning in the Church.[24]

What the Church Congress reports also show, however, is that the tide was turning less fast in some places than in others. The Low Church Evangelicals did not find it easy to see the merits of Secularism, and were quicker to denounce the sins of atheism than to repent of their own. In 1880 the Reverend P. Barker, and in 1881 the Reverend C. Lloyd Engström, both of the Christian Evidence Society, expressed the distinctive Evangelical attitude towards freethought, which was not completely lacking in charity, but was aggressive rather than understanding. The opening paper in the 1881 discussion was delivered by Archbishop Thompson of York. He was a leading Evangelical, who commended the work of the Christian Evidence Society, and urged Christians to refurbish the design argument as a defence of their faith. Though his paper was moderate in tone, it could not escape the assumption that the Secularists were inevitably wrong, in marked contrast to the Guild of St Matthew belief, expressed by J. E. Symes in 1880 and Canon Shuttleworth in 1881, that God was working through everything, including the Secularist movement. Headlam, naturally, put the matter with shocking bluntness in 1891 when he said, 'We Christians owe much to the National Secular Society, it has helped us to overthrow many idols and to sweep away much rubbish.'[25]

Headlam also confessed, a year later, that 'the decay of the narrow Protestant and Calvinist individualism which once dominated English theology, has robbed the secularist controversy of much of the importance which it had in the early days of the Guild'. It was certainly more difficult for traditional Secularist arguments to be employed in the days of Headlam's Guild of St Matthew, *Lux Mundi*, F. W. Farrar's *The Bible, its meaning and supremacy*, and R. J. Campbell's *New Theology*, but fortunately there was no shortage of Christians still prepared to defend the old Calvinism and the old attitude towards biblical truth, as Charles Booth's reporter had noted on Peckham Rye in 1901.[26]

Two societies were founded, like the Guild of St Matthew, to meet the Secularist challenge, but their approach was very different and they did much to remove any favourable impression which the Guild had been able to create. These were the Christian Evidence Society, and the Anti-Infidel League.

The Christian Evidence Society was an Evangelical organisation, founded in 1870 by such men as Archbishops Thompson and Tait, Lord Salisbury and Lord Shaftesbury, to combat 'the present prevalence of scepticism or of unbelief in various classes of society' by adopting the methods used by the Secularists themselves.[17] The Society hired the Hall of Science for weekly lectures in reply to the Secularists, hoping, apparently with some success, to attract the same audiences as attended freethought lectures there. Lecturers were also sent out into the parks and open spaces where the Secularists were at work, to set up a rival attraction.[28] Though the leaders of both Secularism and the Christian Evidence Society were reasonable and relatively moderate men, the proximity of their two bands of followers shouting each other down in the open air

inevitably led to clashes and mutual recriminations.[29] Chapman
Cohen, who experienced a great deal of Christian Evidence abuse
over the years, described the Society's lecturers as 'unscruplous and
foul-minded liars', but they were convinced that their aggressive
attitude to freethought was preferable to the 'kid-glove' approach of
the Guild of St Matthew.[30] Sometimes, free lance Christian lecturers
called themselves 'Christian Evidence' men, and the same sort of
work was also done by the various City and Town missions which,
since the 1830s, had been acting as the spearhead of inter-
denominational Evangelical urban missionary work. The London
City Mission, for example, had an outdoor lecturing station in Old
Street, opposite the Hall of Science.[31]

The Anti-Infidel League was a much smaller body, with less
respectable patronage. It was, in fact, the personal organisation of
William Robert Bradlaugh, Charles's younger brother. This brother
and the League were the inverse of all that the other stood for,
almost to the point of caricature. William Bradlaugh was the black
sheep of the family, who had taken to drink; but on 7 March 1875 he
had signed the pledge, and on 25 March at Exeter Hall he had been
converted by Moody and Sankey. He was given a job at the *Christian
Herald*, of which he became sub-editor, but he was meanwhile
building himself a second career as an evangelist, exploiting his
surname in the cause of his faith, and following his brother round
the country in an effort to undo his work.[32] He issued tracts from his
'Anti Infidel Depot', and in June 1885 he started the *Anti-Infidel*, a
monthly penny periodical 'for the Advocacy of Truth and Exposure
of Error'. In the early 1890s he began the Anti-Infidel League.[33] This
cannot have been very large, but it was symbolic of the extreme
Evangelical position in the late nineteenth century, rejecting not
only Darwin but all modern science and Higher Criticism: 'We
cannot accept the hypothesis that man is only one link in the
unbroken chain of animal life. Neither can we believe that the
Christian Church and the Jewish nation have alike been mistaken as
to the age and authorship of the Pentateuch,' he proclaimed in one
editorial. The object of the Anti-Infidel League was 'To promote
Christianity at Home and Abroad by contending earnestly for "the
faith once for all delivered unto the saints," by means of Bible
classes, lectures and literature'.[34] The Secularists thrived on this sort
of obscurantism; and the Anti-Infidel League made the most of the
problems of Foote and the N.S.S. in the mid-1890s. Relations with
the Christian Evidence Society were not good, for, although W. R.
Bradlaugh thought of himself as extending their work, he could be

something of an embarrassment even to them. He was horror-stricken when the celebrated Christian Evidence coloured preacher, Celestine Edwards, once admitted that he did not believe the Genesis account of the creation of man from dust.[35] One of the Anti-Infidel lecturers, Walton Powell, dragged up the Leeds 'orgies' of 1878 in debate with J. Greevz Fisher in Leeds in 1894. W. R. Bradlaugh's handling of this, both denying any association with Powell and claiming the credit for the trouble he caused G. W. Foote, was sheer opportunism, and one cannot escape the conclusion that W. R. Bradlaugh was a self-deceiving rogue.[36] Yet he was sincere, and spoke for thousands of sincere Christians who felt betrayed by the Higher Criticism, and looked anxiously for reassurance.

Charles Bradlaugh was, of course, a good cause for any aspiring evangelist to attach himself to, and W. R. Bradlaugh was remarkable only in having the advantage of being his brother. Just as John Brindley and Brewin Grant had made careers for themselves out of attacking the infidels from the 1840s to the 1870s, so each generation threw up its self-appointed champions. In the 1870s and 1880s, in addition to the younger Bradlaugh, there was Henry Varley, a Baptist butcher for whom the West London Taberbacle was built in St James's Square. In 1875 he went to evangelise America lest that great nation fall from grace during the absence of Moody and Sankey in Britain; and in the 1880s he exploited religious prejudices to the full in the Bradlaugh case.[37]

## The Secularist reaction

The Secularists had nothing but contempt for such men and their methods. Revivalism, whether practised by Varley, W. R. Bradlaugh, or Moody and Sankey, was almost beneath their notice. This reaction was partly instinctive and partly rational. George Reddalls criticised Moody and Sankey for inculcating piety, not morality; the poet James Thompson compared the appeal of the hymns of the revival to that of the Christy Minstrels—fit only for the infant or negro mind.[38] When Torrey and Alexander came to convert Britain in 1904-05, Torrey was foolish enough to repeat the old stories about Thomas Paine's drunken and dissolute end. Foote wrote pamphlets exposing Torrey, and both Blatchford in the *Clarion* and W. T. Stead in the *Review of Reviews* weighed in against the fraudulent evangelist.[39]

By contrast, Charles Spurgeon received mild, even favourable, treatment. Foote found his defence of the old faith more pleasant and more comprehensible—and, one suspects, more convenient—than the trimming of Dr Clifford.[40] This was to be expected, given Foote's low opinion of Clifford, but quite unexpected is the tribute which Bradlaugh paid to the man who was most nearly his opposite number on the Christian side. In the *National Reformer* in 1870 he wrote:

> Mr Spurgeon is too manly for us to desire to merely worry him. He does not, so far as we are aware, attack us, and to tilt at him without grave cause, would seem like merely using the popularity of his name. Spurgeon does good, despite his religion. We have occasionally attacked his sermons, and may do so again, but we believe that there are hundreds of worse men, and very few more eloquent preachers.[41]

The Secularists preferred an honest opponent, whether Newman or Spurgeon, to one who used dubious tactics, or who was merely liberal and temporising. G. W. Foote, for example, agreed with Gladstone's review of *Robert Elsmere*, but for the opposite reasons. 'When we want a sermon or an essay,' he wrote, 'we know where to get it, and we like it unadulterated.'[42]

The Anti-Infidel League was a minor irritant. Far more serious and more difficult to deal with was the Salvation Army, founded by William Booth in 1878. Foote never liked it. 'It is unparallelled in its vulgarity. The imbecile coarseness of its language makes one ashamed of human nature . . . Its metaphors are borrowed from the slaughter-house, its songs are frequently coarser than those of the lowest music-hall, and the general style of its preaching is worthy of a congregation of drunken pugilists.'[43] The snobbish attitude embodied in this comment is significant, and was not unexpectedly echoed by W. S. Ross,[44] but George Standring adopted quite a different position. Recognising that both the Churches and Secularism had failed to reach 'the common people', he commended the Army's work of social salvation, which provided a 'first step upwards from the abyss of ignorance and degradation'. This admission, which was made in a letter to the *Pall Mall Gazette*, did not please Foote, but it was none the less a significant acknowledgement of the true state of affairs between Christianity, freethought and the people.[45]

The major Nonconformist bodies had in the earlier nineteenth century appeared natural allies of the Secularists in such matters as political radicalism, freedom of conscience, disestablishment and secular education. Methodism was less well thought of, but there were many varieties of Methodist—one did not have to be a freethinker to dislike the priestly pretensions of Jabez Bunting. But there was a marked change in Secularist attitudes from about 1880, prompted by the growing militancy of Nonconformity (now including Methodism) as it tried to assert itself as equal to the Established Church. The 'Nonconformist Conscience', as its enemies called this development, was the product of the old evangelical piety coarsened through involvement in Liberal politics since 1870, and its leaders were Dr John Clifford of the Baptists and the Reverend Hugh Price Hughes of the Wesleyans.[46] From the Parnell case in 1890 to the Torrey–Alexander mission, the revival of 1905 and the education quarrels of Edwardian England, G. W. Foote in particular was incensed by 'screaming pietists' whose 'judgment displays the usual imbecility of religionists'.[47]

The earlier Secularists had not been unduly worried by Matthew Arnold's 'philistines'—they had been philistine themselves in his meaning of the word—but by 1890 both the public mood and the Secularist leadership had changed. At the very time that Secularism may have been becoming more of a lower-middle-class movement, the Secularists were turning against the philistinism of that class. Spurgeon may have satisfied Bradlaugh, but a *Freethinker* review of a new edition of Spurgeon's sermons in 1910 was prefaced by Matthew Arnold's statement, 'Of all the dull, stagnant, unedifying entourages, that of middle-class Dissent seems to me the stupidest'; and the review went on to develop this theme. Another *Freethinker* writer the following year produced an amusing diagnosis of 'Nonconformosis'—an 'interesting disease . . . found mostly among members of the Lower-Middle-Class-Liberal-Backbone-of-the-Nation community'.[48]

The greatest change in relationship between Secularism and Christianity from 1866 to 1915 lay here. In the first part of the period the Church of England as a political institution was the biggest enemy of freethought; by the Edwardian years Nonconformity had taken its place. Though much theological narrowness remained in the Evangelical wing of the Church of England, intellectual and social narrowness appeared to be epitomised by Dissent. This might seem strange, when Clifford, Hughes and Campbell were leaders of a new liberalism in Nonconformity,[49] but both sides were still trading in images; and the image of Nonconformity was shaped above all by what Secularists regarded as its selfish betrayal of religious toleration as exemplified by the education question.

*Notes*

1  For the Church's need for an image to attack in America, see M. E. Marty, *The Infidel* (Cleveland and New York, 1961).

2  W. O. Chadwick, *Victorian Church*, part II, pp. 223, 232, and 'The Established Church under Attack', in A. Symondson (ed.), *Victorian Crisis of Faith*, pp. 91-105; *Christian Evidence Journal*, July 1874, p. 141; P. T. Marsh, *The Victorian Church in Decline* (London, 1969), pp. 51-6.

3  E. g. *F.*, 17 October 1886, 10, 17 December 1911; *Ethical World*, 26 February 1898.

4  *F.*, 11 February 1912; R. Mudie Smith (ed.), *The Religious Life of London*, pp. 200 (C. F. G. Masterman), 302 (Rev. J. E. Watts Ditchfield), 341-2 (George Haw).

5  B. Tillett, *Memories*, p. 26; *F.*, 9 October 1881, 4 June 1899.

6  *Reynolds' Newspaper*, 14 March 1880, quoted in H. M. Lynd, *England in the Eighteen-eighties* (Oxford, 1945), p. 309.

7  *F.*, 17 October 1886.

8  *F.*, 14 April 1889; see also 26 May 1889.

9  *N. R.*, 2 February, 5 July, 29 November, 6 December 1868, 9 January, 12 March 1876, 9 February, 6 April 1879; *S. C.*, 1 March 1879; *S. R.*, 10 April 1880; *L. G.*, October 1912.

10  *N. R.*, 14 May, 11 June 1871, 6 October 1872

11  H. O. 45 10343/140754 no. 2 (23 July 1906); *F.*, 19 May 1907, 6 February 1895, 4 June 1899, 12 March 1911.

12  E. g. *F.*, 20 October 1907; *Methodist Times*, 20 September 1888; *London Quarterly Review*, CVI (1909), p. 25.

13  *Church Times*, 29 January 1892.

14  *F.*, 6–20 July 1890. By contrast, see Bertrand Russell's more sympathetic review of *Lux Mundi* in the *Agnostic Annual* (1891), pp. 48-53.

15  *N. R.*, 8, 22 December 1872; H. B. Bonner and J. M. Robertson, *Charles Bradlaugh*, I, pp. 342-3.

16  A. Besant, *Autobiography*, pp. 122–5; *N. R.*, 24 September 1882.

17  *F.*, 26 January 1890; also 17 August 1890.

18  F. G. Bettany, *Stewart Headlam: a biography* (London, 1926), p. 27; S. D. Headlam, *Charles Bradlaugh: an appreciation* (London, 1907), p. 12; *N. R.*, 30 April 1876; see also 24 September 1876.

19  F. G. Bettany, *op. cit.*, pp. 40, 79; Guild of St Matthew, *Report of Council* (1883), p. 2; D. Bowen, *The Idea of the Victorian Church* (Montreal, 1968), pp. 324-8; K. S. Inglis, *Churches and the Working Classes in Victorian England* (London, 1963), p. 272; P. d'A. Jones, *The Christian Socialist Revival, 1877-1914* (Princeton, 1968), p. 129.

20  *N.R.*, 12 October 1879; S. D. Headlam to C. Bradlaugh, 29 June 1877, B.L. no. 509; 24 June 1880, no. 698; G.S.M., *Report of Council* (1883), pp. 10-12, 17; *F.*, 15, 29 April 1883.

21  E. g. Ross, *S. R.*, 2 January 1886.

22  F. G. Bettany, *op. cit.*, pp. 47-78.

23  J. F. C. Harrison, *A History of the Working Men's College*, pp. 54, 58, 73,

81; *Radical*, November 1886.
24 *The Official Report of the Church Congress* (1880), pp. 345-58, esp. pp. 352-3; (1881), pp. 41-69, esp. pp. 55-9, 65-6; Rev. J. Foxley, 'Secularism, Scepticism, Ritualism, Liberationalism', *Hulsean Lectures* (1881), I, pp. 3-13, esp. pp. 8-9.
25 *Report of the Church Congress* (1881), pp. 41-7; c f. (1880), p. 353; (1881), p. 66; *F.*, 11 January 1891.
26 *Church Reformer*, October 1892, quoted by P. d'A. Jones, *op. cit.*, p. 134; C. Booth, *Life and Labour*, 3rd series, VI, pp. 187-8.
27 *N. R.*, 11 March 1888; M. A. Crowther, *Church Embattled* (Newton Abbot, 1970), pp. 216-17.
28 *N.S.S. Almanack* (1873), pp. 15-16; *Christian Evidence Journal*, June 1874, July 1875; *Anti-Infidel*, August 1888.
29 E.g. *Anti-Infidel*, October 1890.
30 C. Cohen, *Autobiography*, p. 62; *S. R.*, 7 January 1882.
31 'Annual Report of the Infidel-Hall District', *London City Mission Magazine*, 1 September 1882; pp. 199-205, esp. pp. 201, 204.
32 *Anti-Infidel*, March, May 1891; *N. R.*, 16 December 1877; *Anti-Infidel*, December 1899.
33 *Id.*
34 *Ibid.*, June 1892; February 1892 (inside back cover).
35 *Ibid.*, November 1893; also January, March 1894.
36 Walton Powell had alleged in discussion with J. Greevz Fisher that Secularism was degrading because, at the Hall of Science in 1879, boys had been got together and taught how to masturbate 'to make muscular and strong the organs of procreation'. Foote sued W. R. Bradlaugh for £1,000 damages (the sum he needed to complete the purchase of the lease from R. O. Smith), but he was awarded only £30. Bradlaugh claimed a moral victory, at the same time disowning Powell, who had muddled the alleged events with the 'Leeds orgies' of 1878. Bradlaugh then claimed that the case and Foote's failure had caused the mistrust between Smith and Foote which led to loss of the Hall of Science. By 1898 Bradlaugh was convinced not only that he had brought about the closure of the Hall, but that either Powell was a Secularist or 'he has acted like one'. He had previously tried to claim that Powell was a Christian Evidence Society lecturer.—*Anti-Infidel*, November 1893, December 1893–March 1894, May 1894, March, August 1895, January 1898; *F.*, 21 October, 4, 11 November 1894, 24 February, 3, 31 March 1895.
37 See press cuttings in Bradlaugh collection, box 2 (miscellaneous), Northampton Public Library; also *N. R.*, 14 February 1875.
38 *S. C.*, 14 February 1875; *N. R.*, 25 April 1875.
39 *F.*, 10, 31 January 1904; 1 January, 12, 19 February, 16 April, 4 June, 9 July 1905.
40 *F.*, 6 November 1887.
41 *N. R.*, 25 September 1870.
42 *F.*, 6, 13, 20 May 1888.
43 *F.*, 23 April 1882.

44  *S. R.*, 18 August 1888.
45  *F.*, 3, 10 August 1890. When William Booth produced *In Darkest England* in 1890, Bradlaugh criticised it for discouraging thrift—*N. R.*, 23 November 1890; Foote rejected both the theology and the economics of the book—*F.*, 16 November – 7 December 1890, later issued as a pamphlet, *Salvation Syrup; or, Light on Darkest England*. For once, Foote was in agreement with Hyndman—H. M. Hyndman, *General Booth's Book Refuted* (London, 1890).
46  J. Kent, 'Hugh Price Hughes and the Nonconformist Conscience', in G. V. Bennet and J. D. Walsh (eds.), *Essays in Modern Church History*, pp. 181-205.
47  *F.*, 7 December 1890; also 18 October 1891, 9 November 1902; *N. R.*, 22, 29 March, 4 April 1891; see also A. J. Lee, 'The Radical Press', pp. 49-50, and S. E. Koss, '1906: Revival and Revivalism', pp. 77-9, in A. J. A. Morris (ed.), *Edwardian Radicalism*, pp. 47-61, 75-96.
48  *F.*, 24 July 1910, 10 December 1911.
49  J. Kent, 'A Late Nineteenth Century Nonconformist Renaissance', in D. Baker (ed.), *Studies in Church History*, XIV, pp. 351-60.

# XVI

# Education

*Public education and the School Boards*

Though not all supporters of secular education were Secularists, education was, along with the oath, the issue which most divided Christians from non-Christians. As one observer wrote of the political programme of the N.S.S. in 1912, 'probably the Nonconformist section of the Liberal Party would endorse every item except that relating to religious teachings'.[1]

Despite the efforts of G. J. Holyoake in plying W. E. Forster with details of the Dutch system of secular education in 1870, the Secularists were at that time able to make no impact on government policy, or even on the National Education League, which would not declare for the exclusion of the Bible from the new schools.[2] Forster's Education Act of 1870 was a compromise which pleased no one. Bradlaugh denounced it as a farce which would leave rural education exactly where it was before—in the hands of the Church. Austin Holyoake was more favourable to it, but feared the conscience clause might lay parents and children open to pressure, particularly in rural areas. G. J. Holyoake was more positive, and pointed out how Secularist teachers would be able to teach in the new schools as much as anyone else, and he urged Secularists to set up their own schools and to claim the government grant.[3] More realistically, local Secularists appreciated that the new School Board elections, with their system of multiple voting, offered the best chances yet of Secularists being elected to positions of influence in the community.

In 1870 the Birmingham Secular Club decided to put forward their president in the School Board elections as a Liberal, and, when he failed to secure an official nomination, he stood as an independent. He was not elected but, in an election won surprisingly by the Conservatives, he did collect over 7,000 votes.[4] Secularists in other towns—Liverpool, Manchester and Gateshead, for example—also stood unsuccessfully.[5] As more School Boards were formed, however, and more elections held, the Secularists did begin to win seats. It was a tribute to their standing as local radicals that they were able so quickly to make an impact. R. A. Cooper of Norwich was elected to the new Norwich Board early in 1871; William Barker of Bramley was on the Leeds Board in 1872, and got his constituents a new school; Frank Field, an old Owenite and president of the Oldham Secular Society, was elected to the Oldham School Board without a contest in 1876; and in the same year J. H. Tyson, the Stalybridge musician, joined his local School Board; two members of the Huddersfield Secular Society, Thomas Bates and Joshua Haigh, were elected for the township of Sefton in 1878; and in 1879 Jonathan Taylor of the Sheffield B.S.U. branch was elected third out of fifteen successful candidates, with 13,978 votes.[6] By the end of the decade the Secularists had made their marks on Boards throughout the country, but, once elected, they were largely powerless. At best there would be only two or three of them on a Board, not sufficient to influence policy unless they could win the wider support of the non-clerical party. This could often be difficult. The Birmingham School Board, as Charles Cattell grumbled in 1875, was all P's—seven Parsons, seven Purses, one Profession—and no Poor.[7] The Secularist, when elected, was likely to be a poor man, and not until the end of the century did poor men begin to make much impact on local politics.

The School Board which most interested Secularist leaders, and which therefore received most attention in the periodicals, was that in London, which was politically the most important in the country. Edward Aveling was the first Secularist to be elected, for the Westminster division in 1882;[8] but despite this, plans to run a Secularist next time in every division were never realised. The programme of the Secularists was for compulsory, free and secular education, and all these three points were seen to be interdependent. Compulsory education alone, as proposed by Sandon's Bill in 1876, would mean compulsory Church education in the countryside; and free education would simply mean more public money for Church schools. In J. M. Wheeler's opinion, the only correct course would be for free secular education to be financed by the disestablishment of the Church of England.[9]

Whilst there was no division over this matter of free education, other issues proved to be more controversial. Should school meals be provided free of charge? W. P. Ball and Annie Besant argued with each other about this as early as 1884. Bradlaugh's view was that 'The children of paupers ought to be fed, but the children of those who are not paupers ought surely to be fed by their parents'.[10] Foote agreed; but he and Bradlaugh differed over the next issue, which was whether the education provided in private schools should be secular or not. Bradlaugh thought that *all* education should be secular, so that children could make up their own minds. Foote thought this unrealistic, and wished parents to be free to inculcate in their children whatever views—religious or anti-religious—they pleased.[11] This view was shared by Wheeler,[12] but Arthur Moss, who was a London School Board visitor, took the argument one step further and advocated the use of the Bible even in Board Schools. He based this unorthodox conclusion on the reasons given to him by freethinkers who did not withdraw their children from Bible lessons. Not only was such withdrawal 'a cruel punishment' for the child, who lost his good attendance marks and was often shunned by other children; but it was also depriving the child of a knowledge essential to freethought—'The more one knows of the Bible, the less one believes it' was the principle on which many parents acted, particularly when the teachers contradicted each other. Moss put his finger on the mainspring of nineteenth-century freethought when he added, 'It is the hardest thing in the world to convert a "nothingarian" to Freethought. A much easier task is to convert a sincere believer in Christianity.' and 'If the Freethinker's child reads the Bible in the Board school and gets a wrong view of it, the Freethought parent can put it right; at worst he can present the other side of the case. By this method the Freethinker's child is made to *think* at a very early period of its life, and that is a disposition that is worth cultivating.'[13]

This highly practical viewpoint was somewhat eccentric, although it seems in retrospect to have been shrewdly accurate. The mainstream of Secularist thought, so far as public education went, was that it should be secular. In the 1885 Board elections in London, a member of the Westminster branch was elected for his local division, but overall the Liberal/Nonconformist group lost control by one vote to the clerical party, and the Reverend Joseph Diggle became chairman.[14] During the next three years the Secularists played an ambiguous part as allies of the socialists and other radicals against the 'Diggleite' Church party. They were united in their opposition to religious education. Foote was understandably angry when he discovered what examination questions were being set in Religious Knowledge—'Show from the Old Testament that God is long-suffering' (Standard IV); 'What did our Lord teach about prayer?' (Standard V). Such questions were loaded, to say the least.[15] But the Secularists remained divided over free school meals,

which the Metropolitan Radical Federation accepted on Annie
Besant's motion in 1888, but which the London Secular Federation,
led by Foote, rejected along with the proposal that all schools be
subjected to popular control. Behind the latter, apparently
undemocratic, attitude lay a suspicion that popular control of
voluntary schools would negate the freedom implicit in their
voluntary status.[16] The Secularists were therefore undecided in 1888
whether to support agreed radical candidates or to run their own. In
the event they had no policy, but the London Secular Federation
endorsed Hubert Bland in Finsbury and J. H. Ellis in West
Lambeth; and the *National Reformer* endorsed Annie Besant (who
had the support of the East London Secular Society and the Tower
Hamlets Radical Association) in Tower Hamlets, Stewart Headlam
in Hackney, the Radical, W. F. Revell in Chelsea, the Hon. Lyulph
Stanley (leader of the Liberals) in Marylebone, and Mrs Ashton
Dilke in West Lambeth. In the latter constituency the Secularists
were therefore supporting rival candidates, and Ellis and Mrs Dilke
were also faced with an S.D.F. opponent; while at Finsbury some
non-S.D.F. socialists and freethinkers voted for the Radical,
Conybeare, or split their votes between him and Bland. As a result,
neither Ellis not Bland was elected, though Mrs Dilke and
Conybeare were, along with Annie Besant, who topped the poll at
Tower Hamlets, and Stewart Headlam. In all, the elections were a
triumph for the S.D.F., but a dismal failure for the Secularists.[17]

The 1888 elections overall increased the majority of the Church
party to nine. Nevertheless, Besant and Headlam made considerable
progress on the Board, and Mrs Besant reported their doings weekly
for the *National Reformer* in a series, 'The London School Board.
What we do and what we don't do'.[18] One of the first things they did
was to organise a voluntary school meals service. Over the winter of
1888-89, 36,087 meals were provided; and over the first full season,
1889-90, 236,824 dinners were given, and another 26,645 provided at
a small charge.[19] Mrs Besant Secularist protégé, Mary Reed, who
was a school manager in Poplar, appealed for money and clothing,
and explained vividly in the *National Reformer* what misery in the East
End was really like, and why the meals (which cost $\frac{3}{4}d$ each) were
essential.[20] The Church party was also the party of economy
opposed to the scheme, which reinforced support for it among many
Secularists, but not Bradlaugh. Annie Besant also put to the Board a
scheme for the remission of school fees, which moved education in
London towards being practically free. The *principle* of free education
was vigorously opposed, though, by the clerical party.[21] After a

complaint regarding Eyre & Spottiswoode, Mrs Besant and Mrs Dilke also persuaded the Board to deal in future only with firms paying minimum standard wage rates; and Mrs Besant also successfully persuaded the Board to lift its ban on Arthur Moss's spare-time lecturing activities, which the Diggleite majority had imposed the previous year.[22]

By 1891 Annie Besant had turned to Theosophy, and she did not contest the election in that year. Indeed, no Secularists fought at all, though Robert Forder stood as a Radical in Finsbury with a programme of secular education, trade union rates for all contracts, and the provision of evening schools with practical classes. He just failed to be elected.[23] Charles Watts fought Finsbury as a Secularist in 1894, but did worse than Forder in a much larger poll. His only consolation was that he did much better than the S.D.F. candidate.[24] The Secularists were therefore compelled to watch from outside the fight which went on in the early 1890s to prevent the Church majority from increasing the Christian content of Bible lessons in schools. The majority of the Board had originally settled for the vaguest kind of moral and religious education based on the Bible. This compromise was disliked by Churchmen as much as by Secularists, but survived until one clerical member, the Reverend J. J. Coxhead, visited a school which confirmed the truth of what Arthur Moss had said about the state of Bible teaching in the schools. The issue was taken up on the School Board, and in March 1894 new, tighter regulations were introduced. The 1894 election was fought on this issue, the Church throwing large resources into the campaign—the *Church Times* raising over £2,000 for the election fund. The issue was really decided by the teachers themselves, though, when a memorial was signed by 3,130 of them in protest, and when 1,500 teachers at a mass meeting refused to give religious instruction under the new regulations.[25]

Another threat appeared in 1896, when Balfour introduced a Bill in Parliament to increase aid to voluntary schools, to abolish the Cowper-Temple clause in the 1870 Act on which the religious compromise was based, and to transfer the rural Board schools to the county councils. This brought the I.L.P. to support secular education, and united radicals, Secularists and socialists in protest.[26]

A new issue which emerged in the later 1890s was to split the allied opponents of clerical education along lines comparable to the division between the Secularist and Ethical movements. At a conference held at Holborn Town Hall on 19 and 28 July 1898, attended by representatives of the N.S.S., the Freethought Federation, S.D.F., I.L.P., Humanitarian League, Theosophical Society, and various Liberal, Radical and Ethical societies, chaired by Frederic Harrison, a new Moral Instruction League was proposed. One of the prime movers was F. J. Gould, a London Board School teacher until 1896.[27]

Gould had himself suffered as a teacher. He had taught the required Bible lessons in school until December 1887, when the Reverend J. R. Diggle had sent for him and required him to apply to withdraw from religious instruction. Gould was then transferred to a poor school in Limehouse, and for three years he dutifully allowed his headmaster to teach his Bible lessons for him. In 1891 he re-applied to teach the Bible—a move opposed by both clericalists and Mrs Besant, but supported by Arthur Moss. Gould's position was that true education must be Moral Education—'an education inspired by Humanity's entire story—a story which includes the Bible and all other expressions of the genius of our race'.[28]

This is what the Moral Instruction League, inaugurated in December 1897, proposed, and immediately the withdrawal of the N.S.S. was recommended by Charles Watts. The N.S.S. was eventually persuaded to remain and had four members on the committee, but within a year they had withdrawn. The Bible in any form was too much for Secularists to swallow.[19]

The freethinkers experienced both successes and failure in the 1900 Board elections. In London they resolved to run their own candidates, but in the end the only ones they supported were also in the S.D.F.[30] In Birmingham, where the local Secular Society was in conflict with the School Board over the use of a schoolroom on Sundays, H. Percy Ward secured 8,869 votes, but was not elected; neither was their main adversary, the Catholic Bishop of Coventry.[31] In Leicester, Gould, who was now in charge of the Secular Society there, came second out of fifteen successful candidates, with 15,669 votes—in marked contrast to the two I.L.P. candidates, who were not elected.[32] In Birmingham, as a result of the election, the reaction got worse, and on 6 April the Board reintroduced religious, as opposed to moral, instruction for the first time (except for one short break) since 1873; but in Leicester, Gould persuaded the Board to adopt Moral Education, having demonstrated how feeble 'religious' education was.[33]

Education controversies in the Edwardian period were four-sided: Church, Chapel, Secular, and Moral solutions were offered to the problem. The Education Act of 1902 was seen as favouring the

Church, and produced a great outcry from the Chapel. Some older Liberal Individualists, like G. J. Holyoake, supported the Chapel on the principle that there should be no application of local rates to Church schools. The old man even joined the passive resisters, and had a picture seized in lieu of rates at Brighton. Foote thought he was pandering to his Nonconformist friends. Perhaps he was: the hated John Clifford and Holyoake were good friends, and Clifford was to speak at his funeral in 1906. Holyoake's was the reaction of the pre-1870 generation.[34]

By contrast, most of the other Secularist leaders supported the new Act. Foote said the passive resisters were rejecting the principle of democracy (he could favour the majority on those few occasions when they agreed with him); and he thought the Nonconformists were being illogical and narrowly self-interested in demanding 'unsectarian' education. Cohen agreed, and thought the Nonconformists were now suffering the consequences of their own intolerance of the secular solution in 1870. Gould considered the new county councils would be less subject to clerical influences than the old School Boards, and he looked forward to the day when the argument would be about education, not religion.[35] The quarrel of Church and Chapel seemed to offer an excellent opportunity for the Secularists to press forward their alternative solution of secular eduation. In December 1902 and February 1904 they organised public meetings to advocate secular education, and at the general election of 1906 about fifty M.P.s pledged themselves to support it (compared with nearly two hundred Nonconformist M.Ps), but a secular education amendment to the 1906 Education Bill was lost by 477 to 63. In 1870 a similar amendment had been lost by 421 to 60.[36] At a Trafalgar Square rally called by socialists and trade unionists to oppose the Bill, the *Daily News* reported that Foote 'spoke eulogistically of the anti-clerical movement in France. What they had to do in England was to clear the priests and the parsons out of the schools—clear them all out, even, "Archbishop" Clifford.' This was greeted by cheers and laughter. At the end of 1906 the High Church party in the Lords killed off the Bill; seldom can Secularists have been more pleased by the action of the Church and the upper House.[37]

A direct outcome of this abortive Bill was the Secular Education League, formed in February 1907 at a meeting convened by Harry Snell and chaired by George Greenwood, M.P.; on the committee were three Secularists—Foote, Joseph McCabe and Hypatia Bradlaugh Bonner. The League had influential support, with thirty-four M.P.s on its General Council, including such leaders of the Labour party as MacDonald, Henderson and Snowden. Secular education also had the support of the T.U.C. and, from 1910, the Labour Party conference, but it is hard to say whether the League ever had much effect. Powerful forces elsewhere on the political and religious spectrum blocked all attempts by the Liberal government to modify the 1902 Education Act. Runciman's Education Bill in 1908 (the government's fourth) failed *before* the Secular Education League had time to hold its protest meeting, but no doubt this expression of popular radical opinion helped the Liberals to ignore the Nonconformists in their ranks, and Conservatives to feel justified in defending the Balfour Act of 1902.[38]

The Moral Instruction League appeared to make little progress after 1906. By that year, thirty-four local education authorities had accepted the principle of moral education as opposed to narrow Bible instruction, and the Code of Regulations for Public Elementary Schools (1906) made provision for this. Thereafter, the League lost some of its impetus. It was renamed the Moral Education League in 1909, and F. J. Gould, who had left Leicester the previous year, became its full-time Demonstrator—a post he held till lack of funds compelled his dismissal in 1915. During this time, and after, he travelled the world, preaching his gospel of education and humanity.[39]

*Secularist education*

The Secularist ideal of education was that it should be free, rational, secular and humane; but, apart from occasional members on School Boards and later on local councils, or through those who were active teachers themselves, like Gould, or involved in the educational service, like Moss, the Secularists could become active educationalists only during their leisure hours—on Sundays and in the increasingly popular adult night schools. 'All such educational efforts are useful to the branches, and honorable to the movement as a whole,' acknowledged the *National Reformer* in 1883.[40]

Two attitudes to education existed side by side in the Secular societies. On the one hand was the old tradition of the artisan autodidact, who looked to his Secular society for educational leisure of an informal kind. On the other hand, the Secularists ran formal classes, especially in science, which undoubtedly made an important contribution to the education of young men and women who would otherwise have lacked the opportunity. Taken in conjunction with

South Kensington grants, university extension lectures, and the opening up of university education to the suitably qualified poor, this was a new and significant development for which Edward Aveling must in the first instance be given much of the credit.

Most Secular societies and clubs had educational leisure-time activities to offer—one could learn English grammar and logic at Leicester in 1874; singing at the Bradlaugh house, taught by Alice, in 1878; or even Latin at Battersea in 1883.[41] But all educational activities were becoming more institutionalised after 1870, and the Education Act set higher standards of professionalism. When the Walworth Association of Freethinkers started a night school in 1876, they engaged A. W. Collins of the South London Secular Society, a qualified schoolteacher. This Walworth school offered 'a good, sound, practical elementary education' for two hours each evening, three evenings a week. Such a régime must have been too fierce, for attendance fell off during the summer and, although the school was reopened in the autumn, no more is heard of it.[42]

Inspired by the science classes which were begun at the Hall of Science in 1879, a number of similar ventures appear to have enjoyed more success in the 1880s. In Manchester G. and J. Harrop were running classes in biology, chemistry, physiology and French, with over fifty pupils, in 1881; and the West Hartlepool freethinkers were active in the University Extension Scheme science classes run at the Citizen Club in the same year. Successful science classes were reported at Glasgow in 1883; and freethinkers were active as both teachers and pupils in the Royal Society of Arts, and South Kensington classes run by the Rochdale Pioneers in 1885. Other such examples could be quoted, but none matched the achievement in London. [43]

Education at the Hall of Science had begun in the usual informal way, with a Sunday school in 1869. The success of this led to a proposal to start a Secular Day and Evening School, but this does not seem to have come to anything, and in 1870 the Secularists had no school which could qualify for a grant under the new Education Act.[44] They persisted instead with informal evening classes.[45] The Hall of Science school proper was begun by Edward Aveling in the autumn of 1879. Cynics would say that Aveling did it because he needed the money; this was probably true, but he was nevertheless a fine and inspiring teacher. To begin with, the school offered a Chemistry class, taught by Aveling, assisted by Annie Besant; and an Animal Physiology class, also taught by Aveling, assisted this time by a Mr E. Richardson. The Chemistry course was taken by forty-two people (with six ladies, including Alice and Hypatia Bradlaugh), and the Animal Physiology by thirty-seven (with three ladies, including Annie Besant and Alice Bradlaugh). Eleven Queen's Prizes were awarded at the end of the year by the South Kensington department.[46]

The programme for the second year was much more ambitious. The classes (given with their teacher and regular number of students) were Elementary Botany (Aveling, eighteen students), Advanced Physiology (Aveling, seventeen), Elementary Chemistry (Hypatia Bradlaugh, twenty-three), Elementary Mathematics (Aveling, thirty), Advanced Chemistry (Aveling, twenty-three), Elementary Physiology (Besant, thirty), and a Choral and Dramatic class (Herr Trousselle, twenty-six). In all there were 166 students. Alice Bradlaugh later added a French class. The South Kensington examination results at the end of this session (1880-81) were extremely good. Sixty-two examination entries were made, fifty of which resulted in passes by thirty-four individuals, ten of whom were women. At Advanced Level, five of the fifteen passes were in the First Class (including Annie Besant with Botany and Animal Physiology, and W. P. Ball with Chemistry), and at the Elementary Level twelve of thirty-five passes were in the First Class (including Hypatia Bradlaugh with Mathematics and Alice Bradlaugh with Botany).[47] It was this success which encouraged Aveling to apply to the Science and Art Department for a South Kensington grant, rousing Sir Henry Tyler to attack the schools in the House of Commons.[48]

The year 1881-82 started with 212 pupils, all but forty-four of whom were N.S.S. members, and at the end of the year 110 examination entries produced thirty-two Firsts, fifty-nine Seconds and only nineteen Fails. In January 1882 Aveling also started a class to prepare candidates for London University matriculation.[49]

The pupils were mainly skilled artisans between the ages of twenty and forty; in the year 1880-81, only one pupil was under fifteen.[50] A comparison of the results with the national average in 1883 shows how good the schools were. In only one subject, Advanced Botany, was the number of First Class passes below the national average. (All the candidates got a Second Class pass: the average was 9.3 per cent First; 57.3 per cent Second; 39.4 per cent Fail.) And in only one subject, General Biology, Elementary, was the level of failures above the average (25 per cent compared with 24.1 per cent).[51] The science practicals became so popular that Aveling had to move from his own laboratory at 13 Newman Street to the second floor of Bradlaugh's premises at 63 Fleet Street in June 1884, but only a few weeks later, at the end of July, Bradlaugh drummed Aveling out of the movement.[52] The schools were his creation: he inspired them; and it is a credit to his teaching that his pupils, led by Mrs Besant and the Bradlaugh girls, were able to carry on without any noticeable deterioration in standard. In 1885, of seventy results, twenty-three were Firsts, thirty-six Seconds and only eleven were Fails.[53]

The infectious enthusiasm of the Hall of Science pupils was amazing. In January 1884 three of them—Rosina Bumpus, Ernest Davis and Elizabeth Cracknell—started free classes in Botany, Chemistry and Arithmetic on Sunday afternoons at the Milton Hall, home of the North West London branch of the N.S.S. Each class lasted an hour, the courses running from 3.00 p. m. to 6.00 p. m. for twelve weeks. Over three hundred pupils were enrolled.[54] At the same time, the West Central branch was running science classes on Sundays; and Mrs Mary Sowden was teaching science at the Battersea Sunday school.[55]

Elizabeth Cracknell joined the Hall of Science staff in 1884-85, and Mary Sowden a year later. Another newcomer was John Robertson, who taught Political Economy. Ten people were enrolled on this course, but twenty-five were needed from all over the country for the course to be examined by South Kensington, and in 1885-86 the rest of the United Kingdom could not find fifteen candidates to join the Secularists' ten. After Annie Besant's diversion into socialism, she taught less in the schools, and not at all in 1888-89. By this date the schools were in decline, and when Alice Bradlaugh died of typhoid and meningitis on 2 December 1888 they were closed.[56]

This was not quite the end. The schools' physiological models, microscope, chemicals and library of over a hundred volumes were offered to another branch. Camberwell, Nottingham, Portsmouth, Birmingham and Newcastle applied.[57] The Camberwell branch received them, and in September 1889 the science classes were resumed, with John B. Coppock as teacher. Coppock was a member of the Nottingham branch, contemporary with Harry Snell, and had won a national scholarship to Nottingham University after taking his South Kensington examinations with distinctions. There were not many students, but the standard was high: in 1891-92 he had a prize-winning candidate for both Inorganic Chemistry and Advanced Hygiene. The last recorded year of the schools was 1893-94, by which time Coppock was a Fellow of the Chemical Society and on his way to becoming a college lecturer in science.[58] Mary Sowden also gained a national scholarship in 1891 to enable her to follow her studies further.[59]

The achievement of these science classes at Old Street and elsewhere was a considerable tribute to both their teachers and their pupils. At a time when young men (and women) were beginning to avail themselves of the wider opportunities offered for advanced education, the Secularists made an honourable contribution to this chapter of educational history.

## Sunday schools

The Sunday school movement had dominated working-class life, particularly in the textile districts of Lancashire and Yorkshire, since the late eighteenth century. Initially it had provided that elementary education which was unavailable to children and youths at work in the factories on the other days of the week, but, during the nineteenth century as hours of child-labour were reduced and Factory Acts required children to be educated on weekdays, the Sunday schools had become religious schools for children, young people and, to some extent, adults. Radicals had also run their own Sunday schools in the early nineteenth century, as had the Owenites, and some of these ventures were carried on or revived by the men and women who joined the Secularist movement in the 1850s and later.[60]

Many N.S.S. branches and local Secular societies seem to have run Sunday schools at some time in their history, although success was often intermittent. The Halifax, Rochdale, Ashton, Huddersfield and Sheffield societies all had Sunday schools at the beginning of the 1860s, when Bradlaugh wrote in the *National Reformer*, 'We attach more importance to these experiments in schools, than to any work attempted by the Secular Societies.' When the Newcastle Secular Society called a regional conference in 1867, the main subject of debate was the setting up of a Secular Sunday school, and one was opened in Newcastle in January 1869; the Old Street Hall of Science and the Manchester Secular Institute also opened Sunday schools in that year.[61]

The content of teaching varied greatly. At Battersea, where Mary Sowden began with ten children, a school of between sixty and seventy children was being taught, in 1884, Elementary Physiology, Botany, and Sound, Heat and Light. Annie Besant's *Our Corner* was used as a textbook. The children were also given a few lessons about Buddhism! The problem, apparently, was to find subjects which would both instruct and amuse the children. At Poplar in 1887, 'The idea is to collect poor children, with the children of local Freethinkers to act as leaven, and entertain them with little moral songs with instrumental accompaniment, short descriptions of historical incidents and such deductions therefrom as may affect child-life, elementary science with interesting experiments, etc.'.[62]

Behind this programme, with its scientific veneer, was an appreciation of the need for moral education. Annie Besant provided edifying tales in *Our Corner*, and in 1885 she advertised a 'Young Folks Library' of 'Legends and Tales', which mixed classical legends with the stories of the freethought martyrs, Hypatia and Giordano Bruno; while Hypatia Bradlaugh Bonner produced a collection entitled 'Princess Vera, and other Stories'.[63] The master of the moral tale was F. J. Gould, first at the East London Ethical Society Sunday School, then at the Leicester Secular Society Sunday School, and finally in his capacity as Demonstrator for the Moral Education League. In his opinion such work did not need academic qualifications. He recalled of the Sunday school at Leicester:

In dubious grammar, Sarah Perkins taught the children in the Sunday School good lessons. Her hand was ever ready to serve, to wait, to wash, to sew, to mend, 'to warn, to comfort and command'. Quiet-spoken and deliberate, she had the judgment that comes of affectionate rearing of children in a proletarian home.[64]

Mrs Perkins, as well as the superior Aveling ('Edward, D. Sc.'), deserves a place in the history of Secularist educational endeavours.

The heartland of the Secular Sunday schools, like that of their religious equivalent, lay in the textile communities of South East Lancashire and West Yorkshire. In Lancashire some of the great town Sunday schools had survived independent of the Church—as in Rochdale, with a thousand members (including 170 adults), and in Stockport, with five thousand members.[65] In the industrial village of Failsworth, between Oldham and Manchester, the community Sunday school was Secularist. Across the Pennines in Huddersfield, where nearly all the town's children went to one sort of denominational Sunday school or another,[66] the Secularists too had their denominational Sunday school. These two examples, at Huddersfield and Failsworth, are no more typical of the Sunday schools run by the freethinkers than the Old Street Hall of Science classes are of their night-school work; but like them they show the Secularists at their best and most influential.

The Huddersfield Secular Sunday School was started in 1862, and lasted until 1886. Throughout these years it was in many external characteristics similar to, and served the same social function as, the religious Sunday schools of the town. The inspiration for the school was Owenite, and the founding superintendent, David France, is described as 'an old Socialist'. The Huddersfield Secularists saw their task to be to fulfil the promise of socialism as they had known it in the early 1840s.[67] Each year the school celebrated its anniversary with a special service of hymn singing, addresses and a prize giving.[68] Such was its success that larger premises had to be acquired, and Senior's School Room in East Parade was taken in 1865.[69] Gradually the school absorbed most of the local Secularists' time and effort, and in 1878 they solved the problem of loyalty to the N.S.S. or B.S.U. by announcing that the local society would henceforth concentrate entirely on the school, leaving individual members to form branches of the national bodies to conduct orthodox propaganda.[70] In 1878 there were eighty boys and girls in the Sunday school, and twenty-eight teachers, nearly half of whom had been members of the school. In addition to Sunday meetings, they held a singing class on Wednesdays and an elocution class on Mondays. This was the school as young Ben Turner knew it when his family moved into the town from the outlying district. He recalled in his autobiography how the Sunday lessons, held mornings and afternoons, were devoted to such subjects as reading, writing, arithmetic, geography, history, elocution and singing; but, when a national lecturer came, afternoon lessons were replaced by an address from the visiting speaker. In this way, as an impressionable youth, he heard G. J. Holyoake, Mrs Besant, Bradlaugh, Watts, Aveling and Mrs Law, and learnt from them about the land question, perpetual pensions, republicanism, Home Rule, and such topics. It was this, rather than anti-religion, which he recalled. Turner became secretary of the Sunday school at the age of eighteen (1881), and so learned how to chair a meeting. It was a valuable education for a future trade union leader.[71]

The school was threatened with closure in 1883 when its premises were withdrawn. Temporary accommodation was found for the next three years, but when Huddersfield's landlord, Sir John Ramsden, refused the Secularists permission to build new premises in 1886 (the second such refusal in the society's history), the school finally closed.[72] During its quarter-century of existence it had gained considerable local respect, and it was the means by which a generation of old Owenites was able to transmit its ideals to succeeding generations.[73] The school was also a model for other Secularist groups. When the Old Street Hall of Science Sunday School was opened in 1869, the opening and closing hymns were taken from the Huddersfield Secular Sunday School hymn book; and when the Leicester Secular Society was starting its Sunday school in 1881, Sydney Gimson was asked by the committee to give them a report on the Huddersfield school.[74]

The Failsworth Sunday School was unique in the country. The 'Old School', built in 1785, was the community Sunday school, run on non-sectarian lines until 1837, when the Church party built a 'New School' and the radicals of the village (whose memories went back to the 'Jacobins' of the 1790s) took the Old School building by force. Thereafter it became a stronghold of the Chartists and Owenites, and many of its members were associated with the early co-operative movement. These Owenites and co-operators were naturally followers of G. J. Holyoake, and in time the school became identified with the Secularists, especially after 1870 when the Board schools began to take over the educational role which the school had formerly played.[75]

The minute books of the school for 1874-87 show it still to have been providing a basic education for the people of the village. Mainly children attended on Sunday mornings, when they received a general moral education. Adults came as well as children on Sunday afternoons, when the subjects taught included reading, writing, history, geography, singing and sewing. As at Huddersfield, the school was, to all intents and purposes, fulfilling the social function of a denominational chapel—with hymns (from the old socialist hymn book at first but later from its own compilation of secular hymns), a Sunday school anniversary, and all the social life of the chapel, including participation in the famous local Whit Friday walk.[76]

In 1865, 1880 and 1902 the number of scholars was reported to be about 180, and the general level seems to have been between one and two hundred.[77] A new school building was opened in 1880, the foundation stone being laid by Josiah Gimson of Leicester. This gave the school a large hall which would hold 150 people, two ante-rooms and two class rooms. The site was freehold, and a trust deed safeguarded control of the school. Thus protected, the Failsworth people, like the Leicester Secularists, had none of the problems which eventually closed the Huddersfield Sunday school. Further extensions were opened in 1900, providing a stage and kitchens, and the Failsworth school lasted until 1958.[78]

As at Huddersfield, the school was the society. Though there were N.S.S. members in Failsworth who constituted themselves as a branch, the school was independent and possibly all the stronger for

it. Both as a freethought 'chapel' in the community, and as a part of
a tradition of local radicalism stretching back to the 1780s and
forwards into the twentieth century, the Failsworth school is
symbolic of what Secularism was, or tried to be, in the country at
large.

*Notes*

1  Ladbrooke Black, in *Sunday Times*, 21 January 1912.
2  See G. J. Holyoake to W. E. Forster, 8 March–12 March 1870,
   Holyoake papers, Co-operative Union, nos. 1937-40; also nos. 1943-6;
   J. Collings to G. J. Holyoake, 31 October 1869, 1 February 1870, nos.
   1890, 1933.
3  *N.R.*, 13 March, 28 August, 18 September 1870.
4  *N.R.*, 20, 27 November, 4, 11 December 1870.
5  *N.R.*, 20 November 1870, 1 January 1871.
6  *N.R.*, 23 April 1871, 28 January 1872, 7 January 1877; *Secularist*, 20
   January 1877; *N.R.*, 21 January 1877; *S. C.*, 17 March 1878; *S.R.*, 29
   November 1879.
7  *N.R.*, 19, 26 December 1875.
8  *N.R.*, 5 November, 3 December 1882.
9  *Secularist*, 1 July 1876; *F.*, 1 November 1885; see also *F.*, 24 October
   1886.
10 *N.R.*, 9 November, 21 December 1884, 21 October 1888.
11 *F.*, 25 September, 2 October 1887. Some freethinkers thought the
   Board Schools unenlightened places, relying on corporal punishment,
   not teaching ability—see *N.R.*, 23, 30 November, 14 December 1884.
12 *F.*, 30 September 1889.
13 *F.*, 6 November 1887.
14 D. Rubinstein, 'Annie Besant and Stewart Headlam: the London
   School Board Election of 1888', *East London Papers*, XIII (summer
   1970), pp. 3–24, esp. p. 5.
15 *F.*, 6 February 1887.
16 D. Rubinstein, *loc. cit.*, pp. 3-8; *F.*, 14 October 1888.
17 *F.*, 9 September, 18, 25 November 1888; *N.R.*, 28 October, 4, 11
   November 1888; *F.*, 2 December 1888; D. Rubinstein, *loc. cit.*, pp. 21-3.
18 From *N.R.*, 16 December 1888.
19 *N.R.*, 3, 10 February, 10 November, 15 December 1889, 29 June 1890.
20 *N.R.*, 28 April, 1 December 1889.
21 *N.R.*, 21 April, 15 December 1889.
22 *N.R.*, 26 May 1889; *F.*, 10 June 1888, 31 March 1889.
23 *N.R.*, 15 November, 6 December 1891.
24 *F.*, 14 October, 2 December 1894.
25 S. Maclure, *One Hundred Years of London Education, 1870-1970* (London,
   1970), pp. 42, 64; D. Rubinstein, *School Attendance in London, 1870-1914*
   (Hull, 1969), pp. 29-30.
26 B. Simon, *Studies in the History of Education. Education and the Labour*

*Movement, 1870–1920* (London, 1965), p. 160.

27  *Reformer*, 15 August 1897.

28  F. J. Gould, *Life Story of Humanist*, pp. 63-71; *N.R.*, 15 February, 1, 15 March 1891; *F.*, 10 May, 1, 8 November 1891.

29  *F.*, 17 October 1897, 23 January, 6 February, 31 July, 14 August 1898, 9 July 1899.

30  *F.*, 23 September, 7 October 1900.

31  *F.*, 2 December 1900.

32  *F.*, 9, 16 December 1900.

33  *Democracy*, 20 April 1891; F. J. Gould, *op. cit.*, pp. 94-5.

34  *F.*, 3, 17 April 1904; *A. J.*, 30 April 1904. See also S. E. Koss, '1906: Revival and Revivalism', *loc. cit.*, pp. 75-96.

35  *Pioneer*, November 1903; *F.*, 3, 10 May 1903; *L. G.*, 1 June 1904.

36  *F.*, 28 December 1902, 6 March 1904, 3 June 1906.

37  *F.*, 22 July, 16 December 1906. Foote's views are set out more fully in 'Church, Chapel, and Child. The Secular View', *John Bull*, 27 October 1906. Horatio Bottomley, the editor, was sympathetic to the Secularists at this time.

38  *F.*, 31 March 1907, 27 February 1910, 6, 20 December 1908.

39  *Ethics*, 3 February 1906; G. Spiller, *The Ethical Movement*, pp. 124-56; *F.*, 14 February 1915; *L.G.*, 1 March 1915; F. J. Gould, *op. cit.*, pp. 115-70.

40  *N.R.*, 14 October 1883. Individual Secularists also ran their own schools, e. g. Joseph Symes and his wife in Birmingham, 1881—*N.R.*, 6 February 1881; and Ross, George Chetwynd Griffith-Jones and C. R. Mackay were involved in the Whitminster School, 1884-87, under the patronage of Glegg Bullock. Bradlaugh suspected the group of dishonesty, which stimulated them to reply with the libellous *Life of Charles Bradlaugh* in 1888—*S.R.*, 2, 23 August 1884, 7, 14 March, 4 April, 27 June, 12 September 1885, 18 December 1886, 25 June 1887.

41  F. J. Gould, *History of the Leicester Secular Society*, p. 16; *N.R.*, 20, 27 January 1878, 14 October 1883.

42  *S.C.*, 9, 23 July, 1 October 1876; *N.R.*, 9 July 1876. The secretary of the school was William Heaford.

43  *N.R.*, 6 November 1881; *F.*, 25 September, 16 October 1881, 24 June 1883; *N.R.*, 27 September 1885.

44  *N.R.*, 14 March, 18 April 1869.

45  E. g. *N.R.*, 9 January 1870.

46  *N.R.*, 31 August, 12 October 1879, 16 May, 21 November 1880.

47  *N.R.*, 22 August, 17 October, 21 November 1880; 31 July 1881 (reprinted in E. Royle, *The Infidel Tradition*, pp. 119-21), 28 August 1881.

48  *N.R.*, 28 August, 4 September 1881.

49  *N.R.*, 11 December 1881, 23 July, 22 January 1882.

50  A. J. Mundella's reply to a parliamentary question from Sir Henry Tyler, 30 August 1881, quoted in *N.R.*, 4 September 1881.

51  *N.R.*, 23 September 1883.

52  *N.R.*, 8 June 1884; correspondence between C. Bradlaugh, etc., and E. Aveling, 29 July–29 September 1884, B. L. nos. 1127, 1137, 1139-40,

1143-8, 1152-63.

53  *N.R.*, 26 July 1885.

54  *Daily News*, 4 January 1884; *S.R.*, 12 January 1884; *F.*, 10 February 1884.

55  *F.*, 10 February 1884.

56  *N.R.*, 17 August 1884, 16 August 1885, 28 March 1886, 21 August 1887, 2, 30 September, 7 October 1888; H. B. Bonner and J. M. Robertson, *Charles Bradlaugh*, II, p. 104.

57  *N.R.*, 20 January 1889.

58  *F.*, 27 October 1889; H. Snell, *Men, Movements and Myself*, p. 45; *N.R.*, 2 September 1888, 2 October 1892, 1 October 1893; *F.*, 20 August, 17 September 1893.

59  *F.* 11 January 1891. Elizabeth Cracknell had matriculated at London University in 1884—*N.R.*, 10 August 1884; and Hypatia Bradlaugh the previous year—*N.R.*, 4 February 1883.

60  E. g. E. T. Craig, the veteran Owenite, in *N.R.*, 13 January 1884. For Sunday Schools in general see T. W. Lacqueur, *Religion and Respectability. Sunday Schools and Working Class Culture, 1780-1850* (Yale, 1976).

61  *N.R.*, 7 September 1861, 11, 25 January, 26 April 1862, 6 October 1867, 3, 31 January, 7 February, 18 April, 6 June 1869.

62  *N.R.*, 3 February 1884, 25 January 1885, 29 May 1887.

63  *N.R.*, 15 November 1885.

64  F. J. Gould, *Life Story of a Humanist*, p. 87.

65  W. O. Chadwick, *Victorian Church*, part II, pp. 260-2.

66  *Ibid.*, pp. 257-60.

67  *N.R.*, 21 November, 20 June 1863.

68  E. g. *N.R.*, 9 May 1863, 18 June 1864, 24 November 1867, 22 November 1874; *S.R.*, 3 November 1877; *N.R.*, 29 September 1878.

69  *N.R.*, 19 March, 9 April 1865.

70  *S.C.*, 23 September 1877, 14 July, 1 September 1878; *S.R.*, 31 August 1878; *N.R.*, 1 September 1878.

71  *S.R.*, 9 November 1878; B. Turner, *About Myself* (London, 1930), partly quoted in E. Royle, *Infidel Tradition*, pp. 121-2.

72  *S.R.*, 22 December 1883, 19 January 1884; *F.*, 16 December 1883; *S. R.*, 19 April, 3 May 1884, 17 January 1885; *N.R.*, 18 January 1885, 28 March, 1, 15 August 1886; *F.*, 15 August 1886; *S. R.*, 14 August 1886; *N.R.*, 31 October 1886.

73  Through the Balmforth family there is a direct link from Watts, an Owenite and Chartist hand-loom weaver, to his sons, Owen, leader of the local Secularists and Co-operators, and Ramsden, an Ethical preacher and member of the I.L.P.—*N.R.*, 14 April 1889; *F.*, 7 February 1892. It also seems more than a coincidence that Huddersfield had a thriving socialist Sunday School in the Edwardian years—one of only eight in Yorkshire in 1906, with 400 children on its books—F. Reid, 'Socialist Sunday Schools in Britain, 1892–1939', *International Review of Social History*, XI (1966), pp. 18–47, esp. p. 27.

74  *N.R.*, 31 January, 7 February 1869, Leicester S.S., Minute Book II, 8,

14 November 1881.
75  B. Brierley, *Failsworth, my native village*, (Oldham, 1895), pp. 19-20. 22-5; P. Percival, *Failsworth Folk and Failsworth Memories* (Manchester, 1901), pp. 23-5; *Holy Trinity, Failsworth. Souvenir of Grand Bazaar* (1907), p. 25 ; *St. John's No. 1 Sunday and Day Schools, Failsworth. Souvenir of Grand Bazaar* (1903), p, 29.
76  *Reasoner*, 1 July 1865; *N.R.*, 12 January 1868, 7 February 1869; *S.C.*, 29 August 1875; *N.R.*, 29 May 1887; J. E. M. Smith, 'Failsworth Secular Sunday School', *Freethought News*, September, October 1947.
77  *Reasoner*, 1 July 1865; *S.R.*, 6 November 1880; *F.*, 24 August 1902.
78  *S.R.*, 5 June, 6 November 1880, 27 May 1900; F. H. Amphlett Micklewright, 'The Local History of Victorian Secularism', *Local Historian*, VIII, no. 6 (1969), pp. 221-7, esp. p. 223.

# XVII

# Conclusion

'Infidelity as understood a generation ago scarcely exists to-day.' In this manner a contributor to George Haw's *Christianity and the Working Classes* summed up the fate of freethought in 1906.[1] The golden age of Secularism had lasted scarcely ten years, from the Knowlton trial in 1877 to Bradlaugh's admission to Parliament in 1886. No one, not even G. W. Foote, could pretend that things would ever be quite the same again.

Secularism as a philosophical system lacked originality, but attempted to repeat at a popular level the ideas of a rationalist élite. It is doubtful, though, whether those positive teachings which Holyoake had intended to constitute the essence of Secularism ever made a wide or lasting impact on the men and women who joined the freethought ranks, and in the end the secularisation of society made Secularism redundant. As George Bernard Shaw put it, 'When . . . "God is dead," Atheism dies also.'[2] Secularism was not the complement to religion, advancing as religion retreated, but a supplement to it, dependent upon it for its rise and fall.

Secularism was an appropriate response to Victorian religion, which was still dominant and therefore inviting opposition, but which was beginning to loosen its grip, and therefore open to being opposed. The Evangelical Revival, with its emphasis on biblical religion and the Gospel of Salvation, had permeated the fabric of the nation, but the old confidences were crumbling by the last quarter of the nineteenth century as familiar beliefs were questioned and social customs changed. Gradually traditional functions of the Church in society were being transferred to the State, itself becoming more secular as the century progressed. Despite the enormous success of the institutional Churches in recruiting members, organising missions, and inspiring campaigns, they were less central to the life of the nation in 1900 than they had been a hundred years earlier. As the nineteenth century closed, a new Christianity was struggling to be born, no longer the master in its own house, able to control the prevailing political and social structures and ruling ideas, but servant in the house of another and the avowed creed of a decreasing proportion of the population. Secularism had lived to fight the old, assertive religion. 'Bible-smashing is tedious to people who have smashed their Bibles,' quipped Shaw in 1908.[3] Thereafter it survived only as a remnant to fight the remnants of the old religion where they survived in the Establishment of the Church of England, religious education in schools, the blasphemy laws, and the pronouncements of prelates still eager to play their former roles as politicians or as moral censors.

Historians and sociologists of religion, who have seen the Secularist movement as an aspect of religious history, a denomination among Protestant denominations, have highlighted only one side of their subject; for, although the decline of Secularism from the mid-1880s cannot be separated from the decline of the Churches which began at the same time, the British freethought movement was, paradoxically perhaps, as much concerned with politics as with religion. In this respect, Secularism was sharing in, and responding to, a traditional way of looking at men's affairs which was far from secular. The history of Secularism can only be understood as an integral part of the history of popular radicalism as inspired by Thomas Paine and as espoused by the nascent British working class. The nature of the Secularist movement was determined by the nature and experiences of that class—urban, free from many traditional restraints, anti-clerical and radical, its politics shaped by the course of industrialisation in its early stages. With the onset of a fully industrialised, mature capitalist economy, the structure of that class changed, and new social and political creeds became appropriate.

Contemporaries were all well aware of the changes that were taking place at the end of the nineteenth century. 'There has been a great change since Bradlaugh's day,' wrote Charles Booth's reporter of the area round the former Hall of Science in Old Street. 'Working men now turn more to the political attack from the side of Socialism.'[4] George Haw noted in R. Mudie Smith's report on *The Religious Life of London*, a few years later, how the old working men's Radical Clubs were disappearing because 'working men are ceasing to be Radicals'. They were becoming socialists instead.[5] He might also have noted how those members of the old petty bourgeoisie of small masters and shopkeepers, if they were able to survive the competition of impersonal big businesses, were likely to be retreating mentally into a self-defensive Conservatism and physically into the private world of suburbia—what G. W. Foote called 'a general anti-gregarian movement'.[6]

Each generation seems to have believed itself regrettably less serious than its predecessor, but the cry comes so frequently in the late nineteenth century that the historian must pay heed to it. What in fact was happening was the creation of a new working class, itself better educated than before, but not up to the standards of the old working class. The artisan autodidacts looked down with disgust on the products of the new elementary schools. Writing in the *Newcastle Weekly Chronicle*, G. J. Harney deplored the low level of public taste after twenty-five years 'of so-called National education'. 'What would [Robert Owen] have thought,' he wondered, 'if he had lived until now and witnessed the effects of popular education and the triumphs of a free and cheap press?' J. M. Robertson quoted this in the last issue of the *National Reformer*, as he examined the reasons for its closure. A decade later, G. W. Foote was looking back to the middle of the century, reflecting how 'The Mutual Improvement Society of that day is replaced by the cheap double-turn Music Hall.'[8] This cannot entirely be attributed to the increasing wickedness of the younger generation. Their elders had had no choice. 'Unless you went to the dram-shop or the gospel-shop, it was "Bradlaugh or nothing" on a Sunday evening,' wrote Foote in 1896, recalling the position of Secularism twenty years earlier.[9] With the development of alternative leisure time activities, Secularism and the Church inevitably suffered.

Whilst accusing one section of his followers of 'Music Hall-ism', J. M. Robertson offered the opposite excuse for the lower-middle-class readers of the *National Reformer*

Broadly speaking—apart from the reductions of hours in some industries, reductions which are often accompanied by greater stress of labor within the hours worked—men have to compete harder and harder for a living. For the majority of men of fair education, either leisure grows scanter, or the increasing strain of work makes leisure hours more fatigued than they used to be. Again and again I have been told by educated men of business that after a day's work they are too tired to take in a solid *Reformer* article; that they want something lighter and more paragraphic.[10]

The way was clearly prepared for the *Daily Mail*, *Tit Bits* and the *Daily Mirror*.

Secularism was, therefore, the victim of circumstances beyond its control. Far from being a great force to change the world, it was a part of an old world being swept away, along with the dominance of the institutional Church and the Gladstonian Liberal party. But this does not mean that Secularism contributed nothing to those changes which so manifestly occurred during the course of the nineteenth century. Angered by those people who attributed such changes to their being in the air—'like the germs of the influenza'—Robertson correctly insisted 'that there is no way by which ideas can get in the air save putting them there', and his claim was that the Secularists had helped to put them there. Apart from a brief period in the early 1880s, when Secularism became the centre of a major radical political campaign, its main function was as a pressure group. Though the Church of England was not disestablished, secular education not achieved, and the blasphemy laws not abolished, yet the Secularists did help to focus the attention of their contemporaries on these issues, and they served the cause of reform by constantly reiterating the need for change—'for freedom and sincerity in literature; for every extension and consolidation of democracy; for the rights of women; for the extension and reform of education; for the reform and humanising of the penal system; for radical political reform; for the rights of oppressed peoples; above all for Peace', to quote Robertson's list of the campaigns waged by the *National Reformer* in additional to its central objects of Freethought, Neo-Malthusianism and Republicanism.[11] The function of a dissident minority is to challenge that which is accepted unthinkingly by the majority, and to plant the seeds of change. By exercising their right to protest, the Secularists were helping to maintain in Victorian Britain the kind of liberal society which John Stuart Mill had defended so eloquently in his essay *On Liberty*.

*Notes*

1   Silas K. Hocking, in G. Haw (ed.), *Christianity and the Working Classes* (London, 1906), p. 139.

2   *F.*, 1 November 1908. The paradox of secularisation is explored in W. O. Chadwick, *The Secularization of the European Mind in the Nineteenth Century* (Cambridge, 1975), pp. 1-18.

3   *F.* 1 November 1908.

4   C. Booth, *Life and Labour*, 3rd series, II, p. 128.

5   George Haw, in R. Mudie Smith, *The Religious Life of London* (London, 1904), p. 342.

6   *F.*, 9 August 1903. Characteristics of the lower middle class, though mainly the new 'white-collar' class, are discussed in G. Crossick (ed.), *The Lower Middle Class in Britain* (London, 1977), see esp. H. McLeod on pp. 69-70.

7   *N. R.*, 1 October 1893.

8   *F.*, 9 August 1903. For a general analysis of this theme see G. Stedman
    Jones, 'Working-class culture and working-class politics in London,
    1870-1900; notes on the remaking of a working class', *Journal of Social
    History*, VII, no. 4 (summer 1974), pp. 460-508.
9   *F.* 23 February 1896.
10  *N. R.*, 13 March 1892, 17 September 1893.
11  *N. R.*, 1 October 1893.

# Appendix A

*Freethought Societies in Britain,*
*1866–1915*

The accompanying bar-chart, which depicts the annual totals of freethought societies (including those outside the N.S.S.) in London and in Britain as a whole, is based on the *N.S.S. Almanacks* for 1870-93; the *Secular Almanacks* for 1894-1902; the *Secular Annuals* for 1903-04; and the *British Secular Almanacks* for 1878-79. In each case the *Almanack* entry has been assumed to be providing information about the preceding year. The lists of N.S.S. branches and other societies given in the *Almanacks* have been

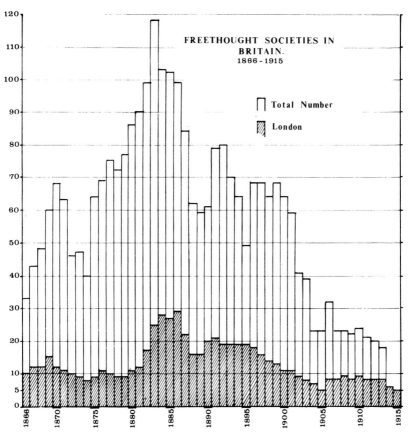

FREETHOUGHT SOCIETIES IN
BRITAIN.
1866 - 1915

☐ Total Number

▨ London

supplemented by reference to the annual reports of N.S.S. conferences, printed in the *National Reformer* (to 1890) and the *Freethinker*. These reports state which branches sent delegates to Conference. A few additional societies have been added from winter and summer samples taken from the 'Reports of Meetings' and 'Guide to the Lecture Room' columns in the freethought press. The diagram illustrates clearly the overall pattern of growth and decline, with expansion in the late 1860s, for a decade following the mid-1870s, and on a more modest scale in the early 1890s; and with contraction in the early 1870s, late 1880s, and in the twentieth century, by which time the collapse of Secularism, especially in the country as a whole, was readily apparent.

# Appendix B
## London Freethought Societies, 1866–1915

The following districts of London each had at least one organised group of freethinkers at some time during the period; where there was more than one society in a district, this is indicated. The years given for activity in each district are those for which positive evidence survives, but it may be that groups did continue in existence throughout short gaps in the evidence. In all there are fifty-eight societies, though the maximum in any one year was twenty-nine (in 1886). These societies are also shown on the accompanying distribution map.

*South London*

Woolwich, 1866–67, 1873–78, 1880–85, 1889–92, 1907–10
Deptford, Greenwich, New Cross (three), 1866–71, 1876–87, 1890–92, 1894–1901
Peckham, 1882–88, 1899
Camberwell, 1885–1915
Walworth, 1876–87
Lambeth (two), 1882–88, 1891–97
Blackfriars, 1866–77, 1880
Bermondsey, 1883–86
Clapham, Battersea (two), 1879–1905

Forest Hill, 1883–87
Crystal Palace, 1882–87
Streatham, 1885–86
Tooting, 1889–1901
Wimbledon, 1893–96
Kingston, 1875, 1880–81, 1883–84

*East, north and west London*

Dalston, 1902, 1906–15
Kingsland, Road, 1883–99
Hackney (two), 1872–4, 1876, 1883–7
Bethnal Green, 1885–1915
Mile End, 1876–80, 1883–1903
West Ham, Plaistow, 1875, 1883–92, 1889–1915

Stratford, 1870–73, 1877–81
Laytonstone, 1884
Walthamstow (two), 1883–84, 1890–94
Edmonton, Tottenham (two), 1890–1901, 1911–14
Wood Green, 1884, 1888–97
Southgate, 1889–91


Finsbury Park (three), 1882–83, 1890–98, 1906–15
Islington (two) 1872–86, 1890, 1892–96, 1910–12
Hoxton (two), 1866–69
Clerkenwell (four), 1866–1905
Euston Road (three), 1866–77, 1884–89
Camden Town, 1882–1901, 1906


Oxford Street, 1883–87
Westminster, 1882–96, 1898
Chelsea, 1867–69
Hyde Park, 1886–91, 1907–09
Paddington, 1866–75, 1883–87
Kilburn, 1881–84
Harlesden, 1902
Hammersmith, 1884–86, 1890, 1892–1904, 1907–08
Brentford, 1870–79

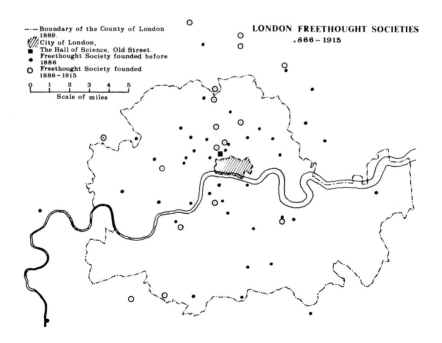

# Appendix C
## Provincial Freethought Societies, 1866–1915

The following towns and villages in the United Kingdom, outside London, had organised groups of freethinkers for at least three years during the period. The years given for activity in each place are those for which positive evidence survives, but it may be that groups did continue in existence throughout short gaps in the evidence. What this list cannot indicate is when these societies were really active and when they were purely nominally organised. The accompanying map of Great Britain shows the locations of 202 groups (there were a further four in Ireland and one in the Channel Isles), of which sixty-five lasted for less than three years (including two Irish). The maximum number of societies in any one year was ninety-three (in 1883).

*Southern England*

Croydon, 1882–85, 1913
Chatham, 1882–1903
Maidstone, 1883, 1885–87
Tunbridge Wells, 1881–83, 1885–87
Brighton, 1879, 1884–94
Portsmouth, 1869–70, 1876–94
Southampton, 1875–89, 1891–92

*West and South West*

Reading, 1883, 1890–94, 1896–1901
Oxford, 1899–1901
Swindon, 1885–89, 1891–93
Cheltenham, 1878–79, 1891–94
Bath, 1893–94, 1896–1903
Bristol, 1866–67, 1869–79, 1881–88, 1892–1900, 1907–09
Plymouth, 1870–73, 1875–1903, 1906

*Wales*

Abergavenny, 1866–68
Newport, 1878–80, 1882
Cardiff, 1869–73, 1877–79, 1881–87, 1889, 1892, 1896–1903, 1905
Pontypridd, 1897–1903, 1905–06

Aberdare, 1871–72, 1880
Merthyr, 1879, 1882, 1905–06
Swansea, 1886–88, 1891–94, 1897–1901

*Eastern England*

Grays, 1884–86
Halstead, 1891–93
Ipswich, 1866–81, 1893–1903
Norwich, 1870–71, 1876, 1882–85
Lincoln, 1876–77, 1879–81, 1910–11
Grimsby, 1867–77, 1880–94, 1896–1901

*The East Midlands*

Luton, 1891–94
Northampton, 1866–1901, 1904, 1910
Wellingborough, 1883–84, 1886–90
Kettering, 1868–71, 1885–88
Leicester, 1866–1915
Burton on Trent, 1869–71, 1877, 1880
Derby, 1869–70, 1874–76, 1880–85, 1887–1903
Ilkeston, 1881–86
Nottingham, 1867–1901, 1904, 1910
Mansfield, 1869–71, 1882–83
Carlton and Netherfield, 1895–1901
Chesterfield, 1896–99

*The West Midlands*

Birmingham, 1866–1913
Stourbridge, 1877, 1879–83, 1885
Kidderminster, 1879–82
Oldbury, 1867–70, 1872–73
Walsall, 1869–75
Wednesbury and West Bromwich, 1868–74, 1881–83, 1885
Coventry, 1869–71, 1886, 1901–07
Hanley, 1870, 1872, 1876, 1882–88, 1891–1903
Longton, 1875–76, 1883
Leek, 1872–73, 1875–76, 1878
Congleton, 1875–79

*The North West*

Crewe and Chester, 1870, 1877–86, 1891–1903
Birkenhead, 1869–71, 1875–77
Liverpool, 1866–1912
Bootle, 1882–86
St Helen's, 1884–87
Warrington, 1869–71, 1875–77

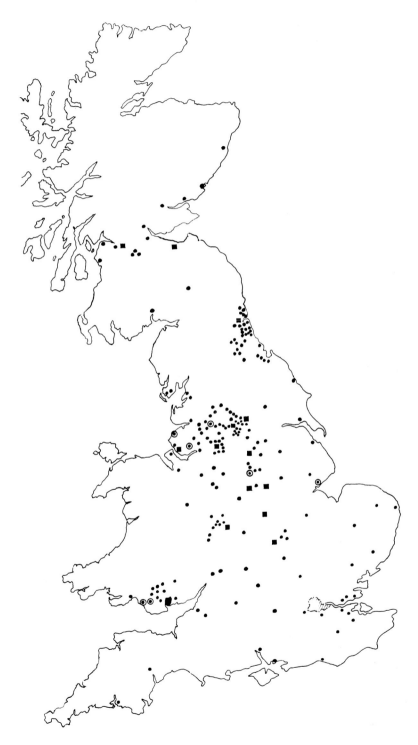

Stockport, 1883–84, 1911–12
Hyde, 1870–71, 1880–81, 1883–84, 1891–92
Stalybridge, 1868–1901
Ashton, 1866–79, 1882–83, 1912–13
Mossley, 1878–85, 1887–88, 1890–93
Manchester, 1866–1913
Failsworth, 1866–1915
Oldham, 1866–91
Rochdale, 1866–73, 1876–1901
Heywood, 1870–71, 1873–74, 1885–87
Bury, 1870, 1879–83, 1908–09
Ramsbottom, 1881–84
Bolton, 1870–71, 1874–87, 1889–1902, 1904, 1908, 1913
Atherton, and Tyldesley, 1881–84
Leigh, 1879–83, 1885–87
**Wigan**, 1878–88, 1891–1903, 1905–06, 1908–09
Preston, 1869–71, 1875–76, 1882–84, 1897–1901, 1913
Blackburn, 1878–92, 1894–1903, 1909, 1912
Darwen, 1870–72, 1875–76, 1878–89
Haslingden, 1875, 1883, 1890–92
Rossendale, 1870–71, 1876–81
Burnley, 1871, 1875–84, 1887, 1908, 1912–13
Nelson, 1888–89, 1899–1901, 1906, 1908–09, 1912
Lancaster, 1869–71
Barrow in Furness, 1877–83, 1885–86
Dalton in Furness, 1877–80, 1883–86


*Yorkshire* (excluding Cleveland)

Todmorden, 1869–71, 1875–79, 1881, 1883–84, 1886–88, 1892, 1895–1900
Sowerby Bridge, 1870–71, 1875
Halifax, 1866–72, 1875–92, 1903
Keighley, 1867–71
Bingley, 1877, 1879–80, 1896–99, 1903
Shipley, 1877–80
Bradford, 1866–1907, 1910, 1912
Stanningley, 1896–1900
Farsley, 1870–78, 1889, 1891–92
Bramley, 1873–75
Leeds, 1866–73, 1875–89, 1891–93, 1896–1900, 1902–04, 1907–08, 1912
Dewsbury, 1866–71, 1878–80, 1884–5, 1889
Batley, 1875–79
Heckmondwike, 1873–84, 1888–93, 1896–1901, 1907
Brighouse, 1882–86
Huddersfield, 1866–1912
Kirkburton, 1869–71

Wakefield, 1876–83
Barnsley, 1875–81, 1883–87, 1893–1903
Sheffield, 1866–89, 1891–3, 1895–1904, 1912–13
Rotherham, 1879–83
Hull, 1867–69, 1874–81, 1883–87, 1889–1903
York, 1877–83

## The North East

Middlesbrough, 1872, 1875–79, 1881–83, 1889–91
Guisborough, 1878–83
Stockton, 1872–88, 1890, 1903, 1905–06
Darlington, 1876–82, 1889–90
Bishop Auckland and West Auckland, 1867, 1871, 1880–89, 1891–1901, 1910, 1915
Spennymoor, 1869, 1871, 1875–86, 1891–92
Tow Law, Crook and Willington, 1870–72, 1877–80, 1890–92
Hartlepools, 1871–73, 1878–92
Seaham Harbour, 1883–86
Easington Lane, Hetton le Hole and Houghton le Spring, 1875–76, 1880–81, 1885–86, 1891–92
Chester le Street, 1888–89, 1891–98
Ox Hill and Stanley, 1889–94, 1896–1901, 1911–12
Washington, 1877–79
Sunderland, 1867–71, 1875, 1887–88, 1890–1901
South Shields, 1869, 1881–83, 1885–1913
Jarrow, 1869–71, 1879–86, 1893–94
Windy Nook, 1869–71
Blaydon, 1880–84
Newcastle, 1866–1913
North Shields, 1875–78
Seghill, 1869, 1876–79, 1881
Cramlington, 1883–95
Blythe, 1893–94, 1896–99
Bedlington, 1867–71, 1873–74, 1876–1901

## Scotland

Hawick, 1878–80
Motherwell, 1896–1901
Hamilton, 1884–86, 1890–92
Paisley, 1866–71, 1877–87, 1889–92, 1896–1903, 1905–06, 1910
Glasgow, 1866–1912, 1915
Greenock, 1866, 1869–72
Edinburgh, 1866–89, 1891–94, 1896–1903, 1906–09

Dundee, 1870–73, 1876–77, 1881–83, 1893–1903
Perth, 1876–80, 1882–87
Aberdeen, 1870–78, 1892–94, 1899–1901

*Ireland*

Dublin, 1875–76, 1882, 1890
Belfast, 1875, 1886–96

*Channel Isles*

Jersey, 1881–87

# Bibliography

*1. Unpublished sources*

*At the Public Record Office (Kew)*

Home Office Papers, H.O. 45
9536/49902, prosecution of the *Freethinker*, 1882–83.
9597/96131, refusal of magistrates to administer affirmation, 1880.
9645/A 36331, meetings in royal parks, 1884.
9682/A 48160, regulation of street processions, 1890.
9989/X 78852, Watford University Press, police seizure of books, 1899.
10332/136764, regulation of street processions, 1882.
10343/140754, Sunday trading, 1906.
10406/A 46794, contemplated prosecutions of *Freethinker* &c. 1887–1908.
10665/216120, prosecutions of T. W. Stewart and J. W. Gott, 1911–14.

*H.O. 144*

114/A25454, imprisonment of Ramsey and Foote, 1883, and contemplated
  prosecutions of the *Freethinker*, 1885–86.

*At the British Library* (Additional Manuscripts)

Ripon papers: 43,618, f. 15 (Bradlaugh).
Dilke papers: 43,909, f. 324 (Bradlaugh); 43,910, f. 326 (Bradlaugh);
  43, 914, f. 271 (Bradlaugh).
Gladstone papers: 44,504, f. 151 (Besant); 44,707, ff. 1–37 (Besant); 44,792,
  f. 106 (Besant); 44,111, ff. 64–155 (Bradlaugh); 44,194, ff. 145, 190–4
  (Bradlaugh); 44,219, ff. 1–76 (Bradlaugh); 44,499, f. 264 (Bradlaugh);
  44,452,ff. 157, 179 (Foote).
Viscount Gladstone papers: 46,016, f. 92 (Bradlaugh); 46,085, ff. 183–259
  (Bradlaugh).
William Morris papers: 45,345, ff. 99, 107, 170, 183, 208 (Besant); ff. 75,
  172 (Bradlaugh).

*At the National Secular Society*

The Bradlaugh papers: over 3,000 letters and papers relating to the life of
  Charles Bradlaugh.

N.S.S., Minute Books, I (17 December 1875–28 March 1878), II (18 April
    1878–29 April 1880), III (May 1886–25 March 1891), IV (29 April
    1891–2 May 1901), V (27 June 1901–24 April 1913), VI (26 June 1913–28
    April 1921).
N.S.S., Organisation Committee, Minute Book (7 August 1889–18 March
    1895).
The Secular Society Ltd, Register of Directors, I (1898–1934).
Minutes of Directors' Meetings, I (14 July 1898–31 December 1907); II (7
    January 1908–13 August 1915).
Bowman, box of papers.

*At Northampton Public Library*

Letters and papers relating to Bradlaugh's election contests in
    Northampton, 1868–86.

*At the Bodleian Library, Oxford*

Miscellaneous Bradlaugh letters, including the originals of some letters of
    which Mrs Bradlaugh Bonner's copies are at the N.S.S.

*At the Leicester County Record Office*

Records of Leicester Secular Society, including: Minute Books, I (13 June
    1852–23 November 1855); II (12 September 1877–27 January 1885); III
    (9 February 1885–2 May 1902); IV (7 May 1902–16 December 1943).
Register of Proposals for Membership (27 April 1885–4 January 1901).
Scrapbooks of printed matter, I (1873–1908); II (1908–09).
Newspaper cuttings, 5 vols. (1899–1909).
Records of the Secular Hall Co. Ltd, including:
Shareholders' Allotment Book (1873–5).
Registers of Members, I (1873–84); II (1885–1904).

*At the Co-operative Union, Manchester*

The letters and papers of G. J. Holyoake (1840–1906).

*At the Bishopsgate Institute*

G. J. Holyoake papers, including diaries (1849–1905).


*2. Unpublished secondary works*

Budd, S., 'Militancy and Expediency—an account of the Secular Movement
    in the Nineteenth Century'. A paper presented to the *Past and Present*
    Conference on Popular Religion, 7 July 1966.
Budd, S., 'The British Humanist Movement: 1860–1966'. A thesis
    submitted to the Board of the Faculty of Social Studies, University of
    Oxford, for the degree of Doctor of Philosophy, Nuffield College, Oxford,
    October 1968.
Campbell, C. B., 'The Conceptualization of Irreligion'. A paper presented
    to the society for the Scientific Study of Religion, New York, October 23,

1970.

Campbell, C. B., 'The Pattern of Irreligious Denominationalism in England'. A paper read to the Society for the Scientific Study of Religion section of the International Congress of Learned Societies in the Field of Religion, Los Angeles, September 1972.

Francis, M., 'British Secularism, 1840–1885'. An essay submitted in partial fulfilment of the requirements for a Master of Arts degree in the Department of History, University of Toronto, May 1969.

Gimson, S. A., 'Random Recollections of the Leicester Secular Society. With Digressions. Part 1 (March 1932); Part 2 (May 1935)—copy in the Leicester S.S. Records, Leicester C.R.O.

Nelson, W. D., 'British Rational Secularism: unbelief from Bradlaugh to the mid-Twentieth Century', University of Washington, Ph.D., 1963.

Stephens, C., 'The Secularist Movement in Birmingham and District, 1850–1885.' A dissertation submitted as part of the requirements for the degree of B.A. with honours in Medieval and Modern History, University of Birmingham, February 1972.

Wilmer, H., 'Dechristianisation in England in the 19th and 20th Centuries'. A paper read at the Ecclesiastical History Colloquium held at Cambridge 24–27 September 1968.


### 3. Periodicals

*The Adult: the journal of sex*, June 1897, September 1897–June 1898, ed. George Bedborough; continued without the sub-title, July 1898–March 1899, ed. Henry Seymour.

*The Agnostic Annual*, 1884–1900; continued as *The Agnostic Annual and Ethical Review*, 1901–07; continued as *The R.P.A. Annual and Ethical Review*, 1908–15, ed. C. A. Watts.

*The Anti-Infidel, for the advocacy of truth and exposure of error*, June 1885–December 1899, ed. W. R. Bradlaugh.

*The British Secular Almanack*, 1878, 1879, ed. Charles Watts and G. W. Foote.

*The Christian Evidence Journal*, 1874, 1875, ed. B. Harris Cowper.

*The Church Reformer: an organ of Christian Socialism and Church Reform*, January 1882–December 1895, ed. the Rev. Stewart D. Headlam.

*The English Leader: a journal for the discussion of stationary questions*, 6 January–14 July 1866, ed. G. J. Holyoake.

*The Ethical World*, 1 January 1898–30 December 1899; continued with the sub-title *devoted to the advancement of democratic morality*, 6 January–17 February 1900; continued with the sub-title *an organ of democracy in religion, education, art, industry and politics*, 24 February–29 December 1900; continued as *Democracy in religion, education, art, industry and politics. An organ of Ethical progress*, 5 January–26 October 1901; continued as *Ethics, an organ of the Ethical movement*, 2 November 1901–17 March 1906; continued as *The Ethical Review, an organ of the Ethical movement*, 24 March–27 October 1906; continued as *The Ethical World, an organ of the Ethical movement*, 15 January 1907–1 June 1916, ed. Stanton Coit.

*The Free Review*, October 1893–September 1895, ed. J. M. Robertson;

October 1895–March 1897, ed. G. Astor Singer; continued as *The University Magazine, and Free Review*, April 1897–December 1900, ed. 'Democritus'.

*The Freethinker*, May 1881–current (consulted in detail to 26 December 1915), ed. G. W. Foote (to 7 November 1915), then C. Cohen.

*Freethought News, a pocket newspaper for the Secular, Rationalist and kindred movements*, February 1947–December 1950, ed. F. J. Corina.

*Half-Hours with Freethinkers*, 1 September 1864–9 February 1865, ed. John Watts and 'Iconoclast'.

*The International Herald*, 2 March–4 May 1872; then with the subtitle *the official organ of the British section of the I.W.M.A.*, 11 May–30 November 1872; then with the sub-title *Liberty in Right. Fraternity in Interest. Equality in Law. We should yield only to the laws of God and the Voice of the People*, 7 December–28 December 1872; then, without the last sentence of the sub-title, 4 January–18 October 1873.

*The Jersusalem Star, being a reprint of a journal published before and after the Flood*, June 1895–16 September 1896, ed. Le Vitty Cuss [i.e. W. J. Ramsey].

*The Labour Annual*, 1899, 1900; continued as *The Reformers' Year Book*, 1901–07.

*The National Reformer*, 14 April 1860–31 August 1861, ed. Joseph Barker and 'Iconoclast'; continued with the sub-title *secular advocate and freethought journal*, 7 September 1861–12 March 1864, ed. 'Iconoclast; 19 March 1864–22 April 1866, ed. John Watts; 29 April 1866–8 November 1868, ed. 'Iconoclast'; 15 November 1868–15 July 1877, ed. Charles Bradlaugh; then with the sub-title *Radical advocate and freethought journal*, 22 July 1877–8 May 1881, ed. C. Bradlaugh; then 15 May 1881–16 October 1887, ed. C. Bradlaugh and Annie Besant; then 23 October 1887–1 February 1891, ed. C. Bradlaugh; then 8 February 1891–1 October 1893, ed. J. M. Robertson.

*National Secular Society's Almanack*, 1870–93; continued as *The Secular Almanack*, 1894–1902; continued as *The Secular Annual*, 1903–04.

*The Northampton Radical*, 30 September–11 November 1874, ed. W. M. Greig.

*Our Corner*, January–June 1883; then with the sub-title *a monthly magazine of fiction, poetry, politics, science, art, literature*, July 1883–June 1887; then with the sub-title *a monthly magazine*, July–December 1887; then with no sub-title, January–December 1888, ed. Annie Besant.

*The Pioneer*, January 1903–May 1904, ed. 'Ignotus' [i.e. G. W. Foote]

*The Present Day, a journal discussing agitated questions without agitation*, June 1883–May 1886, ed. G. J. Holyoake.

*Progress, a monthly magazine of advanced thought*, January–March 1883, ed. G. W. Foote; April 1883–March 1884, ed. E. B. Aveling; April–November 1884, ed. G. W. Foote and E. B. Aveling; December 1884–December 1885, ed. G. W. Foote; then with shorter sub-title, *a monthly magazine*, January 1886–December 1887, ed. G. W. Foote.

*The Radical, a casual publication issued for gratuitous circulation*, February–August 1897, ed. George Standring.

*The Radical Leader*, 4 August–17 November 1888, ed. G. W. Foote.

*Reason, a weekly journal*, 10 March–3 April 1898, ed. George Standring.

*The Reasoner*, January–December 1865, November–December 1868, April–May 1870, January 1871–July 1872, ed. G. J. Holyoake.

*The Reformer*, March 1897–January 1899, ed. Hypatia Bradlaugh Bonner.

*The Republican, a monthly advocate and record of Republican and Democratic Principles and Movements*, 1 September 1870–1 February 1871; then the sub-title without '*monthly*', 1 March 1871–1 February 1872.

*The Republican Chronicle, a monthly journal, advocating Democratic Principles, and recording Republican work and progress*, April 1875–December 1878, ed. George Standring; continued as *The Republican*, January 1879–August 1886, ed. G. Standring; continued as *The Radical*, September 1886–September 1889, ed. G. Standring.

*The Secular Chronicle, a monthly journal established to promote free enquiry into social, political and theological questions, and as a record of freethought progress*, August 1872–October 1874, ed. G. H. Reddalls; then *a weekly journal . . .*, 11 October 1874–17 October 1875, ed. G. H. Reddalls; 24 October–26 December 1875, ed. G. H. Reddalls (senior); then 2 January 1876–24 June 1877, ed. Harriet Law; then with the sub-title, *and record of freethought progress, a weekly journal*, 1 July 1877–24 November 1878, ed. Harriet Law; then 1 December 1878–1 March 1879, ed. George Standring.

*The Secular Review, a journal of daily life*, 6 August 1876–11 February 1877, ed. G. J. Holyoake; 18 February–3 June 1877, ed. Charles Wat s.

*The Secular Review and Secularist*, 9 June 1877–23 February 1878, ed. C. Watts and G. W. Foote; 2–16 March, 1878 ed. C. Watts; then with title *The Secular Review, a journal of daily life*, 23 March 1878–31 December 1881, ed. C. Watts; 7 January 1882–27 December 1884, ed. Charles Watts and 'Saladin'; then with new sub-title, *a journal of agnosticism*, 3 January 1885–29 December 1888, ed. 'Saladin'; continued as *The Agnostic Journal and Secular Review*, 5 January–27 July 1889, ed. 'Saladin'; then as *The Agnostic Journal and Eclectic Review* 3 August 1889–8 December 1906, ed. 'Saladin'; then 15 December 1906–15 June 1907.

*Secular Work, a monthly journal devoted to freethought organisation and social reform*, May 1896–May 1897.

*The Secularist, a Liberal Weekly Review*, 1 January–26 February 1876, ed. G. J. Holyoake and G. W. Foote; then 4 March 1876–2 June 1877, ed. G. W. Foote.

*The Secularist, with which is incorporated The Truth Seeker*, March–May 1902, ed. H. Percy Ward.

*The Truth Seeker*, April 1894–[December 1899], ed. John Grange; January 1900–September 1901, ed. J. W. Gott; October 1901–February 1902, ed. H. Percy Ward; July 1902–March 1907, ed. J. W. Gott; [July–September 1913], ed. J. W. Gott.

*Watts's Literary Guide, being a record of liberal and advanced publications*, November 1885–September 1894, ed. C. A. Watts; continued as *The Literary Guide, a monthly record and review of liberal and advanced publications*, October 1894–June 1896, ed. C. A. Watts; then with the sub-title *a Rationalist Review*, July 1896–December 1915, ed. C. A. Watts.

## 4. Reports of debates

*Eight Hours Movement. Verbatim report of a debate between Mr. H. M. Hyndman
and Mr. C. Bradlaugh. (Revised by both disputants). At St. James's Hall,
Piccadilly, on Wednesday July 23rd, 1890*, London 1890.

*Is Socialism Sound? Verbatim report of a four nights' debate between Annie Besant and
G. W. Foote, at the Hall of Science, Old Street, London E.C., On February 2nd,
9th, 16th, and 23rd, 1887. Revised by both disputants.* London, 1887.

*Secularism, Scepticism, and Atheism. Vebatim report of the proceedings of a two nights'
public debate between Messrs. G. J. Holyoake and C. Bradlaugh. Held at the New
Hall of Science, 142, Old Street, City Road, London, on the evenings of March 10
and 11, 1870.* London, 1870.

*Will Socialism benefit the English People? Verbatim report of a debate between H. M.
Hyndman and Charles Bradlaugh. At St. James's Hall on Thursday, April 17th,
1884.* London, 1884.

## 5. Published sources

Acorn, G. *One of the Multitude.* London, 1911.

Adams, W. E., *Memoirs of a Social Atom.* London, 1903; reprinted, ed. J.
Saville, New York, 1968.

Aldred, G. A., *No Traitor's Gait! The autobiography of Guy A. Aldred.* Glasgow,
1955.

Allen, G. 'The New Hedonism', *Fortnightly Review*, vol. 55, no. cccxxvii, 1
March 1894, pp. 377–92.

Almy, J. T., *Almighty God or Bradlaugh! Being a series of letters addressed to
Englishmen of all shades of political and religious belief—reprinted from the
'Western Guardian'*, August–September 1885

Aveling, E. B., *Darwinism and Small Families*, [London], 1882.

—*The Creed of an Atheist.* London, n.d.

—*Irreligion of Science.* London, n.d.

—*Science and Religion.* [London], n.d.

—*Science and Secularism.* London, 1880.

Ball, W. P., *Mrs. Besant's Socialism. An Examination and an Exposure.* London,
1886.

Barber, T., *Ought Charles Bradlaugh to be an M.P.? An expostulation addressed to
the electors of the Borough of Northampton.* [1877?].

Barclay, T., *Memoirs and Medleys. The autobiography of a bottle-washer.*
Leicester, 1934.

Bax, E. Belfort, *Reminiscences and Reflexions of a mid and late Victorian.* London,
1918.

Benny, J., *Benny on Bradlaugh and Hyndman. A review and criticism of the recent
debate on 'Socialism' between Messrs. Bradlaugh and Hyndman at St. James's Hall
on April 17th 1884.* London, 1884.

Besant, Annie, *An Autobiography.* London, 1893.

—*The Freethinker's Text Book. Part II—Christianity: I. Its evidence unreliable; II.
Its origin pagan; III. Its morality fallible; IV. Its history.* London, 1876.

—*Why I do not believe in God.* London, 1887.

—(ed.), *The Secular Song and Hymn Book, issued by the authority of the National Secular Society.* 2nd ed., London, n.d.

———*A selection of the Social and Political Pamphlets of Annie Besant, with a preface and bibliographical notes by John Saville.* New York, 1970.

*The Biograph and Review,* n.s. vol. I, January 1882, pp. 46–54 —'W. S. Ross'.

*Blasts from Bradlaugh's Own Trumpet. Ballads, Extracts, Cartoons, versified, selected and sketched by 'Ion'.* London, [1882?].

Blatchford, R., *God and my Neighbour.* London, 1903.

—*My Eighty Years.* London, 1931.

—*The New Religion.* Clarion Pamphlets no. 20, London, [1897–98?].

Bonner, A. and C. B., *Hypatia Bradlaugh Bonner. The story of her life.* London, 1942.

Bonner, Hypatia Bradlaugh, *Penalties upon Opinion; or some records of the laws of heresy and blasphemy.* London, 1934.

—'*The War Path of Opinion'. A Reply.* London, 1902.

Bonner, Hypatia Bradlaugh, and Robertson, J. M., *Charles Bradlaugh, a record of his life and work,* 2 vols. London, 1894, 2nd ed., 1895.

Booth, C. (ed.), *Life and Labour of the People in London. First series: Poverty,* 4 Vols. London, 1889–91, reprinted 1902; *Third series: Religious Influences,* 7 vols., London, 1902–03.

Bottomley, H., *Bottomley's Book.* London, [1910].

Bradlaugh Alice, *Mind Considered as a Bodily Function.* London, 1884.

Bradlaugh, C., *The Bible: What it is.* London, 1861.

—*The Freethinker's Text Book. Part 1—Man: whence and how? or, revealed and real science in conflict;—Religion: what and why? or, God = X.* London, 1876.

—*Is there a God?* London, [1861].

—*Jesus, Shelley and Malthus; or pious poverty and heterodox happiness,* by Iconoclast. London, 1861.

—*The Laws relating to Blasphemy and Heresy.* London, 1878.

—*A Plea for Atheism.* London, 1864; 20th thousand, 1880.

—*A Verbatim Report of Mr. Bradlaugh's speech at the Bar of the House of Commons, Friday, May 4th 1883.* Northampton, 1883.

———*Charles Bradlaugh; Champion of Liberty: collected writings and speeches, with comments,* ed. J. P. Gilmour. London, 1933.

———*Humanity's Gain from Unbelief, and other selections from the works of Charles Bradlaugh, with a prefactory note by his daughter, Hypatia Bradlaugh Bonner.* London [1929].

———*A Selection of the Political Pamphlets of Charles Bradlaugh, with a preface and bibliographical notes by John Saville.* New York, 1970.

*Bradlaugh and To-day. Speeches delivered at the centenary celebration at Friends House, Euston Road, London, on September 23, 1933, and the commemoration dinner at the Trocadero Restaurant, Piccadilly Circus, London, on September 26, 1933.* London, 1933.

Bray, R. A., *Labour and the Churches.* London, 1912.

Brierley, B., *Failsworth, my native village.* Oldham, 1895.

*Church Congress. The official report of the Church Congress held at Leicester on September 28th, 29th, & 30th, & October 1st 1880,* edited by David J. Vaughan. London, 1881.

*Church Congress. The official report of the Church Congress held at Newcastle-on-Tyne on October 4th, 5th, 6th, and 7th, 1881,* edited by William Proctor Swaby. London, 1882.

Clifford, J. *George Jacob Holyoake. Full and revised report of a sermon delivered by Dr. John Clifford, M.A., on Sunday evening, February 4, 1906.* London, 1906.

Clodd, E. *Memories.* London, 1916.

Cohen, C. *Almost an Autobiography. The Confessions of a Freethinker.* London, 1940.

—*Bradlaugh and Ingersoll. A centenary appreciation of two great reformers.* London, 1933.

—*Materialism Restated.* London, 1927; 3rd ed., 1943.

—*Theism or Atheism.* London, 1921.

Collet, C. D. *History of the Taxes on Knowledge, their origin and repeal,* 2 vols. London, 1899.

Conway, M. D., *Autobiography. Memories and experiences of Moncure Daniel Conway,* 2 vols. London, 1904.

—*Centenary History of the South Place Ethical Society, based on four discourses given in the Chapel in May and June, 1893.* London, 1894.

Dale, R. W., *Speech of Mr. R. W. Dale on the Bradlaugh Question, February 17th, 1882.* Birmingham, [1882].

d'Alviella, Count Goblet, *The Contemporary Evolution of Religious Thought in England, America and India,* translated by J. Moden. London, 1885.

—'Une Visite aux Eglises Rationalistes de Londres', *Revue des Deux Mondes,* 3rd series, vol. XI, September 1875, pp. 194–218.

Davies, C. M., *Heterodox London: or, phases of freethought in the metropolis,* 2 vols. London, 1874; reprinted New York, 1969.

—*Mystic London: or, phases of occult life in the metropolis.* London, 1875.

Dawson, O. *The Bar Sinister and Licit Love. The first biennial proceedings of the Legitimation League.* London, 1895.

—*Personal Rights and Sexual Wrongs.* London, 1897.

Drysdale, C. V., 'Our New Campaign', *Malthusian,* vol. XXXVII, no. 2, 15 February 1913, pp. 10–11; 'Our South London Campaign', *ibid.,* no. 6, 15 June 1913, p. 42; 'Neo-Malthusianism in South London', *ibid.,* vol. XXXVIII, no. 6, 15 June 1914, pp. 42-3; 'A Retrospect', *ibid,* vol. XLV, no. 5, 15 May 1921, pp. 33–5.

Drysdale, G., *The Elements of Social Science; or Physical, Sexual and Natural Religion. An exposition of the true cause and only cure of the three primary social evils: poverty, prostitution, and celibacy.* 1854, 27th edition, enlarged, London, 1889.

Evans, H., 'Religious Statistics of England and Wales', *Contemporary Review,* vol. LXXI, 1897, pp. 276–9.

Fagan, D. and Burgess, E. *Men of the Tideway.* London, 1966.

Farrar, F. W., *The Bible. Its meaning and supremacy.* London, 1897; 2nd ed., 1901.

Foote, G. W., *Defence of Free Speech, being a three hours' address to the jury in the court of Queen's Bench before Lord Coleridge, on April 24, 1883.* New edition, London, 1932.

—*Flowers of Freethought,* 2 vols. London, 1893–94.

—*Mr. Bradlaugh's Trial and the Freethought Party.* [1877].

—*Reminiscences of Charles Bradlaugh.* London, 1891.

—*Secularism and its Misrepresentatives.* n.d.

—*Secularism Restated; with a review of the several expositions of Charles Bradlaugh and George Jacob Holyoake..* London, 1874

Foote, G. W., and Ball, W. P., *The Bible Handbook for Freethinkers and Inquiring Christians.* London, 1888.

Foxley, J., *Secularism, Scepticism, Ritualism, Liberationalism. Hulsean Lectures at Cambridge, 1881.* London and Cambridge, 1882.

Gardener, Helen H., *Men, Women and Gods, and other lectures, with an introduction by Col. R. G. Ingersoll.* New York and Chicago, 1885.

Gilmour, J. P., *An Apology for his Resignation of the Office of a Vice-President of the National Secular Society. Addressed in the first instance to the Members of the Executive of that Society.* London, December 1896; 2nd ed., revised, February 1897.

Goss, C. W. F., *A Descriptive Bibliography of the Writings of George Jacob Holyoake. With a brief sketch of his life.* London, 1908.

[Gott, J. W.], *Rib Ticklers, or Questions for Parsons.* Bradford, n.d.

Gould, F. J., *The History of the Leicester Secular Society.* Leicester, 1900.

—*The Life Story of a Humanist.* London, 1923.

—*The Pioneers of Johnson's Court: a history of the Rationalist Press Association from 1899 onwards.* London, 1929.

*Guild of St. Matthew. Report of Council for the Year ending August 31st, 1883, presented at the Annual Meeting of Members, September 25th, 1883.* London, [1883]—subsequent annual reports appear in the *Church Reformer* for October each year, 1884–95.

Hardie, J. Keir, *From Serfdom to Socialism.* London, 1907.

Harrison, F., *Autobiographic Memoirs.* 2 vols. London, 1911.

Haw, G. (ed.), *Christianity and the Working Classes.* London, 1906.

—(ed.), *The Religious Doubts of Democracy.* London, 1904.

Headingley, A. S., *The Biography of Charles Bradlaugh.* London, 1880.

Headlam, S. D., *Charles Bradlaugh: an appreciation. Notes of an address given to the Bradlaugh Fellowship by the Rev. Stewart Headlam, Warden of the Guild of St. Matthew.* London, 1907.

Headlam, S. D., *et al.*, *Socialism and Religion.* Fabian Socialist Series, no. 1. London, 1908.

*Holy Trinity, Failsworth. Souvenir of Grand Bazaar held in the Co-operative Hall, Failsworth, in aid of Holy Trinity New Church Building Fund, Thursday, Friday and Saturday, Nov. 28th, 29th, and 30th, 1907.*

Holyoake, A., *Sick Room Thoughts, dictated shortly before his death.* [1874].

—*Would a Republican Form of Government be suitable to England?* London, 1873.

Holyoake A., and Watts, C., *The Secularist's Manual of Songs and Ceremonies.* London, [1871].

Holyoake, G. J., *Among the Americans.* London, 1881.

—*Bygones Worth Remembering,* 2 vols. London, 1905.

—*The Common People: a discourse delivered at the Church of Progress, St. George's Hall, Langham Place.* London, 1870.

—*The History of Co-operation*, 2 vols. London, 1906.

—*History of the Travelling Tax*. London, 1901.

—*In Memoriam. Austin Holyoake, died April the 10th, 1874*. [1874].

—*The Limits of Atheism. or, Why should sceptics be outlaws?* London, 1874.

—*A New Defence of the Ballot, in consequence of Mr. Mill's objections to it*. London, 1868.

—*The Origin and Nature of Secularism, showing that where Freethought commonly ends Secularism begins*. London, 1896.

—*A Plea for Affirmation in Parliament*. London, 1882.

—*Secular Prospects in Death. The Late Councillor Josiah Gimson*. London, [1883].

—*Secular Responsibility*. London, 1873.

—*Sixty Years of an Agitator's Life*, 2 vols. London, 1892.

—*To the members of Leicester Liberal Association*. Leicester, 1884.

—*The Warpath of Opinion. Strange things seen theron*. London, 1896.

Hunt, J., *Religious Thought in England in the Nineteenth Century*. London, 1896, reprinted 1971.

Hunter, W. A., *The Past and present of the Heresy Laws. A lecture delivered before the Sunday Lecture Society on Sunday afternoon, 1st. December, 1878*. [London, 1878].

Huxley, T. H., 'The Interpreters of Genesis and the Interpreters of Nature', *Nineteenth Century*, vol. XVIII, nos. cv, cvi, November, December 1885, pp. 685-706, 849-60.

Hyndman, H. M., *General Booth's Book Refuted*. London, 1890.

—*Further Reminiscences*. London, 1912.

—*The Record of an Adventurous Life*. London, 1911.

Ingersoll, R. G., *Rome or Reason... A reply to Cardinal Manning*. London, n.d.

Jackson, T. A., *God and Gott*. Bradford, n.d.

Jasper, A. S., *A Hoxton Childhood*. London, 1969.

*Journal of Sacred Literature and Biblical Record*, vol. XII, new series, January 1865, pp. 320–43 —'Popular Infidelity in the Metropolis: an unwritten chapter in contemporary history'.

Kent, W., *John Burns. Labour's Lost Leader.*, London, 1950.

—*London for Heretics*. London, 1932.

—*The Testament of a Victorian Youth. An Autobiography*. London, 1938.

Knowlton, C., *The Fruits of Philosophy, or the private companion of adult people*. 1832, 3rd ed., London, 1841.

Legge, M., 'Two noble women, nobly planned', *The Modern Review*, April 1893.

Linton, W. J., *Ireland for the Irish. Rhymes and Reasons against Landlordism, with a preface on Fenianism and Republicanism*. New York, 1867.

—*James Watson. A memoir of the days of the fight for a free press in England and of the agitation for the People's Charter*. Manchester, 1880.

—*Memories*. London, 1895.

Lucy, H. W., *A Diary of Two Parliaments. The Gladstone Parliament, 1880–1885*. London, 1886.

Ludlow, J. M., and Jones, L., *Progress of the Working Class, 1832–67*. London, 1867.

McCabe, J., *Eighty Years a Rebel. Autobiography*. Girard, Kansas, 1947.

—'The Freethought and Ethical Movements in England', *The International*, vol. I, no. 4, March 1908, pp. 319–24.

—*Life and Letters of George Jacob Holyoake*, 2 vols. London, 1908.

McCann, J., *Anti Secularist Lectures. A course of six lectures by the Rev. Jas. McCann, M.A., F.R.S.L., F.G.S., with an appendix containing Secularist objections to the Bible, notes, &c.* Huddersfield and London, 1867.

MacDonald, J. R., *Socialism*, London, 1907.

Macdonnell, J., 'Blasphemy and the Common Law', *Fortnightly Review*, new series, vol. 33, January–June 1883, pp. 776–89.

Mackay, C. R., *Life of Charles Bradlaugh, M.P.* London, 1888.

Mann, T. *Memoirs*. 1923; new edition, London, 1967.

—*A Socialist's View of Religion and the Churches*. Clarion Pamphlet no. 10. London, 1896.

Marx, K., and Engels, F., *Werke*, vols. 31, 32, 36. Berlin, 1965–67. [correspondence, October 1864–July 1870; January 1881–March 1883].

Mearns, A., *The Statistics of Attendance at Public Worship, as published in England, Wales, and Scotland, by the local press, between October 1881, and February, 1882.* London, 1882.

Morris, W., *Art and Socialism: a lecture delivered Jan. 23rd, 1884, before the Secular Society of Leicester*. 1884.

Mudie Smith, R. (ed.) *The Religious Life of London*. London, 1904.

*National Secular Society. Laws against religious liberty, a statement and an appeal.* London, 1892.

Okey, T., *A Basketful of Memories. An autobiographical sketch*. London, 1930.

Pack, E., *A 'Blasphemer' on 'Blasphemy'. The latest Leeds police fiasco*. Bradford, [1903].

—*Pack and the Police. Astounding Admissions, Suppressed Details*. [1903].

—*The Parsons' Doom*. Bradford, n.d.

—*The Trial and Imprisonment of J. W. Gott for Blasphemy*. Bradford, n.d.

Palmer, J. H., *Individual, Family and National Poverty. Reasons why in every family the number should be regulated; the methods that have been proposed, extensively adopted, and found to answer for doing it; together with a few valuable hints for the young*. London, 1875.

Percival, P., *Failsworth Folk and Failsworth Memories*. Manchester, 1901.

Putnam, S. P., *Four Hundred Years of Freethought*. New York, 1894.

*The Queen v. Charles Bradlaugh and Annie Besant*. London, [1877].

Quin, M., *Memoirs of a Positivist*. London, 1924.

*Religious Systems of the World. A Contribution to the study of Comparative Religion. A collection of addresses delivered at South Place Institute.* London, 1905.

*Report of the Union of Ethical Societies*, 1898–99.

Robertson, J. M., *A History of Freethought in the Nineteenth Century*. London, 1929.

—*A Short History of Freethought*. London, 1899.

Ross, W. S., *Sketch of the Life and Character of Charles Watts, by 'Saladin'*. London, n.d.

Ross, W. S. [Saladin], and Taylor, J., *Why I am an Agnostic*. London, n.d.

Rossiter, W., 'Artisan Atheism', *Nineteenth Century*, vols. XXI, no. cxx, February 1887, pp. 262–72, and XXII, no. cxxv, July 1887, pp. 111–26.

St Clair, S., *Sketch of the Life and Labours of John De Morgan, orator, elocutionist, and tribune of the people*. Leeds, 1880.

*St. John's No. 1 Sunday and Day Schools, Failsworth. Souvenir of Grand Bazaar, held in the above schools in aid of New Schools Building Fund. February 25, 26, 27, & 28, 1903.*

Salt, H. S., *Seventy Years among Savages*. London, 1921.

*The Saturday Review of Politics, Literature, Science and Art*, vol. 22, no. 574, 27 October 1866, pp. 509–10—'The artisan and his newspapers'.

*Shall Atheism force on us an Alteration of our Laws? An enquiry respectfully addressed to the constituencies and people of the United Kingdom, by B. W. N.* London, February 26th, 1883.

Shaw, G. B., *Shaw. An Autobiography, selected from his writings by Stanley Weintraub. Vol. 1 (1856–1898)*. London, 1970.

Snell, H., *Men, Movements and Myself*. London, 1936.

Snowden, P., *An Autobiography*, 2 vols. London, 1934.

Spencer, H., *An Autobiography*, 2 vols. London, 1904.

Standring, G., 'Malthusian Memories'. *The Malthusian*, vol. XXXIII, no. 8, 15 August 1909, pp. 57–8; 'Reminiscent Notes on the Neo–Malthusian Movement', *ibid.*, vol. XXXVIII, no. 3, 15 March 1914, pp. 19–20; 'Memories and Musings of an old Malthusian', *ibid.*, vol. XLIII, no. 6, 15 June 1919, pp. 43–4; no. 9, 15 September 1919, p. 69.

Stanton, E. Cady, *Eighty Years and More. Reminscences, 1815–1897*. 1898, reprinted, New York, 1971.

Stephen, J. F., *Digest of Criminal Law*. London, 1877; further editions, 1883, 1926, 1950.

—*History of Criminal Law*, 3 vols. London, 1883.

—'The Law on Blasphemy and Blasphemous Libel', *Fortnightly Review*, vol. 35, no. ccvii, March 1884, pp. 289–318.

Stopes, M. C., *Contraception (birth control). Its theory, history and practice. A manual for the medical and legal professions*. 1923, revised and enlarged 4th ed. London, 1934.

—*Early Days of Birth Control*. 3rd ed. London, 1923.

Streatfield, G. S., 'The Challenge of Secularism', *London Quarterly Review*, vol. CVI (4th series, vol. IX), January 1909, pp. 21–38.

Sykes, D. F. E., *The History of Huddersfield and the Valleys of the Colne, the Holme and the Dearne*. Huddersfield, n.d.

Symes, J., *Christianity at the Bar of Science*. London, 1881.

—*Man's Place in Nature: or, man an animal among animals*. London [1878].

—*The Methodist Conference and Eternal Punishment: do its defenders believe the doctrine? In a letter to Dr. Pope, President of the Wesleyan Conference*. London, [1877].

Taine, H., *Notes on England, translated, with an introductory chapter, by W. F. Rae*. London, 1872.

Thorne, W., *My Life's Battles*. London, [1925].

Tillett, B., *Memories and Reflections*. London, 1931.

Trevor, J., *My Quest for God*. London, 1897.

Tuckwell, W., *Reminiscences of a Radical Parson*. London, 1905.

Turner, B., *About Myself, 1863–1930*. London, 1930.

Varley, H., *An Address to the Electors of the Borough of Northampton*. London, 1881.

—*Mr. Bradlaugh shown to be utterly unfit to represent any English Constituency. An appeal to the Men of England*. 27 February 1882.

Wallace, A. R., *My Life. A record of events and opinions*, 2 vols. London, 1905.

Watts, C., *The English Monarchy and American Republicanism. Reply to the speech of the Right Hon. Benjamin Disraeli by Charles Watts, vice-president of the London Republican Club*. London, n.d.

—*The Freethinker's Text Book. Part III— Freethought*. London, n.d.

—*The Government and the People: a plea for reform*. London, n.d.

—*Republicanism. A reply to Mr. John Bright's letter to the Birmingham Conference*. London, n.d.

Watts, K. E., *Mrs. Watts's Reply to Mr. Bradlaugh's Misrepresentations*. London, [1877].

Willis, T., *Whatever happened to Tom Mix. The story of one of my lives*. London, 1970.

Woodhull, Victoria C., *Life Sketches*. [1881].

### 6. Secondary works

Arnstein, W. L., *The Bradlaugh Case: a study in late Victorian opinion and politics*. Oxford, 1965.

—'The Bradlaugh Case: a reappraisal', *Journal of the History of Ideas*, vol. XVIII, no. 2, April 1957, pp. 254–69.

—'Gladstone and the Bradlaugh Case', *Victorian Studies*, vol. V. no. 4, June 1962, pp. 303–30.

—'Parnell and the Bradlaugh Case', *Irish Historical Studies*, vol. XIII, no. 51, March 1962, pp. 212–35.

Backstrom, P. N., *Christian Socialism and Co-operation in Victorian England. Edward Vansittart Neale and the Co-operative Movement*. London, 1974.

Banks, J. A., *Prosperity and Parenthood. A study of family planning among the Victorian middle classes*. London, 1954.

Banks, J. A. and O., 'The Bradlaugh–Besant Trial and the English Newspapers', *Population Studies*, vol. VIII, no. 1 , July 1954, pp. 22–34.

—*Feminism and Family Planning in Victorian England*. Liverpool, 1964.

Bettany, F. G., *Stewart Headlam: a biography*. London, 1926.

Bittner, E., 'Radicalism and the Organisation of Radical Movements', *American Sociological Review*, vol. 28, no. 6, December 1963, pp. 928–40.

Bowen, D., *The Idea of the Victorian Church. A study of the Church of England, 1833–1889*. Montreal, 1968.

Brown, A. W., *The Metaphysical Society. Victorian minds in crisis, 1869–1880*. New York, 1947.

Brown, K. D. (ed.), *Essays in Anti-Labour History. Responses to the Rise of Labour in Britain*. London, 1974.

Brown, M. G., and Stein, G. *Freethought in the United States. A descriptive bibliography*. Westport, Connecticut, 1978.

Budd, S., 'The Loss of Faith: reasons for unbelief among members of the secular movement in England, 1850–1950', *Past & Present*, no. 36, April 1967, pp. 106–25.

—*Varieties of Unbelief. Atheists and Agnostics in English Society, 1850–1960*. London, 1977.

Burrow, J. W., *Evolution and Society: a study in Victorian social theory*. Cambridge, 1966.

Campbell, C. B., *Toward a Sociology of Irreligion*. London, 1971.

Chadwick, W. O., *The Secularisation of the European Mind in the Nineteenth Century*. Cambridge, 1975.

—*The Victorian Church, Part II, 1860–1901*. London, 1970.

Calder-Marshall, A., *Lewd, Blasphemous and Obscene*. London, 1972.

Cockshut, A. O. J., *Anglican Attitudes. A study of Victorian religious controversies*. London, 1959.

—*The Unbelievers: English Agnostic thought, 1840–1890*. London, 1964.

—(ed.), *Religious Controversies of the Nineteenth Century: selected documents*. London, 1966.

Collins, H., and Abramsky, C., *Karl Marx and the British Labour Movement. Years of the First International*. London, 1965.

Coltham, S., 'English Working-class Newspapers in 1867', *Victorian Studies*, vol. XIII, December 1969, pp. 159–80.

Cominos, P. T., 'Late Victorian Sexual Respectability and the Social System,' *International Review of Social History*, vol. VIII, 1963, pp. 18–48, 216–50.

Cowling, M., *1867. Disraeli, Gladstone and Revolution. The passing of the Second Reform Bill*. Cambridge, 1967.

Cross, C., *Philip Snowden*. London, 1966.

Crossick, G. (ed.), *The Lower Middle Class in Britain*. London, 1977.

Crowther, M. A., *Church Embattled: religious controversy in mid-Victorian England*. Newton Abbot, 1970.

Demerath, N. J. III, and Thiessen, V., 'On spitting against the wind. Organisational precariousness and American irreligion', *American Journal of Sociology*, vol. LXXI, no. 6, May 1966, pp. 674–87.

Ellegaard, A, 'The Darwinian Theory and Nineteenth-century Philosophies of Science', *Journal of the History of Ideas*, vol. XVIII, 1957, pp. 362-93.

Elton, G., *The Life of James Ramsey MacDonald*. London, 1939.

Eros, J., 'The Rise of organised freethought in mid-Victorian England', *Sociological Review*, vol. 2, July 1954, pp. 98–120.

French, R. D., *Anti-vivisection and Medical Science in Victorian Society*, Princeton, 1975.

Fryer, P., *The Birth Controllers*. London, 1965.

Gasman, D., *The Scientific Origins of National Socialism. Social Darwinism in Ernst Haeckel and the German Monist League*. London and New York, 1971.

Gillespie, F. E., *Labor and Politics in England, 1850–1867*. Durham, N. C., 1927; reprinted, London, 1966.

Glaser, J. F., 'English Nonconformity and the Decline of Liberalism', *American Historical Review*, vol. 63, no. 2, January 1958, pp. 352–63.

Glass, D. V., *Population Policies and Movements in Europe*. Oxford, 1940;

reprinted, London, 1967.

Gossman, N. J., 'Republicanism in Nineteenth Century England', *International Review of Social History*, vol. VII, 1962, pp. 47–60.

Grisewood, H. J. G. (ed.), *Ideas and Beliefs of the Victorians: a historical revaluation of the Victorian Age*. London, 1949.

Grugel, L. E., *George Jacob Holyoake. A study in the evolution of a Victorian Radical*. Philadelphia, 1976.

Hall, B. T., *Our Fifty Years: the story of the Working Men's Club and Institute Union*. London, 1912.

Haller, M. H., 'Social Science and Genetics: a historical perspective', in Glass, D. C. (ed.), *Genetics. Proceedings of a conference under the auspices of Russell Sage Foundation, the Social Science Research Council, and The Rockefeller University*. New York, 1968, pp. 215–25.

Harrison, J. F. C., *A History of the Working Men's College, 1854–1954*. London, 1954.

—*Learning and Living. A study in the history of the English adult education movement*. London, 1961.

Harrison, R., *Before the Socialists. Studies in Labour and Politics, 1861–1881*. London, 1965.

—'The 10th April of Spencer Walpole: the problem of revolution in relation to reform, 1865–67', *International Review of Social History*, vol. VII, 1962, pp. 351–99.

Himes, N. E., *Medical History of Contraception*. London, 1936.

Hodann, M, *History of Modern Morals*. London, 1937.

Houghton, W. E., 'Victorian Anti-intellectualism', *Journal of the History of Ideas*, vol. XIII, no. 3, June 1952, pp. 291–313.

Inglis, K. S., *Churches and the Working Classes in Victorian England*. London, 1963.

—'The Labour Church Movement', *International Review of Social History*, vol. III, 1958, pp. 445–60.

Jackson, H., *The Eighteen Nineties. A review of art and ideas at the close of the nineteenth century*. London, 1913; reprinted, 1939.

Jefferys, J. B. (ed.), *Labour's Formative Years, 1849–1879*. London, 1948.

Jenkins, E. A., *From Foundry to Foreign Office. The romantic life story of the Rt. Hon. Arthur Henderson, M.P.* London, 1933

Jenkins, R., *Sir Charles Dilke: a Victorian tragedy.*, London, 1958; revised ed., 1965; reprinted 1968.

Jephson, H., *The Platform: its rise and progress*, 2 vols. London, 1892.

Jones, P. d'A., *The Christian Socialist Revival, 1877–1914. Religion, Class, and Social Conscience in late-Victorian England*. Princeton, 1968.

Jones, G. S., 'Working-class culture and working-class politics in London, 1870–1900; notes on the remaking of a working class', *Journal of Social History*, vol. VII, no. 4, summer 1974, pp. 460–508.

Jones, R. T., *Congregationalism in England, 1662–1962*. London, 1962.

Kapp, Y., *Eleanor Marx. Vol. I, Family Life (1855–1883); vol. II, The Crowded Years (1884–1898)*. London, 1972–76; reprinted, 1979.

Kent, J., *From Darwin to Blatchford. The role of Darwinism in Christian Apologetic, 1875–1910*. London, 1966.

—'Hugh Price Hughes and the Nonconformist Conscience', in G. V. Bennett and J. D. Walsh (eds.), *Essays in Modern Church History in memory of Norman Sykes*. London, 1966, pp. 181–205.

—'A late nineteenth century Nonconformist renaissance', in D. Baker (ed.), *Studies in Church History, XIV: Renaissance and Renewal in Christian History*. Oxford, 1977, pp. 351–60.

Lacqueur, T. W., *Religion and Respectability. Sunday Schools and Working Class Culture, 1780–1850*. New Haven and London, 1976.

Langley, J. S., 'Unbelief in Melbourne', [Sydney] *Nation*, 25 June 1966, pp. 6–7.

Leventhal, F. M., *Respectable Radical. George Howell and Victorian Working Class Politics*. London, 1971.

Lawrence, E. P., *Henry George in the British Isles*. East Lansing, Michigan, 1957.

Lees, F., *Dr. Frederic Richard Lees, F.S.A. Edin.: a biography*. London, 1904.

Lloyd, T., *The General Election of 1880*. Oxford, 1968.

Lynd, H. M., *England in the Eighteen-eighties. Toward a Social Basis for Freedom*. Oxford, 1945; reprinted, London, 1968.

McBriar, A. M., *Fabian Socialism and English Politics*. Cambridge, 1962.

Maccoby, S., *English Radicalism, 1853–1886*. London, 1938.

McGee, J. E., *A Crusade for Humanity. The History of Organised Positivism in England*. London, 1931.

—*A History of the British Secular Movement*. Girard, Kansas, 1948.

MacIntyre, A., and Ricoeur, P., *The Religious Significance of Atheism. No. 18 Bampton Lectures in America, delivered at Columbia University 1966*. New York and London, 1969.

McLaren, A., *Birth Control in Nineteenth Century England*. London, 1978.

McLeod, H., *Class and Religion in the late Victorian City*. London, 1974.

Maclure, J. S., *One Hundred Years of London Education, 1870–1970*. London, 1970.

Magnus, P., *Gladstone, a biography*. London, 1954; reprinted, 1963.

Maison, M. M., *Search Your Soul, Eustace: a survey of the religious novel in the Victorian Age*. London, 1961.

Manvell, *The Trial of Annie Besant and Charles Bradlaugh*. London, 1976.

Marsh, P. T., *The Victorian Church in Decline. Archbishop Tait and the Church of England, 1868–1882*. London, 1969.

Marty, M. E., *The Infidel. Freethought and American Religion*. Cleveland and New York, 1961.

Mayor, S., *The Churches and the Labour Movement*. London, 1967.

Micklewright, F. H. Amphlett, 'The Local History of Victorian Secularism', *The Local Historian*, vol. VIII, no. 6, 1969, pp. 221–7.

—'The Rise and Decline of English Neo–Malthusianism', *Population Studies*, vol. XV, July 1961, pp. 32–51.

Morris, A. J. A. (ed.), *Edwardian Radicalism, 1900–1914. Some aspects of British Radicalism*. London, 1974.

Murphy, H. R., 'The Ethical Revolt against Christian Orthodoxy in Early Victorian England', *American Historical Review*, vol. 60, 1955, pp. 800–17.

Neill, S., *The Interpretation of the New Testament, 1861–1961*. London, 1964.

Nethercot, A. H., *The First Five Lives of Annie Besant*. London, 1961.

Nokes, G. D., *A History of the Crime of Blasphemy*. London, 1928.

Norman, E. R., *Church and Society in England, 1770–1970. A Historical Study*. Oxford, 1976.

Passmore, J., 'Darwin's Impact on British Metaphysics', *Victorian Studies*, vol. III, no. 1, September 1959, pp. 41-54.

Peckham, M., 'Darwinism and Darwinisticism', *Victorian Studies*, vol. III, no. 1, September 1959. pp. 19–40.

Peel, J., 'The manufacture and retailing of contraceptives in England', *Population Studies*, vol. XVII, no. 2, November 1963, pp. 113–25.

Pelling H., *The Origins of the Labour Party*. Oxford, 1954; 2nd ed., 1965.

—*Popular Politics and Society in Late Victorian Britain*. London, 1968.

Perkin, H. J., 'Land Reform and Class Conflict in Victorian Britain', in J. Butt and I. F. Clarke (eds.), *The Victorians and Social Protest*. Newton Abbot, 1973, pp. 177–217.

Pierson, S., 'Edward Carpenter, prophet of a socialist millennium', *Victorian Studies*, vol. XIII, March 1970, pp. 301–18.

Quinault, R. E., 'The Fourth Party and the Conservative Opposition to Bradlaugh, 1880–1888', *English Historical Review*, vol. XCI, no. 359, April 1976, pp. 315–40.

Ratcliffe, S. K., *The Story of South Place*. London, 1955.

Reardon, B. M. G. (ed.), *Religious Thought in the Nineteenth Century, illustrated from writers of the period*. Cambridge, 1966.

Reid, F., 'Socialist Sunday Schools in Britain, 1892–1939', *International Review of Social History*, vol. XI, 1966, pp. 18–47.

Rich, J., 'The Bradlaugh Case: religion, respectability, and politics', *Australian Journal of Politics and History*, vol. XXI, no. 2, August 1975, pp. 38–51.

Richter, M., *The Politics of Conscience. T. H. Green and his age*. London, 1964.

Rowell, G., *Hell and the Victorians. A study of the nineteenth-century theological controversies concerning eternal punishment and the future life*. Oxford, 1974.

Royle, E., *The Bradlaugh Papers. A Descriptive Index*. Wakefield, 1975.

—*The Infidel Tradition from Paine to Bradlaugh*. London, 1976.

—*Radical Politics, 1790–1900: religion and unbelief*. London, 1971.

—*Victorian Infidels. The origins of the British Secularist Movement, 1791–1866*. Manchester, 1974.

Rubinstein, D., 'Annie Besant and Stewart Headlam: the London School Board Election of 1888', *East London Papers*, vol. XIII, summer 1970, pp. 3–24.

—*School Attendance in London, 1870–1914: a social history*. Hull, 1969.

Saville, J., 'Henry George and the British Labour Movement: a select bibliography with commentary', *Bulletin of the Society for the Study of Labour History*, no. 5, autumn 1962, pp. 18–26.

Simon, B., *Studies in the History of Education. Education and the Labour Movement, 1870–1920*. London, 1965.

Sinnott, N. H., 'Charles Bradlaugh and Ireland', *Journal of the Cork Historical and Archaeological Society*, vol. LXXVII, no. 225, January–June 1972, pp. 1–24.

—*Joseph Symes, the 'flower of atheism'*. 1977.
—*Matilda, Agnes and Stella Symes: biographical notes on the women in the life of Joseph Symes*. 1978.
—*Notes on the Symes Family, and Joseph Skurrie*. 1978.
Smith, F. B., 'The Atheist Mission', in R. Robson (ed.), *Ideas and Institutions of Victorian Britain*. London, 1967.
—'Joseph Symes and the Australasian Secular Association', *Labour History*, no. 5, 1963, pp. 26–47.
—*The Making of the Second Reform Bill*. Cambridge, 1966.
Smith, J. C., and Hogan, B., *Criminal Law*. 3rd ed., London, 1973.
Smith, J. E. M., 'Failsworth Secular Sunday School', *Freethought News*, September 1947, pp. 13–14; October 1947, pp. 6–7.
Smith, W. S., *The London Heretics, 1870–1914*. London, 1967.
Sowder, W. J., 'Emerson's Rationalist Champions: a study in British periodicals', *The New England Quarterly*, vol. XXXVII, no. 2, June 1964, pp. 147–70.
Spiller, G., *The Ethical Movement in Great Britain. A documentary history*. London, 1934.
Stewart, W., *J. Keir Hardie, a biography*. London, 1921.
Symondson, A., (ed.), *The Victorian Crisis of Faith*. London, 1970.
Taylor, G. H., *A Chronology of British Secularism*. London, 1957.
Thompson, P., *Socialists, Liberals and Labour. The struggle for London, 1885–1914*. London, 1967.
Thorold, A. L., *The Life of Henry Labouchere*. London, 1913.
Torr, D., *Tom Mann and his Times. Vol. I (1856–1890)*. London, 1956.
Tribe, D., *100 Years of Freethought*. London, 1967.
—*President Charles Bradlaugh, M.P*. London, 1971.
Tsuzuki, C., *H. M. Hyndman and British Socialism*. Oxford, 1961.
Warren, S., *American Freethought, 1860–1914*. Columbia University Studies in History, Economics and Public Law, no. 504. New York, 1943.
Watson, A., *A Great Labour Leader: being a life of the Right Hon. Thomas Burt, M.P*. London, 1908.
Webb, C. C. J., *A Study of Religious Thought in England from 1850*. Oxford, 1933.
Webb, S. and B., *The History of Trade Unionism*. London, 1920.
Whyte, A. G., *The Story of the R.P.A., 1899–1949*. London, 1949.
Willey, B., *More Nineteenth Century Studies: a group of Honest Doubters*. London, 1956.
Williams, C. R., 'The Welsh Religious Revival, 1904–5', *British Journal of Sociology* vol. III, 1952, pp. 242–59.
Wilson, B. R., (ed.), *Patterns of Sectarianism: organisation and ideology in social and religious movements*. London, 1967.
Wiltshire, D., *The Social and Political Thought of Herbert Spencer*. Oxford, 1978.
Wood, H. G., *Belief and Unbelief since 1850*. Cambridge, 1955.
Yeo, S., 'A New Life: the religion of Socialism in Britain, 1883–1896', *History Workshop Journal*. no. 4, autumn 1977, pp. 5–56.

*7. Biographical works of reference.*

*Australian Dictionary of Biography, vol. VI, 1851–1890,* eds. G. Serle and R. Ward. Melbourne, 1976.

*A Biographical Dictionary of Freethinkers of All Ages and Nations,* ed. J. M. Wheeler. London, 1889.

*A Biographical Dictionary of Modern Rationalists,* ed. J. McCabe. London, 1920.

*Dictionary of Labour Biography,* eds. J. Bellamy and J. Saville. 5 vols. to date. London, 1972–79.

*A Dictionary of New Zealand Biography,* ed. G. H. Scholefield. Wellington, 1940.

*Modern English Biography,* ed. F. Boase. 6 vols., Truro, 1890–1921.

# Index